SPIRIT MOVES

04

SPIRIT MOVES

The Story of Six Generations of Native Women

Loree Boyd

NOVATO, CALIFORNIA

14 Pamaron Way
Novato, California 94949
© 1996 Loree Boyd
Cover and text design: Beth Hansen
Cover illustration: Siversong
Text illustrations: Silversong
Back cover photograph: Kauila
Editorial: Katherine Dieter, Gina Misiroglu, and Becky Benenate

Library of Congress Cataloging-in-Publication Data
Boyd, Loree, 1962– ·
Spirit moves : the story of six generations of
Native women / Loree Boyd.
p.   cm.
ISBN 1-880032-59-7 (paperback : acid-free paper)
1. Métis women--Biography. 2. Métis women--History. 3. Métis women--Social conditions.   I. Title.
E99.M47B69   1995   95-9264
920.72'089'973--dc20   CIP
Printed in Canada
ISBN 1-880032-59-7
Distributed to the trade by Publishers Group West

10 9 8 7 6 5 4 3 2 1

THIS BOOK IS DEDICATED TO MY DAUGHTERS,

Layla and Danaelle

TABLE OF CONTENTS

BOOK ONE
Anne

BOOK TWO
Silversong

BOOK THREE
Loree

Acknowledgments

Next to love, acknowledgment is one of the most powerful forces in the universe.

To my family, whose spirit lives in the pages of this book. Each of you holds a special place in my heart.

To my grandmother, Anne... without you, spirit wouldn't move. To my mother, Silversong, who gave birth to my spirit. To my daughters, Danaelle and Layla, and to their father, Danny.

To my brother, James, his wife Cora Lee, and all my special cousins, aunties, and uncles whose names follow: Amber Lee Ann, Sherry, Len, Kathy, Brent, Myrna, Brad, Marge, Nicole, Trish, Sandy, Candy, and Michael.

To my publisher, Marc Allen, and to New World Library. Thank you for being who you are.

To my agent, Manfred Mroczkowski, at InterLicense, for your courage in taking on a first-time writer.

To Katherine Dieter, for your time and talent that allowed spirit to move.

To Gina Misiroglu and Becky Benenate. Thank you for your teamwork, professionalism, perseverance, insight, and faith.

To those people whose lives, words, art, and unique interpretation and encouragement has meant more than you will ever know: Sue Button; Barbara Bazett; Pepsi; Michelle; Kerry; Joeanne Paquette; Eva Lorenz; Angel and Mark; Heaven Fire Productions; George "Coyote" Amiotte; Dr. Gayle Modeleina Randall; Dr. David "Kavika" Deihl; Val and Katy Mijailovic and the "North Star Video crew;" Lei; Brandscombe and Alice "Tu-tu" Richmond and the entire "Renegade Posse;" the Renfrow Family; Jim Clark; Rick Ulrich; Dennis

Boyd; Laura Lamanek; Stephen Green; Dr. Jonathan Weissman; Carmen; Alvin and Ely Marryweather; Thomas Mendoza and the Intertribal Media Lab, S.F., CA; Mike Gray, a.k.a. "Rotten Deal;" Alan Cenci; Berry; Big Mike; and all the rest of my friends from the "Circuit" in Novato, CA; Adriene; Simon; Theodore; Tom and Anne; Marco; Mascarin; Hazel Cox; Kathy and Jerry Kingen.

Special thanks also goes to Kauila; Tantoo Cardinal; the Trudell family; Gardner Compton; Mike Smith; Mr. Alex; C.C.; Robert Redford; and Marlon Brando.

The Indian ways are good ways
We believe in the Earth
The Sun, the Sea and Flowers
All places of our birth

For here at the Center of the World
Moonlight touches our eyes
Warm winds seem to caress us
Beauty fills the night sky

We see the Princess of Dancing Water
Dressed in leather and beads
She teaches us the rhythm of life
To be proud of our deeds

Now riding along into the shadows
Endless as they may seem
We pass our brothers dancing
On the edge of dreams

Oh a Warrior must die fighting
Though always live for peace
We search for the Great Spirit
Our journey will never cease

—"Legends Softly Drifting" by Marty Bluewater

My Own Tribal Wisdom

*M*y *name is Loree Boyd, my native name is Zachćoo, meaning Star-*light and, for me, this story is about the people who have loved, honored, and protected me. In return, the greatest honor I can bestow upon them is to acknowledge their lives.

This story follows the matrilineal line of my family. Each grandmother is like a door that, in a sense, I've had the courage to open, and accept what I see. Their beauty and bravery in overcoming obstacles and challenges shines through this story. It was written with the hope and intention of reaching out and reassuring the reader that she is not alone.

I begin with Bird Song, my great, great grandmother. My great grandmother Margaret follows, my grandmother Anne, my mother Silversong, and finally me. The sixth generation is my daughters, who are coming into their own spirit during a time of great challenge and change in the world. The genocide perpetrated upon the Tribal Peoples of the Americas is common knowledge, therefore I make no apologies for the sketchiness of my earliest accounts. Learning and searching into my history is an ongoing process.

Because many of the people in my story are still alive, I have changed some names and places to protect the innocent. And in some cases names were changed to protect the guilty.

It's funny I should know so much about my great, great grandmother, Bird Song and so little at the same time. It's true what they say, it's in our DNA; before I knew of Bird Song's beginning journey into the new world, her blessings had already been bestowed upon my daughter, Danaelle.

Danaelle was looking forward to spending a summer with her grandmother Silversong. It was the year she would find her spirit name, and she alone would know who she was. Danaelle smiled and giggled when I picked her up one day from Grandma's house.

"I know it, Mommy! I know it! My name is Moon Bird!"

And with that, she showed me who she was in a drawing she had made.

It has been said that "truth" is present with ease for the child and the elder because they are both nearest the Great Mystery One. The child has just come from the Great Mystery and the elder is nearing the time when he or she shall return. Both are near. And so it is that I have mercy for those among us who are in between, and I am always reminded to regard the child and elder, knowing what gifts they have to offer us who are still far from the Creator.

Who cannot see the magic that lives between the child and elder? When their eyes meet and their hearts see clearly that they hold so much of what is precious in the world. You can feel and see their common bond. So it is right that this is a story of many grandmothers and their children, and, of course...those of us in between.

Initially, I began writing *Spirit Moves* as a way to honor both my grandmother and mother. It would not be an overstatement to say I was often in awe of them when I considered the courage, determination, and spirit that not only enabled them to survive the darkest, dark umbra of life, but to go that one step farther—no longer survivors, living next to death, they thrive.

I wanted to understand. I wanted it to matter and so I began to write. At first, it was only ink moving across paper, but soon the words began to take on a life of their own. Spirit had begun to move, and my life and understanding of who I was would also be changed forever. Little did I know that spirit would even change the way I had intended to end this book.

To me, one of the most powerful and valuable lessons I have learned in life is that spirit moves. Spirit moves the planet, it lights up the moon at night, and escorts the sun into the sky at dawn. Spirit moves in all of Creation and is a part of the life, death cycle that completes the sacred circle of life.

On a personal level, spirit moves in many ways, through happy accidents that lead us to a new understanding or a place we need to be, a person we need to meet, or an answer to a question we have.

At times, spirit moves mysteriously through tragedy and triumph. Often through feelings that compel and guide us in a way that can only be described as sacred.

Our instincts, intuition, inspiration, and intellect are often led by this invisible power that not only moves our planet, but moves our spirit so we can experience the things, events, and people that we need in order to feel complete, whole, and alive.

And so it is that this book is the story of spirit moving through six generations of native women and all the special people who played a significant role in creating these lives and experiences.

I believe my family is proof that it is not impossible to get through the most difficult times in life, and that, most definitely, we reach another spirit dimension through our trials and the way we walk through our lives. Poet John Trudell put this sentiment so eloquently:

"Picking up pieces has an effect upon the soul. Each piece places its own weight upon the mind. Each piece an ocean, leaving shore behind. Reality is how we swim, not how we win."

HOW IT ALL BEGAN
Bird Song and Her Daughters

Bird Song was born in 1886, ten years after the Battle of Little Big Horn took place. Already the world which her grandmother had known no longer existed. The Blackfoot Nation, once strong and proud, was starving to death. The people were sick in their hearts, and also their bodies. Small pox threatened those who had survived the plagues of the past and alcohol was slowly poisoning others.

Sometimes it was not a slow process. Many times the reaction these mixtures caused were violent and unpredictable. The whiskey was often tampered with to such a degree that some would go into shock or simply die immediately after drinking the brew. So the white traders became rich, while they watched the Indians pay to destroy themselves with an even greater sickness than the plagues of the past. And for this disease, called alcoholism, for many there is still no cure, and they still pay to die, without even their honor to hold on to anymore.

The Blackfoot people lived in an area spanning from northern Canada to Montana, and journeyed every mile of the way between these two points. They called the plains their home, as did the buffalo. Much of Bird Song's family would eventually settle in Alberta, a northern Canadian province of vast wilderness, with areas that remain virtually untouched.

The first major group of Blackfoot Indians were the Siska, who are known as the Blackfoot proper. They lived primarily in the north. It is said that they were called Blackfoot because the moccasins

7

they wore were often burned by prairie fires that dyed them black. To the south were the Bloods—their way was to paint their faces with the sacred red earth—and farther south were the Piegans, which meant "black robes." Bird Song was born into the Blood Tribe. The Blackfoots were still many in number when Bird Song was born, but many had already died and many were still to die.

They had become victims of germ warfare, both intentionally and unintentionally. Since the first white man set foot on the North American continent, their lives, between birth and death, had become a perilous journey. The white man you could see and fight, his germs you could not see, and you could not run from them.

The only protection they had were the sacred ceremonial objects, places, and spirit to move them toward the day of their death song. Because of the sacredness of their journey, and their acceptance of change and uncertainty, their lives were very rich and joyful, even though many times short in terms of years. They were a nomadic people by nature and this ability to adapt would serve them well always.

There was an infinity to life back then, which is sometimes hard to imagine today with so many considerations as to survival alone. But still the joy of life itself and belief in the power in the places of our birth, were where the peoples' real meaning and strength came from. They lived in truth, simply finding pleasure in the treasures and blessings which we often don't even recognize anymore because of our unquenchable desire for more. Or perhaps we are lost in the material delirium made possible by overwhelming technical distractions.

Really, what more is there than this: to love your family, touch and be touched, and to believe that your life and every substance surrounding you, both plant and animal, and all those who surround you, are here to be either a blessing or a teacher that the Creator has sent, so you can have today? So that today, you live in honor, for tomorrow you may die. Without death, life would be less. So even death can teach us well and walk beside us, and make the day bright. But who can face the light of day or death without honor? Death is not looked on as an end, but a completion of this mortality and a time when our spirit moves on.

When Bird Song was nine years old, she was taken in trade by a French fur trapper to be a helper to his native wife, a Cree. The Blackfoot and Cree Nations had been enemies for some time. Bird Song had never seen a Cree before and had no knowledge of their ways. It took time for her to get comfortable in the strangers' presence, and to live without the fear of being a prisoner in the enemy's camp.

There had been great honor in the trade her father made, and in her heart this made her happy. Before she left her village to live a new life, her mother made her a new medicine bundle. The beautifully beaded medicine bag contained the power that had seen Bird Song through the long illness that had taken so many in her village. She had heard the stories, and seen the fear in the elders' eyes when they spoke of the horror they were experiencing.

"Why must we stay here and become sick?" she asked her mother.

"If it wills, it will follow us wherever we run."

The illness crept into Bird Song while she slept, and for the weeks that followed endless nights of high fevers engulfed her. Time and space lost their meaning.

She lived in this dark dream world until one day a bird, unlike any other bird seen in their land, came to the girl's side. It had the sacred symbol of the moon on its forehead, and it sang the girl's spirit back into her small, frail body.

Bird Song's mother often spoke to her of the Moon Bird's song, saying she must always remember to honor this gift. She was to be like the Moon Bird and see the world beyond her people, see many new things and places, and live with an even greater uncertainty than her ancestors had.

This is how Bird Song received her spirit name. She would go out into the Great Mystery and become part of the past.

Bird Song learned many things in her days with the Frenchman and his wife. By the time she was fifteen years old, she had learned to speak French and also Cree. This made her extremely valuable to the trappers who were looking for a woman, a helpmate. Not many white women were willing to forgo the comforts they were accustomed to for a cabin in the Canadian wilderness.

Shortly after her fifteenth birthday, Bird Song was married to a Scottish trapper. Together they journeyed from Montana north to Fort McMurray, Alberta, where they had their first child, a daughter named Elizabeth.

In the five years that followed, Bird Song gave birth to two more daughters, Edwina and Margaret. These children were born of mixed blood, half-breeds, and came to be known as Metis. The Metis formed an independent nation, a unique amalgam of many cultures and bloodlines. Considered neither Indian nor white, they created a culture of their own out of necessity and pride.

The children played hard and grew strong, but learned early about the responsibilities essential to survival in the wilderness. Although the three girls were close in age, Elizabeth was often relied upon to look out for her two younger sisters. Margaret, the youngest, seemed to enjoy Elizabeth's attention while Edwina resented her older sister's authority.

When Elizabeth was twelve years old, her mother entrusted her to watch over her siblings while Bird Song and her husband made the two-day trip to the trading post. They planned to stop along the way to trade pelts with the natives. Bird Song acted as her husband's interpreter.

Seven long days passed and the initial pride and maturity that Elizabeth felt was replaced by a growing fear. She hid this fear from her younger sisters, knowing that if her parents didn't return soon, she would have to leave them alone and go for help. They were beginning to run out of supplies. Their stomachs reminded them of the emptiness they felt without their mother's daily care and their father's protective presence.

When strangers appeared on the porch one morning, Margaret cried, Elizabeth held her tightly, and Edwina glared hatefully, as they were all told that their parents had been found dead—shot to death and robbed of the fur pelts that were to provide money for food through the winter. No one was ever found responsible for the deaths of Bird Song and her husband, for the making of three orphans, or for changing their lives forever.

The strangers said they would take the children to an orphanage where they could stay together. Elizabeth knew it was only a matter of time before they would be separated. She began to prepare her sisters for the uncertainty that lay before them. She encouraged them to be strong and brave, and promised that they would never lose touch with one another, no matter what.

Shortly after they were sent to the orphanage, Edwina was taken in by a large family who needed domestic help. The father of the family was a river boat captain on the Peace River in Alberta. She woke early and worked late, caring for a family that gave her nothing of love, only a sterile form of Christian charity. The "Captain" believed in a strict and unmerciful form of Catholicism. He was known to be cruel and inflexible. Like the Captain, Edwina grew equally cruel and inflexible as the years progressed.

Elizabeth was adopted by a very wealthy family, the Barnettes, who owned one of the grandest and largest vacation hotels of its time. They also ran a tourist bus line. Elizabeth was raised Protestant and had the finest clothes, jewelry, horses, and eventually cars, that money could buy. She had inherited a light skin tone from her father; her acceptance into a white society went unquestioned.

Margaret's appearance could not be viewed as anything but native. She so strongly resembled her mother Bird Song that the nuns at the orphanage felt it was important she be adopted by a native family. Why make life any harder on her? It was the natural decision. Margaret would return to the land and the ways in which she was raised. The nuns guaranteed, however, that Margaret would be taught reading and writing, and attend church services regularly.

Although Elizabeth did stay in touch with her sisters, as promised, it would be a long time before any of them actually saw each other again.

Alberta, Canada, 1920

Seven years after the death of her parents, Elizabeth met the family that had taken in her sister Edwina. The two families had dinner at the Captain's home.

It was unusual for Elizabeth to take a dislike to someone, but nevertheless, it was clear she didn't particularly care for the Captain or his wife. It seemed to her that the Captain existed solely for his own pleasure, the others serving only as an audience for the Captain's incessant bragging.

Elizabeth's "parents," Theodore and Betty Barnette, sat silently, politely, for the entire, seemingly eternal, evening. Far too well established to offer any show of their own impressive background, the Barnettes knew the Captain's life story before the evening ended.

When the Captain remarked to Elizabeth's father about the honorable deed they had both undertaken, "saving the little half-breeds from their sinful nature," it took Theodore's utmost control to suppress the instinct to whip the Captain like a dog, though Theodore would not have treated an animal as poorly as the Captain treated people. He was thankful these comments were not heard by the children and more thankful when the evening drew to a close.

After they returned home and Elizabeth had gone to her room, Theodore told his wife about the conversation with the Captain. They decided it was best that Elizabeth knew nothing of the Captain's feelings. They would soon all be leaving for Europe and Theodore's business interests would keep them there for two years. It would be a long time before they returned to Canada and

Elizabeth saw her sister again. They knew she felt protective of her sisters and didn't want her to worry.

Shortly after Elizabeth returned from Europe, she planned to surprise Edwina with an unannounced visit. She had exquisite gifts to give her, even the boxes were beautiful. She hoped Edwina would at last realize how dearly she was loved.

Elizabeth's hands trembled as she approached the Captain's house, which was illuminated by a soft glow. Awkwardly, she rearranged the pretty packages that she held in her arms, and reached to ring the door bell. It took only a moment before there was an answer. Elizabeth lifted her chin from the pile of presents and saw the Captain standing in the doorway.

"Well, well, what do we have here?" he said, with a sweeping arm, motioning her into the house.

It was very quiet. The Captain stood silently across from her as she sat fidgeting on the couch. He watched her every movement. Elizabeth grew more nervous, waiting to see her sister. She felt her thoughts might be showing themselves as she attempted to avoid the Captain's gaze.

It will all be worth it, she reminded herself, imagining Edwina opening her gifts. And wait until she hears the good news about Margaret....

She had discovered that their youngest sister had married a man named Desulay, and Elizabeth intended to persuade Edwina to accompany her to meet their new brother-in-law.

The Captain had been drinking. Even from across the room, Elizabeth could smell the whiskey.

"I've come a long way to see my sister. I'm sure you understand how anxious I am to see her. If you would please call her down for me...."

The Captain began to laugh, a crazy laugh that frightened her.

"If you would have sent word of your visit, Elizabeth, you would have known that your sister has accompanied my wife and children to Edmonton."

Suddenly feeling in jeopardy, Elizabeth stood to leave. The Captain grabbed her arm, and when she screamed the Captain's large hand hit her forcefully across the mouth. So intense was the impact, Elizabeth thought she would die. Mercifully, she passed out.

When she awoke, a feeling of warmth surrounded her. Her eyes began to focus. She coaxed her body into movement. Sitting up, she realized the warmth she was feeling came from between her legs. The pool of warm blood she lay in was coming from her own body.

The feeling of warmth quickly evaporated and a bitter chill set into her extremities as she held the arm of a chair and tried to rise from the floor. She had no strength in reserve and soon the room was spinning, darkening, and she began to lose consciousness again.

"Help me, please help me," Elizabeth chanted to herself as she lay on the floor. The room began to fill with light again.

Rising unsteadily, Elizabeth gathered her coat and purse from the floor. As she turned to close the door behind her, she saw the pretty little packages lying untouched on the table.

She closed the door quietly, and began walking toward a distant light. The next thing she knew, a thin, grey-haired woman was hovering above her.

"Honey, who did this to you?" the stranger asked.

Elizabeth was too weak to reply. The woman could see that the injuries were severe and much blood had been lost. She immediately arranged for Elizabeth to be taken to the hospital.

The road to Edmonton, where the nearest hospital was located, was long and bumpy. Elizabeth drifted in and out of consciousness, and when she arrived in Edmonton, she retreated once again into total darkness. The doctors in the emergency room proceeded to do what they could to save her life.

Elizabeth awoke screaming as the door to her room opened abruptly, then closed with a thud. A nurse appeared at her side. Elizabeth's body ached deeply as she tried to reconcile the fear, the hazy memories . . . her family was still in Europe — for this she felt grateful; she wanted to be alone, alone with her shame.

A doctor entered, stethoscope dangling, and took her hand gently.

"I regret to inform you Miss Barnette that you will never hold a child of your own. . . ." He continued talking but his words didn't reach Elizabeth. They echoed in the sterile room while she stared blankly out a small window.

The hospital staff urged Elizabeth to contact her family, but she refused. She asked instead to see Mr. Richard Lawrence, a well-known and respected lawyer in Edmonton. A trusted family friend, he had overseen the Barnette family's business affairs for many years. He arrived at her bedside immediately, and Elizabeth knew she could trust him to handle matters discreetly.

A distinguished-looking man with greying hair and standing six-feet-three inches tall, Richard Lawrence exuded strength.

Having considered the repercussions of publicly accusing the Captain, Elizabeth requested that the Captain be made to believe that if he ever touched her sister, he would be imprisoned for life. She asked Mr. Lawrence to deliver a threat so great and terrible that he would never consider touching her sister. The Captain had no idea of the power the Barnette family name yielded. He had thought that Elizabeth was merely another orphaned half-breed, there to serve his own ignoble desires.

Richard Lawrence recognized the imminent need to protect Elizabeth from further shame, and secure the family's good name and stature, and he proceeded to gather an impressive arsenal of weapons with which to confront the Captain.

Elizabeth secretly felt that these things did not happen to good girls.

Why did this happen? Is this my punishment for having so much while my sisters have so little—to live in silence, in shame? Never to hold a child of my own?

She had been part of a shameful and ugly thing, and she decided to spare the Barnette family and her sister Edwina the disgrace of it all. In addition, she felt guilty for having lived such a privileged life in comparison with her sisters, and this intensified her shame.

Elizabeth made arrangements for Edwina to attend a private girls' school in Edmonton, while Richard made sure that the Captain understood they expected his full cooperation.

While attending the private school, Edwina met and married a man named John Domenick. John was a very talented chef, working for one of the most prestigious hotels in Edmonton. He was a quiet man, well liked, and well paid. Though much older than Edwina, he was impressed by her maturity and sense of duty.

After they were married, they moved into an expensive home, filled with fine furniture and all the modern conveniences money could buy. Edwina became a seamstress of perfection with marcelled hair and bleached skin. For all intents and purposes, she had become white.

There were two things Edwina could never get enough of: repentance and money. Maybe God could forgive someone for his or her sins, but Edwina forgave no one. She hid her native heritage but not her bitterness, and when Elizabeth and Edwina made the trip to see their sixteen-year-old baby sister with the purpose of meeting Margaret's husband, the visit did not go well.

Never had Edwina or Elizabeth considered the possibility that their sister would choose to marry a native, even though they were aware she had been raised by a native family. It was assumed that she would leave this life behind as they had, and marry a nice white man who could give her the comforts that her sisters had come to see as necessities. It was a ridiculous assumption, given that Margaret had been raised in a place so far removed from the world to which her sisters were accustomed, but they held it nevertheless.

Desulay was part Cree Indian and part French. To the older sisters, however, and to much of the world, the mixed blood didn't matter—an Indian was an Indian. Harsh words flew and feelings were hurt, and even though Margaret seemed happily married, Edwina was infuriated.

"My God, that cabin is absolutely horrendous. And the way they communicate—like a flock of birds. Not one of them spoke English...." The conversation continued between Edwina and Elizabeth all the way back to Edmonton. By the time they reached the city, they had agreed that they could not possibly condone the lifestyle Margaret had chosen.

"The girl has simply lost her mind out there with those heathens! And to start a family?! Well, we'll just see about that. It's time she leaves those backwoods savages before it's too late."

Edwina's lip shook as she spoke. Elizabeth sighed in agreement.

"If only we could get her to come here and talk some sense into her, Edwina. I'm sure we could change her mind."

Margaret loved the peacefulness and simplicity of her world. Her idea of comfort was different. Her sisters never seemed able to believe her when she told them how happy she was. It hurt her but she hoped they would understand when they found happiness for themselves. If they could not love and accept her as she was, she would be the one to extend herself, to reach out with understanding and overlook their differences. She felt sorry for them. They seemed to have so much material worth, yet such little happiness in their hearts.

Although they had little contact over the years, Margaret had noticed that Elizabeth, when on her own, was usually quite easy to handle, and tended not to linger on any hard feelings that cropped up. Edwina, on the other hand, seemed to specialize in hard feelings. No one was spared when Edwina was on the war path. Margaret loved her sisters, but facing them together was especially difficult, as Margaret found out when she decided to visit them in Edmonton the following year.

Edmonton, 1921

It was spring when Margaret and Desulay traveled from their home in Fort McMurray to Edmonton to sell his furs at the trading post. Margaret suspected she was pregnant, but fearing her sisters' reactions, she decided to keep the happy news to herself.

When they stopped to visit Elizabeth and Edwina, the sisters convinced Desulay to let Margaret stay on and visit for a few weeks. Desulay knew the trip had worn Margaret out and she looked so happy to see her sisters, he felt good about agreeing to let her stay.

Once Desulay was gone, the sisters set about "remaking" Margaret in their image. They removed her traditional clothing, styled her hair in the latest fashion, and applied some of the cosmetics Elizabeth had brought home from Europe. Margaret hated it. She found no comfort in the strange clothes nor in the personal rituals they performed.

When the transformation was complete, the sisters refused to let Margaret return home. Elizabeth and Edwina were sure that in a matter of time, Margaret would come around and see that she was meant to be a part of their world, not the world of their mother.

Margaret was confused. She had always felt the weakest of the sisters, perhaps because she was youngest. Convincing the two of them that she was being kept from all that was dear to her would not be easy. She became more and more pale, blending with her light-skinned sisters, withering beneath the weight of her pretty new dress and rouged cheeks. She longed for her home and her husband; longed to feel real again.

Edwina refused to acknowledge Desulay when he returned to bring his wife home, and she retreated to the kitchen. Husband and wife were left staring at each other, like strangers. Desulay was stunned at the transformation, more confused than pleased, but he put his arms around his young wife and spoke to her in Cree.

"Your sister's angry with you, isn't she?"

"She doesn't understand, Desulay. Her spirit has grown mean ...and blind."

"Not like you." He pulled her closer. "You see through her hate and find love. She can see only hate through her heart."

Margaret looked up at her handsome husband and returned his smile. It didn't matter that her sisters didn't understand. Desulay did. She couldn't leave, however, without saying good-bye to Edwina.

She spoke softly.

"I love you, Edwina. I'm sorry that you don't understand me. I never meant to hurt you or Elizabeth but I have a home of my own, and I'm happy there."

"Hurt?!" Edwina screamed. "Humiliated is the better word, my dear. Just look at him. He can't give you anything but grief and little brown babies. Mark my words, Margaret, I will never, never allow that man or his children in this house again. In this house, we believe in God, self-respect, and dignity! Your husband disgusts me . . . and so do you. I assume you'll show yourselves out."

She spun around and walked up the stairs to her room.

"Maybe time will give a pair of eyeglasses to her spirit," Desulay joked, "or maybe the white doctors will invent an operation for her."

Margaret's dark feelings began to lift as they walked out, and she felt a subtle stirring in her belly.

Elizabeth had taken Margaret's departure much better than Edwina had. She was deeply disappointed but never capable of the cruelty Edwina displayed. Like most disappointments in Elizabeth's life, this one would be short-lived. There was always something grand and exciting waiting in the wings to replace her feelings of malcontent. This time it would be a trip to the United States.

It was in the place where she found most happiness that Margaret gave birth to her daughter Anne. They lived contented for two years until Margaret became ill with tuberculosis.

It broke Desulay's heart every time she smiled at him through the pain. He felt helpless as he watched the bright light slowly fade from his wife's face. Tearfully, he held her as she took her last, labored breath and her body began to relax, releasing her spirit, as she walked out into the Great Mystery. Shattered, Desulay became one of the walking wounded.

Fearing that Margaret's sisters would attempt to take Anne (as Margaret had warned), he took the child deeper into the Canadian wilderness. The pain of his loneliness grew with each step farther away from the little cabin they had called home. He soon felt too weak with sorrow to care for his child. She looked so helpless without a mother to care for her little body and spirit. He had promised Margaret that her child would not be subjected to the prejudice of Elizabeth and Edwina. Although Edwina had once vowed she would never allow Desulay or his children in her house, she had changed her mind when she heard of Margaret's illness, and vowed to do everything in her power to retrieve the child and raise her in her "white" world.

It was in a state of exhaustion that Desulay thought of Mary and Joseph Cardinal, a Native American couple who had been friends of Desulay's family while he was growing up. When Desulay's own parents died, when he was still a young boy, Mary and Joseph had taken him in and treated him as their own. Their own children were grown and gone.

Confident they would do for his two-year-old daughter what they had done for him, Desulay contacted them. He was not disappointed when the Cardinals readily agreed to care for Anne. He left early the next morning before the sun rose. Anne was still asleep. He knew if he waited too long, she would be awake and it would be even harder to leave her.

Before leaving her with the Cardinals, he knelt down beside his little girl, gently wiping one of her black curls from her forehead. He kissed her good-bye and a tear slid slowly down his cheek. He did not pause to wipe it away; there would be no one to see it.

He walked alone from the house. It was still dark outside. With only the heaviness in his heart reminding him that he was alive, he traveled, becoming purposely lost in the wilderness he knew so well, looking for a place where he could hide from the loss he felt so deeply.

Months passed, and slowly a calm crept into Desulay's sadness as he spent his days following the old familiar trap lines he had done so often in the past. Although sadness was still present, the healing had finally begun. He felt he could once again face the out-side world and decided to visit his little girl. He hadn't communi-cated with the Cardinals since the last time he saw them, but he knew there would be no need for explanation. As always, they would be pleased to see him. As he headed out of the wilderness, he real-ized that there was no place to hide from the loss he felt. Margaret had faced her death bravely; so must he face his life.

Several months passed before Desulay was able to return to the Cardinals' home. Momma and Poppa Cardinal seemed years younger when he arrived. Anne and the Cardinals had developed a warm rapport with one another. Both Desulay and Anne called the Cardi-nals "Momma and Poppa." Anne was taller now, black ringlets swinging. He did not remind her that he was her real "Poppa." When she grew older, he would tell her about her real mother, and about how much they had both loved her. For the time being, he would be a familiar presence in the cabin when he was home. All that mat-tered for the moment was Anne's happiness.

When Margaret died, the future, which Desulay had looked to with such expectations, seemed bleak. As months slipped into years, he was filled with mourning. Five years passed before his grief lifted. Deep within him, Desulay's spirit began to glimmer with a bright hope for a new future. For the first time since Margaret's death, Desulay felt a deep desire to live.

There was a town called Yellow Knife in the Northwest Terri-tories that Desulay had heard stories about. There were many tales of gold and great riches made by men willing to journey that far north.

As always, parting from his daughter was difficult, but he felt it had to be done.

Back in Edmonton, Edwina and Elizabeth blamed Desulay ("the Indian") for Margaret's early death, but no one could tell them where to find their niece. There were no telephones in the Canadian wil-derness and no paper trail could lead them to her.

Anne, for a time, was lost to them in her mother's world.

BOOK ONE

Anne

The door to your spirit is through your deepest scar

CHAPTER ONE

In Anne's Words

I had my earliest memory when I was seventy years old. I guess some- times it takes a long time to find a need to look that far back, so many things lying dead in my mind—locked up memories. But one day I saw a little girl and realized she was me.

The moving picture in my mind is so clear. I see Momma Cardinal sitting on the front porch of our cabin. There are only real sounds, like the gentle calm after it stops raining, and there's nothing but soothing silence and the smell of damp sweet grass in the air. The older woman with a large gray bun in back of her head took care of me and hugged me often with her strong soft arms that felt like wonderful pillows. She was my momma. I knew she was not my real momma but still I called her Momma and I knew she loved me, as I loved her.

I believe when a child is loved as deeply as I was, it becomes imprinted on the soul, a safe place to go, a place where the goodness in life is remembered.

Life was so easy sitting at Momma's feet, my head resting on her apron, cushioned by her softness, as we watched the twilight ever so cautiously close the day.

There were no radios or televisions running interference between our feelings and the world. We were one in that moment, intrinsic to all the beauty the evening called forth that night, just for us. Memories of that evening still evoke strong feelings of security from within me. Yes, life was easy sitting at Momma's feet with my head resting on her lap.

There were no clocks to keep us prisoner and we had no use for calendars. The Great Spirit would speak to us through the trees, telling us when it was time. The wind told us all we needed to know. I feel sorry sometimes for people today, with so many considerations and so little time just to live. So it is, that this was our entertainment. And what a grand show it was, the rich green meadows stretching out beyond my vision, and the smell of cinnamon buns baking. We'd sit back soothed by the silence as we watched our horses perform their dance. I can still hear the bells that they wore around their necks tinkling in the wind. Fluidly, they glide in the gentleness of my memory, no longer lying dead, but alive within my mind, memories now *unlocked.*

Why would a person lock up memories this beautiful for seventy years? I wondered. Then I realized *that* was why—they were too beautiful, too good. I think somehow I knew that if I were to compare this fine little diamond, and see fully all the beauty and pleasure it had given me, I would never have been able to face losing it.

Yet it is a paradox, for I believe without this little buried treasure, I would have died. I knew, even if I chose not to remember, that somebody had loved and wanted me. I never forgot that feeling. It *was* imprinted on my soul.

Doors were opening slowly into my subconscious mind. At first, I saw only glimpses into what seemed like another world to me. I felt like a voyeur peeking into someone else's mind, and then realized it was my own.

It has taken me many, many years to piece together my origins and family ties. I know very little actually, bits and pieces told to me over the years. I know my mother and father both had Indian blood. During most of my lifetime, people of mixed blood were halfbreeds. Now I learn that they were a new people, a race formed independently on this continent with their own government, language, and ways all their own. They were Metis. But like many who have native blood, my culture and beliefs were not honored or held up in any way. Oh, I always knew I was Indian, but no one ever told me to be proud of it.

I believe I have an Indian heart, something only the Creator has the power to take from me someday, and I have accepted and found peace in my life. It may have taken me almost seventy years to get to this point, but I can tell you now that when I look back on those who crossed my path through this life, I'm proud to be an Indian woman, even though it hasn't been easy.

It wasn't until my adult life that I was told my mother's name was Margaret, and that she had predominantly native features, with dark eyes and long, wavy auburn hair. Anyone who knew her always mentioned her hair. I always wished I had been born with her auburn hair, to feel that unseen bond with the one who gave birth to me. She died when I was very young so most of my memories of her are ones I have only imagined. It must have been after my mother's death that my father took me to live with Momma and Poppa Cardinal. I never knew if they were my father's people or just very dear friends of his, but this dear Cree couple became my family.

Our winter home was a log cabin surrounded by beautiful rolling hills. When warm weather came, we would travel for months by wagon. It was like a ritual, repeating the motions of a journey. It wasn't so much going somewhere, as it was a way of life. There were large gathering spots where we would meet up with other travelers like ourselves and for awhile we became a mobile community.

These times when I traveled with Momma and Poppa Cardinal were a very spiritual time for us all. There were many sacred ceremonies that took place once we had all gathered together. There were naming ceremonies and giveaways, where beautiful gifts were literally "given away" as a way of showing thanks and appreciation to the Creator, marriages where men and women were joined together in spirit, solstice celebrations and, the most sacred ceremony of all, sundance.

Along with Momma I would go, like her shadow I would sit and watch, listen, and learn as the women made tobacco ties that would be used in ceremony. I learned how to give thanks in the form of food that was offered to the animals before we ate. I learned to live close to nature's natural cycles, to love the taste of berry syrup on bannock in the summertime, to cure meat that would both satisfy and sustain us through the long winter months. I learned that animals—the winged ones, the four-legged ones and those in the insect world—all had special energy and gifts to give both physically and in the form of lessons. These same things were taught to me concerning the plant kingdom. I knew that the Creator had placed everything we needed here for us to discover their gifts, and by acknowledging their presence, unique abilities, and ancient knowledge, we would in turn receive our blessings.

It was always a thrill for me when we pulled into camp and I'd find children like myself to play with. As other travelers pulled in, I'd stand, watching and waiting with anticipation, hoping for a new friend, hoping for someone my own age to spend the long days of childhood with.

One day my wish came true, the day Ennel's family came to camp. There was much excitement as the men gathered together to help Ennel's father put up the heavy canvas tents that would become their home. Progress, I guess you would call it—no one stayed in tipis anymore. Even backwoods Indians had been touched by modern technology. And there wasn't much buckskin around anymore. Canvas and cotton were taking its place.

The women worked alongside each other in groups, baking bannock, preparing the day's meals, and simply enjoying each other's company.

As soon as the tent was ready, I saw Ennel's father step down from the wagon carrying Ennel in his arms. I only caught a glimpse of her as he opened the flap to their large, dark tent and laid her down. He looked so weary when he stepped back out into the daylight to further set up his camp. The trail had taken its toll on him. You could see he and his wife were happy to be in the company of friends.

How I pestered Momma to let me go in. I so much wanted to see the child behind the heavy canvas flap, but Momma told me I would have to wait, the child was sick and needed to rest. It wasn't long, however, before we met and became best friends.

Ennel had straight dark hair and large deep eyes that looked even more tired than her father's did. Her body was very thin, yet it seemed to stretch out forever under those blankets. Ennel was different from me and all the other children I knew. She always had to rest and I don't ever remember seeing her leave the tent after the day her father carried her in. She was always inside that dark, heavy tent surrounded by the odor of musty canvas. I felt sorry for both of us. The women were always huddling around her bed, bringing medicines and food, and I stood outside waiting to see my friend, wondering what they did in there with all those things. I spent a lot of time waiting at her door.

Whenever I was allowed into Ennel's tent, I had to follow strict rules. I was not to get her worked up or tired out. But once that flap was let down behind us, we entered our own world, a world where only children were allowed. Ennel missed being able to go outside terribly, so I would bring what I could from the outside in to her. I gathered leaves of all shapes, sizes, and colors. Some as big as Poppa's hand, others the brightest shade of red I'd ever seen. Sometimes when I could find the proper leaves, I would show Ennel, as the children that had been there previously had shown me, how to fold the leaves and bite them until a design became imprinted and the leaves could then be opened to reveal an exciting creation. Oh, Ennel was so happy when I brought her my findings. We would lay them out carefully on her bed, surrounding her with the things she missed so badly. We had a new ceremony every time I brought bits and pieces of the world in and shared them with my friend.

When I was kept from seeing Ennel for a week, the special

treasures began piling up in the corner near where I slept. "Why do they keep me from her?" I'd ask myself over and over. There were no other children in camp when Ennel was there, and I missed her terribly. Even though I was much stronger and healthier than Ennel, I felt weak from loneliness. I needed her as much as she needed me.

When Momma denied my request to see Ennel for the eighth day in a row I made up my mind to go see her anyway. Ennel and I had talked about it before; neither of us liked these stupid rules.

I knew that when the tents were raised, there was a little space I could sometimes crawl through, a free space between the stakes and the ground. I was very quiet as I walked alongside the back of her tent and carefully lifted up the canvas and crawled in.

"Ennel, Ennel . . . it's Anne," I whispered. But I heard no words of welcome.

"It's me, Anne," I said, tugging on her nightgown. She felt cold. There was a pan of water next to the bed. I leaned over it awkwardly, trying not to disturb its contents. Ennel's face was very pale, even for Ennel. I held my breath, waiting for her to breathe, until I had to gasp for air. She hadn't moved. There was no rhythm about her body, and I realized she was dead.

I tore the flap of the tent open wide and ran toward Momma screaming. Now I knew why the women cried. Momma opened her shawl, like a great bird stretching her wings outward, and then slowly wrapped them around me as I cried.

That night as I lay on my back, I scooted my head outside of the tent so I could look up at the sky and watch the stars. I didn't yet know the name of God, but I did know that there was some intangible force up there, and it was there that we returned when we died, and I cried happy tears because I knew in my heart that Ennel was no longer trapped inside of that dark, musty tent.

Another memory that stands out in my mind is that of our long trips by horse and wagon. Not many people had cars, in fact, not many of us had ever seen one. Stories traveled by "moccasin telegraph," one person telling another, until eventually the stories drifted into the woods where we lived. They always told of mysterious places and wonderful things that I could only imagine. I spoke only the Cree language as a child, and some French. I had no concept of English whatsoever. You are defined often by your surroundings, and I always saw only familiar things, things I was comfortable with, until on one of these road trips, I came across something I had never seen before and it worried me for a long time.

We came upon an area that had recently seen fire. You could smell a strong, acidic aroma still hanging in the air. I could tell this made the old women worry. As a child, I could always tell when something was wrong by the way the women would begin to huddle, exchanging hushed words and looks. Their looks always spoke louder than their words. I knew there was great concern as we continued walking and soon reached an area that had been totally consumed by fire. A fragile, black form leaned against what had once been a stone chimney.

Fire, the great destroyer, consuming everything in its path with no conscience or concern for the fuel it consumes on its way. Nothing remains, not even the memory of its power, only a vague clue as to its nature, carried by the wind in this wisp of smoke, drifting upwards, leaving behind only the black mysterious remains of what had once been.

In silence, we moved forward, not wanting to disturb the land that now lay naked before us. In this silence, something caught my eye as I looked toward the charred surface of the ground; something began to sparkle. The sun had magically reached down and breathed a beautiful light into a stone, unlike any stone I had seen. I quickly grasped the magic stone and ran ahead to show the older girls what I had discovered.

"Oh, look what I've found," I said, breathless with excitement.

One of the girls looked at me, then at the object in my palm. Her eyes opened wide and she began to shake her head.

"No, no. You must not keep that. You have to put it back," she said, grabbing the melted glass from my hand and flinging it back on the ground.

"But why? Can't you see how it catches the sun? It's beautiful."

"It's very bad, very bad medicine," she said. "Its beauty is only a trick and you must not keep it. It belongs here on the ground."

I knew she spoke the truth even though I did not understand.

As we walked along, an old woman picked up a stick and stopped to poke through a pile of ashes. White bones appeared. It was a bad sign, and for the rest of the day the women were silent and sad.

It wasn't until I was much older that I realized we had come upon a homestead that had been burned to the ground. Yes, these things happened even in my time. We were what they called "backwoods Indians," and anything could happen back in the woods. It was slang with a negative connotation. I imagine it would be like calling a black person a nigger in the United States.

I see now that the older girl was warning me away from a world I had no knowledge of—the white world. It was a frightening place to a young Indian girl who had heard many more stories than I had, and not all the nice ones like those you tell a child. "Bad medicine" that I should carry a piece of that world in my pocket, melted glass in my hand.

Yet, I am part white, another paradox—running away from a world I am part of.

Momma's grown daughter came to visit us from Edmonton where she lived. In all the seven years I'd been alive, she was the most beautiful thing I had ever seen. She wore "flapper girl" dresses that shimmered when she moved and wore her hair shorter than I had ever seen a woman wear it. A long strand of pearls hung around her neck and the memory of my magic rock quickly disappeared upon seeing them. Momma was impressed too. Her daughter kneeled down and hugged me tight.

"So you must be Anne. My name is Cora, but you can call me Corkey, okay?"

She released me, and as she stood up the pearls swung in the air.

Corkey stayed with us for quite some time and told us thrilling stories about the big city—lights and streetcars running up and down Jasper Avenue, houses as big as trees and even bigger. I could hardly believe my ears.

There had been no one special to share with since my friend Ennel died. Corkey became my special companion, big sister, and friend.

The day before she left, I took her string of pearls. I walked down a rabbit trail that Poppa had shown me. I wasn't afraid to go deep into the woods. I knew them well from setting snares with Poppa. To me, the pearls were sacred. I searched for a sacred place where they would be safe until she came back for them. I figured if I kept the pearls, Corkey would have to come back. I just knew it.

When I found the place I was looking for, I used a stick to dig a deep hole. Carefully, I placed the pearls in the damp ground and covered them up. Then, just like Poppa showed me with the snares, I worked the ground with my hands, smoothing the leaves until it looked as if the ground had not been touched.

In the morning, Poppa was busy preparing the wagon for a trip to Lac la Bishe, where Corkey would catch the train to Edmonton. She was dressed in the same clothes she had worn the day she arrived. I heard her call out as I played on the porch.

"Momma? Momma? Have you seen my pearls?" Corkey asked. "I know I set them down somewhere around here, but I don't seem to be able to find them."

Momma came out from the kitchen and they began looking all over the house in odd places. Momma was real upset about the pearls but Corkey told her not to worry.

"Sometimes things just disappear . . . they'll show up when we least expect it," Momma said with a big smile. "Have you seen them, Anne?"

It was really hard for me not to say anything, but I shook my head no and remained silent.

Corkey gave Momma and me a kiss, waved good-bye, flashed us her big, movie-star smile, and was on her way.

It surprised me to discover that she would actually leave without the pearls, but nevertheless I was convinced that she would come back for them, and only *I* knew where they were. She had to come back. I hid my face from Momma, so she wouldn't wonder why I was so damn happy.

I was very lonely after Corkey left. It was beginning to get cold out so I spent a lot of time in our barn made of sod and hay where it was nice and warm. I could sit and stare out at the big fir trees or watch the cloud formations created by the wind. It wasn't unusual for Momma and Poppa to call and call for me to come in and eat. I hung back as long as I could.

Desulay had not been home to visit in many months. Momma said he would be back when it was time. He had traveled far away to work and become rich. Everyone teased him before he left, as he told of all the gold he planned to bring home from his travels. Now he was back, in the kitchen with Momma. He rolled out dough for cinnamon buns and told Momma he thought he was a better cook than she.

"Desulay, you make a mean cinnamon bun, boy, but I'd hate to see you try to cook a real meal. No wonder you come home skinny, you can't stomach your own cooking!"

Momma pushed him aside.

"There's no way I'm going to let some skinny warrior come in here and take over my kitchen. Clean up your mess and get!"

Good memories. Good medicine.

1928

I don't know if it was because of my loneliness and lack of playmates that Momma and Poppa decided to send me to the big city, or if there were other reasons, but I do know that Momma didn't look very happy about it though she tried to pretend otherwise.

"Oh, Anne, you lucky girl, getting to go to the big city! All the people you'll see and exciting, wonderful things you'll do. . . ."

I wasn't happy about it, even if it was where Corkey came from.

"You're coming too, aren't you?"

"No Anne. This is your time, a time for you to go alone to the big city and meet your aunt, Edwina. She's so anxious to meet you. She has children. It will be a good time for you."

She said this very firmly and I knew not to ask any more questions. Much later I would learn that it was Elizabeth and Edwina who insisted I be sent to them.

In an attempt to make me feel better, Momma planned a trip to our friend Tina's. Tina had lived in the big city before she married Stanley. She told me more wonderful stories and it did ease my mind, knowing Tina had survived the trip. Before we left Tina's, she asked me to pick out something special from her house to take with me. It seemed everywhere I looked, new things peeked out at me. But her music box had always been my favorite and I didn't dare ask for it. It was the best of the best. I stood in front of it, frozen in indecision.

Tina reached for the music box and handed it to me.

"Anne, I told you I wanted it to be something special. I know you will always keep it well." Her eyes crinkled up like fans and her smile drifted upward. She hugged me.

Before bed that night, I looked at the music box cradled in my hand. It was made out of porcelain and had a beautiful design of lavender forget-me-nots covering the top. I crawled into my sleeping place and wound it up. My dreams danced to the beautiful music.

When I left with Poppa the next morning, the wind had grown bitter cold. Momma was standing on the porch, holding her big wrap-around apron to her face, wiping tears from her cheeks. I asked Poppa why she was crying and he told me to look at the horses, only forward, never behind.

"She always cries when I leave," he said.

I knew this wasn't true.

Memories from this time in my life are many. Some are recalled with great fondness, others with sorrow. I was about to enter a world in which I would need to depend on the love I'd received from Momma Cardinal and also desperately need the spirit of survival I had inherited from the mother I had never known.

Many children didn't make it. Some killed themselves after being taken forcefully to residential Indian schools. There we learned we were Indian, no longer the People, or the Tribes, but Indian. The little boys had their hair chopped off, and anything that gave us strength, identity, or a feeling of sovereignty over our being was denied. Although I never attended one of these schools, I understand what it feels like to have everything stripped of you.

You see, what a child has is very important to her. These things help her through the hard times, help her hold on, remember, or sometimes forget.

However, mine is a happy story. I made it. I have held my babies and watched my great granddaughter's birth. I didn't do it alone, a little piece of me hid out. The Creator helped my spirit move and kept it safe, in a place where it could not be caught.

CHAPTER TWO

Lucky, Lucky Girl

Bremerton, Washington, 1927

*I*t had been a long and exhaustive search before the lead came in that found Anne. The detective Elizabeth and her new husband, Joe, had hired had by no means come cheap. He was the best money could buy. Joe knew it was worth every cent when he arrived home with the news that Anne had been found and that she would soon be on her way to Edmonton and her new life.

"Do you think she's all right, Joe? They didn't hurt her, did they?"

Elizabeth had not forgotten that the world could be a cruel place.

"I don't think so. From what I've heard, they live quite primitively, but she's been well cared for. However, there are many things we will still have to take into consideration. To Anne, we are all strangers from a strange place, and she does not speak English."

Joe knew that finding Anne would only be the beginning; there would be many other steps before Anne would be able to adjust to her surroundings. Elizabeth was still quite naive, and in many ways spoiled, never realizing the extent of the adjustment Anne would have to face after being taken from her home and all she had ever known.

Elizabeth was greatly relieved that her sister's only child had been found, but her vision of Margaret dying alone in a cold cabin had haunted her for five years. She should have been there. She could have made Margaret leave. She could have done something but it was too late. Margaret was dead, but Anne . . . Anne was alive.

Even after the doctor had told Elizabeth that she would never hold a child of her own, Elizabeth could still not see the price she had paid in attempting to diminish her lingering guilt. Elizabeth knew in her heart that the single act of violence the Captain had committed against her would forever change her future. Yet she still felt lucky. She had survived. She had lived while her sister Margaret had not. Besides money, Elizabeth's guilt was the only real compensation she was capable of giving those she loved, yet in its own way, even her guilt was self-serving.

Elizabeth lay in bed that night wondering why it was that fate had placed her and not her sisters in the Barnette home. Now it seemed as if another cruel fate had blessed her once again. She would become a mother after all, Anne's mother.

Edmonton, Alberta, 1928

It would be several weeks before Anne was to arrive. Joe continued working on the legalities he knew would be required in order for Elizabeth and him to travel outside of the country with Anne. Because Anne had been born in the little cabin in which her parents lived, with only the help of the native women nearby, there was no official record of her birth. This proved to be more of a problem than Joe or their lawyer, Richard, had anticipated. The couple went on to Edmonton to anticipate Anne's arrival.

When the judge learned that Anne's father was still alive, he refused to grant Joe and Elizabeth's request for adoption and would not issue a passport. Upon learning that Anne was being raised by an elderly couple who were not blood relatives, however, he agreed to grant custody of the child to one of the remaining sisters, provided that the child would not be taken out of Canada until the matter could be brought before the court in the presence of the child's father.

As Joe explained this to her, Elizabeth once again felt Anne slowly slipping away from her. It was then that she realized the only chance they had of keeping Anne now rested upon Edwina's willingness to help raise their sister's only child in Canada.

The next morning, Elizabeth sat at the little round table covered in lace looking at her sister's face. She could see the years had been hard on Edwina.

The house was quiet now that Edwina's children had left for school. The morning sun spoke of new beginnings as it danced through the curtains enlivening the room, but Elizabeth could not bear to see the day's promise of hope until the reply she awaited was no longer lingering in the cool morning air.

It was at that table, early in the morning, that Anne's life would be forever changed.

In one chair sat Elizabeth, with her guilt and profound desire to keep her family together pressed upon her heart. Across from her sat Edwina, with her insatiable need for money and status. As the steam rose from their tiny little teacups, they came upon a partnership that would fulfill both their needs.

Little Anne became their project. Elizabeth would provide the finances to Edwina who would raise Anne.

To be Indian was to be bad, savage, horrible, and ignorant. The lowest of human emotions and qualities were ascribed to the Indian. The sisters, however, felt that this was something that one could overcome, and with time, erase. What they failed to realize was that the "Indian" was the creation of the white man.

During the years Anne had been lost to them, Elizabeth had married Joe Redmond, an American. She had met Joe in the United States shortly after Margaret returned home to Desulay when their attempt to remake Margaret had failed.

Meeting Joe had taken Elizabeth's mind off her family problems. He was an entrepreneur, similar to Elizabeth's father, Theodore, in his love for travel. Constantly on the go, Elizabeth had lost track of how many miles they had traveled in the eighteen months since they had been married.

It had been such a beautiful wedding, perfect in almost every

way; but nothing is ever quite perfect. Elizabeth had originally refused Joe's marriage proposal, telling him only that she could not
possibly marry him due to circumstances he was unaware of. Watching the confusion wash over his face that had moments before held
such hope, Elizabeth reminded herself that she was refusing out of
love for him. She could not bring herself to deny Joe, knowing that
if she were to marry him, he too, would never hold a child of his
own. She had never meant for it to go this far but she had been
captivated by his presence from the moment he became known to
her. He stirred within her needs she had never known she possessed,
igniting desires that could no longer be denied. It shocked her how
easily the strong desires she felt defeated the fear she had grown to
know so intimately. Releasing, relaxing, and failing to reflect on
her circumstances, she had fallen in love with him. For a time, it
had only been her heart speaking to her mind, now it was her mind
speaking only to her heart, which lay heavy in her chest.

"I have secrets, Joe, secrets I can never tell anyone."

She spoke these words in her mind and, in her mind, she had
become a prisoner to the shame she felt toward her damaged body.
Joe held her firmly, fearing she would somehow disappear should
he relax his hold on her. The fear rose up within him as he saw her
slipping through his fingers, slipping out of his life. Even the thought
of life without Elizabeth left a haunting emptiness within him. He
felt desperate with desire to know what secrets she held.

Elizabeth tried to pull free from his embrace, but he only held
her closer. She could feel his heart beat, so strong and determined.
Again, he asked her to marry him.

Elizabeth was overcome with emotion, and Joe held her as she
cried a million tears for a child, their child, who would never be
born. As she told Joe about the Captain, Elizabeth realized she had
never experienced such intimacy, or believed such compassion could
exist between two people. It was as if Joe had somehow unlocked a
door through which the shame that had kept her silent for so long
could finally escape.

It took patience and persistence on Joe's part to convince Elizabeth that the only thing that mattered was their love. Joe had found his heart's desire in Elizabeth alone, yet when they began to discuss who would raise Anne when and if she was found, Joe could plainly see Elizabeth's desire to become Anne's new mother. Joe was a warrior in his heart. He knew the love Elizabeth felt for her sister's child must be allowed to grow. He gave Elizabeth hope. Only he knew how delicate she was; only he knew her secrets. He would protect her like a rare and wonderful rose. He would admire her natural need to give beauty and love without demand. Compelled to give her the world without her having spoken a request, he would make her a safe place, where she could bloom.

There was so much to think about now that Anne had been located that Joe's mind swam in confusion as he tried to communicate the essentials to his wife.

"How is she, Joe? How long will it be until we see her?"

Elizabeth hadn't paused long enough to catch her breath.

"Whoa! Slow down a minute, Elizabeth, give me a chance to fill you in."

Relief flooded Elizabeth's face as her emotions broke free and flowed forth in gratitude. For several years she had searched and waited, determined to save her sister's only child from the fate that had befallen Margaret, and in her naiveté Elizabeth believed that it would only be a matter of time before Anne would come and live with her and Joe permanently.

From the outside looking in, Elizabeth was a woman of the world, coordinated to perfection, a pretty little package with every bow in place, still untouched by the realities that walked within her. Elizabeth never saw the connection between the pretty little packages she had brought the night she had gone to visit Edwina and her compulsive need to make things match. Everything had to be perfect. Coordinated with such care and beauty, the pretty little packages adorned in bows were the only thing left untouched, undamaged, and beautiful that night at the Captain's. She had begun a new ritual then; Mondays it might be blue, Tuesdays lavender, but everything would always be coordinated to perfection. Making sure she found the perfect shade or accessory meant much more to Elizabeth than merely looking good; it was something she needed in order to function.

Edwina resented her sister's preoccupation with her appearance. Often she would snicker viciously behind Elizabeth's back at the lengths to which her older sister went to present herself to the world. While her sister wouldn't be caught dead with so much as a hair out of place or shoes that didn't match, Edwina was at home, forever scrubbing floors and wiping runny noses.

It was not surprising to Edwina when she heard her sister's decision to remain childless. Elizabeth had spoken at great length about how unrealistic it would be to raise a child and remain by her husband's side throughout his many travels. Edwina saw it as another symptom of her sister's selfishness.

"Oh, I bet she cries when she breaks a fingernail," Edwina would shriek in fury as she stuck her nose up in the air, doing a caustic impression of Elizabeth. Edwina felt a sick comfort in the role she played so well. She would eternally be the long-suffering martyr, superior to all in her ability to endure unhappiness. She accepted her sister's plan, supposedly out of kindness and Christian charity; the real reason for her acceptance, however, was the generous amount of money Elizabeth promised to give her for Anne's care.

Edwina had three children, Eddy, the youngest, Marilyn, who was eight years old, the only girl and resident princess of the household, and Ronald, who was eleven.

Ronald had little in common with his siblings or his mother, for that matter. He did, however have a great respect and regard for his father, which some of the locals found odd because of the stories that circulated regarding Ronald's birth. The gossip had it that Edwina had been pregnant months before she married her well-known, well-respected husband, John Domenick. If it was indeed true, it might have explained Edwina's obvious lack of motherly love toward her eldest son. Edwina was incredibly cruel to Ronald.

It was easy to see that any respect Ronald had for his mother was born out of fear, not love. In his own way, he was also an orphan, abandoned emotionally by his mother and again by his father, who was always kind to him but never had the strength to be his ally and protect him from his mother.

Even at the tender age of eleven, Ronald had accepted many truths about his life. He had seen firsthand the cruelty his mother was capable of; without notice or provocation, she would strike, attacking him in a blind fury, often over nothing but her own unhappiness unable to contain itself.

It was early evening when Poppa Cardinal and Anne arrived in the little town of Lac la Bishe. Poppa watered and fed the horses while Anne sat on a bale of hay and watched the townspeople. All the patterns and designs of the women's clothes were fascinating. Anne felt proud to be wearing the new dress that Momma had made especially for her trip to the city.

They would spend the night in the livery stable. It was cheap and very near the store where Poppa had to buy one last thing for Anne before putting her on the train in the morning.

Momma had prepared a large basket of food for their trip and they ate until their bellies were full. They had to be sure to leave enough for Poppa's trip home. The sun set too soon for Anne. She pulled the heavy quilt over her head, leaving her nose in the cool night air. The scent of hay surrounded them and Anne felt safe, but awoke several times during the night.

In the morning, Poppa brought Anne a bundle wrapped in brown paper from the trading post. He handed the package to Anne, and she pulled gently on the string and carefully lifted the odd contraption out of its wrapping. She examined it from every angle—so many buttons and holes. She didn't know much about city clothes, least of all city underwear. It took a great deal of concentration, but Anne finally maneuvered herself into the underwear and walked proudly out to see her Poppa, who sat waiting with a shiny red apple in his hand.

As Poppa sat her down in the big train, he handed her the apple. He held her to his heart one more time, then turned and walked down the steps and off the train quickly, without saying a word.

Anne watched him through the window as he jumped from the last step and headed toward the livery stable. The iron wheels ground slowly. Anne covered her ears. As the trees began to pass faster and faster, she couldn't stop the stinging of a tear.

The underwear Anne wore were warm, no doubt, but were all city clothes so uncomfortable? Each bump of the train made the undergarment creep and cut deeper into the skin beneath her chin. She held tightly to the big, red apple for hours as the train rolled along the tracks toward Edmonton. She admired its beauty, its deep red color, and it was comforting the way it fit between her hands, filling both palms and flaring out beyond her fingertips.

No one on the train spoke the Cree language, but one conductor did speak French. He had been told to check on the girl, and dutifully did so when he could. No one else even looked like Anne or her momma.

As time passed, her belly began to rumble, but Anne was unwilling to eat her apple. It was the only familiar thing to hold on to as she traveled into an unfamiliar world.

On the day Anne was to arrive, Elizabeth dressed in lavender. Her fragrance was lilac, and her gloves were lavender, her little hat was lavender, as was her underwear. Even the soap with which she cleaned was lilac scented. She added the amethyst ring that Joe had bought her and some plum-colored eye shadow.

Elizabeth and Joe, Edwina, John, and their three children all waited at the Edmonton train station for Anne to arrive. Eddy whined incessantly until Edwina bought him a sucker that he'd seen in a candy store window.

Ronald stood silently, as he often did, a long, lean figure in the shadow of a family he never fit into. The rhythm of the train in the distance became audible. He wondered what was in store for this little orphan Anne. The scent of lilacs swept past him as Elizabeth swirled in the direction of the coming train.

When the train pulled into the Edmonton station, the conductor came to help Anne with her bag. A tall man entered and introduced himself in French as Anne's "Uncle John." As they stepped down from the train, Anne felt the stares of the small group of strangers awaiting her arrival.

There was much excitement, many words that Anne didn't understand. Although Uncle John tried to explain to Anne what was being said, she remained confused. One of the women reminded Anne of Corkey. She had a beautiful smile, and nice clothes that smelled wonderful. The woman pointed at herself.

"Momma," Elizabeth said, identifying herself to Anne. She wrapped her arms around the child tearfully, nearly suffocating Anne with her thick fur coat. At this moment, Anne was being told that someone other than Momma Cardinal was her real mother. Anne felt tiny and confused. Why was she forced to go to this strange place with strange people? Mamma Cardinal had told her about her aunt, but mentioned nothing of her mother.

The children said nothing, just stared at her, until at last a little boy with a mean face and a sucker jutting out of his sticky mouth leaned toward Anne and yelled in her ear.

"Indian! Indian!" he screamed, and began to poke her with the long, sharp sucker stick that had been in his mouth. Then he grabbed the large, red apple from her hand and began stabbing it over and over again. Anne screamed in grief and disbelief, until anger and a hidden power within her—the desire to survive—ignited. She became like an animal who had been wounded. Screaming, she pounced on Eddy and knocked him to the ground. They engaged in war.

By the time Uncle John and Ronald pulled the two apart, it was clear that the precious piece of fruit was the most seriously injured, lying in pieces on the sidewalk. Anne watched as Edwina picked up what was left and threw it in the garbage. Anne was furious. She didn't care if it was damaged; it was her apple and she wanted it back.

Once the group arrived at the house of Edwina and John, Elizabeth and her husband said good night and returned to their rented suite, while Edwina began to organize the child's belongings and settle her into her new home. She immediately sent Anne to the bath and began to undress her as the hot water filled the room with steam.

Edwina wasn't a kind-looking woman; she was thin with a face of sharp corners, so it surprised Anne when her aunt began to laugh as she removed Anne's dress.

"John, you've got to come in here and see this. Oh you won't believe it! She's wearing boys' underwear and not only that—they're upside down!"

Anne was embarrassed when her Uncle John explained the problem. It was bad enough that these strangers were seeing her body. No one but Momma Cardinal had ever bathed her before. He tried to reassure her.

"Those are very nice underwear and it does not matter if they are boys' underwear as long as they keep you warm." His soothing voice helped a little, but not much.

When John left the room, Edwina began meticulously picking through Anne's black curls. Anne knew she was looking for lice, Momma had always checked her when she had been playing with other children, but this time she felt violated by this woman who was trying to take Momma's place.

Anne sat in the bath water and watched Edwina pick up the clothing, thumb and index fingers pinched together. She placed the dress Momma had made into a bag. Squaw-style clothes. They were little different than the clothes the white women were wearing—a simple blouse tucked into a long skirt. The clothing had made Anne feel safe, like holding her apple on the train.

"Lucky, lucky girl," they had all said when she left her home. As Anne lay in bed that night staring at a strange ceiling, she was beginning to wonder why they had all lied. This was not wonderful or exciting , or even comfortable. Already everything Anne had arrived with had been taken from her, and she sensed deeply that the woman who now bathed her saw nothing good in her.

It's hard to imagine how someone could take a child into her home and reject her at the same time. The woman Anne would come to know as Aunt Edwina rejected her in many ways. It was as if her childhood ended abruptly the day she stepped off the train and into the big city. This was the beginning of her assimilation into the white world.

CHAPTER THREE
Lessons Learned

1929

*A*nne had been living with Edwina a very short time before they all had to move into a smaller house in a cheaper part of Edmonton, known as Riverdale. Edwina was devastated at having to move. She had grown accustomed to a certain lifestyle after marrying John, but the "hungry thirties" were approaching, and people everywhere were out of work and barely able to survive.

The house they moved into in Riverdale was damp and gloomy. Very little light made its way into the dark halls that smelled of mildew. A couple gallons of calcimine had worked well to hide the many imperfections in the walls of the house, but it was poorly heated. There was a constant chill in the air and the whole family, including Anne, wore heavy stockings and sweaters around the house.

Elizabeth was still unable to bring Anne to the United States legally, so she continued to send financial support to Edwina, who relied upon Elizabeth's care money to give her children and herself things that would otherwise be unaffordable. Elizabeth was never able to spend more than a week with Anne before being called to her husband's side to accompany him to some distant land. The trips became more and more frequent, and Joe refused to go without his wife.

She would, however, send long letters on beautiful stationery, and parcels full of the finest dresses, shoes, and accessories a young girl could hope for. Unfortunately, Edwina was offended by these offerings.

"How dare she rub her money in my face. The nerve of that bloody woman!" Edwina raged.

Anne had been told repeatedly that Elizabeth was her mother. Why did she choose to be absent from her daughter's life? It must have been out of guilt that Elizabeth sent her parcels and paid Edwina to raise her. No wonder Edwina resents me so, she thought. She's been carrying the burden of her sister's indiscretion all these years. Anne was sure she had been conceived out of wedlock, and that's why so many secrets surrounded her.

"She's nothing but a selfish, self-involved, spoiled child herself," Edwina said, "she can't be bothered with you; it might interfere with her social agenda, or her love life, the bitch. She has no time for you Anne and you best appreciate the fact that I do. While your mother's out buying new furs and showing off her diamond rings, I'm here working my fingers to the bone, doing her dirty work, and don't you forget it! You think she'd put up with you? Even for a minute? No way. You're lucky I'll have you; your own mother can't be bothered. All she can do is send you gifts and gallivant around the world!"

Elizabeth had no idea how difficult things had become financially for Edwina and Edwina was not about to tell her. She was much too proud to share that information with her sister. It was important for Edwina to maintain the appearance of wealth to the extent that she could.

John was a good man and a talented chef, but the hotel had to let him go. They promised to rehire him when business picked up again. He managed to find work at a little restaurant, and though the pay was considerably lower, he was able to take home large boxes of bread, buns, and pies that had grown too stale to sell to customers, and this helped the family through the winter.

By spring, Anne was nearly eight years old and her English had improved substantially, but she was still often misunderstood.

Edwina used Anne to impress others with her sainthood—good Catholic woman tames backwoods savage—and Anne dreaded these stagings.

She was treated like an animal, being trained, restrained, and disciplined, and eventually expected to perform like a professional, bringing honor upon the woman, the saint, who had tamed the wild savage. This was no simple feat, as the missionaries in Canada would attest. It was nearly impossible, and took great sacrifice on the part of the trainer who would oversee these heathen beasts. Anyone attempting to save one of these lost souls should surely be held in the highest regard. It would take a great deal of time and constant lessons in the form of discipline before one could expect any real improvement, but Edwina was ever vigilant, ever on guard and willing to administer, in a moment's notice, the lessons Anne needed to learn.

Anne never let anyone know her real feelings. She fought like a wildcat with Eddy, trying to protect herself. She bit, scratched, kicked, and screamed—made awful sounds. At first she thought this proved she was indeed a "real savage." It would be many years before she knew better. When Eddy realized he was tampering with something he surely didn't understand, he would run to his mother. That's when the bad times got worse.

Anne had never been spanked by Momma. A slap on the hand maybe, but never a spanking in her life until then. Edwina's spankings were brutal. Anne remembered hearing it said that the difference between the white man and the Indian is that the Indian loves his kids and hits his dog. The white man loves his dog and hits his kids.

When Anne traveled on the wagons with the Cardinals, she had seen men who were bad to their animals. Poppa didn't like it. He was always so kind to his animals. It hurt to watch as the animals were beaten. She knew it was wrong. Now she was the one being beaten like an animal.

Uncle John would do his best to step in and put an end to the abuse Anne was receiving, if he was around. But most of the time, he was not.

The same thing had happened to Ronald as he grew up. The abuse simply happened outside of John's presence. Anne instinctively knew Uncle John loved both of them. But he was a weak man manipulated by a clever wife.

1931

A year and a half passed before John was able to resume work at the hotel, and when he did, the family quickly moved into a house on 92nd and Jasper Avenue in Edmonton. "Twin housing" it was called—large homes were divided in two and shared by two families. It had a private backyard, big windows, and a garden, and the whole family was revived by the move.

Anne was supposed to start school in September, now that she was through her "savage" stage, as Edwina put it. She was beginning to comprehend more of the white world, and she knew it was important for her to go to school as her cousins did, so when illness struck at the end of August, Anne was very disappointed.

After an exhaustive series of tests, it was discovered that Anne had been born with a rare form of anemia that would require several blood transfusions. Initially, going to the hospital frightened Anne. Little red bags of blood hung overhead constantly and she was not clear about what was going on, only that which she overheard. Children were to be seen and not heard, and this was doubly true for *Indian* children. But Anne came to like it at the hospital. She was treated better than she was at home, the nurses could be charming, and the four-wheeled carts in the hallway made great scooters.

Sadly, when Anne had sufficiently recovered, it was too late to begin school. In the following months she heard Edwina tell others that she was too frail to return to school. Not too frail to do the work of a domestic servant, Anne noticed, but too frail for the classroom. Attending school with her cousins was never discussed again.

Edwina was horrified at the prospect of anyone finding out that she had Indian blood. With the fair skin both she and Elizabeth had inherited from their father, it was easy to dissociate herself from the past and her Indian mother, Bird Song. Anne was expected to act as if she were unrelated to the family with whom she lived. Edwina had forbidden Anne and the other children to tell anyone of their true connection.

"It's none of their business. I refuse to have to explain my family history and air my dirty laundry in public. As far as anyone is concerned, Anne is an orphan. That is all the truth anyone need know!"

Anne's English continued to improve. When she mispronounced a word, Edwina would grab her by the face and squeeze until it hurt. She would move Anne's mouth manually, forcing her to imitate Edwina, whose lips were in Anne's face. Anne would repeat the word again and again until Edwina released her grip.

Edwina decided Anne needed a little refinement, so after a day of washing clothes, ironing, scrubbing, cleaning, and cooking, her three cousins would take turns teaching Anne to read and write. Eddy called it "Anne duty." The cycle would begin with Marilyn. She was a year older than Anne. While Marilyn practiced piano and played with her friends, Anne cooked and cleaned, often making Marilyn's bed and cleaning up after her older cousin and friends.

"Listen to me, Anne. You're not an Indian anymore and it's my place to teach you and your place to listen. My mother said so."

After Marilyn, along would come Eddy.

"Oh boy! It's my turn! Am I ever gonna teach you!"

He sharpened pencils across the room from Anne and lined them up in front of him, smiling sadistically. Edwina could hear them working from her room.

"Now this is an addition problem and we will begin by adding the columns on the right."

Edwina was unaware of Eddy's habit of punctuating each word with a sharp stab to Anne's hands as she tried to write out the problems for Edwina's approval. Anne knew better than to try to explain to Edwina. She had tried once.

"Well, I'm only trying to help her and she doesn't want to listen," Eddy whined.

"Well, if that's the thanks you get for trying to help, then off you go and I'll take care of this myself."

Anne then received a lecture on ungratefulness and wasting others' time.

Anne thought Ronald was a saint sent straight from heaven. He was so full of compassion and empathy, always kind and soft-spoken like his father. Anne worked hard for Ronald, trying to impress him with her new skills. They had a special bond. Ronald never got away with anything either.

There were two sets of rules in the Domenick household, one for Eddy and Marilyn, and one for Anne and Ronald.

This was the only "schooling" Anne received. But learning to read was indeed a blessing. She read everything she could get her hands on, teaching herself more as she went. It saved her from boredom and confusion.

As Anne lay in bed one night reading, she heard someone come to the door, and thought the visitor had asked for her. She sat at the top of the stairs and listened as Edwina and the stranger talked. Something looked familiar about the tall, lean figure that Anne couldn't see very well. The streetlight was dim and the man stood outside. He spoke quietly and respectfully to Edwina, who stood before him in her night robe.

Edwina responded vehemently in a hushed voice.

"How dare you come to my home in the middle of the night, and after all this time? You want Anne?"

"Please," the man pleaded.

"If you so much as look this way again, I'll see that you're thrown into jail for abandoning Anne after her mother's death!"

And with that, she slammed the door on Desulay.

He walked down the dark street and paused to search the night sky. He reminded himself that he was not alone, that Margaret was just beyond his reach. He felt her spirit comforting him and asked her to look after Anne.

When Anne asked Edwina who had come, Edwina made it clear that she was not to question these things. Having experienced Edwina's wrath in the past, Anne was reluctant to question further.

Desulay never saw his daughter again. A trapper found him dead the following winter. The cold had claimed him and, in turn, set him free. He too had walked on into the Great Mystery.

CHAPTER FOUR

Welcome to Womanhood

John Domenick's niece Maggie was a real beauty, tall and lean with soft brown curls that framed her face and gentle blue eyes. She was very sophisticated for an eighteen-year-old woman and Edwina didn't scare Anne's cousin one bit. Edwina did not like that at all.

Maggie dropped by the house often to help with chores and check on Anne. Considering how ill Anne had been with her blood disorder, Maggie thought Edwina might work her to death. Anne was responsible for so much while Edwina's children had little required of them. Anne was not one to speak easily about her fears and feelings but Maggie was a soft shoulder. Anne loved the way she fearlessly put Eddy in his place, even if Anne eventually paid a heavy price for it when she and Eddy were left alone once again.

"Oh Eddy, please don't get mud all over the floor. You know it's got to be cleaned when Edwina gets home."

"Oh shut up, stupid! I don't care. It's not my problem if the floor's dirty. That's your job, not mine."

Globs of mud fell from his shoes as he moved toward the pantry and dug into the baked goods stored there.

"Please Eddy, please...."

Edwina was furious when she returned from the grocery store and found Anne on her hands and knees scrubbing the floor with a bucket full of water, now black from the mud on the floor.

"You stupid, stupid girl. How do you ever expect to get the floor clean with that filth?"

She dragged Anne toward the sink, and when Anne began to cry, Edwina slapped her hard across the face, her ring cutting into the skin below Anne's eye. Tears stung as they flowed uncontrollably into the cut.

"Filthy savage! You had hours, *hours,* to get this done, and now you sit here and cry about it."

Edwina noticed the pantry door open and slowly stepped in. There was still a trail of food dropped on the floor and lids lying unreplaced.

"So, now I see why you couldn't get a simple thing like the floor washed. You should be ashamed of yourself, in here like some kind of pig while everyone's out! I told you that these things were not to be touched!"

Her face was red with anger. She swung out and grabbed Anne by the hair, then pressed her face down toward the floor.

"Look! Look at what you've done. We try and try to get through to you, but it's no use, still a little savage. Well, I hope you realize that you're not going to get away with this sort of thing when I'm gone. From now on you will do as you are told!"

Anne tripped on one of the stairs as Edwina dragged her up to the bedroom. In a flash, she held her hand high in the air above Anne, then brought the leather cat-of-nine-tails down hard on Anne's upper thighs and buttocks. Again and again, the leather hit Anne's skin as she tried to curl into a ball to protect herself.

"There will be no dinner for you tonight. You've had it already."

Edwina spun on her heel and slammed the door. Anne lay on the floor for a long time, too numb to feel much. She was amazed at the tiny purple dots the whip had left—so perfectly round, just like the round knots at the end of Edwina's strap. The pattern of bruises left a signature that Anne would not soon forget. Like a gift from the Creator, the ability to retreat into herself came more and more easily to Anne.

After five years with the Domenicks, Anne reached puberty. When she began to menstruate at twelve years old, she became hysterical. She had no idea why she was in such pain, and why blood was flowing from such a private area and she didn't dare tell a soul. She used pieces of an old blouse as bandages and prayed that the blood would stop and she wouldn't die. When Edwina came across the bloodied rags that Anne had tried to hide, she offered no explanation but took her to the basement where the old cotton rags were stored and showed her how she would need to tear thin strips and fasten them together in a bundle and tie them to her panties. It was embarrassing, but Anne watched carefully. It was clear that the procedure would only be discussed this one time and there would be no further talk on the subject.

She began to wonder if perhaps some of the things her aunt was telling her were true. Was she a savage—sinful, wicked, and stupid? If not, why would Edwina keep at her? Why would her own mother, Elizabeth, not rescue her from this situation? Perhaps she was embarrassed by Anne. She started to feel bad about the burden her aunt was carrying—trying to raise a wild animal like herself.

Edwina had often commented on how flat and ugly Anne's native nose was and what a shame it was that it wasn't thin and graceful. Anne looked at herself in the ornate gold-framed mirror that hung in the hallway upstairs. At least it wasn't a pointy beak like Edwina's. The nose became a very important focal point for her aunt, however.

"As part of your grooming routine, I have decided that we will begin to treat your nose in hopes of reshaping it into something more appealing to the eye. At the very least, thin it out a bit."

She handed Anne a small tub of vaseline and brought her to the mirror.

"Now you will take your thumb and pointer finger, wet them, and begin here."

She grasped Anne's nose hard at the bridge and began to slowly squeeze it, pulling her fingers down toward the tip. Anne mentioned how painful this was.

"You're already ugly. What do you expect will happen to that nose of yours if you don't do as you're told? It will grow and grow and grow until all you have is one big, fat ugly nose for a face."

Quietly Anne picked up the small tub of vaseline and began to "thin" her nose.

This routine was added to her daily chores.

When Anne's nose became so raw and swollen that it began to crack and bleed, Anne thought that Edwina had been right; her nose was growing. It was swollen to twice its original size. She looked hopelessly in the mirror. Then in a rage of pain, she worked her nose like a piece of meat, brutally trying to change herself.

After hours of staring at herself, running her fingers up and down her nose as she was shown, squeezing and trying to make it thin, trying to make it look pretty like white noses, Anne's self-hatred reached new heights. It seemed to Anne that Edwina was right; she was terribly ugly. With the only strength she had left, she stood crying, and began to talk to the awful image she saw in the mirror.

"You are so ugly! I hate you! I hate you! Please die!" She continued until she fell to the floor exhausted.

Elizabeth had no idea of the reality of Anne's life at Edwina's. She didn't know about the beatings, the humiliation, the monitored phone calls. Whenever parcels from Elizabeth would arrive for Anne, Anne would be summoned to the bedroom where Marilyn and Edwina awaited her. She had learned that if she pretended she hated the dress or blouse she actually favored, she would get the dress she pretended to detest and Marilyn would get the other.

Elizabeth was still making yearly visits, which lasted a week, no more. Edwina would prepare for the visit like a mad drill sergeant. Anne would be told exactly what to do and say. Then upon Elizabeth's arrival, Anne would be given more freedom than usual, being allowed, for example, to walk to the market alone.

It was on one of these solitary trips that Anne met Mary, who had recently moved into the neighborhood. Normally, Anne would have declined the invitation for someone to join her—it was such a treat to be alone—but Mary seemed a kindred soul somehow, and Anne agreed to let her come along.

Mary had just moved from British Columbia to Edmonton with her mother and stepfather. She was tall and blonde with eyes a brighter blue than the sky. She was fifteen years old and knew exactly what she wanted—to return to Kamloops, British Columbia, the little town she had just left behind. Anne envied the confidence she heard when Mary spoke. When they parted that day, Anne knew they would see each other soon, and as soon as Elizabeth left town, Anne sought her out.

They became fast friends on the sly, sharing their unhappiness and their hopes for something better. Mary told of the beatings she received from her stepfather, and her mother's inability, or unwillingness, to stop the violence. Anne eventually felt safe enough to entrust Mary with her experience of life with the Domenick family.

"You should just teach that old bitch a lesson," Mary said, "otherwise it sure ain't gonna get any better. If you ask me, it's time we both skated out of here while we can."

Being younger than Mary, Anne tried to hide her shock at this statement. She didn't want Mary to think she was a baby.

"You're damn right," Anne said half-heartedly.

"Now you're talking, Anne. See, I figure with the both of us together, we'd have no problem making it to Kamloops and once we're there, we can stay with friends of mine until we get jobs. . . . We're going to have to do it soon, though. I can't take it much longer."

There was a long silence.

"So? Are you in or out, Anne?"

"But Mary, how will we get there? I don't have any money."

"I know you don't have any money. I'm not stupid, you know. I've figured it all out. All you have to do is listen to me. We could leave tomorrow night at midnight. Yeah, let's definitely leave tomorrow night! I'm going to."

Mary stood up, then Anne, slightly dazed. Mary placed her hands on Anne's shoulders and looked deeply into her eyes.

"Don't be late Anne, or I'll figure you chickened out, and I'll leave without you."

Anne nodded her head in solemn agreement.

At 11:40, Anne quietly left her bed and began to dress. The house was so silent, she thought Edwina might hear her heart pounding as she stepped carefully past her door and down the stairs.

"Anne, over here! Come on, we've got to get going," Mary whispered loudly from behind a bush. The two girls hustled down dark alleys for thirty minutes before they reached the train yard.

Light from the yard revealed to Mary how Anne had dressed for their escape.

"Oh, for Christ's sake, I don't believe it," she said. "I told you to dress warmly and wear good shoes. Good *walking* shoes. Here you are in a wool suit and penny loafers! Jesus, it'll be a miracle if we make it out of here without you freezing to death. No wonder you can't keep up with me. What were you thinking?"

"Well, you don't have to have such a fit about it. I'm sure once we're on the train, I'll be perfectly comfortable."

"Well, little Miss Patent Leather Penny Loafers, we'll see what you think when you're freezing your little socks off in the back of an unheated railroad car!"

Mary headed for the tracks and Anne stumbled after her.

"Mary, wait up! What do you mean unheated? Mary! . . . "

"Quiet, Anne. You know what they do if they catch you out here? Those big sticks they carry aren't for swatting flies, you know."

They had to crawl through gravel on their bellies to get past the linekeeper's tiny office. Once they were a safe distance from the shack, Mary began checking each train car, searching for one that was unlocked.

"Damn it. They're all locked," she muttered.

Anne was frightened by Mary's frustration and intense

determination. She gave a thought to returning home, but the image of Edwina in a rage quelled the impulse immediately.

Suddenly, the train lurched forward and startled both girls. Mary began to run alongside the train as it picked up momentum.

"They'll be stopping soon," Mary yelled back to Anne, "if we just climb on and get a good hold, we can ride till it stops and then find a car that's open."

Mary grabbed a passing ladder and hoisted herself up. Crying and falling farther behind, Anne was no longer concerned about appearing immature.

"I can't do it, Mary. I just can't. I'm scared."

"I'm going, Anne. I'm going. . . . Just give me your arm, Anne, before it picks up more speed."

Anne reached forward, acutely aware of the cold steel wheels turning at her side. As she reached for Mary's outstretched hand she prayed that she would be able to clear her feet in time, and wouldn't be sucked under the train.

Anne leapt to Mary's side, and struggled to find a foothold as the train shook her about like a rag doll. She clung to the cold metal bar with all her strength.

"You're a baby," Mary yelled above the noise of the train.

"Who cares if I'm a baby when I'm dead?" Anne sobbed.

"Well, I don't care what they say about you when you're dead, either. And that's just what you're going to be, if you don't hold on tight. If you keep up that sniveling, I might just kill you myself."

The wheels roared beneath them. On and on, the train traveled the dark track. Anne's hands grew numb.

"Mary, I don't think I can do it. I can't feel my hands anymore. I think I might let go. I can't tell anymore, Mary. I can't tell if I'm even holding on."

"You're going to be okay, Anne, you're just cold. So am I. We'll be stopping soon, you'll see. Just hold on a little longer. We're just about there. . . ."

When the train downshifted, Mary looked at Anne doubtfully.

"We have to jump now, Anne, or else we'll be caught and if we ain't caught—God knows when they'll slow down again. There's no other choice, now, you're just going to have to do it. I don't care if you're scared, you've just got to do it, damn it. Now!"

And with her words still hanging in the air, Mary jumped from the train.

More frightened than she had thought possible, Anne tried to let go of the bar but her fists remained clenched, frozen in place. Her friend quickly disappeared from sight, and Anne panicked. Again, she commanded her hands to release their grip, and with a forceful thud, she was suddenly on the hard ground.

"Come on, Anne," Mary said breathlessly, "we've got to move away from the tracks. They'll be checking."

She grabbed Anne beneath the arms and placed her on her feet.

"I saw a light back about a mile or so. I think it's a linekeeper's shack. We'll have to take a chance and make up a story or we'll freeze to death out here. With any luck, we'll be able to spend the night."

By the time they reached the brightly lit cabin, they had devised a story. Mary did most of the talking while Anne stood near the stove trying to chase the awful chill from her bones.

"Well, we were traveling with my uncle to British Columbia when his car broke down," Mary began. "And because it's so cold out, he told us to see if you would maybe put us up for the night until he got it fixed."

The woman listening didn't look very impressed with the story, but agreed to set them up in a room.

"I don't think she bought it," Mary said, closing the door behind them. "We better be long gone before she wakes up."

When the woman's husband returned, she relayed the girls' story. One phone call to the Royal Canadian Mounted Police confirmed his suspicions. The girls had been reported missing.

Anne slept like a baby in the overstuffed bed until voices from downstairs wafted up to rouse her. Mary was out cold, so Anne shook her.

"They're here, Mary! The RCMP. I heard the woman call him 'Officer.'"

Mary shot to her feet. She was still fully dressed from the night before. While Anne dressed, Mary pried open the bedroom window, which was sealed shut with several coats of paint. When half of her body was out the window, the bedroom door flew open and one of the RCMP rushed in.

Still in sad shape from the previous night's adventure, Anne started bawling the moment she saw the officer. Mary abandoned her escape and brought her leg back in through the open window. Still hoping to talk her way out of things, she threatened her weepy partner.

"I swear, I'll throttle you kid, if you don't shut up."

But nothing Mary said could frighten Anne more than the thought of Edwina.

The police escort back to Edmonton seemed tormentingly slow for Anne. She braced herself for the beating she would receive.

With every smack of the leather hitting her flesh, with every vile word that poured forth from Edwina's twisted mouth, Anne vowed that next time she would be smart, next time she wouldn't be caught.

"Discipline is what the little savage needs," Edwina declared.

It was decided that Anne would be sent to a Catholic orphanage for troubled girls for the summer.

The orphanage was out in the country. There were two wings in a large, old brick building. One where the good girls slept, and the other for those who had been in serious trouble with the law. Because Anne was only twelve, she was placed in the good girls' wing. Except for the nuns and two Ukrainian groundskeepers, there was no one around for miles.

Anne soon learned that even the "good" girls were expected to work hard for their room and board. The dark halls and endless wooden floors became well known to her as she spent hours on her hands and knees making sure all was clean.

Working hard had never bothered Anne, and although the nuns
were strict they seemed to be fair. She did her share gladly, and found
camaraderie and friendship with the other girls. When the work day
was complete, they were allowed to play with abandon. Romping in
the beauty that surrounded the orphanage and playing little-girl
games was something Anne had never before been a part of.

Susan and Janice were also twelve years old. The three girls
soon became inseparable. One of their favorite things to do was go
out in the large barn in the field about half a mile from the orphanage. In the barn, they would laugh and giggle and play in the hay,
jumping from stack to stack.

One day, the groundskeepers showed up. One of them jabbed a
pitch fork into the hay near the girls.

"If you ever tell anyone, we'll kill you," the other one said.

Anne and Susan shook their heads. Janice stared eerily into a
corner of the barn, unable to respond.

One by one, the girls were raped.

When the two men left, Anne and Susan clung to each other as
they cried. Janice sat in a corner without tears. Lovingly, Anne went
to Janice's side and began to dress her. Their pinafores were ripped
and torn. Together, Anne and Susan helped Janice rise awkwardly
to her feet, and they all walked back to the orphanage. They sang no
happy songs. They played no little-girl games.

Anne and Susan changed their clothes, then helped Janice remove hers. Janice refused to leave her bed.

"She's been feeling sick all afternoon, I think she needs to rest,"
Anne told the sister who came to check their rooms when they
were late for dinner.

That evening after they had gone to bed, Anne woke to hear
Janice moaning and went to get help. Janice was burning with fever, so Anne carried her to the bathroom at the end of the hall and
ran some cool water. The moment Janice's little body touched the
water, she shrieked. When the nuns came running, her friend
couldn't speak of her ordeal but just continued to cry in pain.

Anne and Susan listened from their beds until Anne couldn't stand it anymore. She got up to go comfort her friend. Susan grabbed her from behind. The moon was shining through the window onto Susan's fearful face.

"Anne, please, don't tell. You know what they said. They'll kill us."

"I have to Janice. If I don't, they may come and kill us anyway."

It was a scandal beyond comprehension—three girls brutally raped at a Catholic orphanage. It didn't matter that the men were not religious people; the parish had hired them and therefore bore the responsibility. It was decided immediately that the girls would be removed from the grounds and the whole incident covered up as quickly as possible.

Anne was the only one of the girls capable of becoming pregnant, and thankfully she didn't. She spent several weeks recuperating in another girls' home and was then returned to Edwina. The incident was never spoken of and Anne had no idea whether Edwina had been told or not. The routine she had previously known quickly resumed, only now she was watched even more closely than in the past.

CHAPTER FIVE
A Royal Family

December 5, 1934

A parcel from Elizabeth arrived for Anne's birthday. It was a birthday picked at random to satisfy the paperwork filed for Anne's guardianship.

The package contained a beautiful navy blue suit, finely tailored, and an ivory blouse that tied in a large bow at the neck, and a little navy blue hat that was trimmed in ivory. There was a small ivory purse to match the blouse. Elizabeth had been careful once again to enclose the perfect accessories—navy blue kid leather gloves.

When Anne tried it all on, she looked far older than thirteen. Elizabeth would have been proud. Of course, Edwina touted the usual your-mother's-no-good response, and Anne felt almost guilty for having received another gift.

Anne sunk into a familiar despair. Soon even Ronald would be gone. He was joining the Royal Canadian Air Force when he graduated. Edwina didn't know this yet, but she would know soon.

Anne carefully placed her new outfit on a hanger, taking care to smooth out any wrinkles. It was really going to be awful in the house once Ronald left, she thought.

That night as Anne lay in bed, a peaceful assurance came from deep within her. She too would someday break free from Aunt Edwina's grip. She had been well trained. She knew how to run a household, even if she was only thirteen. She could clean until it sparkled, scrub until it shined, and iron out any wrinkle you threw her way.

The next morning, Anne began scanning the Help Wanted ads in the *Edmonton Journal*. She was careful to do this privately. An ad appeared that made her heart quicken.

> *Mother's helper wanted. Room and board. Duties*
> *will include food preparation and caring for four*
> *children. Cheerful attitude preferred. Contact Mr.*
> *and Mrs. King for interview....*

If she timed it right, she just might be able to apply and make it home before Edwina did.

Anne took a deep breath and knocked loudly on the door. Mrs. King opened the door and greeted Anne graciously before inviting her in. The Kings' house was a large, inviting home. Anne immediately informed Mrs. King that she was a hard worker and more than qualified for the position.

Mrs. King was charmed by her enthusiasm. She asked Anne about her family and Anne told her that she was an orphan with an elderly aunt who was unable to care for her.

"Children, come down here," Mrs. King called up the stairs, "there's someone I'd like you to meet."

Little feet scurried and soon they all bolted haphazardly down the stairs.

First there was Sonny, the oldest of the lot at age eleven. Then Barbara, who had just turned nine years old and seemed a little shy. Bob and Tom were four-year-old twins with impish grins.

"Well, when can you start?"

Anne was stunned. How easy it had been! She sprinted the eight blocks back to Jasper Street and took the steps to her room two by two. Edwina was not yet home. Anne said a silent prayer of gratitude and changed quickly out of her navy blue suit.

When Edwina left to join John for lunch the next day, Anne took down her small suitcase, packed the essentials, and hurried out of the house. Edwina would not be happy when she discovered Anne had run away once again. Anne put the thought of Edwina tracking her down out of her mind and focused on a bright future.

Mr. and Mrs. King treated Anne as if she were part of their family. The children were affectionate, and she was valued as a human being who was capable of accomplishing many tasks. Two months after she arrived, Anne was thriving.

The second week in November, when the snow lay heavy upon the ground and the air outside was frigid, Mr. King walked in his office and found Mrs. King grieving. News had come via telegram just an hour before; her mother was seriously ill. They would have to leave immediately for the United States.

Heartsick, Mr. and Mrs. King called for Anne to join them. She knew that something had been terribly wrong since the telegram arrived. Mrs. King had been barely able to control her emotions. Her face was swollen, her eyes brimming with tears. Mr. King held his wife's hand as he spoke.

"We've received some very sad news today, Anne. And if you feel it's possible, we're going to need your help. Emaline's mother has taken ill, she may not live through the month. Mrs. King and I would like to leave as soon as possible. . . . Please don't feel you have no choice in this. I'm sure my sister would be more than willing to watch over the children in our absence, but they're so comfortable at home here with you that I thought by chance you would agree to watch over them while we're in the States."

He began to ramble out of nervousness, mentioning the many details he would have to oversee before they left. Anne stopped him midsentence to respond to his request.

"I'm sure the children and I will make out just fine, Mr. King. I hope you'll rest assured of that."

Dabbing at her red and swollen eyes, Mrs. King expressed her gratitude with a nod.

Anne knew the loneliness of being in the world without a mother.

Anne cooked breakfast in the morning and the older children helped the twins dress. Everyone pitched in when it came time to clean. In the evening, after the twins were tucked into bed, Mr. King's sister, Kathleen, would come over with her daughter Caroline to sit with Anne, sipping tea and knitting.

Anne felt so grown up as she sat with Kathleen, watching her intently. She imitated her mannerisms, careful to hold her cup just so, making sure her pinkie was held delicately out to one side. She hoped Kathleen didn't notice that Anne knew only one stitch. She would watch Kathleen, and practice new stitches when she was alone.

When three weeks had passed, Mr. King sent word that Emaline's mother had died. They planned to stay on for the funeral and arrive home on Anne's fourteenth birthday. Kathleen suggested a birthday party. They could surprise Mrs. King, whose birthday was only days later.

"It will be a coming-of-age party," Kathleen said, thinking Anne would be turning eighteen.

When Mr. and Mrs. King approached the house, all was dark. It looked as though Anne and the children had gone to bed early.

"Welcome home!"

Anne swung open the door, Sonny and Barbara stood behind her. Someone threw the light switch and "surprise" echoed throughout the house. Mrs. King was startled as all her friends came rushing from hiding places. Another group emerged from the kitchen and another round of greetings were exchanged.

Mrs. King wept. There's weeping with pain and weeping with relief. The crowd of friends were washed with her relief.

At Mrs. King's urging, Anne sat to open a brightly wrapped box, a gift from the States. The children had opened their gifts and now it was Anne's turn. Everyone waited, relaxed and smiling.

Anne gently pulled the string, peeled back the soft paper, and lifted the skeins of angora wool and new knitting needles from the box. The colors took her breath away.

"Oh, Emaline, how beautiful."

Anne was so moved, she didn't notice that she had called Mrs. King by her familiar name.

Anne greeted more guests and served hors d'oeuvres until the children went to bed. Once they were snuggled in, Anne joined them and read "The Night Before Christmas."

Anne was walking a different path than her mother, whoever she was. But then, every daughter must.

She was disappointed when the twins fell asleep before she finished the story. Still a child herself, the time she spent with the children was more play than work.

Not wanting to disturb them from sleep, she lay beside them silently, thinking of how lucky she had been to find this home and family.

Two weeks after the Kings arrived home, Anne awoke in the night with a terrible pain radiating from her throat. The throbbing grew stronger as hours passed slowly until at last the sun rose into morning. Every time Anne swallowed, the raw skin that lined her throat became more inflamed. Her temperature rose as the infection took hold. She began to shiver and a cold sweat beaded across her forehead. She prayed it would pass.

When Mrs. King found her still in bed, Anne's tonsils were so big she was having trouble breathing. Her ears ached as Emaline tried to comfort her.

"Dear, you have to listen to me now. Try not to upset yourself so. You're very ill and we must take you to the hospital where they can give you medicine and make you all better again."

They wrapped Anne in a soft cotton quilt. On the way to the hospital, Emaline asked Anne the name of her aunt. She should be notified, Emaline said.

Anne turned away from Mrs. King and began to cry.

"Please don't send me back," she sobbed. "Please, no. I would rather die."

Emaline put a hand to Anne's forehead tenderly, wishing she could change things, and knowing she had to contact her aunt.

"Dear, sweet child, we'll see that you are well taken care of and that you get better real soon, you'll see. Worry about nothing but getting better. Trust me, Anne. We must go to the hospital now."

"If I have to, I'll come right to your aunt's house and get you, if that's what it takes," Mr. King said as he placed her carefully in the backseat of his car and patted her on the shoulder.

Soon Anne was swimming in ether. A nurse dropped it on some cotton gauze, placed it in a mask, and covered Anne's face, and Anne dove into a dream world of anesthesia.

When she awoke, partially, she was staring at a giant, crusty dinner roll. Anne, in her semi-conscious state, was unaware of the sign posted at the foot of her bed that said Absolutely Nothing by Mouth. Apparently, the nurse who had delivered her tray had not seen it either.

Anne was famished. She sat straight up in bed and quickly desecrated the large roll in front of her, eating wildly, swallowing large pieces.

The crusty dinner roll ripped poor Anne's already tender throat to shreds. Her bed was covered with blood when a group of nurses surrounded her, shouting questions at Anne and each other.

"What did you eat? Can you answer me? Did someone give her dinner?"

"Someone brought her dinner," another nurse shrieked. Anne could hear the voices but couldn't speak. Moments later a mask was once again placed over Anne's face and she tumbled into unconsciousness.

The Kings contacted Edwina.

When Anne was leaving the hospital, she received a parcel from the Kings containing a soft, lavender robe, matching slippers, a photograph of the King family, and the following note:

Dear Anne,

We're so happy that you've recovered. The children send their love. They miss you a great deal; we all do.

I'm so sad to tell you that your aunt would not agree to your return. Because you are underage, we have no authority over you. We can only trust in God to keep you well and someday Anne, you will be eighteen. I've spoken to your aunt. She is aware that we will under no circumstances tolerate any abuse of you and that if we learn such a thing has taken place, we will see that she answers for it.

I'm sorry we couldn't have done more.

With loving thoughts and all our prayers,

Love always,

Emaline

Anne had talked to Emaline, to the extent she was able, about the way she was treated by Edwina, but in reality, Emaline didn't know the half of it. Some things were just too difficult to mention.

As Anne regained her strength, her confidence grew also. Having been threatened by Mrs. King, Edwina was less inclined to outright physical abuse, but instead left Eddy in charge whenever she left the house. Eddy had grown taller, leaner, more beautiful, and nastier than ever.

Ronald, Anne's only ally, spent less and less time at home as he prepared to enter the Royal Canadian Air Force.

To Anne, the title "maid" represented status. No longer content to be a baby-sitter or a mother's helper, Anne decided she would be a professional. She was still only fourteen years old, but her spirit whispered encouragement.

She envisioned herself in a black uniform with a little white apron and cap. She began reading the want ads on the sly once again and there it was—her next job. Once again, she would leave Edwina's without a word.

She could hardly wait for the front door to open so she could see inside. The McDillon estate was a beautiful Victorian beyond Anne's imagination. From backwoods savage to maid of the mansion, she thought as she waited at the front door.

A heavyset woman with a plain round face answered the door. She was wearing a cotton shift and worn slippers, and had her hair pulled back in a tight little bun.

"You must be Anne," she said, smiling pleasantly.

She wiped her hands on her dirty apron before reaching out to shake Anne's hand, then motioned Anne into the home, and turned and limped ahead of her into a large, elegant room with marble floors and a baby grand piano in the corner.

Floor-to-ceiling windows flooded the room with morning sun. Sitting daintily on the sofa, Anne carefully removed her navy blue kid leather gloves and folded them neatly in her lap.

"My name is Frances," the woman said, "but you can call me Frankie."

She settled into a large, overstuffed chair that nearly swallowed her. Anne was concerned that the lady of the house might find this inappropriate, but perhaps Frankie had been with the family for years and now enjoyed such privileges.

"You know . . . Frankie, I'm very efficient. I can dust, mop, wash clothes, anything except cook, I don't have much experience there, but if you'll teach me, I'll do that, too."

When the interview was nearing its end and Anne was convinced that Frankie thought she was right for the job, Anne leaned close to Frankie and whispered her request, hoping to clench the job.

"Do you think I could meet the lady of the house today?"

Frankie began laughing uncontrollably, tears running down her chubby cheeks. She tapped her leg with her hand, trying to regain composure.

"Oh, Anne, do I really look like I'm the cook?"

Anne was confused.

"Well, you certainly do. And a very professional one at that."

Again Frankie roared with delight. She took Anne's hand in hers and spoke as one speaks to a child.

"I think you and I are going to get along just fine, dear. We'll even get you a uniform, how does that sound? That way no one will mistake you for the cook, eh?"

"Oh yes, Frankie. And it should have a white hat too, don't you think?"

"Oh, we'll play it to the hilt dear."

Elated, but still somewhat confused, Anne gathered her things to leave.

"I'll be interviewed again, then?"

"Oh, Anne. I'm not the cook, nor the head housekeeper, nor the gardener—I'm Mrs. McDillon, dear. But I insist you call me Frankie."

She could hardly believe that this crazy little woman owned such a magnificent mansion.

The McDillons were mentioned on billboards throughout Edmonton. The owner of the largest local construction company, Mr. McDillon had died suddenly at one of the construction sites. No matter how much money he made, it was important to Mr. McDillon that he work side by side with his employees. It was a freak accident, a cable snapped, a sheet of metal fell. He left Frankie a fortune and a business to run, which she did with great confidence.

Frankie was in her late sixties with four grown children. She loved to cook and could usually be found in her kitchen come mealtime, preparing something for her sons, Westly and Ernie. The kitchen was a warm, relaxed place to congregate, and the boys and their mother got such a kick out of the escapades of their socialite sisters, Alberta and Louise.

The grease monkeys, their sisters called them, all grease, grime, and grins. They preferred to spend their time in a garage near their mother's home or at the corner pub sipping Labatt's Blue.

"Wonder what the grand princesses are up to today, Mother?"

Wes poured himself a hot cup of coffee and joined his brother at the table.

"Oh, you know boys, the usual—brunch with the queen, a few cocktails, the symphony, then home before the car turns into a pumpkin!"

"Alberta's got a new dress," Frankie went on, "designed by the guy who makes dresses for that movie star she met last week."

Frankie flung the dishrag over her shoulder and waddled toward the brothers, swinging her hips like Alberta.

"Simply to die for . . ." she said, batting her lashes.

Alberta and her sister, Louise, used the main portion of the house, the upstairs, library, and sitting room. Frankie kept a large suite of her own, and the boys had their apartments set up in the basement and used the back entrance as their front door.

At first Anne thought it was dreadful, the way they all treated each other, but soon she realized that they meant no harm and simply took great pleasure in teasing each other.

Frankie apologized for having to put Anne up in the pantry, but the pantry was roomy, with shelves on one side and a large window on the other. She shared a bathroom with Frankie.

Anne looked exactly like the maids she'd seen in the movies with her little black dress, white apron, and maid's cap. She modeled for Frankie and the brothers.

"Oh, something's missing," Frankie said, grabbing a feather duster from the broom closet.

"It's important that you hold it just so," Frankie demonstrated, and they all laughed when Anne followed suit.

Over the next week, Anne learned to serve from the left and clear from the right, how to address guests properly, and everything else a proper maid should know. The sisters planned a dinner party and Anne helped Frankie prepare.

"Oh, it'll be fun, Anne. You'll get to see firsthand how they carry on."

Frankie opened a silver container from the fireplace mantle and lifted out a cigarette dramatically, then offered one to Anne. They were each tipped in a different shade of pale pastel satin. Anne played along. Neither of them smoked and they choked, laughed, coughed, and laughed some more as they imitated the sisters.

Frankie was startled when she looked at her watch.

"Oh boy, we don't have much time, Anne. I'm going to start dinner. We better move it."

When the guests arrived, Anne served hors d'oeuvres while the girls snapped out orders.

"Yes ma'am, right away sir . . ." It was just like in the movies.

Anne loaded up her silver tray in the kitchen, and with Frankie laughing behind her, she resumed her dignified air, and returned to the wonderful play taking place in the other room.

The two grease monkeys, the cook, and the maid finished the evening telling each other stories in the kitchen and gathering around the piano after the guests had left.

Anne could hardly believe her ears when Mrs. McDillon began to play piano so sweetly. Her chubby hands didn't miss a note. The music seemed to magnetize the air around them.

"You have a beautiful voice, Anne," Frankie said when she'd finished playing. Anne blushed.

Maybe these are my people, Anne thought. They don't seem to care what my nose looks like or that I was born brown. Maybe I have found my people.

The feeling of belonging didn't last. Soon after the party, Frankie approached her and for the first time since they had met, Frankie looked very sad.

"I've had a phone call, Anne. I suspected you were underage when I hired you. I know that you must have had a very good reason to leave your aunt's house the way you did, but she insisted on coming over immediately, and I didn't feel I could deny her that. She's on her way now."

Anne felt sick. She had no idea how Edwina had found her.

Mrs. McDillon walked slowly into her room and changed into a nice linen dress, combed her hair, and put on a dab of lipstick. When the doorbell rang, she asked Anne to go to her room until she came for her.

Anne struggled to hear the conversation. Edwina was extremely polite when she introduced herself to Mrs. McDillon. She was well aware of the McDillon name. When there was a knock on Anne's door, she was relieved to hear Frankie's soothing voice.

"Anne, would you please come out here? Your aunt would like to speak to you."

Anne opened the door, swallowing hard, reluctant to make eye contact with Edwina. Suddenly, Edwina went off.

"Mrs. McDillon, I can hardly believe a woman of your means could find no other place for my niece to sleep. You put her in a pantry? And you have the nerve to tell me she's happy here and you want her to stay?"

Edwina's voice had never been more vicious, and Mrs. McDillon was shocked at the sudden fury that erupted. She was speechless. Edwina ordered Anne to gather her belongings quickly and meet her outside, then stomped out of the house.

Frankie and Anne settled for a silent good-bye. No words were capable of expressing the feelings of sadness and frustration.

Refusing Edwina the satisfaction of her tears, Anne watched numbly as the McDillon mansion faded from sight. She knew now that it was only a matter of time. She would never give up. She would never surrender her spirit to Edwina. Someday she would have something of her own, something that Edwina could never take away from her. Her spirit was growing stronger, and one day it would carry her away for good.

Anne was beginning to feel the haunting sense of Margaret's love for her. She could not identify it, but it was as if her mother's spirit stood invisibly beside her, guiding her, giving her the confidence she would need to continue on. It was a nurturing feeling, as if Margaret was reaching through the veil that stands between heaven and earth . . . whispering words of encouragement to Anne's spirit.

Anne felt her mother's strength envelop her like a warm shawl on a winter's night. She remembered when Momma Cardinal spoke to her about the natural laws that were given to the People by the Creator. These truths, like spiritual seeds that Momma Cardinal had helped Anne plant within her consciousness when she was a young girl, had finally begun to blossom.

Anne had never been allowed to forget that she was an Indian. Now it was time for Anne's spirit to step out from behind the fear and insecurity of the past. She remembered running through fields of wildflowers, and the ceremonies and the symbology that formed the sacred architecture of her people. Like soothing medicine on a throbbing wound, Anne recalled the smell of sweetgrass and sage burning as the drum beats rang out into the sky and the People chanted their prayers to the invisible force that now held Anne's hand.

Slowly, intuitively, she began to move back to her center, to the place where she stood strong in her spirit. She was ashamed of nothing. She was beginning to remember what being Indian was all about.

CHAPTER SIX

The Moon Bird

Alberta, 1938

Edwina and John had known David and Laura Lamanek for many years. The Lamanek family owned the grand McDaniel Hotel where John was head chef. Unlike the owners of many other hotels and businesses in Edmonton, they had survived the depression relatively unscathed. Showing good faith, the Lamaneks had rehired many employees as soon as they were able. John Domenick was one of them.

It was this unique situation that made it difficult, in fact, downright impossible, for Edwina to deny a request from Mrs. Lamanek. Edwina was always a gracious hostess when they were around. The Lamaneks represented money and freedom, pure and simple, and they were the reason that her husband was finally able to bring money home again.

"Edwina, I'm sure you know that Mr. Lamanek and I will be spending the summer at our place on Elk Island in central Alberta, and I'm looking for someone to give me a hand around the house. I was wondering if perhaps you would consider allowing Anne to join us?"

Edwina spilled hot tea on her dress and attempted to swallow the piece of crumpet that had lodged in her throat.

"Why, I can't ... I can't think of a reason to decline, Mrs. Lamanek ... certainly. A splendid idea."

Anne was restraining herself. She quickly stifled the excitement she felt, fearing that if Edwina saw how happy she was, she would find some way to sabotage it. Anne had always liked the Lamaneks.

They included her in conversations, asked her questions, and treated her kindly, as if she were important. Anne liked it when they came to visit, and couldn't help but get a quiet satisfaction out of the way Edwina bowed and squirmed before them.

After they left, Edwina approached Anne with the news, pointing a sharp finger in her face.

"I swear to it, Anne, if you do anything, I mean anything, to embarrass your uncle or me, you will regret it. Mark my words."

The next morning Anne had taken care to dress herself appropriately before leaving the house to walk the twelve city blocks to Mrs. Lamanek's for her interview. By the time she arrived at Mrs. Lamanek's door, she had beads of perspiration popping up on her forehead, although she looked very smart in her navy blue suit. Taking a moment to gather her thoughts, she wiped the perspiration and smoothed her skirt before ringing the door bell.

Greeting her with a little grin, Mrs. Lamanek invited her in. "I'm so happy to see you dear. Come and have a seat, I'm going to make us a nice glass of iced tea." Mrs. Lamanek seemed genuinely pleased to have Anne in her home, and it was not long before Anne was lost in its surroundings.

Sitting down on a sculptured red velvet chair, she began to look more closely about the room. There were so many beautiful things, paintings like Anne had never imagined existed, and sitting on a glass shelf she saw a porcelain music box covered in lavender for-get-me-nots. Gently she lifted its tiny lid, and delicately the notes began to break the fragile silence of the room, filling it with beautiful music. For a moment something deep inside Anne's spirit moved, a forgotten memory . . . something too beautiful to remember that could only now haunt her with its melody. It was the same music box that Tina had given Anne when she left Momma and Poppa Cardinal.

As if breaking the spell the little music box had placed on Anne's heart, Mrs. Lamanek's words brought reality once again into view.

"Your Aunt Edwina gave that to me for my birthday. I believe it was the first year you lived with her. Beautiful, isn't it? Certainly a rare treasure, that one." Then, almost absentmindedly, she continued. "Oh, how silly of me! I was going to bring us some cookies to go with our tea."

To Anne, Elk Island was Never Never Land, completely surrounded by water, accessible only by boat. Her spirit expanded within her chest and a wonderful feeling of freedom filled her when she saw it. They paddled a small boat across the water toward the island, breathing in the fresh cool air. There were so many trees.

As they neared the shore, a bird's song began to echo longingly across the island carried on the wind. A special gift for Anne. A greeting, a welcoming. The song was so strong and steady with power that it even made the water sparkle like polished silver reflecting the sun. This was Anne's special moment, all just for her, and she knew it instinctively.

Summer had turned the sky bright blue and the sun outlined the Lamaneks' large, white house. Who could wrap the world any better than the One who created it?

Three people lived on the tiny island. Mr. and Mrs. Lamanek, and Chaz, a nineteen-year-old Cree from the Indian community of Marlboro, a poor community with no running water or electricity. It consisted of tar paper shacks built in the dense Canadian wilderness of Alberta. Very few residents were able to read or write or speak English. The Lamaneks had known Chaz since he was fourteen years old. He had come to them looking desperately for work so that he could feed his elderly parents and younger brothers and sisters.

Whenever the Lamaneks left Elk Island at the end of summer, they knew Chaz would be there, taking good care of their property until they returned. They had developed a deep bond with Chaz, born out of respect and trust that had grown over the years. Mr. and Mrs. Lamanek had not been able to have children. It was a sad fact that they had come to accept, and Chaz was like a son to them.

Chaz was slight in build, handsome, strong, and proud. His mixed blood had given him startling green eyes that shone out from his deep brown skin. Knowing how hard times had been for his people, and feeling a great honor when he could make life easier for his elders, Chaz worked hard for the money he made. And as always, he shared with those who had less. There were many native people who lived near the island and Chaz made sure they all got what they needed, be it food, clothing, or money for a doctor.

For Chaz, there was no "way" other than the one he had learned as a child—the tribal way, the way of his people. A true warrior would not see a man, woman, or child go hungry, even if it meant that he would suffer an empty belly to feed one of them.

It pleased Laura Lamanek to look through the large glass window in her living room and see Anne smiling, carefree, romping around the island with their old dog Queenie. She suspected that life for Anne had not been easy and had watched how hard Anne worked while the rest of Edwina's children played. She knew the true story of Anne's mother and her death. She had known the Barnette family before they adopted Elizabeth. She knew Elizabeth was not Anne's mother and thought it a crime to tell the child otherwise, but felt it was not her place to say so.

Laura Lamanek could not change the facts of Anne's life, but perhaps, for one summer at least, she would give Anne a childhood.

"Momma and Poppa Lamanek" they asked to be called. It rolled off Anne's tongue easily.

When Anne met Chaz Belcour, nothing seemed to roll off her tongue. Laura knew that Anne was shy by nature, but never had she seen her as shy as the day she was introduced to Chaz. And in a similar way, Chaz was suddenly unable to speak in complete sentences in Anne's presence. By the awkward exchange of greetings and glances, Laura could plainly see that they were quite taken with one another. Nothing like young love, Laura thought to herself, remembering what it was like to be Anne's age, and all the exciting, confusing, dreadful feelings that accompanied it.

A week passed before Chaz found the courage to ask the Lamaneks if he could take Anne on a date. Not only did Momma Lamanek allow Anne to go out with Chaz and his friends, she encouraged it! There was no hesitation; she went with the Lamaneks' blessings.

Anne had never before experienced such camaraderie. The group of young people were close to her age, and perhaps even more importantly, they were Indian. Here among these brown faces, native people, Anne felt the acceptance she had so longingly sought.

Still, in many ways, she was a stranger to her own people. Sometimes it frightened her when Chaz and his friend Dennis talked about a spiritual world she was not quite in touch with. When Anne was young, she had known her people's ways and believed as they did in a Creator who did not limit himself to one face, as Edwina's god did. This Creator came in many forms, had many faces, and lived in all places, but she had been beaten for believing her god had no limitations and slapped for speaking her language. Edwina's god said that her native language was the language of the devil, the dark spirit, and that Anne would not be allowed into heaven if she did not speak proper English. No matter how many times Edwina had slapped her for speaking her native language, instinctively she knew this wasn't so.

She was haunted by the idea that she would always be a stranger to both worlds. Like the salmon, she swam upstream, continually searching for home.

Where do I belong? echoed from a quiet, dark place within her.

It was true, the Kings, the McDillons, and the Lamaneks loved her, as did Ronald, but she still felt an emptiness inside herself, as if she were perpetually on the edge of life, not in it.

Often the young people that Chaz and Anne went out with spoke in Cree, bursting into laughter on occasion. Anne would smile, pretending that she fit in while she tried to hide her feelings of isolation. She had lost her ability to understand her own language.

One evening Chaz, Anne, Dennis and his girlfriend, Lillian, went to a bar. Even though the drinking age was twenty-one, Anne didn't want to be left behind. The others had been in before. Anne agreed to have one drink.

The bar was crowded. Lil grabbed Anne's arm and dragged her to a table filled with friends who had just returned from a baseball game.

"Relax, Anne. No one's going to bite you."

The bartender approached their table with a pitcher of beer and several glasses in hand.

"Here you go, young lady." He poured Anne a glass of beer and for a moment their eyes met.

Anne's heart beat. She quickly took a sip, set the glass down, and bolted out the door.

Chaz found her crying behind a large tree at the side of the bar.

"I've been looking all over for you, Anne. Why on earth did you go running out like that?"

"My aunt would kill me if she ever found out I was in a bar, Chaz."

Chaz chuckled, put his arm around her, and started toward the moonlit lake across the road. Anne relaxed when it was clear they weren't headed back into the bar.

They could hear the distant music from the little bar as they rounded the lake. Anne told Chaz about running away from the Domenicks, and about being caught and punished.

As Anne described her beatings, Chaz realized there was nothing to chuckle over. He held her tightly at her shoulder, and as he did, the empty place in Anne's spirit grew small.

As autumn began to close in on Elk Island, a dread of returning to Edmonton enveloped Anne. Edwina, backbreaking work, Eddy's presence, Ronald's absence—there was nothing there to nourish Anne's spirit. Nothing.

Chaz had been so kind and caring, and Lil and Dennis had become like family to her. Lil was four years older than Anne and had been like a big sister to her. When Dennis and Lil announced their plans to be married, Anne cried with happiness for them both.

The two couples had become inseparable that summer, and Anne's love for Chaz had grown. Chaz found himself unable to bear the thought of Anne returning to Edwina. Determined to see that Anne would at last be forever free from her aunt, Chaz and Dennis and Lil helped Anne form a plan. She would run away, far far away, and with their help, perhaps this time, she wouldn't be caught.

Momma and Poppa Lamanek had been so good to Anne. The thought of leaving them to face Edwina's wrath alone seemed a betrayal and it tormented her as she stood at the door with her tiny suitcase in hand. She lay a note at their door.

Good-bye Momma. Good-bye Poppa. I love you both so much. Please forgive me. Anne

Queenie watched from the living room, and Anne ran to embrace her sad friend. She lay her face on her woolly shoulder and whispered in the dog's ear.

"Oh, please don't look so sad, Queenie. I'm relying on you to take good care of Momma for me. I love you, Queenie, and I'll never forget you, girl. Never. Good-bye."

Anne picked up her suitcase and closed the front door, and a low, lonely moan escaped from Queenie.

She made her way through the cool night air. Chaz was waiting at the pier ahead. The moon was full and shining brightly, illuminating her path so she wouldn't stumble.

Pausing when she heard the call of the Moon Bird, Anne looked back toward the Lamaneks' house. The moon had breathed a brilliant blue wash over the Moon Bird and the white house, making both appear luminescent. They seemed to glow.

Cocking its head to the right, the Moon Bird studied her, and time stood still.

At last, the Moon Bird's wings stretched out into the night, slowly, powerfully. As it flew directly at her, Anne's heart began to pound. Suddenly the Moon Bird came to her side, sweeping a wing tip across her shoulder as it veered up and out into the indigo night. As it swept past her, Anne shook. She had heard it speak, not in words, but to her very soul, and it gave her strength. The message had come swiftly, but stood crystal clear in her mind.

"As the Moon Bird takes to flight, the Moon Bird does not fear the night because the Moon Bird's made of light. Speaking softly, you'll hear me say, I will make a brand new day."

Anne knew it was the Moon Bird; there was no mistaking it. She had heard Chaz and Dennis talking about the magical bird, how it is a source of strength, a guardian angel to those it chooses. Listening as they talked about the mystical bird, Anne thought it was simply a legend, but Chaz told her that Moon Bird is a woman's spirit, a guide who journeys between heaven and earth, with powerful wings that bear the symbol of lightning and the full moon shape formed in feathers on her forehead.

Anne knew it by its other name, the owl, but this owl was unlike any other. Half woman and half bird, she was capable of shape-shiftings and commanded powers that mortal man could only imagine.

The legends told that Moon Bird was once a woman, found abandoned at birth, taken in by a family and used as a slave. She was later sold to an evil man who disliked women. Although she was treated as the lowliest being among her clan, the Great Spirit saw the beauty that lay beneath her burdens, and guided her spirit to a place where she would be blessed for her gentleness. The man beat her regularly and gave her little food, yet she found it within herself to share with the animals.

The summer was hot with no rain, the winter had grown mean and cruel. Everyone was hungry. Hiding a meager portion of food beneath her clothing, leaving the food in a sacred place that she found while gathering wood, she would make offerings to the animals. The others in her clan thought only of what they could take from the animals, never giving to them, not even gratitude.

Birdlike in her own features, with a thin graceful body, the woman longed to be an owl—the Moon Bird—afraid of nothing, not even the night. She would watch as it circled in flight, wishing that she too could soar between the heaven and earth.

The animals, especially the winged creatures, gave of themselves to her and asked for nothing in return. They serenaded her soul, many times singing her back to health as she recovered from a beating.

One evening, after escaping from the evil-spirited man with whom she lived, she ran deep into the woods. There, at her sacred place, she cried out to the moon, begging it to evoke its powers and set her free. The moon heard her cries and sent her a great white owl as a messenger. It's said the owl is the messenger from the Great Mystery.

When she saw the great Moon Bird descend from the sky, she fell to her knees.

"Take me if I am worthy," she cried.

Looking into her spirit, the messenger outstretched her wings, embracing the woman. In that moment, she became the Moon Bird.

When she was born and then abandoned, no one but the sky had praised her beauty.

When she was a child, only the birds sang her lullabies.

As a woman, she had known a woman's pain.

As the Moon Bird, she would come to guide and heal women. Because women bear the seeds of tomorrow and the beginning of a new day, new life, and a new way.

As expected, Chaz was waiting at the pier when Anne arrived. Anne had thought the Moon Bird was only a make-believe myth. Now her eyes filled with tears as he embraced her.

"It'll be okay, Anne. We'll send word once we're married, and Momma and Poppa will understand."

"I know Chaz. I saw the Moon Bird."

Anne breathed in deeply, allowing herself to find the strong place within herself. Sighing deeply, she released the turmoil she felt.

"You saw the Moon Bird?" Chaz asked quietly, his eyes scanning the night sky.

"Did she see you? Did she look into your eyes? Your spirit?"

"Yes," Anne replied.

Chaz was silent, alone for a moment in his thoughts.

"You're going to be okay, Anne. The Moon Bird knows who you are and, no matter what happens in your life, she will be your guide and look out for you always. She heard your sorrow and looked into your soul. She knows you are worthy, just as I do."

Anne had big medicine, and in a way, it frightened Chaz. Not many can have Moon Bird medicine. The Moon Bird had imprinted her spirit's sign upon Anne's soul. Few women had such power, and fewer were brave enough to look into the Moon Bird's eye.

Allowing it to peer into her soul, Anne had proven she held such power; she had survived all that her short life had offered her. She had known a woman's pain, and she was not quite fifteen years old. The Moon Bird would continue to help her survive the pain of the years to come.

Separate beings, melded together in a moment of time, Chaz and Anne glided silently across the water toward a distant shore, in that moment—one. The moon shed silver light that danced on the water.

CHAPTER SEVEN
Searching for Her People

Dennis and Lillian were waiting on shore when Chaz and Anne arrived. Wasting no time, the girls quickly crawled into the back seat of Dennis' old "Indian squad car" while Chaz took the co-pilot position. Sitting on the floor boards, Anne and Lillian pulled a blanket over their heads and Dennis put the old beast in motion. They headed down a dark dirt road toward Marlboro, a tiny Alberta Indian village where both Lillian and Chaz had grown up.

Dennis' car seemed to moan, as if it were begging him to pull over and put the old thing out of its misery. Suddenly, it began to jerk violently.

"Oh shit! Wouldn't you know it? My brother warned me this might happen, but I thought we'd make it to Marlboro before I had to deal with it."

He pulled to the side of the road, opened the hood, and surveyed the damage as Chaz moved his Zippo lighter in a circular motion.

"Start her up," Dennis called to Lillian.

She climbed into the front seat and turned the ignition. The sound of metal against metal hurt Anne's ears, but at last, the old engine turned over.

"I think that will hold her until we get to my brother's place in Gun," Dennis announced as he climbed back into the car and pulled back onto the road.

On the way to Marlboro, they arrived in the tiny town of Gun

95

at three o'clock in the morning and went directly to where Dennis' brother, Billy, lived and operated a mechanic's shop. Anne was embarrassed to disturb Billy, but after Dennis explained the situation, Billy was more than happy to help them out.

They all camped out in Billy's living room and when Anne and Lillian awoke in the morning, Dennis, Billy, and Chaz were already down at the shop working on the car.

"This is what it looks like," Chaz told Anne, "Billy says he'll waive his fee, but parts alone are gonna run about seventy dollars—"

"Seventy dollars?! You've got to be kidding," Lillian burst out. "Where are we gonna get that kind of money?"

"Now, there's no need to panic. It's just going to take longer than we expected."

Chaz explained that Billy knew of an outcamp a few hours away where Chaz and Dennis could get work. The girls could stay with Billy's girlfriend, Nora, and help her parents out at their restaurant.

It took almost three months before the group had saved enough money to send for the part they needed, and winter was soon approaching. They were about to celebrate when Dennis announced that it would be another two weeks before the part arrived. It was cramped at Nora's and Anne was beginning to worry.

"I've talked to Billy and he said we could borrow one of his cars. I think we should head back to the island. Dennis and I can get temporary work there."

"Chaz," Anne's eyes were filled with fear, "you know they're going to be looking for me, for us."

"It's only for two weeks, Anne. We can stay at my cousin's place. They're not home right now. As long as no one sees you girls, it'll be all right."

It was dusk as they drove through town. Once again the girls hid under a large blanket in the back seat. Slipping and sliding as they drove through the heavy snow, they made their way up the long driveway that led to Chaz's cousin's cabin.

They built a fire and gathered around it.

"Tomorrow, Dennis and I are going into town to look for work. If anyone asks, we've been in Gun working and haven't seen you since we left Elk Island," Chaz said.

Anne was exhausted. She placed a gentle kiss upon Chaz's lips before going into the bedroom that she would share with Lillian.

At about four-thirty the following afternoon, Dennis and Chaz arrived back at the cabin carrying several bags full of groceries. Although it was late afternoon, the sky had already grown dark. Winter had arrived and would not leave soon. The land around the cabin had turned into a hard sheet of ice. Anne could feel the cool air sneaking in through cracks in the cabin walls.

While the girls were in the kitchen making supper, Chaz called out suddenly.

"Anne! Lillian! Get your coats! It's the RCMP!"

Dropping the knife in her hand, Anne ran to the window to see them approaching. Yanking at the back of Anne's sweater, Lillian dragged her away from the window and guided her toward their bedroom where they climbed out the window and began running through the deep snow.

Looking over her shoulder, Anne saw the RCMP making their way up the long snowbound driveway that led to the cabin.

"Lay down, Anne, they'll see you!"

Lillian pulled Anne to the ground. Lying on their stomachs on a sheet of snow-covered ice, the girls watched the cabin.

"Your name is Chaz Belcour?" The officer had a heavy French accent.

"Yes sir. What brings you to my cousin's home?"

"This is your cousin?" he asked, motioning toward Dennis.

"No sir. My cousin isn't here. This is my friend. We're staying here until my cousin returns."

"Is there anyone else here with you?"

"No sir. Just my friend here."

"Your friend, eh? That wouldn't be a young lady by the name of Anne Domenick would it?"

"Anne? No. I haven't seen her since I left for Gun with Dennis over two months ago," Chaz said, trying to look puzzled.

"Her aunt, Edwina Domenick from Edmonton, has reported her missing. She was staying with the Lamaneks on Elk Island when she disappeared. Her aunt thought you might know where she could be found."

Hearing the wind moan outside the window, Chaz's thoughts were with Anne, lying out in the cold, as the officer dawdled about the living room.

"You boys won't mind if I check the bedroom, eh?"

"No sir. Please do."

At least half an hour passed. Lillian had a heavy coat on but Anne had only her thin sweater.

"I'm freezing, Lil."

Anne's lips felt thick as she spoke. Lillian felt sorry for her. Even with her heavy coat, the cold wet snow seeped in to chill her bones. She opened up her coat and the two of them began huddling together to fight off the cold.

"Leave, leave, please leave," Anne chanted to herself, calling for help from the Great Mystery.

Her body began to grow numb, but this would not force her to surrender. Guided by the Moon Bird, Anne began her journey to a sacred place within her, the place where her spirit lived. Now impervious to the physical discomfort of the worldly plane, Anne was on Indian time . . . touching eternity, a place where the past, present, and future seem to meld into one. She heard the sounds of the drums beating as the People sang their sacred songs.

Anne knew the Creator heard her prayer. Chanting silently in syncopation with the song she heard echoing from the sanctuary of her spirit, Anne drew strength, as memories became alive, carrying her away from the cold.

The officer stepped out from the bedroom.

"I see there are some women's clothes in there."

"Yes sir. My cousin's married."

"Very well. You give me a call if you should happen to see Miss Domenick, eh?"

The officer raised his eyebrows and tilted his head back.

"Certainly," Chaz replied as he walked the officer to the door and watched him head back out into the snow.

The RCMP patrol car pulled out of sight, and when the car lights disappeared, Dennis ran out of the cabin and began calling.

Anne was groggy, wanting very much to sleep as Dennis and Lil dragged her toward the cabin. Chaz stoked the fire and gathered blankets. He brought Anne a warm cup of tea as her hair began to thaw in front of the fire. Large drops of water fell on her face.

"We're going to leave first thing in the morning. We'll take Billy's car to Marlboro and be married on the way. The four of us—a double ring ceremony . . . then no one will be able to take you away from me."

Anne's face glistened with melted snow. She nodded her head in agreement. She hoped that it would happen the way he described.

Simultaneously, the four looked at each other. The sound of a car was nearing. Dennis ran to the window.

"They're back! And with another car behind them. You've got to hide again."

Chaz panicked. He knew Anne was not strong enough to go outside again. The memory of a root cellar threw Chaz into action. He began to search frantically for the trap door that led to the cellar. To his great relief, he found it under a throw rug in the main room and opened it quickly. He rushed the girls down into the darkness, and was replacing the rug when a violent knocking began.

As Chaz stood on the rug that concealed the opening, Dennis answered the door. It was Edwina. Elizabeth had not yet discovered that Anne was missing, and Edwina was not about to let her find out. She was not going to be swindled out of the money she received for Anne's care.

"You know, Chaz, you're in a lot of trouble. Knowing your kind, that's nothing new. But you're out of your league this time, boy."

She began circling Chaz. The officer stood silently at the door, watching.

"I haven't seen your niece in two months," Chaz said firmly.

Anne and Lillian huddled together in the dark, listening through cracks in the floor above their heads.

"How dare you stand there and lie to me? As if I don't know you've hidden her somewhere. You think you can get away with this?"

Anne wanted to stop the attack, even go with Edwina to spare Chaz such venom. But the strength of her friendships began to encircle her.

"Whispering softly I hear it say, I will make a brand new day," the Moon Bird's words echoed, coaxing her to hang on, until tomorrow, just until tomorrow.

When Edwina and her RCMP escort had driven off, the four packed their belongings and headed for Marlboro.

"Anne, we're here. Wake up."

Chaz's voice intruded upon her consciousness as Anne was coming out of sleep. Her neck was stiff from being cramped in the back seat for hours. Marlboro. They had made it.

They were married in a little farming community just outside of Marlboro. A double ceremony. When they were pulling into Chaz's village as man and wife, a trace of fear lingered because Anne had lied about her age, but for the most part, Anne felt safe for the first time in a long, long time.

They passed shack after tarpaper shack as they drove through the forest to Chaz's parents' cabin. Anne squeezed Chaz's hand as the car pulled up in front of Momma and Poppa Belcour.

They greeted Chaz and his new wife warmly. Speaking little English, Momma Belcour held Anne's face close to hers, feeling its contours with her hands as she spoke.

"My eyes are sick but I can still see Chaz has a very pretty wife."

"I'll be a good wife to him," Anne said quietly, "and a good daughter to you."

"Poppa's been sick, Chaz. It's good you've come home and brought your wife."

She led Anne to a room in the back of the cabin.

"You and Chaz will stay here until your cabin is built. Come now and help me cook dinner."

As the months went by, Anne tried hard to fit into her new home and make Chaz's people her own. Momma and Poppa Belcour tried to make this task easy for her, but Anne soon discovered there were those in Marlboro who did not embrace her presence as her in-laws did.

She was Indian but raised white. She was different, and some people in Marlboro didn't like it. An Indian who doesn't speak the language? An Indian who reads and writes, dresses, speaks, and acts like a white woman?

It wasn't Anne's fault she had been raised white any more than it had been her fault she was born brown. Living between day and night, Anne experienced a sense of alienation that perhaps only she would ever understand.

Hoping that with time those who looked at her suspiciously would see that she meant no harm and had simply come to live and be a part of their community, Anne persevered.

Anne enjoyed the time she spent with Momma Belcour. She never doubted Momma's love for her, and she had become one of Anne's protectors. Even though they were far apart in age, a special bond grew. Anne knew that Momma Belcour had experienced a woman's pain and she often gave the words to Anne's heart when Anne was unable to explain her own feelings and fears.

Although her eyesight was failing, Momma Belcour's mind was alert and she was eager to share her knowing wisdom with Anne. There was so much to learn about life, and Momma Belcour was a wonderful teacher. Anne had great respect for her, for she was a talented storyteller and Anne would easily become mesmerized by her words and the metaphors she used in the stories she related.

She would often find solace in Momma's words after she had trouble understanding the harshness of this tiny town.

"Wahh ... whwass, eigh ... Moonieasquaw! Moonieasquaw!" the women would chant, headed by their ringleader Emily, a woman in town with a notorious reputation for wild, wicked ways. Like a ritual, it began when Chaz finished building their cabin. The group of squaws would come to the house to visit and leave when the cupboards were bare. Pointing at her apron, her clothing, the way she combed her wavy hair, they would speak in their Cree language and laugh.

They were her husband's people, and she wanted to be accepted. One night before bed, she asked Chaz what "Moonieasquaw" meant.

"Where did you hear that? Tell me? Were those women over here again today? Damn it Anne, I told you they're nothing but trouble."

"Tell me what it means Chaz, or I'll ask Momma Belcour."

He looked at Anne sadly. He had hoped these things would pass and they would be left in peace.

"White bitch," Chaz said.

The words stung.

Slowly, a sick feeling set into the pit of Anne's stomach. There would be no acceptance here. Not for her. Listening to the birds singing in the forest, she pondered her future. The Great Spirit gave Anne a song. She hummed along.

Tell me where you belong. Living life between dusk and dawn? Neither day nor night, neither Indian nor white, where do you belong?

Anne still realized that she was part of the Great Mystery that she heard Momma Belcour speak of. "The Great Mystery is layered in meaning and symbology; it is how many natives describe that which can never be fully understood through the use of language and can only be conceptualized," Momma would say. "In essence, it is our divine spirituality; the invisible form through which the greater power affects our lives.

"The Great Mystery is exactly that—a great mystery. It is also the place where our spirits walk on when we die. It is Indian for heaven."

With this simple explanation of life, Anne's confusion dissipated and a deep sense of knowing gave her peace. Someday she would find where she belonged. Someday she would find her song.

CHAPTER EIGHT

Love Medicine

Marlboro, Alberta, 1936

*A*nne *was going into her seventh month of pregnancy. She was fifteen* years old. Lillian was in her ninth month and ready to deliver any day. They lay on Anne's bed and compared their bellies. Watching the baby roll and wiggle beneath her skin, Anne wondered out loud.

"You know, Lil, there's just one thing I'm really worried about," Anne said, "I'd just like to know, when the baby comes out and my belly button unravels, well, how will I ever get it back in again?"

Lillian struggled to roll over onto her side. Seeing Anne's face, she realized it was a sincere question. Stunned that someone seven months pregnant could be asking such a ridiculous question, Lil tried to find words that wouldn't sound condescending.

"Anne, babies aren't born from your belly button," Lillian couldn't help but giggle when she heard herself. Anne's confused expression turned to alarm when Lillian explained the birthing process. She quickly turned away.

"Oh, thanks a lot Lil, now I'm really scared."

"Oh, honestly Anne. Women have babies every day. You'll see, before long you'll be good as new."

Dorothea was born prematurely in the dead of winter. Ill at birth, she was small and fragile, like a beautiful doll.

Momma Belcour stood silently admiring her granddaughter Dorothea.

"She's perfect, Momma," said Anne, "ten fingers and ten toes. Why do you look so serious? She's small, but she'll grow."

Looking at Anne with an intensity that worried her, Momma Belcour tried to smile kindly.

"I don't mean to scare you, Anne . . . but she is beautiful . . . such beauty is sometimes too fragile to live in this world."

Silently Anne looked at Momma Belcour as a chill ran down her spine. Momma's premonition had scared her, but out of respect she remained silent. Momma Belcour knew that Anne was upset, but it was her duty to prepare Anne for the future.

The Old Ones had spoken of fearing such beauty. Never had Momma seen a child so perfectly formed; she was flawless. And sadly, Momma realized, too perfect to be a part of this world.

Anne made a bed out of a shoebox. She lined it with rabbit fur and placed the child near the warm stove. Instinctively she had created an incubator. The snow was heavy but Dr. Burkell was able to make it to their cabin.

He shook the snow off his sandy blonde hair and congratulated Anne on the birth. He looked too young to be a doctor, but he had a good reputation and denied no one care, no matter what color he or she was or whether or not he or she had any money.

Anne saw the concern in his young face as he examined Dorothea. He suggested Chaz retrieve some olive oil from town.

"It'll help keep her body heat in, until she's stronger. I want you to bathe her in a heated room, no drafts, and in olive oil only."

He demonstrated with a cotton swab from his bag.

"Sometimes it takes many months to build a preemie's strength, so you stay rested too. And it wouldn't hurt you to put on a few pounds," he told Anne.

By spring, both Anne and the baby had put on a few pounds, but still, Dorothea struggled; she was small for a child five months old.

Anne was careful not to throw open the windows as she was inclined to do after a long winter. The sky was clear and blue, but there was still snow on the ground and possibly more to come.

Dorothea was growing, there was no doubt about that. Anne wiggled her toe making her giggle and coo.

"Hang in there little one, hang in there and grow strong."

Emily—the woman who lived in town—would visit occasionally, always unannounced. Emily was still a thorn in Anne's side.

"I saw Chaz in town yesterday," she would taunt. "He sure seemed to like that new waitress at the hotel. Looked like they had known each other for years."

"Well, he found his way back home last night, Emily, if that's what you're getting at."

Almost as the words left her mouth, Anne realized that she had grown up fast in Marlboro that first year. As reality collided with fantasy, Anne realized that the love that had once made her feel so safe and secure in Chaz's presence was disappearing before her. Fear and insecurity welled up within her as she contemplated an uncertain future. Chaz was slipping away from her, deeper into the dark, hazy world of smokey bars. The world that Emily ruled.

No matter how Anne tried to sweep away her anger, it would fester until Chaz got home, and the familiar argument would start again.

"Emily came by today. She said she saw you in town last night. Making new friends, are you?"

"Anne, I stopped for a few beers with the guys. That's all. What's this all about anyway?"

"Emily. That's what it's about. You know she would like nothing better than to see me leave...."

"I should have known as much. I told you that woman's a troublemaker. Always has been. Look what she's done to poor Ricky."

Chaz poured a cup of coffee. "Everyone knows she's got love medicine on the poor guy."

"Love medicine? Oh, really?" Something in Anne had a really hard time grasping the concept of love medicine.

"You should see him, Anne. He's left his wife, his kids, he's like a crazy man, spending all his money on booze for her and that ugly sister of hers. He's a totally different person. Two weeks and he was hooked."

"Ricky can't stand the sight of her, Chaz," Anne replied skeptically.

"I don't care what you say, Anne, it's true. She's got love medicine on him."

As Anne was rolling her eyes, Chaz took her face in his hands.

"At first you thought the Moon Bird was only a legend, didn't you? Well, I'm telling you, these things happen. Emily has medicine. Bad medicine, but medicine nevertheless."

The Moon Bird was real, Anne knew that, but to believe Emily had cast a spell of love on a man? The whole idea was far-fetched for Anne, but she would keep her theories to herself. Although she wouldn't admit it to Chaz, she felt that perhaps there was a tiny grain of truth in what he had said. What else would drive an otherwise sensible man crazy with thoughts of desire for a woman he detested?

Momma Belcour had walked up to the cabin as they argued that night. Blind as she was, she knew the lay of the land and found her way around easily. Her ears made up for what her eyes now lacked. She stayed with Chaz and Anne that night. She waited until the house was silent and the others were asleep, then she took one of Chaz's jackets and carefully covered the heart area with black India ink. This would protect him from Emily's love medicine; it would protect them all.

She felt better as she lay her old body down to sleep. She had seen things like this before. Chaz was right, it was bad medicine. And Emily had the power and lack of conscience to use it.

Emily had four children, each with a different father. She would have had more if it weren't for the self-induced abortions done with sharpened birch limbs and powdered alum. She often left the children alone for weeks at a time. Neighbors brought the children food to eat and wood to burn.

When Anne told Lillian what Chaz had said, she laughed along with Anne but knew that these things were real in ways that Anne didn't understand. She hoped Anne would heed Chaz's advice to keep her distance from Emily.

"Power . . . magic, huh? The only power that woman has is right here!" Anne said, pointing between her legs.

Lillian let out a long and heavy sigh, and shook her head in mock disgust.

"So, what are my girls up to today?" Chaz inquired as he stepped through the doorway.

"To what do we owe this early visit?" Anne asked.

"The company has decided to move camp. Weather's improving. I know it's not the best of times, but I can't say no Anne, we need the money."

Anne could tell Chaz was uncomfortable.

"Look, Chaz, we have to do what we have to do. The baby's getting stronger now. We'll be okay."

"Well, Anne, that's one of the things we need to talk about. I thought it would be best for you and the baby to go and stay with my aunt and uncle, Shar and William, in Blue Ridge while I'm gone. Shar can help you with the baby and the company would do you good."

Blue Ridge was a small community in northern Alberta, mainly a farming community with one hotel and a post office. Anne had met Chaz's aunt and uncle before, and knew they would welcome her, but having her own home was something Anne treasured. It might not have seemed like much with no water and no electricity, but to Anne, it was the only thing other than Dorothea that was all hers.

Anne agreed reluctantly to pack up in the morning.

The next day, while Dorothea slept, Anne began to pack everything that they would be taking to Blue Ridge. She came across one of Chaz's jackets and held it up to see if it needed to be laundered.

She was shocked to find a huge ink stain across the front of it. She looked closer, yes black ink. How strange, Anne thought, as she examined the jacket closer. How on earth did he manage this?

Deciding the jacket was worthless, she tossed it into the fire that burned daily in the little cabin. The flames cracked and popped, then black smoke began to roll. It formed strange shapes as it moved and Anne shivered at the images of Emily that vividly appeared in her mind's eye.

For a moment, she heard something . . . the very distinct sound of Emily's cackling, teasing her from the fire that greedily engulfed what remained of Chaz's jacket. The sound slowly drifted up and out with the black smoke. Forcing her eyes away from the hypnotic flames that arose as the last of the jacket was consumed, Anne finished up her packing quickly and bundled Dorothea for the long trip ahead.

Shar had three grown sons and little Willy, who was ten months old. She was eager to take Anne under her wing and share her expertise. Anne fussed nervously over her baby, not allowing Shar to even hold the child. Shar expressed her concern to her husband William.

"She's gonna make herself sick Will, you see her? Day and night, 'my baby this, my baby that.' That baby is Cree. It must be taught to survive, made strong and tough like my Willy. No wonder the kid is so small, she hasn't given her any room to grow."

"Well, it's her first one Shar, you just better let her be. That baby's pretty fragile, the doctor in town said so, so maybe it doesn't hurt to be extra cautious."

"Well, I don't care. It's just not healthy. . . ."

The following morning Shar approached Anne.

"You know what that baby really needs, Anne? A good old-fashioned bath. No more of that olive oil. It's not healthy for the baby, only being bathed in oil like so much fried bread."

"Oh no, no, no Shar! The doctor said she must only be bathed in oil until she puts on more weight."

Anne was near tears and Shar found it annoying.

"Anne, there's no need for alarm. Honestly, a little water's not going to hurt her."

Anne was bone tired. It seemed like the last five months of sleepless nights had suddenly caught up to her. Shar convinced her to lie down, offering to watch Dorothea until nap time. She made Shar promise not to bathe the baby and when Anne was satisfied with her sincerity she handed Dorothea over and crawled into bed with a sleeping Willy beside her. She pulled the large, soft blanket over her shoulders, and let out a deep and grateful sigh.

Anne awoke when she heard the door slam. She crawled out of bed feeling refreshed, and walked out to greet William returning from work.

"Hi William. It looks like a cold one out there today, eh?"

Anne walked toward Dorothea who lay sleeping in her crib.

"Damn right it's cold. Snowed all day, made a mess of the roads. I had a hell of a time getting home, finally ended up walking. Left the car stuck in the snow over by the post office."

William took off his coat and Anne reached to stroke Dorothea's sleeping face. Her heart dropped. The baby was burning up with fever. There was no response as Anne gently rolled the child over and she began to scream.

"She's sick. Oh God, please!"

The child lay silent and pale.

William ran to the crib and Shar came running from the kitchen where she had been preparing dinner. William spoke as she entered the room.

"She's still breathing, Anne."

Anne looked up at Shar in horror. The blood was draining quickly from Shar's face.

"Did you bathe the baby, Shar?"

There was no answer.

"Did you bathe the baby?" William asked.

"Yes," she replied in a whisper.

"How could you—"

"I'm going to get Sam at the post office," William said.

"We'll get her to the clinic Anne. Just hang in there. She needs you."

William bolted out the door. Shar stared blankly out the window as she watched him walk through the heavy snow.

It took two hours for William and Sam to return with a truck. Holding Dorothea close to her, Anne climbed into the cab of the pickup.

The drive through the snow seemed excruciatingly slow. Even as she stood at the door to the clinic and waited for someone to answer the door, time seemed to tick by in slow motion.

A nurse finally answered.

"The doctor's not here this week," she apologized. "You'll have to come back next week."

She began to close the door. Sam stepped forward.

"This lady's got a sick baby here."

Sam pushed the door open again and ushered Anne and the baby inside. The nurse put her hands on her hips and responded sternly.

"I'm sorry. I told you, the doctor is not in."

"Well, Mrs. Greenwell," Sam read from her tag, "I assume those initials R.N. mean something. *You'll* just have to do."

He continued into the clinic toward the nearest examining room.

"Please," Anne pleaded, "my baby is so sick."

Mrs. Greenwell would not look at Anne but responded to Sam.

"She can lay the baby over there. Unwrap her and call me when you're ready."

When the nurse returned, she gave the baby a cursory examination.

"This baby is going to die, that's all there is to it."

Anne began to sob; Mrs. Greenwell continued talking to Sam.

"Even if these people had money, and you know none of them do, I doubt that she would make it to the hospital in

Edmonton." She looked momentarily to Anne. Sam was reaching for her hand.

"She has money," Sam said, "what do we do?"

"I'm telling you, it's worthless—"

"I'm telling you lady, goddamn it, you're going to go in there and call Edmonton and tell them we're bringing in a sick baby, now!" Sam screamed.

Anne held the baby on a pillow to cushion the ride. They drove in silence, except for the sound of Dorothea's labored breathing. Snow fell around them.

"Let me carry the baby, Anne. I have good boots on."

He lifted Dorothea gently from the pillow. Anne was pale. Her mind danced in a night-long prayer.

Before Sam left in the morning, he contacted Momma and Poppa Lamanek at Anne's request. He tried to convince Anne to eat something, but she wasn't able. She thought if she stopped her prayer, Dorothea might let go. Sam drove home as the sun was rising, anxious to see his own daughter. He wanted to hold her in his arms for days.

Momma Lamanek entered Anne's hospital room. It seemed like such a long time since they had last seen one another.

"She's beautiful, Anne."

Unable to contain herself, Anne collapsed into Momma Lamanek's warm embrace.

"Yes, she is too beautiful, Momma," Anne sobbed.

Momma Lamanek smoothed back a strand of Anne's black hair.

Poppa Joe had informed the staff at Edmonton General that Anne was his daughter and money was no object. He insisted they do everything possible to save Dorothea. A specialist was called in. For three nights and four long days, Anne stayed at the baby's side. There were small signs of improvement. There was much talk around the hospital about the Indian woman with a small, sick child and bigshot connections.

"Come home for one night's sleep, Anne," Momma Lamanek said quietly. "A few hours, then you can come back, okay? We have a room waiting for you."

"She looks better, don't you think?" Anne had asked Momma Lamanek before they left the hospital. Momma didn't answer.

It was a beautiful room with a canopy bed that was curtained off, lovely paintings and fresh-cut flowers.

Anne tossed in bed, unable to sleep. Finally, she was pulled into a deep darkness where she slept restlessly until six A.M.

When she first awoke, she thought she had slipped into a wonderful dream. She was a maid in a beautiful mansion. Then reality crept forward. She remembered where she was and rose to her feet. Her body ached; particularly her arms when she combed her hair. They ached for Dorothea.

Momma and Poppa were at the table drinking coffee.

"I called a half an hour ago," said Momma, "she's still hanging in there."

Momma offered Anne some food. She turned away.

"You have to eat something, Anne."

"I'll eat on the way to the hospital," Anne said, grabbing an apple from the counter.

The phone rang. Anne's heart stood still. Momma answered it.

"Oh . . . oh, I see . . . oh . . . I see."

She hung up the phone, turned toward Anne and opened her arms. Anne knew.

She dropped the apple and ran up the stairs, closing the door behind her. Momma and Poppa listened helplessly as Anne began grieving.

"Please, no. Don't take my sunshine away."

CHAPTER NINE

Spirit Moves

*M*omma brought Anne meals but they sat on the night table untouched. Poppa offered to get in touch with Chaz but Anne wasn't interested in seeing him. She didn't know where to find him anyway, the out-camp was always on the move, and Chaz was changing. Was it alcohol? Was it love medicine? Probably both.

Poppa sent a radiogram. It was expensive, a medium seldom used. It traveled throughout Alberta and into British Columbia. Barbara, the owner and bartender of the Hinton Hotel, heard the message come over the airwaves.

"Anyone knowing the whereabouts of Chaz Belcour of Marlboro, Alberta, is asked to contact their local RCMP. There is a family emergency regarding his daughter. His wife is in Edmonton."

Barbara grabbed the hotel master keys and walked up to room 105. She entered without knocking. Empty bottles and garbage filled the room.

"What do you think you're doing, you old bitch?" Emily cursed.

"Shut up, Emily. Chaz, get your ass out of that bed and get dressed."

She picked up Chaz's pants from the floor and flung them at him.

"Your wife and baby are in Edmonton. Something's wrong with your daughter. You're supposed to contact the RCMP."

Barbara turned and left. Chaz dressed in confusion, ignoring Emily's protests. Hungover, he borrowed a car and went to find his wife. Chaz was no longer the man Anne had married. Alcohol and Emily had changed him.

Chaz missed the funeral by three days.

When at last he arrived, Anne simply looked at him, almost as if she didn't recognize him, and then rolled over in her bed and faced the other way.

"She's not well at all, Chaz," Poppa Lamanek told him. "She's better off with us right now. We'll make sure she gets what she needs. It isn't physical, it's emotional."

Poppa Lamanek explained everything that had happened and Chaz left feeling as empty as the liquor bottles that littered his life. Looking desperately for someone to blame, he blamed Emily, and her evil ways. But Chaz, drunk or not, was a man, and knew he would have to live with the choices he had made.

Months passed without meaning. Chaz returned to Edmonton a number of times to convince Anne to come home, but she refused. She didn't know about his affair with Emily in the Hinton Hotel, but something in her spirit warned her that she must be careful, and she was angry that Chaz had left Dorothea and her alone in the first place.

Edwina called, her voice dripping with sympathy. She had given up the search for Anne when she was informed of Chaz and Anne's marriage. Anne had no desire to see Edwina, but Ronald was about to be sent to Germany and Anne hadn't seen him since before she was married, since before she had become a mother, and then a childless mother.

Uncle John picked her up at six o'clock on his way home from the hotel where he worked. John squeezed her hand as if to give her some of his strength, and told her how sorry he was. He had always been kind to her and she would have been comfortable had Edwina not been waiting at the other end of the ride.

"Oh dear, it must have been a terrible ordeal for you. You've been in all of our prayers."

Edwina's kindness seemed cruel—so sweet and soft spoken after so many sharp, cold exchanges.

If I owe you anything Auntie, this is it, I'm here. And even this seems like a lot to ask under the circumstances, Anne thought, entering the house with John.

Little had changed at the Domenicks. Everything in perfect order. Anne was seized with the desire to grab her coat and run. Then Ronald entered the room and opened his arms to her.

"I'm so sorry," he said, as Anne fought back her tears.

"I'll get through it, you know. It's just going to take some time, I'm afraid."

Marilyn entered and offered her condolences, and Eddy soon strutted into the room wearing a flashy suit. He looked at Anne briefly, then strode past her without so much as a hello, and sat down at the dinner table. Everybody followed. They sat around the table mired in tension—just like old times.

Anne grew more and more unsteady. As she raised her teacup, her hand began to tremble. Anne tried to get a grip on her emotions, but it was no use. She had little strength to draw on. Her lip began to quiver.

"I'm sorry Aunt Edwina. This is a lovely meal, I just don't feel well."

"You've got to keep your strength up, Anne. At least try to eat something."

Edwina's voice was so gentle, it provoked Anne to cry softly. Too little, too late, Auntie. It almost seemed as if she meant it.

Metal bounced sharply off a china plate. All heads turned from Anne to Eddy, who had just thrown his fork down in disgust.

"Oh, for Christ's sake, Anne. It's not like you'll never have another one. You'll probably have another ten!"

Ronald shot up from his chair and grabbed his brother by the collar, lifting Eddy out of his seat. He held him up against the wall by the neck.

"How dare you say such a thing to Anne? I won't tolerate it. If you don't have anything better to say, you damn well better keep your mouth shut, you little bastard."

"Let him go Ronald," Edwina screamed, "you're hurting him."

As Anne and Ronald left the house, Anne said softly to Eddy, "I hope you never experience the pain of losing a child."

"You didn't have to leave with me," Anne said to Ronald.

"No, I didn't. But the only reason I came tonight was to see you. That house has never held anything for either of us but bad memories. . . . I'm just sorry another one was added tonight."

Ronald looked so handsome and mature. They both looked back at the house on Jasper Avenue as they walked toward Ronald's car. Anne knew that she would never set foot in Edwina's house again.

Neither Anne nor Ronald spoke, but she heard a voice, as if someone were whispering in her ear.

"Look forward, Anne," the voice said, and the sound of a bell on a horse's collar tinkled. But there were no horses nearby. Is it the Moon Bird, she wondered?

As they were driving, Ronald swerved abruptly, pulling the car over to the side of the road. He leapt out and scaled a vine-covered tree until he reached the top. Straining every muscle, he grasped a brilliant white, solitary blossom illuminated by the street lights. He brought the last bloom of autumn to Anne.

"This is you, Anne. A beautiful mourning glory."

Anne was touched deeply. At last, she had been given a spirit name—Morning Glory. Nature provided the ceremony and the sacred symbology of a single white blossom that had defied death. The Creator had even seen to it that Ronald would be the guardian of this private ceremony. There was no one else Anne wished to honor her with her spirit name. Anne was touched by the sincerity of his gesture.

As she slept that night, Anne saw herself standing at the foot of Dorothea's grave, which was covered in snow. Looking up, she saw it was also the threshold of her own death. But unlike her daughter,

Anne would be able to choose between life and death. She stood still.

The flutter of wings sounded in the sky and a great creature landed at the foot of Dorothea's grave. As it stretched a beautiful wing into the night, Anne saw the face of an angel with the symbol of the moon on her forehead. Looking deeply into Anne's spirit, the angel began to speak to Anne's soul.

"Lay her here gently at your feet although her heart no longer beats. You will know she does not lie here in a hard, cold bed. I have built for her a silver sled.

"Carrying her through Father Sky, Grandmother Moon no longer cries. Do not fear her snowy grave. You now must be forever brave.

"You've been strong Anne, and I can see your strength is like this great oak tree, giving shelter and providing shade, and looking down on what you've made.

"Life at times seems cruel indeed, but you my dear bear precious seeds, born sometimes from sorrow. You contain our hope for tomorrow.

"As your roots grow deep and strong, you'll remember my words and know that I was not wrong.

"So Anne, I will tell you dear, how important it is that you do not fear. For as long as the moon shines bright, I will not leave you, not even in your darkest night."

In her dream, Anne saw the great wings of the Moon Bird had opened. She swooped low, the tip of one wing brushing against Anne's heart. In Grandmother Moon's eternal light, Anne watched as a silver sled took flight and disappeared with the Moon Bird.

Anne's grieving was sensed by the Moon Bird. She was a messenger, a guide from the Great Spirit and Grandmother Moon. Anne knew that she would never be alone, she had found her Indian Angel. In fact, the Moon Bird would never leave her, or her family. Instinctively Anne knew that this was an eternal legacy that would be passed on to future generations.

CHAPTER TEN

Native Child
(The Birth of Silversong)

Marlboro, 1939

Chaz was a good man when he wasn't drinking. Perhaps he was not the brave warrior Anne had once envisioned, but he could be kind, considerate, and compassionate. And he had freed her from her past.

It was winter when Anne returned to Marlboro to be with Chaz. She was eighteen years old. She had just spent what seemed like an eternity with the Lamaneks grieving the loss of Dorothea and recovering from what many had termed a nervous breakdown. It was hard to believe she had been with the Lamaneks about a year.

Her homecoming was subdued. She organized the cabin, finding Dorothea's booties, packing away the tiny clothes in the shoebox Dorothea had slept in. Each item tugged at her heart, but Anne stood strong and wiped the tears from her cheeks.

A package arrived from Elizabeth, and Anne had to go to the Obed post office to pick it up. Obed was about ten miles from Marlboro and possibly the smallest town in Alberta. There was a gas pump, a small motel, a restaurant, and the post office. That was it.

"All the way from the U.S.!" Carl said, as he handed the parcel to Anne.

People called Carl Walker "the mayor" because he was the only person who owned anything in Obed.

Anne hadn't seen Elizabeth for two years. She opened the pretty parcel slowly: a brown seal fur coat and a black satin evening gown.

To wear in Marlboro! Anne laughed out loud. Who but her mother would send such a thing? The gown had a daring slit up one leg and delicate white and lavender flowers that flowed from one shoulder to the floor. She slipped the fabric across her skin to feel its softness.

Anne sensed that though her mother gallivanted around the world, she too was lost.

Marlboro had not changed much, but thankfully the women who had harassed Anne no longer came by. And she avoided them as much as possible, especially Emily.

She liked the peacefulness, the sound of animals at night, the sight of the forest; even the walk to the well was something Anne took great pleasure in. Chaz often worked out of town and she enjoyed the solitude.

Anne became pregnant again.

It was a difficult pregnancy. She had no serious physical problems but the first signs of new life that stirred in her filled her with intense delight and unspeakable grief. She relived the moments of Dorothea's short life and wept.

1942

It was the end of May when little Lance made his way into the world. He was kicking and screaming, his chubby little body shaking along with his strong little fists.

"Nothing fragile about this guy." It made Anne smile.

For a time, it seemed that Lance's birth had breathed new life into Chaz and Anne's marriage. Lance's birth was good medicine. Prayer is medicine, laughter is medicine, family is medicine, as is any person, place, or thing that reminds you of the sacredness of life and power of love. Making good memories is always good medicine, and it seems that there is always good somewhere ... if we look hard enough. There were good days, watching the baby grow, hearing his first sounds, seeing his first steps. And although Chaz was hardly present, Anne was happy.

Anne took the baby everywhere with her, and it was not un-usual for her to pack him on her back when she went to the com-munity well, an empty bucket in each hand.

One day near the end of summer when the sky was clear blue and the fresh air crisp, Anne sang to herself, and to Lance, on the way to the well. Forest animals watched from the bushes, scurrying over and under them, birds scattered through the trees.

When she reached the well and was filling her pail, something sharp hit her above the right eye. Warm blood began to seep from her brow and into her eye, blurring her vision.

"Moonieasquaw! Moonieasquaw!"

Emily stood from her crouched position behind a bush. She had a whiskey bottle in hand. Her sister stood up next to her, and they both began to curse and laugh and pelt Anne with rocks.

Anne begged them to stop. She was afraid Lance would be struck. She wrapped her body around Lance to shield him as rocks bounced off the water pails.

A pickup truck veered off the nearby road and roared into the well area where Lance and Anne were huddled. Dennis' cousin Dan, who worked for the forestry department and whose jurisdiction in-cluded the Marlboro area, spotted trouble. He slammed on his brakes and threw the door open near Emily and her sister.

"Get the hell out of here. Now!"

The two women sneered at Dan, then turned and staggered back into the woods. Dan went to help Anne and Lance, who were both crouched at the well crying.

Dan helped Anne to her feet, picked up a water bucket, and began to fill it. Anne made a compress for her bleeding eye.

"This forestry job's got me out in this area every other day. Please don't hesitate to call me anytime, rather than put yourself and your son in danger."

He set down the first bucket and started on another. "There's just no telling what those women might be capable of."

After driving her back to the cabin, Dan drove up to Emily's place to set her straight. He told her in no uncertain terms to stay away from Anne Belcour. But Emily didn't scare easily.

"Cavalry to the rescue, eh?"

She slammed the door in Dan's face, and Dan left cursing.

That night Anne awoke to the sound of glass breaking. She grabbed Lance from his crib and once again cradled him for protection. Glass shards flew in all directions. Emily's laughter echoed from outside as she left.

The day before this happened, Chaz had been paid at the outcamp, and stopped by his parents' house to give them money on the way to the grocery store. He had plenty left when he got to the grocery store in town, and plenty left afterward when he crossed paths with Emily, and she began taunting him.

"Haven't seen you around Chaz, what's up? Not allowed to go out, eh? Is that educated woman of yours ruling the roost? I suppose she figures you're too stupid to make your own decisions."

Chaz didn't understand why she got to him so with her wicked teasing. Why did he let her get to him? A group of men from Marlboro were entering the Hinton Hotel across the street. Emily got their attention.

"I guess now that Chaz's married to a white woman, he's too good for us."

"What will it take to get you off my back, Emily?"

The men began calling out to Chaz, urging him to join them.

"One drink, Chaz. That's all."

Chaz hesitated.

"What's wrong, Chaz? Afraid you'll go 'Indian'?"

She was right. He wasn't good enough or smart enough for Anne.

When Chaz awoke two days later, surrounded by empty bottles, he had two wadded-up bills in his pocket. He checked out of the Hinton Hotel and headed back to the cabin where Anne had covered the broken windows with pieces of scrapboard.

He learned from her that Emily had been terrorizing his wife while he waited, drunk, for Emily to return to his hotel room.

When Anne finished telling him about the ordeal, Chaz got his coat and, feeling he would drown in confusion and self-pity, left without saying good-bye. Anne had no idea when or if he would return.

"Oh, it's only a matter of time, he'll be back," Anne said to Lillian, her eyes stinging with tears.

"I suppose he's working in the bush again."

He had been gone two weeks now, and had left Anne and Lance without money or food. Anne had been rationing what food they had left, her son getting most of it. She was weak and hungry when Lillian arrived with two large brown grocery bags.

Lillian set the bags on the table and gave Anne a hug. She could feel the new bulge of life that had formed under Anne's blouse.

"Dennis and I will help you. It'll be okay. It always is . . . in the bush working, eh?"

"I assume."

Lillian turned to face Anne squarely.

"You aren't going to take him back, are you? After leaving you and Lance? And you, in your condition?"

"Please Lillian, not now. I just can't take it. What am I supposed to do with two babies to feed? It's not like I have choices right now."

"You always have choices. You know Anne, you're like a sister to me. It doesn't seem my place but damn it—"

She stopped putting away groceries and held Anne by the shoulders.

"I hope you would do the same for me . . . Chaz is in Edson with Emily."

Anne blinked. The news came in slowly and settled in her belly, then rose up and seemed to stick in her throat.

". . . How could you even say such a thing, Lillian? Chaz can't stand Emily."

"He's crazy Anne. Just like Ricky. Emily has medicine on him."

Lillian had no doubts about such things. Throwing her shoulders back, Anne opened the door.

"Love medicine. Get out of my house!"

"Anne, I'm sorry. I really am."

Lillian shook her head. It seemed everyone but Anne knew where Chaz had spent the last two weeks.

Another week passed before Chaz returned. Anne heard the screen door open and Chaz walked into the house quietly. The words ran in her conscience: *Be a good girl, Anne. Just don't say anything. For the sake of the children, Lance and his future sibling. Keep your chin up. Try not to feel anything. It's easier that way.*

"I'm going to be going out to camp next week," Chaz said emotionlessly.

"I want you to pack up whatever it is you and Lance will need. You're going to stay with my cousin, Henry, and his wife, Olive. They'll help you with Lance and I'll send for you when I get back."

Anne looked deeply into Chaz's eyes as he spoke, and saw an emptiness. It frightened her deeply. She nodded her head in agreement and began to gather her belongings. There was no use fighting. It was a man's world, Anne thought. This was simply the way things were done.

Olive and Henry had five children. Anne felt burdensome, two more bodies in their tiny cabin, two more mouths to feed. She brought an offering of salt pork and beans, and it eased her mind that Chaz had provided his cousins with meat many previous winters, but still she felt awkward.

They were poor but generous people. Anne worked side by side with Olive, cooking for twenty men who worked at a nearby farm. Three times a day, the men came to be fed. All day long, Anne and Olive cooked and the older children looked after the young ones.

Olive said she didn't know how she ever got along without Anne's help and, after talking to her boss, got Anne a wage. It wasn't much, but she knew it would help and Anne was grateful. She felt proud that she could pull her own weight as her pregnancy progressed and in five months she had peeled enough potatoes to buy a bus ticket back to her cabin. She was in her seventh month of pregnancy.

When the Greyhound stopped in front of the Hinton Hotel, Anne held tightly to Lance's little hand and scanned the street looking for a ride to her cabin outside of Marlboro, less than an hour away. She missed her sad and lonely cabin; at least it was home.

Not only did she find a familiar face standing in the middle of a circle of men, her old protector Dan, but also the black satin evening gown that Elizabeth had sent her. There was no mistaking it—the unique pattern of flowers ran from shoulder to hem.

Emily had crudely cut and hemmed the floor-length gown so that it now hung unevenly at her knees.

"Ma'am, is this your only bag?" the bus driver asked.

"Yes, thank you," Anne mumbled.

Holding Lance's small hand ever tighter, she began walking quickly toward the Pine Cone Inn.

Dan slipped in behind her and took the suitcase from her hand before she realized it.

"Anne, is that you?"

He patted little Lance on the head and cooed.

"My, my, you certainly have grown."

Anne blushed, placing a hand on her expanding stomach.

"Not you, Anne. I was talking to Lance!" Dan chuckled.

"Is someone picking you up or can I give you a lift?"

Dan had long, lean legs, dark wavy hair, and a smile that could melt an iceberg. He picked Lance up and set him on his shoulders as they walked to his truck.

As they drove through the countryside to the cabin Chaz had built for her, Anne was filled with peace. Even the betrayal of seeing her gift on Emily disappeared into her warm spirit.

When Dan pulled up to the cabin, Anne stumbled out in

disbelief. The cabin door hung from a single hinge and broken glass sparkled in the sunshine everywhere. Every window had been shattered; shards of glass lit up the yard. Her Pyrex and a few pieces of china lay broken.

Anne was unable to speak. Lance tugged on her arm. Dan offered to help her clean up, but Anne wanted to be left alone with Lance.

He didn't know her well, but Dan found it difficult to drive off. When he passed Dennis and Lillian's place, he saw them outside, and abruptly pulled his truck to a stop in front of Lillian.

"Anne Belcour is home," he said. "Someone has ransacked her cabin, broke all the windows and robbed her blind. She wouldn't let me help but, you know, she's pregnant again, it's rough. Chaz is nowhere to be seen."

Lillian thanked her cousin for the information, left the children with Dennis, and walked over to Anne's place. She wasn't going to let the fact that Anne had thrown her out stand in the way of a beautiful friendship.

Without a word, they embraced. They both glanced around the battered room, and Lillian suggested Anne and Lance come home with her. Anne could feel the outline of her unborn child's foot as it moved in her womb. Taking a deep breath, Anne found the strong place within her expand, making room for the little life force within her to move.

Lance hugged her leg, and she knew that nothing of real value had been lost.

Marlboro, 1944

When Anne was about to give birth, Chaz walked back into her life. He apologized. She accepted. Lillian said nothing.

Awkward days passed; they felt like strangers. Feelings of betrayal lingered. Chaz no longer stayed behind to drink with the boys. He played with Lance. Only time could heal . . . or reveal what would be.

Cars only left Marlboro fully loaded. If someone was going into "town," word went out and soon a small party was formed. Few people owned vehicles, and pitching in for petrol made it easier for everyone. Dennis and Lillian were ready to go. Chaz was checking to see if Anne needed anything. Lance rested on her big belly as she pulled a pair of clean pants on her son. She pushed a wild lock of hair out of her face.

"I know this sounds crazy Chaz, but I've been dreaming of biting into a big, red, juicy apple. I can just taste it."

"Well, we don't see many apples in these parts at this time of year, but I'll give her a try."

When Chaz and Lance drove off, soundlessness settled in. Like a medicinal balm on a throbbing wound, it worked its magic. Anne's head felt heavy on the pillow as she lay down in bed. She tried to find a position that would relieve the pressure from her back. Dull pain wrapped itself around her like a girdle. Unable to sleep, Anne rested, as her stomach began to do a slow, rhythmic dance.

The squeezing grew stronger. Sleep sounded so sweet but would not bestow its comfort on her. She became damp, followed by more pain and pressure. Anne's labor had begun.

Fear rose up like a wave, crashing over her body with each contraction.

"I can't give birth to this baby all alone."

The screen door slammed. Chaz was back from town. Anne called out, her voice shaking.

"Chaz! The baby's coming!"

He rushed to the bedroom, grocery bags in his arms, and lost his footing as he entered the room. The bags hit the floor and burst open, and apples began to roll like snooker balls. Chaz danced over them.

"Oh, God, gotta get Dennis," he said.

He handed Anne an apple and absentmindedly patted her on the head, then ran out the door to chase down Dennis and Lillian so they could notify the neighborhood midwife.

Marlene Shirley Bernadette Belcour had a powerful cry. "A big handle for such a little pot" some people would say. When her voice boomed out of that tiny body, Anne feared nothing of the future. This baby, like Lance, would live, and with that realization, Anne's head no longer felt heavy upon her pillow and she fell effortlessly into a sweet sleep. Her baby's cries faded gently into the air, until they became so soft, and drifted into Anne's dreams as a song.

Anne awoke when a pungent odor penetrated her sleep. She opened her eyes slowly. The elders had been called in by Chaz, and they stood at the foot of her baby's sleeping place. Chanting softly, they made their medicine as they moved about. They performed their ceremony and anointed the baby's feet.

This continued for three days, then the elders left, with no fanfare or explanation. They gathered their sacred objects and sage, and left the house. It made Anne uneasy.

"Tell me why, Chaz. Why did they come? What were they doing?" she asked.

"Perhaps even they don't know, Anne. Some things are meant to be a mystery."

It was true, some things were meant to be a mystery. But as the mystery began to unfold, Anne realized that the presence she felt was that of the Moon Bird. Walking to the window, she searched the night sky, and found the full moon rising, still shadowed by pine trees. Smiling to herself, Anne felt the strength of her daughter's spirit and wondered where this spirit would lead her.

BOOK TWO
Silversong

A fantasy is something that is not available

A vision keeps you from perishing

A dream is the symbology that comes to you

that must always be obeyed

And strength . . . strength is telling yourself the truth

CHAPTER ELEVEN
In Silversong's Words

I was born at the end of our world. February 6, 1944, the month of the hungry moon, born under the sign of Aquarius, my Christian name is Marlene Shirley Bernadette Belcour, the time, World War II, just after the thirties—distress, loss, grieving, hard times.

The Tribes, the People, could not respond to what they knew was right. Since the beginning of time, the Creator had provided everything, provided all we needed for the journey of life—food, water, shelter, clothing.

What was left up to us was our relationships, "all our relations" were left up to us.

By the time I was born, the life my people had once known had come to an end. No longer caretakers of Mother Earth, our food source was intentionally eliminated, starving the People into submission and dependency. We watched as the buffalo were shot by thoughtless men and trained buffalo hunters who wantonly slaughtered the sacred buffalo while the People died of starvation and disease.

No longer allowed to even respond to the Creator, their beliefs and ceremonies were outlawed as they were confined to concentration camps called reserves. I was born hungry.

I remember the Old Ones speaking of a time without fear, a time when they could worship, hunt, and feed their families. But that was before their sacred objects of empowerment were confiscated, eventually showing up in museums under glass where people would pay money to see them. Some of our grandfathers ended up the same way; even our deaths were not respected. Many simply quit making the sacred aids of empowerment because they knew they would end up desecrated . . . everything else had been.

People often shake their heads in amazement.

"Why don't the Indians of today follow and do the beautiful, powerful ceremonies and art of the past?"

As if we were lazy or something. These questions only show the ignorance of those asking, they don't "get it." For tribal people, art and life are one. There is no separation.

Some elders were wise—they hid their beautiful hearts from harm, kept what beauty they could salvage from the fragments of the past and hid it, with the intention of saving something for their grandchildren. Much was lost, but many precious, sacred ways were protected in this way.

Food became a commodity, requiring conditions and laws. Laws that were stronger than the men upholding them.

Their laws did not care that the People were starving. If you didn't have a hunting license, you couldn't feed your family. If you fed your family without a license and were caught, you would go to jail, and your family would starve. Hunting times were controlled. The *laws* did not particularly coincide with the ideal time to hunt for the betterment of the herds, land, or the People.

My father, Chaz Belcour, would slide out on the frozen lake on the darkest nights. There he would make a hole and fish to feed the People. It wasn't that he had a dishonest heart, but rather that he was still powerful enough to break the law—the People would eat those nights.

Threatened, intimidated, and all the while we were being taught in our new schools to memorize verses from the Bible such as "Perfect love casts out all fear."

Death-bringers, I thought. Putting to death all things of life.

I was born at the end of our world.

I was told when I was little to be patient, that the white man was only passing through on his way to the moon and other planets.

"They think their scientists will keep them alive for eternity, so they won't need their spirits."

The People, by living, struggling, praying, enduring, and honoring through ceremony wove themselves into the design of the Creator.

Artists and dreamers can still follow the path that the Ancient Ones have left in symbols and glyphs. The white man will always be a foreigner until he acknowledges the spirit of "place." When he ceases to possess everything he sees and stops trampling the fragile and delicate to get it, he may find his spirit.

My spirit is like a runner that goes between the Creator and my body. I don't need to be told what to do, because if I remain still enough, I'll hear clearly as my spirit delivers the true meaning of what it is I need to know in a given moment. I don't need to be "plugged in" because I have never been disconnected. Only when I turned from my spirit voice, did I get into any real trouble.

It was on the radio all the time: war, death, tanks, soldiers, bombers, gas chambers. And the uniforms—forest rangers, the Royal Canadian Mounted Police, government people, even the good guys from the Salvation Army had uniforms of authority.

The People would gather around the radio, listening for word on how our troops were doing, and discussing the war and what might happen. It was then that I realized how much had already been taken. The power of the People now belonged to a stone pony and the weight lay heavy on our hearts.

Waiting for the end to come was not the stuff little girl dreams were made of, so perhaps because of that, I was born "old," and clung to what truths I could find. Sometimes there were very few. The People had become so poor, I remember them taking turns carrying a battery from one house to another. There was fear, a fear you could feel . . . as everyone had lost someone in the war.

My mother was one of the few native people who could read

and write. Long lines of wagons would come for her services, bringing with them loving thoughts for her to write, or long letters from overseas for her to read to them. Some of the people came from far off, so they would set up camp in our yard.

My mother told me about an old woman who had brought a goose prepared in the traditional manner for her grandson. It was the first time he'd been away from home, and he had written to his grandmother telling her how badly he wanted a goose. Not realizing the consequences of the miles that lay between them, the grandmother brought the goose to Mom in a lard pail, and Mom appealed to my father for advice.

"Go ahead and send it Anne, it doesn't matter what shape it's in when it arrives. It's the fact that she sent it that will make him happy."

The packages had to be wrapped several times in heavy canvas and sewn together before being addressed in permanent India ink. That way, if the ship carrying the mail was bombed, the parcels had a better chance of being retrieved.

My parents' marriage ended too. Survival now replaced dreams and visions, survival next to death. That's how close we came to the death-bringers. Some weird kind of strangeness came about, acting as if and pretending you didn't know what living was for. *Reason* came to the People, who from the beginning of time had lived beyond reason, lived *beyond* . . . in spirit.

I was born in a log cabin that my father built. Days after my birth, the "long hairs" came. They still followed the old ways and hadn't cut off their hair. Mother said she was concerned as to how to feed all of them, as was the custom. She was sometimes ill at ease in their presence. She had been taken away from her people at such an early age that it scared her, these ways, this power, these people, her people.

She had already lost one precious baby daughter, my sister Dorothea, and she did not want anything she didn't understand around "this baby." Yet she trusted my father, who knew, understood, and trusted the ways of the spirit world.

My mother's instinctual self had been shamed into hiding, yet the spirit of gratitude for what little we had was a matter of fact. My mother honored God, Jesus, and the Great Spirit. She taught us at an early age that it was this invisible force that guided our every moment.

When I was a week old, our house caught on fire. Jip, Mom's German Shepherd, saved our lives. He crashed through the window and would not stop barking until he'd alerted the neighbors and awakened Mom. By the time the neighbors arrived, Mom's nightgown was on fire and had to be extinguished.

Somebody was always looking out for us, Mom let us know that early on. Only one week old and already I was teetering between life on earth and walking on into the spirit world.

One of my earliest recollections is thinking I had been picked up by an eagle. My father's beaded, buckskin jacket with the long fringe off the arms moved like feathers as he swooped down and picked me up. He smelled good, like smoke and the outdoors. He was always nice to me, I can never remember him any other way. I knew instinctively my parents' marriage would be ending. As I said, this small child's eyes spoke of endings.

The people were trying to live within reason, everyone had their "reasons," like the elders who held the secret sundances.

One time, when the elders were holding their secret sundances, the colored cloth was stolen off the sacred tree. The medicine man came out of the sweat lodge and told his helpers exactly who did it and where it was. The helpers went into town and retrieved it from underneath the mattress of the white people who had stolen and hidden it. These people knew nothing of the "spirit." They thought the ceremonies were merely superstition. *That* got my attention, as did similar stories, stories now referred to as "gossip."

For me, stories held hope of enlightenment and empowerment. I think it was the Old Ones that attended my birth who imparted a continuum of truth to me, and through their ceremonies, kept me from losing my mind so I could make it through the "mind-fields" of my future with a clarity—a clarity that would provoke the ones I loved most. Try as I would to assimilate, it never worked for long, and a deep and profound sadness would come upon me. A sadness that I could not hide and was too young to understand or explain.

Mother protected us from her personal confrontations with Chaz, and the rest of the world. She kept us warm, fed, and convinced that the Creator was on our side. Before I started school, Mom had to find work so she could support my brother Lance and me on her own. There was no welfare or assistance of any kind at the time, and there were no jobs in the Indian community. Alcohol abuse was so prevalent in the new Indian lifestyle, that life had become harder yet.

My father was a well-known "good provider" for the People. I believe that the Indian women were afraid to lose him, and that is partially why some of those women disliked Mom. Others were threatened by her "white" knowledge, which reminded them that they too had one foot in another world, a world they did not understand. Something so trivial, Pyrex cookware for instance, could be a problem for them. Mother thought they hated her; it was bigger, it went deeper . . . and it went far beyond my mother.

My mother was alone most of the time, and there was always the threat that what she held most dear would be taken from her, but I think the rejection by the Indian people cut the deepest. Everything she had always hoped for—belonging—was dashed. All her fantasies of that which is "Indian"—related to all, in harmony, connected to the Great Spirit—never took into account what five hundred years of genocide and assimilation does to a people, stripping away all faith and foresight. The wisdom was overshadowed for this generation of the Tribes. No longer *beings* filled with dreams, they were now the depositories of stereotypes and slogans: squaw, buck, lazy, ignorant, sneaky, drunk . . . the list goes on.

If the average American wants to know about the Tribes, who they are when they are not fighting for survival, all they need to do is take everything they have ever been told about "Indians," and reverse it.

CHAPTER TWELVE
A World at War

A few years before Marlene was born, word spread into the backwoods —the world was at war. Listening to the mortars explode over the radio was terrifying, and it seemed as if the war was on their back doorstep rather than on another continent. There was fear in the People's hearts. The depression had weakened an already tired people and war was more than many could bear. Mothers cried as they bid their sons farewell, fathers "kept their chins up," standing strong and stoic as boys became men the brutal way. While some people were desperately looking for work on this continent, others were dying in a distant land.

The reality that blared through the radio was in sharp contrast to the cool, quiet woods that surrounded Anne and Chaz's cabin. When Marlene was still very young, she had already shown qualities of being extraordinary. While the other children swam in the fish pond, Marlene floated in the ocean. She asked startling questions and had insight that sometimes unnerved her elders. She was born both extremely intelligent and talented, a combination that can sometimes kill a person if she is unable to come to terms with her own questions.

As the children grew, Anne and Chaz's relationship deteriorated. Chaz would only show up at home to get food. "Chaz, we'll starve to death, we have little ones who need to eat! Little ones who need shoes!" Anne screamed as she watch Chaz fill a box full of food from her pantry.

"They're my people, Anne. It's my responsibility!" was his familiar response.

Anne was angry. "Why? Why should our children suffer?"

"Someday we may need their help. As a man it is my duty, you don't understand." Chaz picked up the large box and headed out the door.

Staring at her now-empty pantry, Anne fought the feeling of defeat that began to engulf her. Anne didn't understand, and she was confused. Chaz was like two people. One honorable and sober, the other drunk with no conscience. Anne felt alone. It seemed as if Chaz was either gone "working," leaving her with nothing, or coming home to clean her out of what little bit of security she had hidden in her pantry.

Another familiar week passed with no word from Chaz. Leaving the children with Lillian, Anne headed out find him, ready for a fight. Once she had been young, once she had forgiven him, but this time was different. Anne was a little angrier and a whole lot wiser.

As she approached Emily's cabin, she saw Chaz's truck. Hearing their drunken laughter filtering its way out of the cabin and into the night, Anne made her way through the snow.

Never pausing to knock on the door, Anne slammed the door wide open as she walked in. Sickened, she looked around the room and saw immediately where Chaz's paycheck had gone. Never in her life had Anne seen so many bottles of alcohol. Walking toward the table, as Emily began cursing her, Anne grabbed up two full bottles of whiskey. "How dare you take food out of my children's mouths?" Anne screamed as she brought the bottles out to her side and then smashed them together in front of her. With a thundering crash, alcohol and shards of glass splattered around the room. Anne smashed bottle after bottle with an angry force that had never been released. Not stopping at the whiskey, Anne continued on until the last beer bottle had been broken, then she turned her attention toward Emily.

Grabbing her by the hair, Anne yanked Emily up from the bed

and threw her against the cabin wall. Chaz screamed. "You can't do this, Anne! . . . You can't!" Anne held Emily by the throat and began to slap her, as Chaz continued. "You have no right, Anne! You can't come in and do this!"

Anne released her grip on Emily, and turned toward Chaz. "I already did." Without another word, Anne walked out the door.

Something inside of Anne had broken with the last whiskey bottle she left lying behind her on the floor. These were not her people. There has to be something better than this, Anne thought. She was determined to find a place in the world where perhaps her children would have a chance. It seemed to Anne that there was no future in being Indian, only pain.

It was over. Anne had to face it. She was alone in the world with two children to raise. Gathering her courage about her like a cloak, her strength would guide her through the dark days ahead.

Anne started working as a waitress in Edson, Alberta's Commadore Restaurant, a small local restaurant that was really nothing more than a mom-and-pop coffee shop. Lance and Marlene were left with a baby-sitter while their mother was at work. One day, Chaz arrived to pick up the children. Unaware that Anne had not been informed of this arrangement, the baby-sitter was happy to be relieved of her duties early. Chaz and the children left without so much as a good-bye to Anne, and traveled to Edmonton where some of Chaz's people lived. There the children were left with a family named Paquette while Chaz looked for work. The beds there were pissy, wet, and cold, and soon after they arrived, the teenage children quickly understood Marlene's fears. They were left in charge while the parents went to town, and saw how alarmed Marlene would become whenever news of the war came on the radio. Marlene would ask them if the army had gotten to her mother and if it would be long before they came to get Lance and her too. The teenagers told her that the army couldn't get her if she hid in the cupboard under the sink and stayed there.

It was a ritual—each day after the parents left, Marlene hid. She didn't question where her brother hid, or why she and her brother were safe when the parents were home. She just did what they told her to do, in hopes it would keep them both safe. She never questioned what was going on nor spoke to anyone about it, it was as though silence was a necessary element of safety. It wasn't long before Marlene got bedbug bites, lice, and painful sores, all the while clinging to the idea that someday her mom would come back.

In the meantime, Marlene had Lance, and as long as she had her brother, she knew she'd be okay. He made it bearable.

Lance got Marlene through it, as he would many times as the two grew. He became Marlene's hero; he was always there for her. Marlene thought it was remarkable that the adults around them couldn't provide the stability that her brother provided effortlessly.

It took Anne three months to find her children and once she did, she couldn't bring them home. She had exhausted all her money just getting to Edmonton. The Paquettes told her that Chaz owed them money for the children's care, and they were held hostage until Anne paid up. They demanded not only money, but also insisted that she buy them a cow. They were poor, they said. But everyone was poor.

After Anne went to work and saved up, she retrieved her children and moved to the tiny town of Obed. Anne was the postal person and also worked for the highway department. An elderly man she got to know had such compassion for the family that every week he would drop by with provisions of some kind. He knew Chaz. He was like a grandfather to them; the kids called him Grandpa Joe. He spoke kindly and was a gentle spirit, helping many children. It wasn't long before all the little ones called him "Grandpa Joe Kerr."

When Marlene was still quite young, her father stole her from a baby-sitter once again. Chaz still believed in the old ways, where in the case of a divorce, the man kept the girl child and the woman the boy. After taking Marlene, she was sold over a barroom table to an elderly white couple for the sum of two hundred dollars. They were very fat and cooked all the time. Marlene was terribly lonely for her brother, but it was nice to be spoiled a bit. She often asked them about Lance, wondering when she would see him again. She looked in their eyes when she asked about her brother. She wouldn't talk to them about her brother unless they looked in hers. They said they would get her another brother if she stopped crying, and she said, "If you get me another brother and I look into his eyes, Lance will not be in there."

She knew about those things, even then.

With the help of the RCMP, Anne eventually found Marlene and brought her home. Grandpa Joe Kerr gave Anne a two-room log cabin in Hinton, Alberta, that he had acquired from the highway department. The cabin was about forty or fifty feet down in a valley between two hills. On one side was a very steep hill, and on the other was a path that led to town. About twenty feet from the cabin was Happy Creek, the main water supply. Marlene and her brother would go up the creek and collect coal. At Happy Creek, her brother once again took care of Marlene's fears.

One day, as Anne journeyed the mile into town for supplies, an absolutely horrendous storm struck. Lightning bolts the size of poplar trees stood for seconds at a time. The air came alive. Everything danced and moved to the sounds of thunder and lightning, which had become one; there was no time lapse between them. The children sat huddled, listening to the thunder and counting, trying to see how long it took before the lightning struck, gauging how many miles away the storm was. This time, they were *in* it.

Lance took immediate action. Without hesitation he got an apple box, a blanket and some nails. Using his mother's hammer, he nailed the blanket over the window to spare Marlene the horror of it all. It helped not to see the frightening power engulfing her. She felt safe once again, like in the cupboard.

Suddenly Lance was hurled across the room in a brilliant flash of lightning that lifted and moved the floor. The lightning moved through them ... they were suspended in a surge of pure energy ... then suddenly dropped to the floor.

The storm stopped in an instant and only far off rumbling sounds could be heard. All this happened in three or four seconds. When Lance said, "It's over now, it's over," Marlene knew she could trust him.

1948

It didn't take Anne long to figure out that it was going to take more than mere toys to feed Marlene's soul. She sought out and bargained for the services of a ballet teacher who lived in Edson. Little Mar became a star.

She performed her first public recital at four years old, singing, dancing, and reciting poetry while standing on an apple box. She performed flawlessly and for a time was lost in the applause, happy that she had pleased the people so. She had no stage fright.

Shirley Temple was the rage at the time, and Marlene was looked upon as that sort of child. She was small for her age, so she really charmed people. She liked seeing people happy; it was such a wonderful distraction from the people surrounding her whose daily lives had become a struggle for survival.

The fears that Marlene had were not those of the usual child. While other children feared the dark, Marlene was worrying about the state of the world. Anne was ill often, as the rare anemia she had suffered as a child resurfaced. With the illness came the dreams. There was always blood, pools of blood she was drowning in ... they were terrible nightmares. Being a sensitive child, Marlene worried that at any time her mother might leave her and die. Marlene now had a new fear to add to her growing list.

As a child Marlene understood creating art was a worthy purpose. She felt useful, needed in fact. She sensed the enormous function creativity had in the enhancement of life. What would the world be without flowers? Without dreaming? Dreams are dreamed by the artist within each person. Her mother taught her how to recognize the beauty and good things in life that many parents unintentionally taught their children to forget—they had other things on their minds. So much surrounds children, and so much is often lost. Anne showed her daughter how to see. The artist was born.

Marlene could read a bit before she started school. She would hang around Lance when he was doing his homework until eventually she learned. Lance was always an action-type guy. His interest went beyond learning proper English, and it was tedious for him.

Marlene had not yet started school when Anne found her hiding under the kitchen sink, huddled in a ball and holding her head.

"Marlene, we've been looking everywhere for you. Why didn't you answer us? Why have you been hiding?"

"The war . . . it's here, Mom, I hear it."

Her little body shook with sobs and she took large gulps of air, trying to calm herself.

"But Marlene, the war's over. It's only a radio program."

Anne tried to comfort her. Marlene had been this way ever since she returned from the Paquettes, and Anne could only hope these fears would subside. But regardless of what her mother said or did, Marlene knew the war was real.

Another change that Anne had become aware of since Marlene's return from the Paquettes was her insistence that she be called by her spirit name, Silversong. Her spirit name and the personal ceremony she experienced to receive her name were the last gifts she would receive from her father and his people.

Luckily for Silversong, her mother was an extraordinary and inventive teacher. Unlike her own home schooling program, Anne fashioned learning games for her children that were fascinating and full of knowledge. Her own love for books had never waned, and she took time to find the appropriate material she would need. She traveled around the world with her children while they sat in front of the fireplace in the evenings.

It was the way it was supposed to be, wonderful and exciting.

Anne was thrilled to find a map of the world tucked inside a magazine. Proudly, she hung it on the wall and watched as her children took turns putting colored pins in the various countries as they took their journeys, traveling page by page.

Although Silversong was stronger than little Dorothea had been, she was still a very sickly child, often prone to bouts of pneumonia. There was only one other child who had survived more cases of pneumonia than Silversong. His name was Bobby Seals, and he also lived in Hinton, near Happy Creek. Anne was sure that if it had not been for the discovery of penicillin, Silversong would have died from the same disease that took Dorothea.

Anne had to fight to get medical care for Silversong. The native people had little money, so they didn't get the medical care that those with money did.

The nuns in the hospital would take Silversong down to the pantry and set her up on the counter. They would all come and visit her there, asking her questions and waiting silently until she spoke. She had learned all the Christian stories from her mother, the same stories that Anne heard as a child at Edwina's, the same stories that Anne knew white society would expect Silversong to know in order to be accepted. Silversong told the nuns she knew Jesus had died and that when he was in church he amazed the scholars. She also told them about the time he got really angry at the moneychangers and they nailed him up. She wasn't happy about the church, but she really liked Jesus. It seemed to her he acted like a native. He taught on hillsides and by streams, he baptized out in creation, in the river. He even went into the desert for days and vision-quested. He sundanced to his death.

Silversong knew what he said was how he lived, and she could trust him.

The Cree people were named "Kristineau" by the French, because they were Christ-like in their beliefs. Over time, the moniker was shortened to "Cree." The Cree followed the same ways that

Jesus spoke of, but had different ceremonial objects. Where Christians had incense and myrrh, for instance, the Cree had sage and sweet grass. This seemed to make Christians nervous.

The nuns asked Silversong so many questions that she became frustrated. She finally told them that if they had husbands and kids of their own, they wouldn't have to ask her all these things. It seemed so basic to Silversong. They didn't have kids of their own to help them out. Their eyes grew large when Silversong suggested this. They drew back. They told her that if she was good, when she got older she could marry Jesus like they had. At that point, Silversong could sense the protective atmosphere that surrounded the sisters. They were safe, and so Silversong thought that maybe someday she too would become a nun.

They served her cookies, and when a bell rang, she was promptly deposited into her room, where she listened to the sound of shuffling feet and stiff, starched habits hurrying off to vespers, mass or prayers. There was so much order compared to the life Silversong knew, it was odd.

It was also the first real experience she had with the "outside" world.

She experienced the outside world once again when she started school at five years old. She was so excited. Anne had impressed upon her the importance of an education and the excitement of learning new things. A picture was taken the day Lance and Silversong stood on top of the steep hill their first day of school. Anne was so proud, and Silversong felt really grown up and included.

All her friends were happily seated about the classroom, and Silversong was assigned her own desk. About an hour into the class orientation, she became thirsty, so she got up and took a paper cup full of water.

She had just gulped it down when Miss McNeely hurled her around by the arm and slapped her full in the face. Silversong's joy died. It burned ... and pain shot in an instant through her whole mind. Had Miss McNeely not held her by the right arm, her feet would have left the floor when she was struck. Her nose began to bleed and did not stop for a long time. Silversong's friend, Sherry, jumped on Miss McNeely when she saw her teacher shove Silversong aside like a rag doll. Still in shock, Silversong watched Sherry wrestle her teacher to the ground.

Anne was furious when she found out what had happened and wasted no time in going to confront Miss McNeely. As it turned out, the teacher thought Anne had sent her daughter to school underage, because she was so small—still wearing clothing that fit most three-year-olds. When Anne showed her Silversong's papers, Miss McNeely changed her tune and began crying (perhaps afraid that Anne intended to beat her up as well). Miss McNeely's mother eventually stepped in and claimed her daughter was suffering from a nervous breakdown. Silversong's formal education had started off with a real bang.

After that, Silversong began to ignore it when people treated her badly. She assumed it was just a part of life. Occasionally, she might try to change their minds or make excuses for them, rationalizing that they were hurt. She thought being nice was the answer and that if she were pure and good enough, God would see to it that people liked her and would protect her. She would be safe.

Silversong and her friends talked about these things, and decided, or rather convinced each other, that they were nun material. That was their future ... until they got caught pulling down their pants. She was then informed just how seriously evil a person she was, and she began to pray harder, trying to be better, all the time sensing that it was a lie, yet further convinced that she was a very bad girl.

She was learning her catechism. Questions and answers became an intense investigation for her. She was looking for solutions to problems she didn't understand. Studying the past, fearing the future, it seemed as if the "now" was the worst place to be. According to the Bible, in the past, God was with the people. He spoke to them from burning bushes and clouds. And in the future, he would be waiting, but not much was said about the now. It seemed to Silversong there was no room left for living, lessons, or experience. Straight-line thinking—a beginning and an end. Mother Earth doesn't matter. She will be destroyed and we will all be lifted up from the holocaust.

The People's thinking is different—it's circular, like their Mother. And every seven years, one cycle of life is completed.

The first seven years, their needs are minimal. We require someone who loves us, enough food to keep us alive, water, and shelter.

The next seven years, their priorities change. Food turns to growth, family extends to friends and relationships.

Then begins the next cycle, with each seven years giving them a chance to add or subtract what is or isn't necessary any longer. They learn and grow, constantly changing as they move around the medicine wheel of their lives.

Linear thinking, "straight line" thinking, leaves no second chances. It assumes one only sits and hopes that when things get really bad they'll be lifted up out of the tribulation. There's no way out but up. No responsibility for the next seven generations or for Mother Earth. Silversong kept thinking about the Second Coming of Christ.

I thought that when they told me He would "come to live in my heart the day I accepted Him," that referred to the "Second Coming." He already lived in me, so as far as I was concerned, He had already come again to earth. I couldn't look up at the clouds waiting for Him to return and fix everything, because if I believed He was in my heart, He has returned.

I believed God is Love. If you are in deepest Africa and you love, that is God. God understands Swahili, Cree, Sioux, Blackfoot, and even old English. Love in any language is God. This is what He said to me.

It's much easier not to do anything, to sit back and wait. But it is up to us to love one another.

Of all the things Silversong learned as a child, music and art were what moved her to the place of peace she was seeking. It was always her art that she would return to when she had questions that no one could answer.

Old Pauline knew the ways of Silversong's people. She was a Cree woman who took care of Silversong often when Anne was ill. Pauline spent their time together teaching Silversong how to think like the People. Great Mystery stories, old ways, stories about the animals and trees, mountains and lightning. Silversong was already aware that there were two worlds, the white and the native; and she also knew that the native world made her mother uncomfortable. For her mother, it was a world best left behind.

Silversong would lie on her stomach for hours and watch the fish that flowed so thick, they had to squirm side by side upstream. So abundant were they, Silversong actually thought she could walk across the stream on their backs.

It seems that the youth see more clearly; they more accurately reflect back to society that which it has given them. They are closer to the truth than when they become older and learn to cope. Indian people used to have an idea of who they were—a part of everything around them. According to Indian tradition, every drop of water in their bodies had been a river, a cloud, or an ocean over eternity.

The minerals and soil surrounding them holds the very elements of their ancestors, sustained by the echo of life. Nothing is taken from the earth without acknowledging what had been created for them to share, for all things are related.

Silversong saw that the tribal way reflected harmony. Honoring the strength of the buffalo, sight of the eagle, and the sun . . . raising their hands up to the Creator, palms down, as they gave prayers of gratitude—not palms open and wanting more. Made by the same forces that created the mountains and forest, they respected all God/ Great Spirit's creations.

It was easy to see the conflict between the Tribes and white mainstream thinking at that time. The Peoples' most sacred beliefs and ceremonies were laughed at as some kind of strange, sick joke. So the People learned to keep their beautiful thoughts hidden. It is easier to keep safe that which is secret, than regain that which is lost.

Silversong decided she would keep secret the old ways of looking at life that Pauline had taught her; the songs, the drum, the prayers taken up in smoke, and the ceremonies.

She never forgot any of it, although many times it might have been the smart thing to do. She remembered Pauline telling of the Old Ones on horseback making their pilgrimages to places of power and enlightenment, safe places the Creator had made. What the Old Ones recognized as sacred made much more sense to Silversong. Especially when compared to the places she was being taught to honor in school. They all seemed all to be places of death.

Scientists now generally agree, on some level, as to the existence of Sacred Ground. Their technology has informed them of certain atmospheric conditions that exist. Silversong believed these conditions tuned up bodies at a subatomic particle level. She could feel it. The Old Ones knew it long ago, long before technology was born. The whites should have taken more than the land, Silversong thought, they might have really learned something.

Silversong remained in her safe, silent place. A sacred place in her mind.

She had been taught never to align herself with anything that could be broken, and she was also taught that looking can blind one and sometimes keep one from seeing. But her most important lesson perhaps was to come: discovering that a fantasy is something that is not available, a vision keeps you from perishing, and a dream must be obeyed. And strength, strength is telling yourself the truth.

CHAPTER THIRTEEN

Haunted Haven

*A*nne was lonely much of the time. As time went on Anne thought of herself as a single mother, although the term had not been coined yet. New visitors began to replace the old, and it wasn't long before Anne started see her old protector, Dan. Their relationship was awkward at first, but as Dan and Anne overcame their initial shyness with one another and began to express their feelings they found happiness. Life was good once again. Dan and Anne had formed a new family from the fragment of the past.

Anne and Dan had two children together. Ron was born first and then two years later Patty was born. Ron bore a strong resemblance to Dan. He was always tall for his age, long and lean. Anne named him after Ronald, her saving grace during the years she spent at Edwina's. She said it was her way of honoring him for always being there for her as a child. Patty was precious, with thick curly black hair that Anne would wrap into ringlets. She was a sweet, happy child—they both were, but Ron had a quiet intensity about him.

Anne was happiest with Dan. He was her true love, but it was an ill-fated relationship. Dan was loving and kind but had trouble keeping a job, and Anne saw a bleak future ahead if she stayed with him—more children, more hungry mouths she could not feed. She chose instead to take responsibility for the lives she had already brought forth, but the fact that her life could not be spent with Dan always hurt her, and after they parted while Patty was still a baby, Anne resigned herself to providing as stable a family as she could, though it lacked the passion she had enjoyed with him.

Brule, Canada, 1953

Anne met Terry Lawsen when Silversong was nine years old. He came into their lives while Anne was very sick with her anemia, in and out of the hospital.

Terry pretty well took over and always treated Lance, Silversong, Ron, and Patty as if they were his own children, and Anne felt indebted to him. He was the only real "Dad" the children ever knew.

Even early in their relationship Terry was in the grip of an alcohol addiction. Alcohol isn't prejudiced; it isn't a disease reserved for Indians. Terry Lawsen was a lumber-jacking Swede, a small man with light hair and blue eyes. But he found out that when there's no place else to go a whiskey bottle can make a good hiding place. It was the vehicle that transported him through a maze of emotions, and finally, to the place where nothing at all matters, nothing hurts. He would be empty, like the whiskey bottle, void of all considerations. There were similarities between Chaz and Terry, but there were differences, too. Although Terry drank, he was a good father and a consistent provider.

It was Terry who moved the family to Brule, a small town in the mountains, and there the clan became known as the Lawsen family. Even with his drinking, there were happy days and a sense of security. Although they lived way out in the Canadian wilderness, they had an exquisite school marm and she taught ballet. Silversong was totally intrigued and began taking ballet lessons in exchange for cleaning and chores.

It took six months for her to get a record of "Blue Danube" that was to accompany her dancing at a Christmas concert. She also played hockey at the time. An odd combination—hockey and ballet.

There was a lot of diversity in the life Anne had created for herself and her children. The diversity of the different cultures Silversong grew up with always intrigued her, and she saw them as vast resources of new understanding.

They had never known a life as good as the one they had with Terry in Brule. The children called him Dad and his coworkers called him "Top Dog" because he was one of the lumber mill's main supervisors. For once, Anne wasn't alone, and the stress and strain of the previous years drifted into memory. She was really happy. They all were.

When summer arrived in Brule, the heat was more than merely inconvenient and uncomfortable, it was dangerous. Insurance companies knew the potential for catastrophe was great and refused to insure the mill for the months of June, July, and August. During those hot months, Terry's job focused solely on protecting the mill from potential fire. Even operating the machinery posed a great risk of fire.

Everyone knew how hazardous it was, but nothing could have prepared them for the moment of stupidity that led in mere seconds to an inferno. Years later Terry said he remembered it as if it were happening in slow motion.

One of the new employees fired up a chain saw and it began to throw sparks. The sparks lit up the dry shavings that ran along the large beams overhead, and suddenly flames shot down the length of the beams. In an instant, it was a raging storm. There had been no small fire, no hope of containment, no middle ground, just suddenly a conflagration—tinder-soft shavings, igniting in a single moment. There wasn't even time to scream "no" before it was out of control.

Immediately, Terry turned and ran for the shed that held his tools. They represented a huge investment of money and a lifetime of work. They brought the food home to his family's table.

"Don't do it, Terry! You'll never make it," one of oilers shouted.

Terry later said he remembered looking in the oiler's eyes, sensing the man was going to try to tackle him. Terry never gave him a chance, and he got out of there with most of his important tools in tow.

Lance had been playing nearby when he saw smoke rising from the lumber mill. He ran to see what was happening just as his step-father came bolting out the door with his tools. Terry screamed at Lance, telling him to get away.

"That car's going to blow up!" Terry hollered.

The owner of the lumber mill had his new car parked close to the building. The heat was so intense that Terry was sure it was going to go, but Lance hopped in, started her up and drove to safety.

After the car was a safe distance away, Lance took charge and saved the main house from burning down, keeping it watered for hours while the rest of the crew and townspeople helped the volunteer fire department put out the blaze.

Lance never acted like a kid. For as long as Silversong could remember, he always seemed like a man. Maybe this was because, until Terry Lawsen became Lance's dad, Lance had been the man of the family. He was eleven years old when Terry came along, and now Lance had an ally. Terry Lawsen treated Lance as his equal; he taught Lance how to be a hero.

And Lance was hailed as a hero—the radio station in town talked him up and the local newspaper ran articles. He was even awarded a special watch. Everyone was very proud of him, but there were no two ways about it, the burning of the lumber mill was a tragedy and made for a tough winter. The only meat the family had was what Lance and Terry could trap, and the only money came from peeling ties—taking the bark off trees so they can be put through the saw mill. They ate a lot of mashed potato sandwiches and Anne looked tired, but she never stopped working. She was out there with Terry, unloading huge ties from the horses, and peeling them. Silversong could remember their conversation.

"How you doing, honey?"

"We can do some more," Anne said.

"Do your hands hurt?"

"No, they're too cold, can't feel them anymore."
Anne kept right on working.

Lance found a bird with a broken wing, and he named it Blinky. He was bound and determined to nurse that bird back to health, which he did, but Blinky never flew again. He would just pluck and cluck around the house, and the kids tried to teach him to talk. Lance was a real mother hen.

"I know something's wrong with Blinky. It's his feet, look at him. It's as if he's up to something; I can't figure it out."

They couldn't understand what Blinky found so appealing about stomping in a mud hole for hours at a time.

It was a sad day for all, especially Lance, when they discovered Blinky had stomped himself into a deep clay hole and not made it back out.

The following year, Terry got hired as the foreman for the S&N lumber mill in Edson. The pay was much less than he had been making before the mill burned, but it was his only option.

All year long, Lance, Silversong, Ron, and Patty had been having major fights. Things kept mysteriously disappearing and they all suspected one another. When it came time to move, Terry attempted to repair a loose wallboard and, to the family's surprise, he discovered every single item that had been missing. All the tiny, shiny treasures the kids had suspected one another of taking over a period of a year were behind that wallboard—Silversong's ring and Patty's badge, three of the boys' trucks, and some hair clips; if it had caught Blinky's eye, it was there. Lance was stunned.

Blinky was by then dead and gone, so they couldn't choke him for all the grief he'd caused, but they were all guilt-free once again. No longer did they peer at each other out of the corners of their eyes, sure that if they watched closely enough, they would catch the culprit that was snagging their special junk. For the first time in a year, they all liked each other again.

They moved into their new house out on Grand Prairie Trail,

only a stone's throw from Edson, right before Christmas. Anne and Terry couldn't get over their good luck at having found such a large place to rent for such a reasonable amount of money. They were only paying about a third of what was normally asked for such a huge house. The only drawback was that one room was sealed off.

"That room's under renovation," they were told.

Well, it was only a matter of time before Anne's curiosity got the best of her, and she pried the boards off to take a look.

There wasn't a damn thing wrong with that room and it really got to me. I mean, why waste all that perfectly good space? It was Christmas time and I knew we'd be having company over. Terry was always dragging the boys home for a party during the holidays and I figured it would make a darn nice guest room. I dusted and fixed up the bed and threw a rug over the stain that had soaked into the wood floor.

Later that day, the kids and I unpacked the Christmas decorations and hung white streamers throughout the living room. We were really pleased with our efforts, even found some large white paper Christmas bells and placed them right in the middle where we could admire them.

Sure enough, Terry brought home a couple of the guys and they had quite an evening so the fellas decided to sleep over. I gave them a couple pillows and directed them to our newly acquired guest room.

It wasn't quite light outside when I got up that morning and came into the kitchen to put the coffee on. I damn near tripped and fell on Terry's friend Bud, and then I saw that Al was also there on the floor sound asleep. I couldn't figure it out. I woke them up and asked them what in the hell they were doing sleeping on the kitchen floor when we had a perfectly good guest room?

Well, they both took a moment to look at each other, and I could see when they finally began talking that it was embarrassing for them to admit to me that they'd both become frightened.

They said that every time they were about to fall asleep, they would begin to see terrible things, like nightmares. Finally they both just gave up, came down and went to sleep by the stove.

It seemed after Christmas our luck got downright grim. First Silversong got sick and landed in the hospital with hepatitis. It was later discovered she had gotten it from the well water. We thought we might lose her for awhile there, she looked so awful, big black circles under her brown eyes and jaundiced.

No more did Silversong recover, and the rest of the family was hit with the Asian flu. It was bad that year ... it took all we had to hang in there, helping each other out as we could.

And then there was Terry's accident, where he lost his middle finger at the first joint.

It all happened so fast. He was unable to get over the fact that he had been caught in the machinery like that. Terry took a great deal of pride in knowing his job and it just didn't make any sense to him.

A couple months later, Terry and I stopped in the pub to get to know some of our new neighbors and have a couple of drinks.

I mentioned that we'd recently moved into town from the house out on the Grand Prairie Trail in Tolertin.

Well, right then several people at the bar just stopped what they were doing and looked at us.

"You mean to say you people lived out there in the Grand Prairie House?"

"Yeah, we rented it."

"You know, they've never been able to rent that place before. Used to be the morgue, you know?"

I looked at Terry with a raised eyebrow.

Terry said, "Holy smoky, cross-eyed, Mexican Christ!"

He looked at his missing middle finger and began waving it in the air.

"I knew it, Terry, I knew it all along. I could feel it!" I said, as Terry sat there staring at his finger.

*"I knew it too woman, but I just couldn't put my finger on it!
All those things happening to us out there, and those bastards
never told us a damn thing!"*

Anne told everyone about her dream about the house out on
the Grand Prairie Trail.

"That goddamn place burned right to the ground!" she said,
looking pleased.

Then her best friend Teresa came in the door.

"Anne, you'll never believe what happened last night. That
goddamn house burned right to the ground!"

No one was living there and there was no electricity.

"Must have been a transient, probably built a fire to warm himself," Teresa said, trying to comfort herself.

"Yeah, yeah, must have been," Anne agreed, but neither of them
believed it.

CHAPTER FOURTEEN

Teddy's Spirit Moves

Edson, Alberta, 1959

*A*s *Silversong entered her teenage years and her artistic talent became* evident, she felt an intense responsibility. She began to see that she could best respond to life through her art. She always believed it was a gift from the Creator. Its impact, the power to communicate and share understanding on any level, seemed important to her. And as temporary and precarious as life was, she felt a strong desire to ease the pain of mortality.

Everyone is on a vision quest, whether he or she acknowledges it or not.

Lance and Silversong were the only two Indian children from Edson that made it to high school. As a fifteen-year-old, Silversong felt she was "wasting away" in the wilderness. Although she was surrounded by the majestic beauty of the Rocky Mountains and lush green forest, she wasn't captivated by the beauty, but rather, felt it was holding *her* captive. A tortured soul, no one in Edson or in her family seemed to understand her. Often she grabbed her paints and headed off to the woods, determined to paint herself out of the place, at least for a couple of hours. As she painted, she would contemplate her identity, which was already in crisis.

Even at school she was treated differently. She and her brother were often kept after school by their teachers. There was no genuine reason for this, but they were Indian and because they were Indian, the teachers assumed they needed extra help. They were singled out, and Silversong felt they thought she was stupid. She didn't like their patronizing ways, and decided that people do some of the cruelest things with smiles on their faces.

As she painted, she heard an ancient drum beat somewhere inside of her—the voice of her people warning her of the false shadows that fall across the white man's face. It was a warning she had to ignore as she packed up her paints and headed back toward the house. She chased the thoughts away; they were carried off in the cold north wind.

"Time to wake up and stop thinking like an Indian," she would say to herself as she walked in the front door of her house.

The family had moved to the S&N lumber mill when Terry was promoted to foreman. The house at the mill wasn't fancy but Anne, as usual, knocked herself out making it a home, spending as little money as possible. There was very little to spend. She painted the old linoleum floor by hand with a sponge, creating a new design, and the results were charming and comfortable.

Lance didn't seem to have the problems at school that Silversong was having. It seemed her brother was able to ignore everything.

He also made sure he was better at everything than anyone else and that helped him cope. He worked harder than anyone Silversong knew, proving to the world he wasn't "a lazy Indian." He and Silversong never talked about this, however.

Actually, the fact that they had native blood was never talked about. It was a secret in their house. Neither Anne nor Lance would discuss it with Silversong, and she wondered what was so wrong with being Indian. She wondered what was wrong with *her*. She was not supposed to speak of anything Indian, which was not easy. Every time she looked in a mirror, she saw an Indian. Her hair was black, her eyes and skin were brown. She saw the contrast between the girls she went to school with and herself.

The years of pain and shame had taken their toll on Anne. She had seen what thinking, acting, and being Indian had done to many of the young beautiful children she remembered from the years she lived in Marlboro with Chaz. Now she would see them occasionally in town, heading into a bar, their eyes cloudy with alcohol, the look of hopelessness. They had no future. Many of them were dying young.

Anne didn't want her children to die. And somewhere along the line being "Indian" once again became something to overcome, something to erase. Silversong now began to ask the same questions Anne had asked as a native child.

Anne was very proud of the way Lance and Silversong were accepted into one of the best groups of young people in their town. They were friends with all the "nice" girls and boys—doctors' daughters, businessmen's sons, but most importantly, white people. Anne forbid her children to hang around with, or even speak to, any of the "Marlboro people." Marlboro was the Indian reservation near where they lived. Marlboro was where Silversong's natural father lived. Silversong would always remember the time, deep down when she would retreat into her spirit. She never spoke to her mother about what happened, but she could always recall it as if it just took place.

I am walking up main street to meet my girlfriend at the soda shop. I walk past a small group of young people from Marlboro. They look at me silently and I avoid their gazes and walk a little faster. Near the entrance are the "nice boys" standing in a group, anticipating the weekend. They are laughing and joking. I hear one say, "It's Saturday night, let's go rape a squaw." It's not the first time I've heard this said, and I tell myself again that it means nothing, it's just a saying.

All the girls I go to school with are what I call "Sandra Dees"—blonde hair, blue eyes, and highly sought after. I am invisible.

One day at school, this boy who is really cute talks to me and I am so surprised that I can't speak. Finally a sound breaks through. It's a squeak, and from now on my nickname is "Mousy."

Christmas Eve. It's very cold out but everything looks so

beautiful, wrapped in a pure white blanket of fresh snow. I am so excited. I've been invited to a Christmas party by the most popular group of kids in town. For once I feel truly accepted. Everything's so magical and extra special this time of year. I feel like Cinderella as I dress. I can hear Mom humming and singing Christmas carols. Even Dad is feeling fine tonight. Geez, I can't believe I've been invited. They must really like me.

The party is at a boy's house whose parents are out of town for the night so everyone feels really grown up. Some of the boys are even drinking beer. Everybody feels cool, we're all having a really great time. The night flies by and everyone decides to head home.

"I'll give you a ride home," this boy says. "Come on in here for a minute, I want to talk to you."

He motions for me to go into the kitchen with him. We talk for awhile and then we go toward the living room to leave. Something is wrong—the living room is full of boys from my tenth grade class. All the nice girls are gone. The boys are talking and laughing again like the day out in front of the soda shop—Saturday night and squaws and what they're good for.

They hold me down and systematically rape me. They take turns repeatedly. In a blur of horror, I look at each face. Everything is in slow motion now. I am looking for a protector, someone who will make them stop. There is no one, no hint of concern.

I leave my body and see it from above, my arms held straight out like Jesus. How stupid I was not to protect myself. How stupid for not knowing I was a squaw and it was Saturday night.

I hover above, about three feet away. I speak softly to myself, yet I am not speaking at all.

"I wonder if they'll kill her? Look at their faces—they're insane. Is it a performance? A ritual? A sporting event? An act? Like the games, yes, like sports, showing off for one another. She is frozen. How hard it must be for her. Even God can be no part of this."

The smell of beer and cigarettes nauseates me. I move farther away, no longer hovering above myself. Confusion and pain remain. It's all that exists now.

When the "activity" is over, I see they are scared.

"If you tell anyone, we'll kill you," the nice boy says.

I was like a robot. I couldn't feel my arms or legs, yet they responded and I dressed myself. I looked at each one of them and I walked out the door.

It was cold, a cold that burns like fire, like hell. Even the Christmas lights seemed to mock me. I had never walked home alone before but this time I walked. I walked alone.

Nothing mattered anymore. What else could they do to me? I had left my house a sixteen-year-old virgin and returned, no longer a virgin and knowing I would never really feel sixteen years old again.

The physical pain kept me connected, or I would have drifted far away. The moon was full. I heard the snow moan beneath my feet. I couldn't even cry. The snow cried for me that night.

It was very late when Silversong walked in the front door that night. She looked at Anne and said absolutely nothing. Anne had been scared, and when Silversong came home she was relieved enough to be angry, and she slapped her.

Silversong thought she was special. She thought she was talented. She thought she was a worthy person, now all she felt was confusion. Anne never understood why Silversong wanted so much from life. And now that Anne was not feeling well, she became impatient with Silversong. She would often tell her daughter, and anyone else who happened to be around, that Silversong thought she was the Queen of England. She nicknamed her "Queenie."

Little did anyone realize that Queenie had been a dear four-legged friend to Anne when she was Silversong's age. But without an explanation, it seemed to Silversong as if her mother was being cruel.

"What's wrong, Queenie?" Silversong would often hear.

"I am not a queen, and this sure as hell isn't Buckingham Palace."

"What's wrong? The S&N not good enough for you, Queenie? Edson's not even good enough for you, eh?"

Silversong was ungrateful and selfish, Anne said that night, and it was absolutely terrible what her daughter put her through. Again, Silversong said nothing about the event that had just taken place a few hours earlier.

In the morning, the family opened presents. Silversong hugged her brother and sister. They took pictures and Anne cooked and organized until she was exhausted. Silversong listened, as usual, to her stepfather's dumb jokes and laughed. She played Monopoly with Lance, even though she knew he was cheating her out of a hotel every time he whistled. And she heard a new voice in her head. It said, "It doesn't matter."

She started making a new prayer. She convinced herself that it would be okay if she remained silent. It would become a bad dream. She felt so humiliated and ashamed. There were times she felt like she couldn't breathe, like she was suffocating. She trusted no one, only her suffocating silence. None of them could know. Her mother was ill, her stepfather was an alcoholic, and her brother Lance would have killed someone had he known. And she loved all of them, and was afraid she would lose their love if she spoke about the incident.

She was determined to do the best she could. Her temple had been destroyed, everything felt broken and violated, but she was convinced she would show everyone that she was of value. And she would never again forget that she was a squaw.

She grew moody and distant, wore long sleeves and a big sweater to keep herself covered. She lay around a lot, saying she was sick. She was teased, and called selfish, lazy, extravagant, and vain. Extravagant, because she tried to love and pamper herself in order to heal. Vain, because she was always trying to look clean and groomed to perfection, thinking that if she looked really nice, people would respect her, and not know how ugly she felt.

Anne was the same in many ways, but for her it was a matter of acting white. If she acted white, people would respect her more. Anne's vow of silence had been to deny her Indianness. Silversong now had her own, equally dangerous, vow of silence.

She felt her reality had been warped, and it was hard for her to feel special any longer. It was hard for her to feel good . . . it was hard for her to feel at all.

From then on, she was "Mousy the Varmint" at school and "Queenie" when she walked in the front door to her home.

She and her classmates were studying "The Vanishing American," learning how "savage and cruel" the Indians had been. She didn't believe the stories. She knew there were reasons for their stoicism. She would close her eyes and put her face straight up to heaven and ask the Creator why she was born between the white and the Indian, between night and day, living at the edge of dawn waiting for the light. In the light, she felt she would see clearly.

You couldn't be "sort of Indian" in Edson. You either were or weren't. Lance and Silversong were oddities, some mutant breed. In 1959, there were no other "minorities" in Edson; the Indians were the "niggers" of Canada.

Silversong had been spiritually wounded, but no one noticed, and she could not tell anyone because of her prayer of silence. It was all she had, and she hung onto it. The Creator answered her prayer of silence by sending her Teddy.

Teddy was Lance's best friend. Whenever anyone described Teddy, they always said he had hair so blonde that in the summer it would turn pure white, that he had a great sense of humor and was very happy-go-lucky, always smiling.

Teddy was like a foster son to Anne and Terry Lawsen. Although no one knew for sure, the story was that Teddy's parents had divorced and, somewhere along the line, the Lawsens became his family. The Lawsens began a habit of "adopting" stray kids from the neighborhood, kids that had nowhere else to go because home life was too scary or uncertain. Teddy had become a favorite to Anne and Terry, and they thought of him like their own son.

Lance and Teddy had an old beat-up car that they decided to make into a convertible by hacking the roof off. They used one of Anne's brand new comforters to cover the jagged edges, and spent the whole summer with their hair blowing in the wind as the only kids in town driving a convertible.

When Silversong thought of Teddy, she felt gratitude. She wanted to thank him. No one could have been better, or whiter. He was so white his eyelashes were snowy against his sky blue eyes. She would forever see him in winter snow and blue sky.

Teddy always said that life was too long to spend it unhappily. He even told Silversong once that if she wanted to cry when he died, she had better plant onions on his grave. He never wanted to cause anyone tears.

He had told Silversong that he knew she was hurting. Often, when she was baby-sitting for a neighbor, he would come by and try to talk with her. They had crushes on each other but since he was Lance's best friend, and Anne and Terry treated him like a son, Silversong tried to think of him as a brother, and he won her trust. Had she looked at him as a white boy instead of as her foster brother, she would have felt threatened.

He used to hug her a lot and laugh because she got so stiff when he did it. He loved to tease her. Again and again, he would ask why she got so stiff. What had happened to her? He sensed something, or maybe he was the first person to hear her silent prayer.

Teddy's nickname was "Little Angel." He carved it into a leather weight-lifting belt he made. He got the nickname because he was actually a little devil in a way that made Silversong like him even more. She was very committed to her unhappiness, and he couldn't bear it, nor could he bear her silence. One day when she was baby-sitting, he came to see her.

"I love you, Silversong, and I would never hurt you. You are so beautiful and sweet, but so sad. Why? Why? Why? I want to help you. You're safe with me."

He said if she didn't talk about it, she would never be happy her whole life.

"Ted, what if I am nothing that you think I am?" she said. "Would you still love me? Or do you only love the person you know of?"

She looked closely at his face.

"The person that I know is the only person there is. That's you, Silversong, and I love you. Nothing will change your soft brown eyes and your warm satin skin, the sound of your voice or the smell of your hair, and those things make me happy."

So she told him the truth of what had happened to her.

He studied her, held her, and told her there was nothing he could say or do but cry with her, which he did.

She envisioned him in the snow and in the blue sky. The snow and Teddy knew, and they both had cried for her.

He held her tightly. They talked for a long time and he explained to her that the boys had never really touched her, that she was still the same person, and that making love was beautiful. What Silversong had experienced was an act of violence.

He talked about how when two people are in the same spirit, their souls touch. He didn't want her to spend the rest of her life afraid, making herself sick. He said that people are made to make each other happy, and that to make love when you are loved and protected is something special.

"Don't let them kill you, Silversong, try to *feel*, change it."

During that year, which seemed to last a lifetime, Teddy never betrayed Silversong. He comforted her and understood. The following fall, at the end of September, they made love. Everything was exactly right—the understanding, the trust, the safety, the love. Silversong believed they would get married.

She told Teddy how she had learned her catechism in the Catholic Church—the Act of Love, the Act of Contrition, the Act of Hope, and many more prayers. It had been a very proud moment when, at age ten, she dressed in a white lace wedding dress and was married to Jesus. She kissed the Bishop's ring. She was confirmed and she believed. She realized then that she could never be married and have children because she would then be an adulteress, betraying Jesus. It seemed to Silversong that Jesus had had enough betrayal, having been nailed to the cross. She felt pure, holy, special. No matter how difficult life was, she knew that there was a sacred place in her heart. She would be faithful and would become a nun.

"Silversong," Teddy had said, "in the first place, it's against the law for a ten-year-old to be married, and in the second place, if God is Love, what is done in love is what counts. You have to think for yourself, like Jesus did."

He was right, Silversong decided.

They had a feeling that Jesus was against the whole idea of child brides and according to what they could find in the Bible, Jesus had never said anything like, "Marry me."

Often Ted and Silversong would talk about these things. They decided that the grown-ups were pretty confused. Silversong guessed that two world wars in a row had left those on the white side as bad off as those who suffered the Indian trauma. Silversong and Teddy actually made a united decision not to let confusion prevail. They wanted the best of both worlds for each other and that's what they gave each other.

When Teddy went off to work in British Columbia, Silversong couldn't stand being in Edson anymore. Anne told people that Silversong had run away, but she hadn't. Silversong had told her mother she was leaving, and had gone with a girlfriend who said they could get great jobs in a little town in British Columbia called Cashe Creek.

They got jobs and worked hard, but were barely able to manage staying alive. Every penny went to pay for room and board. But being in Edson was still too painful for her. She needed to breathe and she couldn't breathe in Edson. There had to be a better place somewhere. She and Teddy had given themselves one year to work things out.

Ted and Silversong finally met in Kamloops, British Columbia. She got a job in the nearby town of Dawson Creek cleaning a radio station. It was Christmas time when she realized she was pregnant. She had been out of contact with Teddy, and wasn't sure where to reach him. As much as she hated the idea, she knew that she had to return to Edson. She had been advised of a girls' home there where she could stay and no one would ever know. She had been urged to put the baby up for adoption.

Although she was not married, she could not bring herself to give up her baby. She called home.

Anne was so happy to hear from her that she just said, "Nothing matters honey, come home."

When Silversong got home, Anne hid her from everyone. Anne knew how hard it was in a small town, and she wanted to protect her daughter. Anne would walk with her at night so she would get exercise and have a healthy baby. When asked about the baby's father, Silversong became so upset that Anne could see it was bad for the baby, and let it be.

Loreen Ann Lawsen was born in Hinton, Alberta, on June 2, 1962. It made Silversong happy because even the name Edson was repugnant to her. Hinton was where Teddy was from, and it made Silversong feel connected to him. She gave her daughter her stepfather's last name, and never was a baby more welcomed into a family.

It was not Teddy's intention to abdicate responsibility at that time—he was protecting Silversong's wishes, which were for him to go out and make a life for himself with the hope that they could one day share it. When he came home that summer and discovered his baby, he laughed more, smiled more, and was happier then he'd ever been. Only Silversong and Teddy knew that the baby wasn't

Teddy's, that she had actually conceived the baby during the horrible "squaw rape," but this was their own precious secret, a secret she would keep for a long, long time. No one would ever know the truth, and Silversong wanted it that way. She wanted to believe that Loreen really was Teddy's. After all, fantasy often is less painful than reality, and sometimes fantasy is safer when it becomes your own personal truth.

Silversong was baby-sitting about eight kids of various ages for a week, and Teddy came to help her. They would walk over to Anne's house, about a quarter mile away, with a trail of kids behind them, Teddy carrying Loree, the name he referred to her by and which would forever stick. He said they were practicing because they were going to have twice as many children! When they arrived at Anne's, he was unable to contain himself and raised Loree up in the air, exclaiming, "Look at my baby!"

There was a moment, a brief moment, when Teddy and Anne made eye contact, and the world stood still, in utter silence. The noise then resumed. Maybe this happened in Silversong's heart alone—moments frozen in time, memories that hang in the gallery of one's heart like paintings. These moments are masterpieces.

Teddy looked sheepishly at Silversong, and saw her love. He just kept looking at that baby of *his*. He knew she understood; he could tell. There are times in life that cannot be in bondage to reason. There was no reasoning strong enough to hold back the declaration, "Look at my baby."

Teddy had to go back to British Columbia to work, and also wanted to locate his mother. He had heard she was living in a town called Kelowna. Silversong and Teddy knew that one day things would work out, and they were in full acknowledgment that the relationship was in flux. Moving locations was only a process, like their relationship. It was what had to be done, and there were no teary good-byes. He was in her heart and she was in his. They understood these things. They were together in spirit and as close as a thought.

A few weeks after he left, Anne woke Silversong up very late one night.

"Teddy's home. I heard him out in the bunk house. He still has the cough he had when he left."

They moved to the window to see if the light was on. It was cold out and Anne didn't want him getting any sicker sleeping out in the bunk house, which was poorly heated. She roused Silversong out of bed to go with her to get him. Silversong was pretty comfortable, not anxious to get out of bed, but she finally complied.

"Yeah, you're right, Mom. He should come in, it's way too cold out there tonight."

As Silversong stood on the porch, she realized, as did Anne, that there were no footprints in the snow. They both knew that the snow had lain even for days.

"But I did, I did hear him. It was Teddy." Anne was sure of it. They thought that perhaps he had come in from the north and crawled through the window, so they circled the cabin silently. No footprints. They both felt odd.

Two days later the word came.

Teddy was traveling to Kelowna to tell his mother that he'd had a child. He caught a ride, but the car he was traveling in went over a cliff. He broke many bones and survived for about twelve hours before dying as a result of his injuries. All he said before dying was, "Please get the Lawsens," but no one knew who the Lawsens were.

Silversong was hysterical when she phoned Anne at the Legion hall and told her to come home. She said something terrible had happened. Anne pulled up in front of the house and when she got out of the car, she could hear the kids crying from inside the house. When she walked in, Ron and Patty were holding each other on the couch, like a couple of kids hanging on for dear life.

Lance was out in the bush, working in a camp. Anne wasn't

sure if it was him they were crying about, or what exactly had happened. But when she saw Silversong, she knew someone they loved had died. She couldn't understand Silversong's words until finally, in a whisper, she said, "Teddy, it's Teddy, Mom."

For a long time Anne didn't want to believe it. Please, she prayed, not our Teddy.

When Silversong first heard about Teddy's death, she didn't cry. Teddy used to say that she was too sweet, and if she ate dill pickles it would help. She just stared at the produce spread out on the table and picked up an onion. She thanked him for all he had given her and reminded herself that when someone is in your heart, there are no good-byes.

Silversong never told anyone that Teddy wasn't Loree's father. She was afraid people wouldn't understand. She thought that Lance might feel Teddy had betrayed him. She also feared the details may become distorted over the years, confusing the baby, and she wanted to protect Teddy's image; it was sacred to her. Teddy had never let Silversong down; he had given her strength and protection that she intended to return to his only child.

In love, there is a sanctuary where everything is protected, sacred, and cannot be violated. This gift of sanctuary is what Teddy gave Silversong, and bequeathed to their daughter. Sometimes life is very short, but the spirit is forever. Silversong remembered hearing that tears are the blood of the soul.

Silversong could not hate the white man after Teddy. He changed all that. She discovered there were good people no matter what their skin color; warriors not merely physically powerful, but mighty and loving. Silversong thought about this.

Many times I was not lovable. Before I told Ted everything, I used to scream at him, pound his chest when he hugged me. I even bit him once. He never changed his mind about me. I guess he thought I was worth it. When someone understands your heart, trouble is halved. Can you measure how much can be given when love is present? No, what was given to me in my two years with Teddy will affect our family through generations yet unborn.

A single act of kindness and mercy will immortalize the giver.

> *Do not stand at my grave and weep*
> *I am not there, I do not sleep*
> *I am a thousand winds that blow*
> *I am the diamond glint on snow*
> *I am the sunlight on ripened grain*
> *I am the gentle autumn rain*
>
> *When you wake in the morning, hush*
> *I am the swift uplifting rush of quiet birds in*
> *   circling flight*
> *I am the soft starlight at night*
> *Do not stand at my grave and weep*
> *I am not there, I do not sleep*

—Unknown

CHAPTER FIFTEEN

Rhinestone Indian

Her grandmother Elizabeth was the closest Silversong ever got to knowing a real queen. She was regal . . . immovable in her position, she had a type of authority that was unquestionable. Her life worked and that was all there was to it. She was always very clean—her hair done to perfection, nails immaculately manicured, always a little makeup, lipstick, and blush.

"Look bright and cheerful," she would say. It was her motto, and she believed it showed the world you cared.

When Silversong was about five years old, Elizabeth and Edwina were trying to settle some long-ago power struggle, and Silversong's hair represented the current conflict. Was it going to be pigtails or ringlets? Elizabeth won, and Silversong got the ringlets, which she really liked.

Although Elizabeth seemed very approving, everyone walked softly around her, as if she might reveal another side when you weren't paying attention. She visited Anne and Silversong annually, driving a stately black Buick—a three-holer, they called it, because it had three holes in a row running down the front bumper. Silversong was always excited to see her roll in the front gate.

When she left, her last kiss always included a whisper to Silversong alone: "If you ever need me, you let me know."

Silversong believed those were the words that Elizabeth herself had longed to hear whispered in her ear as a child.

When things got tough, those words would swoop through Silversong's head like a sparrow.

Edson, Alberta, 1963

Silversong and Loree were still living with Anne when Loree was a year and a half old—curly, light copper-colored hair and big brown eyes rimmed with dark lashes. Anne was wonderful with her and as far as anyone in town knew, Loree was one of the Lawsen kids. No one really questioned it much, as there were always so many little ones in their home. Anne and little Loree were like mother and daughter, while Silversong was still trying to come to grips with her reality and do that last little bit of growing up herself.

Silversong wanted to take Loree away. She wanted to build a life for the two of them and give her the chances in life she knew wouldn't be available to her in Edson. It hurt Silversong to know her baby wouldn't have a father, so when Loree began calling Terry "Daddy," it made her feel both happy and deeply sad.

She sure picked the right family to come into, Silversong thought as she lay in bed unable to sleep. It was nearly midnight when she heard a knock at the door. She opened it enough to see that it was the police. HMS it said on the officer's chest, Her Majesty's Service, followed by RCMP.

Without so much as making eye contact, Silversong slammed the door shut and went to get Anne. She didn't trust anyone in a uniform. It seemed to her that the RCMP always brought bad news.

"Terry, Terry, it's the RCMP!" Anne said, rousing him from sleep, "the boys are in jail."

"He said it wasn't an emergency, Mom. He's waiting outside on the steps."

She fumbled in the dimly lit room, looking for her slippers.

"Christ, woman. You mean to tell me those boys done landed themselves in the hoosecow?" Terry said, lighting up a cigarette from the bedstand.

"Hurry up, Terry, Silversong wouldn't even let them in the door."

Silversong peeked around the corner from the hallway and saw Anne open the door. The officer who spoke to her acted very supportive. He encouraged her to keep boyhood screw-ups in perspective, and suggested that the Lawsens let the boys, Lance and Jerry (another one of the Lawsen's so-called foster kids), cool off in the clink overnight.

Silversong's curiosity piqued. She continued to listen from another room, occasionally peeking around the corner. Every time she did, that damn RCMP officer would be looking right back at her. He never gave her a chance to satisfy her curiosity and see if he was on official business or only patronizing her mother.

It was a silly game of hide and peek. Silversong's anger started to rise, and the last time she peered around the corner, their eyes locked in a steadfast gaze. This time, she refused to retreat. Instead of dropping her eyes from his, she continued to hold his stare and came out from the hallway. She narrowed her large brown eyes to slits and hissed at him, "How could you?!"

She whipped her head around with such force that her long black hair struck her face like a whip. Then she was gone. Silversong wasn't sure if she was angry at the young officer for arresting her brother, or at the nonchalant smile on his face that for some odd reason both fascinated and infuriated her.

Silversong laid for hours in the dark, her eyes wide in wonder . . . Her Majesty's Service. The RCMP were uniforms, guns, and protection. She liked the idea of that last part, protection, but she still couldn't discern her mixed feelings.

She saw the officer not long after that. Their cars passed driving down Main Street and he touched his hand to the brim of his Smoky-the-Bear hat, in some sort of salute. She had to admit that he was extremely attractive.

Silversong got a job at the new Motor Hotel that had just been built in town. It was the first of its kind, changing forever the old hotel/pub proprietorships, like those seen in old Westerns. The new

Motor Hotel brought a little piece of the modern world into their backwoods town.

Silversong liked her job serving food in what was called the Flame Room. It sounded extremely exotic. It was so beautiful to her—everything was brand new and sparking. The first two hours of her shift, she worked the coffee counter.

She was breezing around, humming a tune that played softly in the background, when two customers walked in. She picked up a large pitcher of water and headed toward their table. She was horrified to see Alan Pearson and Corporal Redmond, the two officers who had been at the house when the boys were in trouble. Silversong nearly dropped the pitcher of water she was holding, and wanted to cuss. She knew she'd have to be nice to them; they were customers. Smiling broadly at her, Alan looked her square in the face once again. There were no two ways about it—he was devastatingly handsome.

Keeping her chin tucked into her neck, she raised her eyes slightly, her face burning with embarrassment. She took their order and left as quickly as possible.

"I know where you can reach me for lunch from now on," she heard Alan say to his partner as she retreated to the kitchen.

It wasn't long before Silversong learned his schedule.

Alan thought nothing of taking two days off to backpack fifteen miles into the wilderness to assist some old trapper who needed help.

"Do you get extra pay for that kind of work?" Silversong asked him.

"No, that's part of my job, the part I like best—public servant."

Most of his work centered around solving problems in the community. It was the paperwork that he didn't like. Everything required a report of some kind or another. But when he spoke of his days, he was always understanding and supportive.

Serving the people, Silversong thought . . . what a wonderful man.

He finally got around to asking her out to a drive-in movie. It was hard for her to believe, although she had hoped it would happen. She suggested the following Wednesday, her night off work.

When Wednesday rolled around, Lance and his entourage of musicians and mechanics were hanging around as usual. There was a lot of space at the Lawsen house, and no neighbors around, so they had the freedom to express themselves.

The whole gang rose to their feet when they saw Alan pull in the driveway . . . what in the hell now?

Many of them thought nothing of driving without a license, and it wasn't unusual for them to be drinking beer, even if a few of them were underage. There was an air of apprehension as Silversong put on her coat, and every eyeball in the room followed her as she headed out.

"There's a squad car out there, Silversong," Lance announced.

"Oh, I know. Alan and I have a date," she said smugly, enjoying the fact that this was cramping her brother's style.

"Great, just great! Is he going to be hanging around here from now on?"

"Well, I imagine he'll be driving me back home tonight," she said, and sashayed out the door.

As it turned out, Lance and Alan got along quite well, and Lance became very close friends with Alan's supervisor. They hung out working on cars and making music, and soon discovered they had a lot in common.

Like Silversong, Alan was raised as a Catholic, and also like her, he was short. He joined Her Majesty's Service determined to follow in his father's footsteps. So important was this to him that he actually had himself "stretched" for two years to gain the vital inch he needed in order to join the force. His sister was a nun, his brother a journalist, and his father was the commissioner of the RCMP throughout Canada, a position equivalent to the head of the FBI in the United States.

Silversong thought Alan was great. She saw no games or subtle messages that left her wondering. He was straightforward, and she admired his values and beliefs. They went everywhere together, including to all of his RCMP functions within the "police world." He thought it best not to socialize with the public because there was too much of a chance for favoritism. Officers were reassigned every four years to ensure that the public had unbiased public servants. Silversong was impressed with his sacrifice for what the RCMP believed in: justice for all.

She used to help him out and sometimes, if he had to leave the station, he'd ask her to listen to the police-band radio.

"When I call '10-17,' that means I love you."

Silversong was so pleased. She never heard "I love you" again; it was always "10-17."

Alan wanted marriage and loved children. He asked Silversong to go to a wedding with him in another province five hundred miles away. A good buddy of his from the RCMP boot camp and an old family friend were getting married. It was the first time she would meet his family and their friends. She was more confident about their partnership than ever.

She had to beg Anne to let her go, because it was for an entire weekend and it was so far away. There was never a question about whether they would be chaperoned. The issue of sex before marriage was still a taboo concept.

The drive through the mountains that weekend was incredible. They cruised along in Alan's small sports car. They talked, laughed, stopped to play in the snow, exchanged sweet kisses on cold cheeks. They bundled up in heavy sweaters so they could keep the top down on the convertible. They were *extra* close, Alan seemed *extra* kind—the hugs stronger, the looks longer. But then Silversong sensed a shift in him: a mixture of sadness, anger, and fear that seemed so unlike him. And with each mile they drove, he became more and more sharp-edged and distant.

Arriving in the town where the wedding was to be held the following day, Alan dropped her off at the home where she was to stay.

Alan said his friend who was about to be married had a message for him from Alan's father. Silversong knew Alan and his father had exchanged strong words the previous week, but she didn't know what the disagreement was about. Alan seemed very upset but reassured her, and himself, that his father really did love him and that they would work it out—that his father would change his mind.

Silversong didn't press him for details; it was too important. She figured he would tell her in his own time. She had complete confidence in Alan, and knew she could trust him with anything.

Later that night Alan called the house.

"Is everything okay?" Silversong asked.

"Yes . . . yes." But she could tell by the tone of his voice that he was upset.

"Am I going to see you tonight?" Silversong was hoping they could go have coffee, even half an hour together would be reassuring.

"No, I'm dealing with way too much right now."

"The message from your father . . . was it good news?"

"No," Alan replied flatly.

There she was, far from home, surrounded by strangers. She needed reassurance.

"What could possibly be so horrible? No one died, did they?" It was time he told Silversong what this was all about, and so he began.

"I'm the only son, the only one who can follow in my father's footsteps. He has big plans for me . . . he thinks I'm letting him down."

"How? Where?" She got angry. "There has never, ever, ever been a better officer than you, Alan—"

"It's more than that. . . ." His voice cracked and he sounded defeated.

"You know that my father's the most powerful man as far as my career is concerned, and you know how important the police force has been to me . . . . Well—"

There was a long pause. Alan took a deep breath.

"My father says I'll go nowhere in the force if I choose . . . if I choose to ignore his advice—"

"My God, Alan, can't you compromise? Can't you work this out?"

Silversong felt the weight of his emotions lying heavily upon her heart.

"He says if I choose to marry a native, there's no way an Indian can rub shoulders in our society—"

"Society?! Society?!"

"I'll see you in the morning." Click.

The shock of his words hit Silversong physically. She felt like she'd been slapped, and then a numbness set in.

The moon was full that night. She let it shine down on her through the open window as she lay in bed, still numb, speechless from the pain. She was told never to go to sleep with the full moon shining upon her, because it would curse her. As she laid there examining the dark corners of her mind, she remembered a story that her mother had told her years ago. It was the story of the Moon Bird.

At this moment, she decided to beseech the Moon Bird for protection and intuitive guidance. Although she did not know what the future would hold, she sensed that the Moon Bird could somehow guide her. She felt that the blood that was pumping through her veins was rich with mysteries and ancient knowledge that were just beginning to reveal themselves.

I'm already cursed, she thought, as she closed her eyes. Maybe the Moon Bird can remove a curse, too.

Alan came the next morning, his breath thick and smelling of strong liquor. The veil had fallen between them.

"You can't be seen with me today. It's too complicated. Just mill about, do your own thing. I've arranged for your host to entertain you today. We'll leave in the morning."

All day long, Silversong looked across the hall at Alan as the events took place around them. She did her best to become invisible. Alan was the ideal comrade at the full-dress officer's wedding. The bride and groom dashed beneath drawn swords. It was a perfect wedding, right down to the last grain of rice and champagne toast.

Her heart was as fragile as the crystal goblets held by the guests and it fell to the floor and shattered into a million unsalvageable pieces. The shards made her eyes water. No, she thought, please don't let me cry in front of these people, please.

There was no place to go, no place to hide, nowhere she could cry with her shame, humiliation, and pain. She couldn't change her skin, couldn't change the blood that flowed in her veins. She hated herself, and headed back to her room, the proverbial back of the bus.

Alan picked her up the next morning. She was silent, well beyond tears. They drove and drove and drove. She knew he felt bad, compensating by shifting hard, turning quickly, and accelerating on every straightaway. Finally talking to the silent ghost that was left of her, Alan verbally filed the report he received from his father as he slugged liquor from an elegant silver flask in a deep brown leather case that Silversong had never seen before. He repeated to Silversong the same words his father had told him when he said he wanted to marry Silversong.

"Report A: There's no way an Indian can rub shoulders with . . ."
He left it at that.

"Report B: Here's the six-page dossier, a background check on your family done by my father.

"Report C: There is no recourse."

She was too hurt to speak. Her thoughts confirmed the truth—if she were to be with Alan, he would lose everything—everything he had worked for, everything he knew, everything he wanted.

She had once felt safe and protected in his world. Their relationship had given her back her dignity. He loved children and her child was not a problem. He had accepted her, her child, and all the circumstances of her life.

Not any longer.

"I'll take you away, far away and we can still build a life together."

He was grasping at straws.

Silversong told her mother what Alan had said. Anne didn't
like it.

"You can't run away. I'm sorry, Silversong, but this will always
be between you, no matter how far you go."

She knew what Anne said was the truth, and she was filled
with disappointment, heartache, and fear.

"If you ever need me . . . ." Elizabeth's words swooped down on
her and she knew it was her only way out.

Elizabeth sent her a train ticket the following Tuesday. Silversong was on her way to the United States.

1964

It was a long, fearful journey. She was running away from Canada
and leaving everything she knew and loved—her baby, her family,
her love—desperately looking for a place without a history. Confused and hurting, Silversong may not have known what she wanted,
but she knew what she *didn't* want in her life.

It was cold the day she left; the snow was dry and deep. It seemed
as if all the world spoke to her as the train moved across the land.
As she reclined in her seat and stared through the frosty windows,
she saw not only the scenery go by, but the moments of her past
that had led to this point in her life.

In a half-sleep, the images moving along the window took on
a movie-like quality. The trees resembled millions of buffalo; the
sound of the train rumbled like a stampede. She sat up and was
startled to see her own reflection added to the picture. The frosted
window began to weep as the heat in the coach came on.

As the train slowed, the wheels moaned against the cold steel
and hard snow, crying out like a woman wailing. Silversong knew

that once again the snow was crying for her, because she could not. She listened, her anguish unleashed, creating an escape for her thoughts, which were full of a pain she was unable to express. She was twenty years old and going to the United States of America. It might as well have been the moon, as little as she knew about the world she was about to enter.

Arriving in Seattle, Silversong felt odd not to be surrounded by snow. It seemed like springtime, and made it easier for her to consider the possibilities that lay ahead.

Grandma Elizabeth and Grandpa Joe met her at the train depot near Pioneer Square. Everywhere she looked there were people and traffic; everything except the huge, cliff-like buildings seemed to be in motion, and it made her dizzy.

Most of her life, Silversong had been surrounded by the familiar. Through her artist's eye, the unfamiliar territory took on a surreal quality, like a carnival that had come to town. Nature, it seemed, was only an accent here and there.

They left the train depot and boarded a large ferry. It was like entering the belly of a whale. The ferry ride to Bremerton, where her grandparents lived, took an hour and a half.

Her grandparents had been in the restaurant business for many years and consequently knew a lot of people, and proudly showed her off to them. Silversong felt special, yet there was so much she kept inside, silent.

Elizabeth said that she and Grandpa Joe were buying a new restaurant across from the navy shipyard. She wanted Silversong to pretend that it belonged to her. Her grandpa felt she could learn more about life in a restaurant than she would learn in college.

Silversong threw herself into a new life. Her favorite comic strip was "Little Dot," so she decided she would be like her. She named the restaurant "The Red Dot" and by the time she finished decorating, there wasn't a table cloth, curtain, or uniform that wasn't white with little red dots covering it. The atmosphere was charming, people really got a chuckle out of it, and Elizabeth and Joe were as happy as she was.

There were two cooks, a dishwasher, and six waitresses working at The Red Dot. Elizabeth was the hostess and Silversong worked as a waitress. She worked every day except Sunday (which was church day, according to Elizabeth). She looked forward to seeing the regular customers. It was a simple, uncomplicated life and she liked the fact that she seemed to make people happy. Life inside The Red Dot was good.

Sometimes she would overhear the customers talk about black people struggling for equality and civil rights, and she couldn't help but think about her own people, how she had seen them struggle—yet she never mentioned this. She had come to the States to discover another reality. Nobody seemed to notice Indians much; it wasn't a part of their consciousness, so it was easy to remain silent.

As the months went by, Silversong cried alone at night. She was homesick and heartbroken. Every time she called home, it seemed to make her feel worse. Loree would be sick, or something else would be wrong. She knew her family loved her, and that knowledge was her only comfort. She hung on to the thought that some day things would work out, that she would have her daughter back, and they would have a different life with new opportunities. She was a Lawsen, and she knew that she was strong. Her mother had always said that Lawsen women had backbone. She would remind herself of this as she strapped on her red-dotted apron, and put a pretty smile on her face.

Bremerton, Washington

The following summer, the restaurant was hired to cater a banquet for a group of celebrities who were in town for a rodeo. It was expected to be quite an event. Joe Redmond knew the governor of Washington, which was probably why they got the job.

Rex Allen, a famous movie cowboy, was the featured entertainer.

Joe joked with Silversong, "You are so beautiful, I'm sure you're going to get 'discovered'."

She knew he was teasing, but she had to admit she was excited about the evening.

The banquet was held at a sprawling ranch just outside of Bremerton. Silversong was supposed to pass hors d'oeuvres around and was happy to find the atmosphere so relaxed and pleasant. The crowd gathered in small groups here and there, and she tempted them with her Silversong tray of delights.

About two hours after the banquet had begun, a middle-aged gentleman who was rather portly asked her what her name was, and also asked what kind of Indian she was. She was a little embarrassed to think that she stood out from the crowd. She had tried to forget the fact that nobody else looked like her, with long black hair and brown skin. She started to excuse herself, but when she turned to look at Grandpa Joe, who was close by, she saw he had a big grin on his face.

"He's looking for an Indian princess, just like you. Are you interested?"

She figured Joe was kidding, so she flipped her hair and head around saucily and said, "Sounds great to me."

"Are you afraid of crowds?" the man asked.

"Oh, heavens no," she said without hesitation.

"I mean, thousands of people?"

"I love crowds, and people, thousands and thousands of people. The more the merrier."

Silversong shot a grin in Joe's direction. She was really enjoying this now.

"As a matter of fact, I'm going to be famous someday anyway. It'll be good practice."

The man laughed along with her.

"Looks like we won't have to worry about you being shy. You've got some kind of energy, young lady. Most of the native people I've worked with have been quite shy and subdued."

"Nope, not me. Certainly not me."

"You are simply delightful," the man said, as he motioned his valet for a phone. Joe approached her.

"I see you're doing just great. Quite the little conversationalist."

"The joke's on you, Grandpa. Getting one of your buddies to pull my leg. I caught you this time."

Hanging up the phone, the man returned.

"I'll need to talk to your family," he said.

As if you don't know Grandpa, Silversong thought.

"Well, this is my grandfather."

By this time, Elizabeth had joined them and the man introduced himself.

"Hi, I'm Wilson Self, Rex Allen's manager. We're looking for an Indian princess for the show. Rex wants to meet her. If it's okay with you, I'll run her over. It should only take about a half an hour, and I'll be happy to explain all the details when I get back."

Silversong was stunned. This was not a joke.

"Excuse me for a moment," she said in a wee little voice, "I'll be right back."

"Well, I'm not sure," she heard Elizabeth say as she left. "She's not American, you know. She's Canadian."

The next thing she knew, she was standing in front of a mirror with her hands to her face.

"Now, you've really done it!" Silversong scolded herself as she splashed cool water on her face. *Somebody* does these sorts of things, she told herself, why not her? I know what I'll do . . . I'll just act "as if" like I learned as a Catholic—the Acts—faith is living prayers in action. She emerged from the bathroom, determined to follow through.

A limousine was waiting to take her to meet Rex Allen. It was the first time Silversong had ever seen a man putting on makeup. He was so beautiful that she couldn't imagine he needed it, but that was show biz, she figured. His outfit was shimmering beneath the dressing room lights, a cream-colored, sequined, studded, fringed suit and two-thousand-dollar Nudie boots.

There she stood, all five feet of her, nothing but a foot of jet black hair as her only glory. They talked, and although she was nervous, the conversation went well. Before she knew it, she was being fitted for a white rhinestone-fringed dress and headband, complete with feather.

"Hold your hands up like this as I sing 'Son, don't go near the Indians,'" Rex instructed. "I'll be riding my wonder horse Cocoa and I'll swoop you up and you can sit behind me as we ride around the arena. When we're finished, we'll go sign autographs and do our publicity shots."

"Uh ... okay," was all she managed to say before being whisked back to the banquet.

When Silversong returned, she found she had become the talk of the party. It was like Cinderella at the ball, they said. Wilson Self said it would be a sensation. He wanted her to be a surprise addition to the evening's show.

"The only girl in the show. And a real Indian at that."

Silversong felt it was all so strange, these two worlds she lived in. She couldn't understand why the fact that she was Indian was suddenly revered. It was a brief but poignant encounter with the great paradox. She'd suddenly become so special; it was less than a year ago that she had been despised for the same reason. Being Indian had prevented a marriage to the man she loved. Now, suddenly she was a rhinestone Indian that everyone loved. It was hard to know which reality to believe in. She was neither a "bad" Indian nor a rhinestone Indian, but somewhere in between.

She never spoke to anyone about these feelings because she instinctively knew that no one could tell her what was really going on.

Grandma Elizabeth thought that Silversong's participation in the rodeo was "unreal"—a bad idea, and flatly told her so: "I'm your guardian and I will not allow this to be anything more than a brief experience."

Silversong thought long and hard about what Elizabeth said about "reality." In Silversong's mind she was surrounded by fantasy—*Gilligan's Island, My Three Sons, Laugh-In*. What did they have to do with reality? she wondered. Thousands of young men were dying in Vietnam, and the Indian people were fighting for the right to worship in a traditional manner. The only things she knew were real at the time were her child and herself. But there was no recourse, Elizabeth had put her foot down, and that was that. When the rodeo ended that night, her "career" was over.

CHAPTER SIXTEEN

The American Dream

*I*t was 1965. A year had passed since Silversong had come to live in the United States, still wanting to let go of the fantasy she had about Alan. Silversong tried hard to stop the looping around and around, the thoughts and feelings that plagued her mind. She had to look to truth in a ceremonial way. She had to feel the loss, accept it, and say good-bye.

She carved his name in a beautiful shell and dropped it from the Bremerton ferry into the deep dark waters of the Puget Sound.

Silversong saved up all her tips and bought Loree a chantilly lace Easter dress with matching bonnet, and sent Anne money to help with Loree's expenses.

One of the waitresses she worked with at The Red Dot asked if she would go on a double date with her. Silversong hadn't been out for quite some time.

"They're real nice fellas, both in the navy," her friend said.

She knew that Amy had been dating a sailor for some time and she was curious.

"Listen Amy, I'll go with you but you know how my grandmother feels about sailors, so you best not mention that they're in the navy. I'll just tell her that we're going to a movie and as long as I'm home early, why worry her?"

The following Saturday night, Amy and Silversong left to meet Amy's boyfriend, Randy, and his shipmate, Jason Lowe. Jason was from South Carolina and spoke with a southern accent. He had already been drinking, and Silversong was rather put off by his actions.

They all talked a little, and after a short time Silversong was back home in her bed, sound asleep. She woke up when the phone rang the following morning. Amy was crying. Apparently, after dropping her off the previous evening, Randy noticed Amy had left her purse in his car and foolishly grabbed the steering wheel from Jason in an attempt to turn the car around. They careened off the highway, down a steep bank, and landed in someone's backyard.

Speaking almost unintelligibly, Amy asked Silversong between tears if she would drive her to the navy hospital to visit Randy. Silversong needed to pick up a special meat order for the restaurant, so Joe and Elizabeth thought it would be fine if she took Amy for her visit. They knew Randy had no family in the area; perhaps that's why they allowed her to go.

She'd never been on a military base before and it felt like they were entering another world entirely as they drove through the gate.

Amy spent hours giggling, talking, and reading to Randy behind a closed curtain. Silversong just sat waiting, feeling uncomfortable and stupid. Some of the navy patients were flirting with her, with low whistles and teasing, and it made her squirm and become stiff, not knowing where to turn her attention. Then she saw Jason Lowe in a nearby room. He seemed happy to see a familiar face and was very sweet.

"Would you like to read to me? You can sit over here as if you're visiting me, if you like," Jason ventured.

He smiled and Silversong smiled back. He's far away from his home and family just like me, she thought. He was probably just blowing off steam the other night. He seems kind and sensitive now, a total gentleman.

He reassured her with pats on the hand, and made steady eye contact as they talked. Both his legs had been broken, the left one in twenty-two places, eleven inches of bone completely shattered. The doctor had inserted a steel rod to reinforce the fractured area and he was expected to be in the hospital, flat on his back, for at least a year. Silversong thought he was handling it very well.

She began visiting Jason every time she took Amy to see Randy. For the entire length of their courtship, Jason was in a full body cast. After a year had passed, he asked her to marry him.

The thought of marriage scared her, but she felt that she had to do *something*. Loree was already three years old. She felt she didn't have much time left if she wanted to be the kind of mother she wished to be. She decided it was a chance worth taking. She was hoping it would solve at least some of her problems.

Jason was released from the hospital a month before Christmas. Silversong went back to Canada and told her family that she was going to be married on New Year's Day. They were shocked, but her mind was made up.

Jason arrived and they were married. But the moment the ceremony was over, he began to drink, and a deep, familiar fear rose up within her. Jason hadn't drank so much as a glass of wine in over a year, but by the time they arrived at the hotel room, he was smashed, and Silversong couldn't for the life of her bring herself to get undressed.

Looking for an excuse to leave, she said, "I forgot something at my Mom's," and then caught a cab home.

No one was there when she arrived. She just sat in her room and cried. A half an hour later, Anne and Terry came home.

"What in the hell are you doing here?" her stepfather asked.

"I ... I ... I needed to get something. ... Can I stay here tonight?"

They looked at each other.

"We didn't want you to get married, Silversong—you insisted. You're now a married woman ... a *married woman*." The look on Anne's face was one of bewilderment mixed with painful familiarity, a far-away reminder of life with Chaz.

Then Anne tried to reassure her.

"You just relax, it'll be okay. You've had a rough day. Just get your things and Dad will drive you back."

Silversong had the feeling that Anne wanted to hug and slap her at the same time.

Terry drove her back to the hotel in silence. When she got out of the car, she looked back and he locked the door while looking her straight in the eye. The finality of her situation sunk in fully.

As he drove off, she went to the hotel room and knocked on the door. When there was no reply, she tried the door but was unable to open it. She knocked and knocked, but there was still no reply.

Finally, she got angry and began to kick the door, yelling. When people started looking out their windows, she felt totally humiliated. How bizarre it must have been to see a bride kicking a door down on her wedding night.

Thankfully, the door popped open. Evidently, ice had caused it to freeze shut and all her kicking had knocked the ice loose. She found Jason passed out cold, dead drunk on the bed wearing nothing but boxer shorts and a full metal leg brace that ran from waist to foot.

1966

Jason, Silversong, and Loree boarded a train headed for the States. This time, Silversong was not alone. She had her daughter and her new husband with her. She still felt much of the same fear that she felt the first time she left, plus a new sense of guilt and responsibility. Somewhere deep inside, she felt as if she were doing the right thing; it was the only solution she could imagine.

Saying good-bye to her little Loree was one of the hardest moments of Anne's life. She was so innocent, with big brown eyes and a presence that filled the emptiness in their home. It was easy to love her, and even easier to believe she was "their" baby. Anne knew that Silversong was hurting and confused in ways that were beyond her help. She had made her a promise and would have to keep it. Anne and Terry had told her that when she had a home of her own, they would give Loree back to her. After three years, the time had come.

It wasn't Silversong's fault, but neither Anne nor Terry could deny the pain of separation. The younger kids, Patty and Ron, screamed at Anne, making things worse.

"How can you let them just take Loree away?"

It seemed as though there had been a death in the family. Patty cried her eyes out, Ron just stopped speaking, and Terry began drinking heavily.

So there was Anne, aching to hold Loree, worrying whether she would be safe. To Anne and Terry, the U.S. might as well have been South America. Silversong was her daughter, but she could not help but think of Loree as her own, and for the life of her, she couldn't understand what Silversong was searching for. . . or running from.

Silversong, Jason, and Loree settled in California, and Silversong immediately sent word to Anne that Jason had been hired by a private company, after being discharged from the navy. Knowing that Loree would be even farther away left Anne feeling helpless. And Terry's drinking was out of control—at his worst, he would aim his verbal attacks at her.

"It's *your* fault that Loree's gone. You wanted your freedom. You didn't want her."

It was ugly and there was nothing Anne could do to prevent it.

Ron's drinking had also escalated. He started talking about going to the States to see how Loree was doing. As it turned out, however, it was Patty who first made the trip to California. Loree was like a little sister to her. She was only thirteen years old, but managed to convince Anne to let her go. It was unheard of, in those days, for someone that young to be traveling to the States.

When she returned from California, the news wasn't good.

"We need to bring Loree home, Mom. I don't feel good about her being there. I don't know what it is, but I just don't feel good about it."

Patty didn't feel comfortable with Jason. The fact was, none of the family really knew him, including Silversong. There was nothing Anne could do but pray.

Anne hadn't been feeling well, but the doctor in town told her not to worry about the bleeding that she began to have. Her relationship with Terry was deteriorating, right along with her health. Ron and Patty were now both in their teens. When she felt that the situation had become unbearable, she left to find work in Edmonton.

She was hired at the McDaniel Hotel as a waitress, and soon began working in their banquet rooms. The health problems she was experiencing worsened, however, and although she wasn't yet eligible for medical benefits, she decided to see a specialist.

It was then that Anne discovered she had advanced cancer of the cervix.

Silversong was stunned when Lance phoned and told her that Anne had almost lost her life. As soon as she heard the word "cancer," she imagined the worst, but Lance quickly informed her that she had had an operation and subsequent treatments, and was already recovering.

Silversong was furious that she hadn't been told sooner. She couldn't understand why the family had kept this from her. Anne insisted she would have told her had the situation been worse than it was, but it frightened Silversong to think that Anne might have died alone, not wanting to be a burden to her daughter.

They were all loners in a sense. There were many things that had begun to unfold in Silversong's own life which she'd chosen not to mention to the family. She knew they were struggling financially and emotionally, just like she was.

California was so far removed from anything that she'd ever known. It was as if a great shadow had cast itself over her life. It crept in silently, insidiously, and she felt it begin to steal her inner light.

Loree was her daughter, yet she always felt fear surrounding her. Was she a good mother? Did she do the right thing? She knew she had reasons for her actions, but . . . .

Listening to the Supremes sing "Love Child," on the radio one afternoon, she began to cry.

"What's wrong, Mommy?" Loree asked.

"It's just that this song reminds me of you, honey, and it makes me so happy that I cry."

"Does this song make my other mother cry too?"

She was missing her grandmother.

Cucamunga, California, 1967

Anne hadn't seen Loree for well over a year. It had been difficult, but she knew that for herself and Loree, and Silversong too, they needed the time apart to adjust.

Patty and Anne sent parcels to Loree for her birthday and Christmas, and many cards and letters. Anne sent her a beautiful Mackintosh plaid kilt and matching cap, and a doll's outfit made from the same fabric. She wanted to send a little of Canada down to California.

Anne had always tried to keep her own family life separate from the life she had lived with her aunt Edwina and "mother" Elizabeth. She had known for many years that Elizabeth was not her natural mother, but they kept in contact and occasionally saw each other when she was in Canada. Anne loved her, and understood why Elizabeth hadn't been in her life as much as she would have expected a birth mother to be. Anne chose to honor her contribution to her life, and continued to call her Mother.

When Elizabeth heard of Anne's illness and Silversong's move to California, she decided to surprise Anne with the gift of a wonderful trip. Elizabeth always loved surprises, so she insisted that no one tell Loree that she and Anne were coming to visit. Somewhere inside, Anne knew that Loree should be prepared to see her, but she dwelled instead on the fact that she would soon see her girls.

When they arrived at Silversong's house, Elizabeth decided to go into the house first and tell Loree she had brought her a surprise. As Anne stood behind the door, she could hear Loree squeal with delight. When the door flew open, Loree became suddenly silent and her eyes grew large. Elizabeth asked her if she recognized Anne.

"You brought my real mommy."

Anne tried to stay calm as she got down on her knees and Loree wrapped her arms tightly around her neck.

"You are my really, really mommy, aren't you?"

Anne took a deep breath, trying to gather herself as she wiped the tears from her face. She looked at Silversong and gently released herself from Loree's hug. She held her out, looked in those big, brown eyes, and smiled.

"No, honey, but I am your really, really grandma."

When it came time for Anne to leave, Loree had it in her mind that she was going home with her. She found Loree hiding inside her big, old suitcase and gently coached her out, trying to act as if she had made a joke. Anne pretended to laugh, and could see that Loree knew it meant something was wrong.

Perhaps because of Anne's own confusion as a child growing up, she was concerned about how confusing Loree's life had become. She told her granddaughter that Ron was planning on coming down to stay with her, and that knowledge made her very happy.

"Will he be here tomorrow?"

"No, but see this—" Anne wiggled Loree's loose front tooth. "When that tooth falls out, it will almost be time for Ron to be here."

She seemed satisfied with that. When Anne turned to look at her a last time, she was waving with one hand and wiggling her tooth with the other.

Jason thought that Silversong gave Loree too much attention. He seemed to resent the child. If she cried, he'd tell Silversong to ignore her. If she didn't eat her food or if she threw it on the floor, he wanted her plate put on the floor from then on. Anne was concerned that Jason had not stopped drinking since their wedding day. There were many heated arguments when Silversong wouldn't comply with his authoritarian commands. He was beginning to beat her. She was beginning to see what little value women represented in Jason's world, and she was used to that. She'd rarely been treated as if she had value.

The first time Jason hurt my mom I was four years old. I woke up in the morning and went into the bedroom to see her. She was in a funny position, and looked odd as I came near, still dressed in the clothes she had worn the day before. I saw her face first, then the blood. Although the wound was still wide open, the blood had congealed above her left eye, but not before it had made its way across her cheek and run down onto the pillow her head was resting on.

Was she dead? Maybe a burglar had broken into the house last night and done this to her? I noticed more blood on the sheets and bedding, a red trail that traced the movements she had made through the night. Shaking her softly, I gently spoke into her ear. She looked shaken and she whispered to me, telling me to talk quietly.

Jason had thrown her into the coffee table and she had hit the corner of it and slashed her eyelid. I knew Jason was dangerous and we must be careful around him. Mom and I continued to talk quietly. She said she would figure out some way for us to leave safely.

We tried the best we could to go about the business of living while her wounds healed.

Jason cried and begged her to forgive him. He promised not to break the promises he had already broken, and broken again . . . the cycle repeated itself, always ending the same way—violently.

For a few weeks at a time, or sometimes for months, he would be nice. In fact, he would be so nice he made it easy to forget what had happened. Everyone was anxious to forget anyway.

CHAPTER SEVENTEEN
Baby Blue

1968

Silversong had been in mild labor throughout the day, if there is such thing as mild labor. During the evening, her contractions became stronger and there was little time between the pains when she asked Jason to drive her to the hospital. It was 11:45 P.M. when they arrived in front of the emergency room. When Silversong tried to get out of the car, Jason began protesting.

"If you only wait fifteen more minutes, I won't be charged for an extra day of parking!"

Silversong was furious; she could barely control her body between the contractions as she walked through the emergency room doors at 11:55. Her water burst all over the floor. She was hurt, humiliated, and angry. She screamed at the hospital staff to get Jason out of the labor room. Jason tried to peek into the room and Silversong screamed again.

"Get him out of here! He's the one who got me into this in the first place. Out!" A few hours later, Jason Jonathan Lowe was born.

They laughed about it afterward, but Silversong never laughed very loud. She thought that perhaps if she *tried* a little harder in their marriage, Jason would understand, and would love her more for her efforts.

In the meantime, she found solace in her paintings. She began taking night courses at nearby Chaffe College. Her classes never interfered with preparing dinner or getting the ironing done, but

Jason didn't like the fact that Silversong's talent was the one thing he could not threaten to take away or control; it was all hers. He squinted his hazel eyes and his face became a strained instrument as he spoke.

"Just what in the hell are you trying to prove, Silversong? You've got everything a woman could possibly want! *Me*, baby. Somebody to pay your bills."

He laughed, but nothing was funny.

Silversong painted when Jason was at work, and tried to keep believing in herself, but it was getting harder and harder to protect herself physically and even more so mentally.

"Go play with your paintbrushes if you want, but remember you're only really good at one thing baby, and you can't do that standing up, can you now?"

Jason seemed to enjoy this game and often he would continue on and on.

"You're lucky I even put up with you—nobody else would want you now. A woman with two children who's going on thirty years old. You don't have any choices left. You just better hang on to me real tight.

"You want to use your Indian name? I'll give you an Indian name—Chief Spread Eagle. Now that's you, Silversong."

He was punishing her. "I'm God, I'm white, I'm a man; you're nothing but a squaw."

Once again there was no one to protect her and nowhere to go; she was too ashamed.

Silversong looked desperately for something to hold on to and believe in. Instead, she found *their* faces—she was a squaw, and it was that tragic Saturday night all over again.

She would just try to survive.

Shortly after J.J. came home from the hospital, Silversong and Loree began planning his future. They had great things in store for him. First off, they joked that since he was so much work as a baby and so demanding of them, he would repay them by becoming their slave once he was bigger. That one never did pan out.

They should have known he wasn't planning on cooperating with their plans right from the start when they both went to his cribside and began to serenade him. He let them know directly he wished they would shut up. At first, they didn't want to believe that this baby didn't like their singing, and they were feeling more than a little crushed at the thought, so they decided to test a theory out. Surely a little newborn had no way of discerning his preferences at such an early age, they thought, and once again began to serenade the little duffer. It was only a matter of moments before the truth became obvious. Every time they began to sing, he began to scream, and when they stopped, so did he.

By the time J.J. came along, the family was living in a little three-bedroom, ranch-style house in Cucamunga, California. They had moved there a few months after Jason received his discharge from the navy.

In front of the house, there was a decorative brick wall that sheltered the entrance way. The wall was attached to the house by several large wooden beams, and a banana tree grew below them. There was a circular driveway lined by large olive trees that shed an abundance of fruit on the pavement in the summer. Loree would forever remember the smallest details of the house—the greasy, little round spots left behind after the olives had been baking in the hot sun, along with bits and pieces of crayons she strategically placed, hoping they would melt into an abstract rainbow.

The front yard was almost totally covered in a lush bed of dark green ivy. Loree loved the way it tickled her ankles when she ran through it, especially in bare feet. Silversong would scream at her.

"Get out of there! Right this minute," she'd say. "You're lucky a black widow didn't get you. You should go out in the backyard in the playhouse where it's nice and cool in the shade."

Her favorite part of the house was the living room, and everyone who came by to visit seemed to agree with her. The entire back wall was glass with glass French doors that led out into the back-yard where her playhouse and tree swing were. She spent a lot of time out there, spinning in circles, staring at the sky.

It was an incredibly hot, dry time of year. The landscape seemed to change with the winds. It was like magic, after weeks of heavy smog and smog alerts, the wind would come and carry it all away.

Silversong had heard from the family in Jasper that Ron was in trouble. He wasn't coping and the drinking was getting worse. She hoped that if he could somehow get away, perhaps breathe a little and sober up, he'd be okay.

Even though Ron had a great sense of humor and could be quite a socializer, there was a part of him that was inaccessible. He rarely spoke about his feelings, yet he felt deeply. Ron became a father for the first time when he was seventeen and fell deeply in love with a young girl named Candice. By the time he was nineteen they had two children. Ron arrived in California, twenty years old and heart-broken over his recent breakup with Candice.

Jasper, Alberta, was mainly a tourist town and, at one point, the entire family, except for Terry, worked for one resort or another in town. For awhile, Anne worked for two resorts at the same time, trying to make ends meet.

On top of Ron's problems, Terry was beginning to lose the battle with alcohol himself. Anne had her hands full. It seemed that when it came to the men in her life, she always seemed to choose those who tore down her spirit in an intangible way. She could some-how never put her finger on it. It wasn't easy, but working as hard as she did, she managed to tolerate the unmanageability of life around her.

Terry would go on binge after binge with the grocery money and "the boys," and would come home ornery and hungover. He seemed to unleash an awful, unsubstantiated revenge on Anne. It reminded her of the saying, Things change, yet they stay the same.

Ron was giving birth to his dark side. It started out gradually at first, like most things, but finally went out of control as the years passed. By the time Ron was fourteen years old, he had become Terry's "drinking buddy."

Anne was furious the first time she found them drinking, but quickly learned she would have no say in the matter. Now she had two of them to fight with.

"Oh, for God's sake woman, it's only one little beer," Terry would say. Unfortunately, he never noticed how much of his life was focused on that "one little beer."

"Stop at the store, gotta get some beer."

"After work, we're going to go and get a beer."

"It's the weekend, let's get some beer."

"I'll do it right after this beer."

"I'll be there, just let me finish this beer."

There was only one variation to the scenario, and that was when the family was on a road trip. Then it went something like, "Stop at the next restroom—and by the way, we need to pick up some beer."

Ron was shocked when he woke up at Silversong's house and saw the mountains revealed in the distance, mountains that were not visible the day before.

Those were good days, when you woke up in the morning to see the mountains and breathed fresh air.

"Boy, they'd never believe this back in Jasper," Ron would say.

It must have been hard for Ron, feeling so inadequate while surrounded by such magnificence. It was the first time in his life he had ever been in the States, or even so far from home and the rest of the family.

Edson, Hinton, and Jasper were very close together, yet the little towns considered themselves very independent from one another. There was a strong sense of honor in which town one chose to call home. Although they had moved from Edson to Jasper after Loree permanently moved to the States to be with Silversong, the Lawsens—Anne, Terry, Ron, Lance, and Patty—still felt an alliance with Edson. It didn't matter that the family actually lived in Jasper now.

Edson was home . . . except for in the mind of the constant exception—Silversong.

She left nothing of herself in Edson except that which was taken from her. Silversong knew all too well how devastating a small town could be, how hard it could be for people to see beyond their own private little "Peyton Places," how hard it could be to feel alive in a place like that.

Once you were able to look beyond the neon signs and bar fronts in Jasper, it was truly spectacular, with the beautiful Rocky Mountains as a backdrop and some of the cleanest air and freshest water in the world.

Ron slept in the living room on a couch that pulled out into a bed. He worked at a gas station in the evening. He seemed to enjoy his stay with Silversong, even though his thoughts were not always happy ones. Silversong used to fix him special dinners and take them down to the station and surprise him. She did this so often that it was no longer a surprise, but he always acted as if it was.

Ron and Jason didn't get along very well, but they managed for the most part to avoid one another. Sometimes Loree would hear Jason talking to Silversong about Ron, and didn't like what she heard. She just kept hoping Ron would stay for a long time, at least until she grew up and could go back to Canada with him.

When Ron moved in with Silversong the beatings stopped for a time, simply because there was another man in the house, and Ron was bigger than Jason. Ron was always Loree's special hero—Uncle Ron, a tall, dark, handsome Indian who wasn't afraid of Jason.

Silversong loved Ron, and Loree simply adored him. Years later Loree remembered that, with his first paycheck, he bought her a yellow "slip-n-slide" lawn toy that she wanted so badly.

The only thing Loree and Ron disagreed about was Loree's cat, Charlie Browne. Ron didn't like Charlie and Charlie didn't like Ron. It didn't matter where Ron would attempt to hide his shoes, Charlie would search them out, find them, and promptly pee in them. The only thing that saved Charlie's life was the fact that he belonged to

Loree, and that he had a little talent. She had trained the cat to do several dog tricks. Although the whole family agreed this was impressive, Loree never could get him to stop peeing in Ron's shoes. Unlike Jason, Charlie Browne was not the least bit intimidated by Ron's stature.

Over time, Ron formed a band and named it Blue Moon. Sometimes the guys who were in Ron's band came over and practiced in the garage. They were pretty good, but even Loree at six years old knew they would never make it with a name like Blue Moon.

One afternoon when the band had finished practicing, Silversong decided to take advantage of all the extra muscle, and she put the young men to work. Loree's playhouse had begun to fall apart, so they decided it was best to tear it down. As they took up the floorboards, they were horrified to discover a nest of black widow spiders. Silversong's eyes grew big and she walked around with a strange look on her face for a few days after that. Loree imagined that she was thinking about all those times she yelled at her to get out of the ivy and go play in the playhouse.

Nineteen sixty-eight was a real scorcher. Ron decided it was time for him to go back to Jasper for the tourist season. It was clear he and Jason had become like oil and water. He was homesick in California, even if he wouldn't admit it.

Loree wasn't very happy that her "hero" was going back to Canada without her. She walked to the end of the block to play with friends. When it came time for her to head back home, the afternoon sun had heated the pavement. Not only had she forgotten to tell anyone where she was going, she had also forgotten to wear shoes.

When they finally found her, she was standing in a little patch of shade. She could only fit one foot on it at a time and was bawling her head off. She had been trapped there for an hour, screaming for somebody to rescue her. It was torture. Unfortunately, her hero was still planning to return to Canada.

CHAPTER EIGHTEEN
The Rain Dance

January, 1969

J.J. *was two months old. Christmas had been neatly packed away* in an ugly cardboard box for another year. Shiny new toys were strewn throughout the house. The dreadful summer heat had been replaced by cool rain and shades of gray

Loree had been stuck in the house for days. The rain had come at last, and now it seemed it would never stop. She got dressed and headed for her swing. Silversong caught her on the way out.

"Stop right there! You're not going anywhere today. It's too wet out."

She looked like she meant it.

Loree tried pouting, but it didn't work; Silversong wasn't budging an inch. Begrudgingly, she turned on the TV and watched another cartoon. Silversong was edgy, kind of stiff again. She kept walking to the window that faced the street in Loree's bedroom, staring at the water running down the gutters. Little rivers with a life of their own were forming in the street as Loree began whining to go outside again.

Again, Silversong said no.

There had been very little rain in the area for years. But the storm that came that winter brought more water than the small town of Cucamunga could possibly welcome.

Silversong worried about the land being so void of trees and brush and the ground being so hard and dry. She suspected there would be nothing to absorb all the rain.

The doorbell rang and Silversong answered. It was Harold Black, "Harry" as he was called, an elderly neighbor who lived just a few houses away. Harry was in his eighties and had recently been discharged from the hospital after undergoing triple-bypass heart surgery. Silversong hadn't been able to contact Jason at work and was happy to see Harry, grateful for the company. She invited him in, winking as she motioned him to enter.

"Come on in Harry, looking good . . . ."

"How you doing, kid?" Harry asked. His old face crinkled like a raisin when he smiled.

"Heard you added a new pup to your pack, eh?"

"Yup, a little duffer. With any luck, he'll grow up to be a dirty old man like you, Harry."

Silversong put on a pot of water for tea.

Harry had a soft spot in his heart for Silversong. He thought of her as a daughter. Silversong never let him down, always going out of her way to make his birthday or hospital stay and recovery an event. She would make posters and cards that were a delight to Harry. He loved the special attention. Everybody seemed to love Harry.

Harry said he was concerned about all the heavy rain; it was creating major problems. Knowing Silversong had two young children to care for, he felt it was important she not be alone. Even at his age, Harry was a warrior in his heart, a protector of the women and children.

His eyes were a bright blue, in sharp contrast to his Silversong hair which was often covered up with an old brown hat that matched his old brown sweater. Both were favorites of his.

By the time Harry arrived, Silversong had been trying to contact Jason for over an hour. Jason worked over an hour away from home and Silversong feared he might not know how severe the weather situation was getting. Dialing Jason's work number again, Silversong wondered if maybe she was overreacting. No, she decided she would feel better once he knew.

Unable to get through, Silversong shook her head in dismay and hung up the phone. It reassured her that Harry was worried too. Jason couldn't say she was just being a hysterical woman.

A commercial had just come on when the electricity went off, and they heard a loud cracking sound. Silversong, Harry, and Loree turned to look out the glass doors into the backyard, and saw it coming directly at them.

It looked like the ocean wave on *Hawaii 5-0*, only it was crashing over the fence into their backyard. Behind the house, there was a large empty field, and an orange grove that employed dozens of migrant fruit pickers.

The water must have gained a lot of momentum as it crossed that empty field, gaining strength along the way until it crashed into their home and into their lives. As if in slow motion, they watched the wave, spotted with oranges, break through the fence and continue toward them. In seconds, they were in water up to their waists, and it was getting deeper.

Silversong waded into the back bedroom where J.J. was sleeping, brought him out, and placed him on the china dresser where Loree was perched. She asked her to watch him. Water was everywhere. In a moment of panic, she reached for the front door.

"No, no!" Harry shouted, "Don't open it."

He explained that if the front door was opened, it would create a suction through the house powerful enough to carry them all away. Still weak from surgery, he struggled to find the electrical box to turn off the power.

The water was getting higher, and soon Loree and J.J. would no longer be safe on top of the dresser. Loree screamed at Silversong as the water began to splash on them. She didn't know how to swim, so she said a prayer.

Silversong half-waded, half-swam over to J.J. and Loree, picked J.J. up in her arms, and told Loree to jump in the water and hold on to her shirt. Loree didn't want to get in the water, but jumped courageously.

The water was black and seemed to be alive. Pieces of debris scraped against their bodies as they moved. Things that had been in the living room five minutes earlier rubbed against their legs in the water. It splashed over Loree's face as she concentrated her grip on Silversong's shirt. It was almost above her neck. They made their way slowly to the kitchen window. Harry was near total exhaustion, but continued to make his way from room to room, searching for coats and blankets, knowing it would be important for them to stay warm once they made it to the roof of the house.

The kitchen window was small and high up on the wall, close to the ceiling. Silversong wrapped J.J. in a blanket and knotted it at the top. Then she looked at six-year-old Loree, wet and scared. She knew that she had no option other than to trust that Loree could hold onto J.J. while Silversong climbed to the window. Once she climbed through, she balanced herself on the support beams that attached the house to the entry wall.

The beams were wet and the wind was strong as she tried to find her balance. She looked down toward her feet and saw a whirlpool forming beneath her. She told Loree to hand J.J. up to her. Loree was scared and crying; she said she was afraid she might drop him and fall in.

The water was rising fast and Loree had trouble keeping her footing as she reached up to hand J.J. to Silversong. She couldn't get a hold of the blanket; she tried, but it just kept slipping out of her reach. They would both have to reach out farther. Finally, she was able to grab the knot at the top of the bundle that held little J.J.

Loree was crying and Harry was becoming disoriented. He no longer seemed to hear Silversong as he held on, his body partially floating on top of the refrigerator. There was only two feet of open space between the water and the ceiling.

"Mom, please," Loree screamed, "the water's getting bigger!"

Loree was perched on the kitchen windowsill. "Hang on a few more minutes," Silversong yelled as she took J.J. over to where the support beams met the roof and could safely set him down.

Silversong was five feet away from the roof when she heard Loree cry out again. She was panicking, and as Silversong watched helplessly, Loree jumped from the windowsill and hung onto the beam, one hand on each side of it. The rain was still coming down hard, covering her face and making it harder for her to grip the beam. The water swirled below her feet. Silversong knew that if she lost her grip, she would be swept away and drown.

Seeing no other option, Silversong threw J.J. onto the flat part of the roof and went back for Loree. J.J. landed about six inches from the edge of the roof, and she turned again toward her daughter. She made her way across the beam back to where Loree was suspended. She kept screaming at her to hold on tight. Loree was tired and told Silversong she wanted to let go.

When Silversong reached her, she stood above her and tried to pull her hands free from the beam, but they were locked in place. She bent down, trying to keep her balance, holding both of her wrists in her hands, and telling her to drop one to the side so she could pull her free. Loree was too scared to let go; the fear had become paralyzing.

Silversong was finally able to persuade Loree to trust her. She released her hands and Silversong pulled her up onto the beam. They walked as if on a tightrope across the beam over to where J.J. had landed. Both of them were in an ice-cold sweat.

When they opened up the bundle that held J.J., they found him smiling. He appeared to be fine for the moment, and in that moment, so were they.

Silversong piled the blankets and coats Harry had gathered on top of Loree and J.J., and returned to help Harry onto the roof. He was at the window and his head was the only part of his body not covered in muddy water. Silversong pleaded with him to let her help him up onto the roof, but he was too exhausted to help her lift him out of the water and she couldn't do it alone. His skin was becoming translucent and he looked more and more pale as the light from the gray sky above reflected on his dear face.

"Go now and be with the children. You can't leave them there alone. I'll just hang in here, Silversong. Please do as I ask, now."

Harry was determined not to change his mind, once again showing that old stubborn streak his friends loved to hate. Silversong went back over to where the children were and got a blanket for Harry. She figured if she could at least get him sitting up on the windowsill, they could warm him up a little and perhaps cooperate and work with her to get him out of there.

When she got back to the window, Harry was gone. She stood there alone for a moment, feeling her warm tears mixing with the cool rain, as she cried for her friend.

The water circled the house forcefully while the first outside rescue attempts failed. Every time Loree lifted the blankets off herself and J.J. to see what was happening, Silversong would yell at her to get back under and stay covered.

Loree wondered where Harry was. The wind whipped against the blankets and she looked at J.J.'s little face, amazed that he slept so soundly. She said another prayer and told herself that Jesus would protect them and wouldn't let them die today.

Loree peeked out again and saw Silversong waving a coat above her head, hoping someone would see her—a tiny speck in a ocean of water. The rest of the neighborhood was already gone, and the force of the water surrounding the house grew. From under the blankets, she heard Silversong yell.

"Over here! We're over here!" Silversong screamed again and again.

There was a buzzing noise overhead. It was a helicopter and the crew was trying to lower a rescue basket. It was almost impossible to hear anything else, but they struggled to communicate.

It was useless. The helicopter tried to hold its position precariously close to the house. The wind blew the helicopter around at random and, finally, the crew had to abort the rescue attempt, turning the helicopter around and flying away.

The water rose, then receded, then came back up again even

higher. In the distance, Silversong and Loree could see that the water was becoming deeper. She lifted the blankets and climbed under them with her children. Loree looked up and told her that she loved her, and that she didn't think Jesus was going to let them die. Silversong told her that no matter what happened, they would stay together and yes, Jesus loved and would protect them. If they were going to die, Silversong didn't want her to be frightened, so she did her best not to show her own fear. Silversong told her that Harry had gone to get help for them and Loree asked her why they couldn't go with him. She didn't answer her. Instead, she talked to her daughter about Jesus and heaven, as she held her.

A very long time passed. Then, finally, they were assisted down from the roof by some of the migrant orchard workers. The water had temporarily receded but was still up to their necks and higher in some places.

The workers formed a human chain and passed them, one by one, down the line. There were fifteen or twenty men forming the chain, and they held on tightly to each other. Silversong, Loree, and J.J. were about half way down the line of men when Silversong lost her footing and the water began dragging her back. Loree was behind her and she grabbed Silversong with a little fist full of power and literally hung onto her until she got back into position. Silversong looked ahead and saw J.J., still in his little bundle, nearing the end of the chain.

They were evacuated to the Otis Elevator Company, where the upper floors had been turned into a temporary emergency shelter. People were wandering around in shock. Most were only partially clothed, no shoes, no *anything*.

Silversong kept hoping that she would find Harry somewhere. When the migrant workers came to rescue them, she told them Harry was missing, and they said they would put him on their list and keep searching. They were finding people hanging onto cars, bushes, and rooftops.

J.J. was hungry and looked like he was getting sick. He wouldn't stop crying. What an introduction to the world—it was all starting to take a toll on his little body. There was no food or milk, but Silversong found some instant coffee creamer and some sugar, mixed them with water and filled a plastic baggy, fashioning a bottle out of it. Small children, the elderly, and those with medical problems were placed in a back room to be transported out of the flooded area as soon as possible. Unfortunately, when the big trucks came, they forgot about everyone waiting in the back room. Silversong and her children were the last ones out.

They walked outside toward giant trucks and the driver told Silversong that she and the baby should ride in the cab where it was heated. Loree began to cry. There were so many strangers; she didn't want to be separated from J.J. and her mother.

Someone came and touched my shoulder. A kind, black lady smiled at me and told me that she was a grandma and that she was very lonely for her grandchildren. She said she would really appreciate it if I'd keep her company on the ride to the other shelter.

"Honey, it's okay. You come with me and I'll take care of you. As soon as we stop you can be with your mom and baby again, darlin'."

I held her hand and we walked to the back of the truck. Once inside the giant truck, I sat on her lap and we talked quietly. She had a very pretty voice. We drove on and on through the night.

When the truck finally stopped, men came and helped Silversong and her children out onto the road. Loree ran the length of the truck looking for her mother and found her crying uncontrollably, standing with Jason.

Jason kept saying, "Where's Loree?" over and over again. All Silversong could do was cry. It had been nineteen hours since the water came.

Loree was standing between them, tugging on Jason's coat but in all the confusion, he didn't notice she was there. Finally she yelled as loud as she could.

"I'm right here!"

Jason looked at her as if he had seen a ghost—he imagined that she had drowned.

For the first week afterward, the Lowes stayed with friends while Silversong contacted Anne to tell her the good news. They were all safe. Anne had no way of knowing if they were alive or not. She and Terry watched the news silently as awful pictures of the flooded area bombarded their TV screen, and they knew that the president of the United States had declared the area a federal disaster.

Terry and Anne applied for a bank loan, so that Silversong's family could fly up. But Silversong knew money was tight for everyone, and said she needed to stay in California and sort out what remained of their lives.

However blissful the reunion of Silversong, Jason, Loree, and J.J., reality set in fast—they had no place to live, no clothes, nothing except the nasty case of pollution poisoning that Loree had developed. It took a week to come on and a painful shot to get rid of.

They moved into a motel while waiting to hear from the authorities about when they would be permitted back into the area to see what, if anything, could be salvaged from their home. Jason was already talking about rebuilding. Silversong remembers the somber day when they were finally allowed back into their house:

The neighborhood looked like an alien planet. Everything was scarred. Nothing would ever be the same. But we were lucky to be alive. Harry's body had been found, a half mile from the house.

The currents had carried the truck away and it was found with the frame bent beyond repair, a mass of useless metal. The section of the house where we had waited to be rescued had collapsed. The rest of the house was, in some places, three-quarters full of mud and debris.

Often, when a tragedy strikes a family the community comes to their aid. But when a disaster strikes an entire community, the process of recovery changes dramatically. Any survivor of such devastation will tell you, you can easily get lost in the numbers game. One becomes a statistic—just one in a long line of victims waiting, and grateful for anything that comes your way.

There was very little to be saved. Many of our belongings had been washed away or simply destroyed. Our insurance company paid for a contractor to restore and rebuild what was left, and the state sent prisoners from a nearby jail to help with the clean up. They were easy to spot roaming around in small work parties, wearing bright orange jumpsuits.

Our house was several miles from the Vin Rose winery, which had also been damaged by the flood. There were large wooden wine containers scattered throughout the neighborhood. Reports of several unbroken bottles of vintage wine were discovered in the mud, and this helped encourage everyone to keep digging. When it came time for us to move back in, I still had a lot of fear. It would never feel like our house again.

The rebuilding went very slowly, and for a long time the contractor was at the Lowes every day, finishing up some of the smaller jobs.

One day he came in and told Loree he had a surprise for her, and to close her eyes. He had found some of her little stuffed animals and gave them to her. Loree thought they all looked different, yet familiar. He had cleaned them and replaced the eyes that were loose, and generally rebuilt them for her. It was a gesture of kindness that she would never forget.

It rained the first night they were home, and Loree awakened to hear her mother crying. She also heard Jason yelling.

"Stop being so hysterical! What the hell's wrong with you anyway?" he screamed.

"I'm scared, I can't help it, Jason ... I don't want to stay here. Please can't we just stay in a hotel tonight?"

"Stop acting like such a goddamn baby, Silversong. You're going to have to deal with it. What do you want me to do, just sell the house and leave?"

Still sobbing, she answered yes.

"Grow up, Silversong. We aren't going anywhere."

As the rain beat down rhythmically on the roof, Silversong wrapped herself in a warm blanket in hopes that her body would stop shaking so violently. She lay down on the couch in the dark and listened.

Jason hadn't been in the flood area when it happened, and he hadn't known Harry like they had. He never understood. He never even tried.

CHAPTER NINETEEN

Moonlight, Motorcycles, and Moving

The Lowes' house was very empty and quiet, except for J.J.'s on-again, off-again cries and the occasional conversation of neighbors who would stop by to see what kind of progress had been made to the house.

Often they would share the stories of how much their lives had changed in that one long, rainy afternoon. There was a lot of bitterness and confusion at how quickly they could lose control over their lives. They could no longer surround themselves with comfortable reminders of who they were. There were no more pictures, no more mementos to mark the special moments in life. Only memories were left.

It was discovered that a flood gate had malfunctioned and the decision was made to divert the water in the direction of Cucamunga rather than letting it flow into an adjoining affluent area. They figured if it had to go somewhere, why not let it wipe out all those little homes in Cucamunga?

Many people were suffering from Post-Traumatic Stress Disorder after losing their homes and nearly their lives, although the clinical term for what they were experiencing was never mentioned. There was little understanding or help available. Many moved, while some, like Silversong's family, stayed and suffered, attempting to rebuild their lives.

They learned how to make the best of a bad situation and the value of having a sense of humor. Amidst the destruction, there were various articles of clothing strung from branches and bushes, and new outdoor toilets deposited in backyards. Life became somewhat of an adventure; they never knew what they might find while digging through the mud. The whole contour of the neighborhood had changed.

One night after Jason and his best friend Frank had been drinking, they decided to go motorcycle riding in the moonlight in an empty field behind the house. It was only a matter of minutes before Frank had thrown himself over the handlebars of his motorcycle. He also got run over by it as it kept going without him, running right over his back, and Frank carved a major new gully in the field with his body.

Frank was forced to recover lying on his stomach, while the tire tread that was imprinted on his back healed. Silversong couldn't help but giggle a little, knowing that he had, technically, run himself over.

Jason and Frank had first met when they were both in the navy. When Frank heard there were good job opportunities in Southern California, they both decided to move their families there and begin civilian life as neighbors.

Loree always liked Frank a lot. She thought he was really handsome and that he looked just like Dean Martin. His wife, June, was a real character and even though Loree was a kid, the two of them were good friends. She had very pale skin with yellow-blonde hair that she teased to an unnatural height. False eyelashes were the rage at the time, and Loree thought that June would wear hers out, batting them at Jason.

Frank and Jason spent so much time together that eventually June and Silversong became good friends, but it's not as if they made a conscious decision about it.

June was having an affair with one of the men in town and she confided in Silversong about how crazy things were getting. Considering all the stepping out the "boys" had been doing, Silversong understood how June could find the idea appealing.

June confided to Silversong that she had a hot afternoon rendezvous planned with Mark, her mystery man, and she came over to the house beforehand so Silversong could fix her hair. Silversong was really good at hairstyling; she could tease it higher than June could. As a finishing touch to her "look," June went into the bedroom and changed into a brand-new pink mohair sweater that she had bought especially for the occasion, and off she went to meet her man.

A little later in the afternoon, Jason called from the local tavern and asked Silversong to come down, have a drink, and go out for dinner.

When Silversong arrived at the tavern, she noticed Frank sitting at the bar next to Mark, whom Silversong knew June had met with that afternoon. When Silversong went up to order a drink, she overheard Frank asking Mark if he had been rolling around on a pink rug or something. He began to pick pink mohair balls off of Mark's shirt.

Silversong tried to act nonchalant when she made her way to the ladies' room to use the pay phone. Frank was just walking out the door when Silversong ran back up to the bar to get some change. She lied, saying it was for the cigarette machine, and dashed back to the phone. After three very long rings, June answered.

"June, this is Silversong. Don't ask any questions, just get that damn sweater off now!"

The next morning after Jason and Frank had left for work, June called to ask what the previous night's phone call was all about. Silversong began to explain the events as they had taken place. June was grateful for the warning, but Silversong let her know it was the last time she could participate in her extra-marital curriculum. June was the one having the affair, but Silversong was the one worrying out about it.

Moral of the story according to Silversong:

If you're planning on screwing around on your husband, forget the mohair, or at least go for a nice neutral color that blends

*easily, and always carry an extra quarter—in case of an
emergency, you'll be able to make a phone call.*

1970

Jason and Frank became disillusioned with their jobs and the
California commute. They heard about promising work opportunities in Seattle, and decided it was time for a change.

It had been about a year since the flood when plans for the big
move were finalized. Once again the two families set off, this time
north on I-5, rather than south. The boys were in one car, the women
and children in the other.

The women didn't seem to mind having some *real* company, even
if it meant listening to the kids whine for fifteen hundred miles or so.

Using the money from the sale of the little house in Cucamunga
as a down payment, the family began house hunting. Everywhere
they went, the trees followed. It was beautiful. The world was bright
blue and emerald green.

The first time Loree saw the house on Seventh Avenue, she noticed the large tree in the yard, full of lilac-colored flowers the size
of her hand. She could see it through the large plate glass window in
the living room. Silversong was surprised to find the house much
larger than it appeared from the street. There were three bedrooms,
two on the main floor and one upstairs, and a full basement that
held a family room complete with a second fireplace. The upstairs
room was built over the garage and was paneled in a rich cedar. There
was a pencil sharpener on the banister that Loree thought was rather
spectacular, and immediately claimed as her own.

It all seemed absolutely perfect—the perfect neighborhood, the
perfect home, and, best of all, no bad memories.

The backyard was incredible, much larger then the front, and it
had a little river running through it with a tiny bridge crossing over
it that was absolutely charming. It even had a tennis court. The
deck out back ran the length of the house. It was redwood, as was
the trim on the predominantly white house. You could either go

down the stairs from the deck and into the backyard, or take the stone steps that wound around the side of the house.

It appeared as though everything had finally fallen into place, the papers were signed, and they moved in.

Silversong's life seemed somewhat charmed for awhile, having found such a nice home and having the opportunity to begin again, maybe get everything right this time. Everyone seemed somewhat subdued during the first few months, as they settled into the new house and Jason settled into his new job.

Loree got to know her new neighborhood, and made friends with Wendy Wheeler. Wendy was one year older than she was, and lived right next door. Loree saw Wendy as her opposite. Wendy had blonde hair and blue eyes.

Loree thought they both had perfect houses and perfect yards. She also thought Wendy had the perfect brother, perfect mother, and perfect father—those things she felt she *didn't* have. And during the years they lived on Seventh Avenue, the differences between the two families became excruciatingly apparent.

Wendy's parents never fought or disagreed about anything. They were always immaculately groomed, and Loree would have sworn that they never had sex, or even thought about it . . . maybe Wendy had been adopted? Loree couldn't be sure but . . . Wendy's mom? She couldn't imagine it. Mrs. Wheeler would never have dreamed of wearing makeup like her mother did. And, unlike Loree's mother, who was uninvolved in local organizations and patriotic to nothing, Mrs. Wheeler belonged to the PTA and every other socially acceptable, respectable association in town.

Wendy was what Silversong described as a "Sandra Dee." Mrs. Wheeler was always cleaning methodically while Mr. Wheeler hung out in the garage or kept neighborhood watch. They could have been the Cleavers; it was like walking into a fifties time-warp, one yard over. And although Loree was sometimes uncomfortable around the Wheelers, she secretly wanted to be like them, in that little world where everything is always perfect.

That's when Jason began beating Silversong again. Loree would later recall her mother's beatings with crystal-clear clarity:

I wake up to the sound of glass breaking, and lie in bed upstairs listening to them fight below, trying to measure by the tones of their voices how bad it's going to be.

Is he hurting her? Where is J.J.? Is he about to wake up . . . or has he already been awakened by their voices? Uh-oh . . . it's getting worse now, Mom's screaming . . . he's hurting her.

I walk down the stairs a bit to listen further. I peek around the corner and see them. He's hitting her body with his fists.

"Please stop! Please, you're hurting my mother! You're hurting her," I holler.

He tells me to shut up, then slams my mother's face into the bathroom door.

I hear J.J.'s screams over my own, and then see him standing in the doorway of his bedroom watching the fight.

I run down the stairs and slip in blood. Jason screams at me to leave before I'm "next."

"Leave my mother alone!"

For a moment, I feel very brave. I can stop him. He will listen to me.

He turns and comes after me. Suddenly his body lies at my feet. He has slipped in blood. He grabs my ankle, trying to pull me down. I kick myself free and run.

"I hate you! I hate you, you bastard!" I yell. I'm too angry to be scared anymore . . . but he comes after me again. My mom stops him. He turns, pounding his fists into her stomach. I can see her body silhouetted by smudged blood, as his fists slide from her body onto the door behind her. Her eyes find mine and she screams.

""Run . . . run, Loree . . . run!"

Barefooted, with only her nightgown on, Loree ran to the Wheelers' house and pounded on the door crying.

"Please help my mother!"

They looked at her with such distaste, like some strange alien from a distant planet. Silversong was still being beaten. Everyone could hear her screaming.

"So, your Mom and Dad are arguing, Loree, what's it about? . . . Now calm down, Loree, it's late, you'll wake up Wendy, and we wouldn't want her to see you like this, now would we? Really, now, Loree, this is between your parents—"

One last time Loree pleaded. "Please, *please* just call the police, *now!*"

"You head on back home now, Loree . . . I'm sure things will settle down."

Loree left, and sneaked around the back of the house where the screams were coming from. She sat on the back deck of her perfect house, waiting and listening, listening and waiting.

It took an hour before the police decided to arrive. By that time, Jason had seen the squad car coming and went to meet the "boys" at the door with a smile.

"Yeah, little fight with the ol' lady . . . got a little carried away . . . yeah, sorry about that, everything's cool now."

The officers didn't like being involved in domestic disputes; it was too dangerous. And it wasn't as if there were any *real* laws governing spousal abuse at the time. It was apparent that the officers were anxious to leave as quickly as possible. They told Silversong that she could go down to headquarters in the morning and file a complaint, but that they could not make a man leave his own house.

Apparently, they could not make him stop beating his wife either. Loree was totally disillusioned. They all seemed to give Jason permission to hurt her mother. Where could her mother go? Whom could she call? Nobody. A women's shelter didn't exist; there weren't any abuse hotlines. They were on their own.

Silversong spent the following day immobile in bed. Jason was quiet and apologetic. Loree didn't talk to her mother about how she felt. Silversong cried, and looked at the world through red slits surrounded by purple and black welts and cried. Her lips were cut and swollen, and it hurt too much to talk.

North Seattle, 1970

Jason came home from work one day and the children immediately had the sense that the evening was going to be different somehow. After living for awhile in uncertainty, the children became comfortable with being uncomfortable. Both Silversong and Loree felt the most frightened when nothing was happening—the anticipation, the calm before the storm, the silence one senses before a tornado hits.

That night J.J. and Loree were hustled off to bed early, and Loree laid upstairs in her room breathing in the smell of cedar from the dark wood that lined the walls, anticipating what the evening's conversation between her parents might hold.

She dreamed big dreams in her upstairs world, listening to the radio and lip syncing to her favorite songs. With an array of outrageous costumes, she danced in front of her mirror for what seemed like hours, until she fell into a deep sleep.

The next day Silversong explained that Jason was being transferred to Chicago, and that it was important to the whole family. It was to be a temporary move; they would rent out the house for two years and then return to Seattle.

Two years ... Loree thought about how old she would be in two years—ten years old —and she began to imagine what her life might be like in Chicago. Another chance? Perhaps another fresh start? Silversong had those same thoughts, though she didn't admit it openly.

Chicago, 1971

When they moved into the apartment in the small suburb of Wheeling, everything was new—the apartment complex, the scenery, the people, everything.

They lived on the second floor, and Loree had a view of the

Flamingo Hotel across the street from her bedroom window. A glowing pink neon sign became her night light. Robert Frost Elementary was going to be her school, about a twenty-five-minute walk from their apartment.

At first, Silversong drove her to school, but the day soon came when Loree had to walk by herself. She was scared that she might get lost and put up a fair fuss about it until her mother came up with the bright idea of writing their telephone number and address on Loree's thigh in ink so she wouldn't lose it. And, of course, Silversong couldn't help but draw an elegant flamingo next to it, in flaming pink ink.

All day long, whenever Loree felt worried, she tugged her dress up a little to see the flamingo's feet peek out.

It came in handy, too. Loree wondered what crossed that kind lady's mind the afternoon she came to her door, lost and crying, lifting up her dress when she asked her if she knew her phone number, showing her the elaborately designed flamingo.

Shortly after, one of the major soup companies in the nation poisoned Loree, J.J., and Silversong. Somehow Jason managed to escape, as usual, unscathed. Things were not off to a great start in Wheeling.

Loree had walked home from school for lunch—a simple sandwich and a nice, large bowl of cream of celery soup. She returned to her classroom, and after an hour or so, her stomach felt like it was tied in knots. There was a pressure that made her feel as if she might implode at any moment. The opposite happened, and she began to throw up violently. She could barely walk to the nurse's office. Once there, she laid on a hard little cot waiting for someone, anyone, to pick her up. Even the motionless walls made her wretch.

She was surprised to look up from her bucket and see Jason standing at the foot of her cot, ready to retrieve her. It seemed early for him to be home from work, but he quickly explained that Silversong had called him to pick her up because J.J. and Silversong had also become ill.

When Loree arrived home, it was an awful scene. The three of them were throwing up, weak, and getting sicker by the minute. Silversong was beginning to get quite frightened and upset when she saw how severe the children's symptoms were becoming.

"You've got to get us to a doctor, Jason. Something's wrong, very wrong."

Jason was still pissed off that he had had to come home from work early.

"Oh, for Christ's sake, Silversong. You've got the goddamn stomach flu and I have to get back to work."

"Jason, please. We need to see a doctor," she said again, but Jason was unmoved.

"Then I'll call an ambulance, you asshole!" Silversong screamed, staggering toward the phone.

"Okay, okay, you win. I'll find a doctor," Jason said, grabbing the telephone book.

They finally loaded themselves into the car and Jason drove to the doctor's office. They laid Loree out on an exam table in one room, and Silversong and Lance in another. By then, they could not stop vomiting and were convulsing.

They were transferred to the Harrison Memorial Hospital, and there it was discovered that they had severe food poisoning.

The first twenty-four hours were hell. They wanted to clear out their systems and restore body fluids, so they were hooked up to intravenous feeders. J.J. was only two years old, but it took three nurses to restrain him to find a vein. Then they had to tie him down so he wouldn't rip out his I.V. It seemed more traumatic for the nurses than it was for J.J. The hospital was so full the day they were admitted that Loree was placed in a steel crib right next to J.J. They weren't allowed any water by mouth until the first twenty-four hours had passed, at which time the nurse brought in a small Dixie cup that was half full. Loree drank it greedily, and still felt as dry as the desert.

J.J. recovered most quickly, probably because he hated cream of celery soup and hadn't eaten as much of it as Silversong and Loree had.

Two days later, J.J. and Loree, still in identical steel cages, were moved to a new room. The staff decided they could stay together because J.J. was entertained having his sister on hand to witness his antics. In their new room, they were separated by a clear plastic window, and J.J. was fascinated by it.

Once they were allowed to eat again, a nurse brought in a bowl of oatmeal and a small assortment of other tasteless items. She made the mistake of leaving J.J. alone with a bowl of oatmeal. It only took a minute—Loree looked over toward J.J. and couldn't believe her eyes. He was totally covered in the sticky white paste. It tasted so horrible, J.J. decided he would use it for something else.

Not only did he seem to like the feel of the paste against his skin, he had large globs of it in his hair, and when he discovered these, he began to finger paint on the clear partition between them, smearing and swirling large wonderful designs. Loree hadn't seen him smile so much since the morning she found him sitting on their shag carpet, mixing grape Kool-Aid, lard, and coffee grounds into the carpet with a large wooden spoon.

By the time the nurse realized her mistake, it was, literally, all over. Loree never did feel the same about oatmeal or cream of celery soup again.

Winter arrived with snow flurries. The apartment was quiet one night—J.J. was asleep and Jason was working late. Unable to sleep, Loree crawled out of bed and headed toward the kitchen for a drink. Something had been bothering her, so when she saw her mother reading a book silently on the couch, she decided to ask her why there were no baby pictures of her in the house.

"Come here and sit down by me. You're getting to be quite a grown-up, aren't you?"

Loree nodded her head silently.

"You know, Honey, I knew that someday we would need to have this talk. I love you, Loree, and I know what I am going to tell you is sad, and we might both cry and that's okay."

Scared by what she might hear and seeing her mother already near tears, Loree blurted out her worst fear.

"Are you my real mother or am I adopted?"

"I am your real mother Loree, and, no, you weren't adopted. But Jason . . . Jason is your stepfather. Your real father died when you were a baby. He had blonde hair, as white as snow, and eyes as blue as a clear summer day in the Rockies. He was Norwegian like Grandpa Lawsen."

Somewhere in the back of her mind, Loree knew that her dad had been a good guy, like her grandpa. They both cried, but Silversong cried the hardest.

Loree and Silversong hugged each other as they wept.

Before going to sleep, Silversong said a prayer of thanks to Teddy. If he would have lived, he would have been a great father. But even in death he had the power to provide Loree a protective veil. She had a father, only he was in heaven.

After that, Silversong and Loree didn't talk much about Teddy. It upset Silversong so much to think about what she had lost, not only her childhood, but the hopes that went with building a family with the one man she ever really loved. And then there was the silent secret. The white lie.

A few months before they were to move back to the house in Seattle, word came that Patty was pregnant. Anne Lawsen flew to Chicago from Edmonton. Silversong and Loree felt especially comforted to have her there. Anne and Loree reunited in a special way, often taking long walks together. One day in particular, they took an awful pair of shoes that Jason had made Loree wear and threw them into the river. Loree hated those shoes and Anne knew it. Taking full responsibility for their actions, Anne wore a huge grin as they each took one shoe and gleefully watched it sail through the air. Of course, they didn't tell Jason or Silversong. Instead, they walked into the apartment, heads hung low (hiding their secret satisfaction), fully ready to explain that the shoes had simply gotten up and walked off on their own as they played in the grass. Anne told her that she would replace them.

They entered the living room just in time to see J.J., filled with glee, dash out from one of the back bedrooms and run to the sliding glass door that led to the patio. He unlocked it, and from the expressions on the faces of Jason and Silversong, there was trouble in River City. Jason's face was bright red, and Silversong looked like she was ready to choke someone.

Apparently, about fifteen minutes after Loree and Anne had left for the park, little J.J. had casually closed and locked the sliding glass door while Silversong and Jason were outside. Anne could well imagine the game of hide-and-go-seek and peek-a-boo that they must have played with him to get him to unlock the door.

They used to call J.J. "Angel Boy," which was kind of a sick joke. He was awfully cute, like a little puppy with his big brown eyes rimmed in dark lashes. He'd look up and suddenly his parents would change their minds about strangling him, and give him a big hug instead.

One time, J.J. found his parents' wedding rings in the bedroom and promptly flushed them down the toilet. Because they lived in a new apartment building, they had yet to put traps in the sewer system to catch such things. Perhaps J.J. was a lot more intelligent at the time than he was given credit for.

At last, the day came when the family headed back to Seattle. As they piled into the van that Jason had bought for the trip home, Silversong knew it wasn't going to be easy. She and Jason had had a huge fight the day before, so they weren't speaking to one another. Two or three thousand miles to go. . . .

The ice breaker came when they hit Lincoln, Nebraska. They pulled into a little gas station and Jason bought everyone a soda.

Before giving Loree hers, however, he took one long, long swig from it.

Loree was furious. He passed her polluted pop back to Anne, who passed it back to her. They were just pulling out of the parking lot as Loree grabbed the soda pop, and with a big huffy pout, threw herself back dramatically against the wall of the van to show the world her displeasure.

She had actually thrown her back against the back doors of the van, which swung open, leaving the family staring at her two legs sticking straight up in the air as she exited, rather ungracefully, from their presence.

The family gathered around her, concerned. It lasted about five seconds, long enough for her to get to her feet before they burst into a chorus of hysterical laughter.

A day later, Jason, exhausted, turned over the reins to Silversong and crawled into the back to sleep. Loree wedged herself in between her mother and grandmother as they drove through the night.

They only drove for about ten minutes before silently pulling over at a hamburger stop. After eating, they climbed back into the van unnoticed by J.J. and Jason, who slept soundly, and headed off back into the night. Unfortunately, they went in the wrong direction.

They drove for almost an hour before realizing what had happened. Silversong immediately turned around and accelerated. They made it about thirty miles past the point where Jason had fallen asleep when he woke up. Luckily for the family, he never did figure that one out.

Somewhere in South Dakota, Silversong bought a copy of the book *Bury My Heart at Wounded Knee* by Dee Brown. It is one of the greatest, saddest books ever written about native people; and it was all the more poignant that she began reading it as they traveled through Indian country.

Silversong was becoming more radical with every page she turned, every mile they traveled. As she read, there was, in essence, a new Indian war beginning: It was him against her, cowboy against Indian, wrong against right.

It was a small victory, but a victory nonetheless when, after hours of arguing, Silversong refused to stay in the elegant hotel Jason had picked out because it honored a man who had become a hero for butchering people. There was absolutely no way Silversong was going to set one foot in the Custer Hotel.

It took them over an hour to find a room available elsewhere, and when they did, it was in a little motel called the Thunderbird. Silversong and Loree were both pleased. Loree felt certain that the beds in the Custer didn't have coin slots that made them vibrate.

Angry about losing the skirmish, Jason hurriedly drove the family to Mount Rushmore the next day. While he took J.J. to a lookout point, Loree and Anne stretched their legs and checked out the gift shop. Silversong protested, refusing to so much as set a foot out of the car or in any way honor the dead presidents carved in stone, or their government, which had condoned, and *still* condones, such atrocities against the indigenous people.

Silversong felt that moving back into the house on Seventh Avenue was like entering a time warp again. Nothing had changed. Mrs. Wheeler still had the same hairstyle and not so much as a blade of grass in the Wheeler's yard had grown beyond its designated height.

It was only a matter of moments before Wendy herself came bubbling out of her front door, bouncing toward their car. She stopped right at the edge of her grass however; it was her safety zone. You never know what might happen to a nice white girl over there in Indian country.

Try as she might to continue her friendship with Loree, there were certain realities that Wendy Wheeler just wasn't accustomed to dealing with. She was a sweet kid though, and as they grew older, Loree would sometimes notice a look cross her face, as if Wendy wanted to reach out to her and didn't quite know how. Loree felt the same way. They were red and white, two separate realities, divided by a perfect line of tulips and an immaculately groomed bush.

Loree now knew better than to run to the Wheelers when Jason went on the war path. Instead, in her nightgown, she'd run three blocks over to Tina's, whose mother and father had taken a liking to her. Tina's mom was Alaskan Aleut, and she was much more like Loree's mother than most of the women she knew. Unlike the Wheelers, they didn't seem to hold her personally responsible for her parents' actions.

Several months after they moved back in, Silversong, J.J., Loree, and Anne drove to Edmonton to pick up Patty and her new baby, Amethest. Patty's eyes welled with tears as she held the little bundle that contained her daughter, and they all drove away from her in-laws' house.

Her breakup with her husband Steven had been painful, but not without its rewards—she admired Amethest's little hands, perfectly formed and reaching out as if to comfort her mother, who was crying wholeheartedly as they hit the main highway.

On that trip, Silversong met Ron's new wife, Monica, a tall, lean, beautiful blonde, a lady who was articulate and extremely intelligent. At last, Ron had found the real thing. And it seemed the feeling was mutual.

Time moved in fast-forward for everyone. No longer a thirteen-year-old hero receiving praise from the local paper, Lance had married his high school sweetheart, Karen, and was now the proud father of a beautiful daughter he named Sierra.

Sierra and Loree watched Ron and Monica cook dinner, clowning around like a couple of kids as they tried to fry pork chops with plastic forks that kept melting. They had just moved into their new apartment in Edmonton, and Sierra and Loree were their first official guests.

Approximately a year after Amethest was born, word came that Ron and Monica had a brand-new baby girl, "Little Nickel." Her name was actually Noel, but at the time, a little paper that circulated throughout the Seattle area was called the "Little Nickel" and somehow the nickname stuck. No one in the family could describe it, but there was an unsettling undercurrent that seemed to be picking up speed slowly as life went on. Patty spent her time in the States ferrying between Edmonds and Kingston, while Silversong worked as a cocktail waitress at the Kong Chow Restaurant in North Seattle.

Jason had received a prestigious promotion and became the youngest executive at Ingersol Band, a heavy-duty equipment company. He began a never-ending cycle of traveling overseas for extended periods of time. He would be gone to Switzerland or off to Paris or Germany for sometimes four to six months.

It was a time for the family to be themselves and not exist in a constant state of tension and terror, waiting for him to walk in the front door.

Jason always was an ego-maniac, which on a good day gave him a strange, arrogant, good guy, bad guy appeal. The corporation was impressed by his "kick ass, take names later" persona, so they paid him a lot of money and gave him plenty of perks, something Jason found very appealing. Ingersol Band knew that Jason could be depended on, whether it meant relocating, a last-minute business trip, or even a three- or six-month overseas assignment. He wasn't one of those wimpy guys who whined anytime one of his children got sick. Jason wasn't the type of man who took into consideration how the demands of his job would affect his family. His career took precedence, and with that single priority in mind, there were no other considerations. It was a man's world, and he was king of his castle.

When Jason came home, the peace treaty was broken.

Loree woke up in the middle of the night to the sound of glass shattering and her mother's screams. Jason had been expected to arrive home on a seven o'clock flight from Paris. Silversong had dutifully waited at the airport for his arrival, only to come home alone three hours later without a clue as to where he was or when he would be home. Not really anticipating a problem or even thinking ahead that far, she had made the fatal mistake of locking the door before crawling into bed. When Jason arrived home at three o'clock in the morning, he was drunk, mad, and in a mean mood.

He picked up J.J.'s bicycle from the front porch and threw it through the six-by-six-foot plate glass window in the living room. Screaming, he climbed through the window, jagged glass still protruding from the window frame, and he began to beat Silversong.

Sitting on the back porch waiting for the police to arrive, Loree hoped he wouldn't kill her mother, or come looking for her.

Frightened, in shock, and completely numb, Silversong endured the worst beating of her life. By the time it was over, she was unrecognizable. Her eyes were beyond swollen, but black slits revealed broken blood vessels. Her lips were completely mangled, and she was unable to speak. It hurt to cry.

In the weeks that followed, Silversong painfully recovered. It's time to leave, before it's too late, Silversong said to herself as she examined the bruises on her face that were now beginning to fade. He will never hurt me again. At that moment, Silversong had decided to divorce Jason. It was only a matter of waiting until the right moment . . . when Jason left for Europe. Only then would it be safe for her and her children to leave.

CHAPTER TWENTY
Happy Birthday

My aunt Patty divided her time in the States between our place in Seattle and Grandpa's place in Kingston. In our two homes, she found time to heal from her divorce and began to make plans for her and Amethest's future.

Patty loved Kingston beach as much as Grandma and I did, and she absolutely adored her baby. Patty could be near tears, and then boom! Amethest would wake up from her nap and Patty would look like the happiest, luckiest, richest person in the world, and in those moments she was.

When Patty had regained some balance in her life, she decided to move back to Edmonton to start nursing school. Everyone was sad to see her go, but there was no holding Patty back. It was time for a change, a time for decisions.

I had a hard time getting used to Patty's absence. When she stayed with us, Patty, Amethest, and I all shared my room. She told me bedtime stories, and I watched Amethest while she took a shower or caught up on some sleep. Sometimes we would go out and play what we called "superball" in the backyard, and I was never lonely.

I didn't see them for a year. By the time they flew home for Christmas, it seemed as if they had been gone forever. The whole family was happy and expectant. Whatever turmoil had been going on was set aside.

Patty gave me two of my favorite singles that year, "Bye, Bye,

Miss American Pie" and *"I've Got a Brand New Pair of Roller Skates, You've Got a Brand New Key...."* *We sang our hearts out to those two songs, late into the night, eating popcorn.*

Patty and Amethest got matching pajamas and robes. They were light blue with tiny little mauve roses. Mauve was Patty's favorite color.

Mom gave Patty a ring of hers that Pat had admired for a long time and Mom joked that she had to give it back when she came home from school, but she actually had decided to give it to her for keeps. It was all part of the fun.

All of the women, even the little ones like Amethest and me, sat around the table sipping tea and painting our fingernails. We spoke of the future. Patty only had three months left of school and money was tight as usual. She was having problems finding good, affordable child care for Amethest. Grandma was quick to offer to care for Amethest, and Patty knew it was the best choice she could possibly make for both her daughter and herself. She knew Amethest would be well cared for and loved, but it didn't make things any less painful. She didn't want to leave her baby.

We reassured her and reminded her how fast the next three months would pass.

Patty was nicknamed "Pat" by Silversong, and "Mercer" by Ron when he was little. Silversong always wondered where he came up with that nickname. Patty was the youngest of the siblings, and the last time Silversong saw her, she was getting on an airplane to fly back to Canada to finish her college courses. She intended to be a nurse, specializing in pediatrics. She looked so grown up, so determined, and full of purpose.

How Patty cried when she gave Amethest a kiss and turned to walk down the dark hallway and leave. She was so torn having to leave behind a child that she desired to be with above all else. But she realized that to meet the responsibility of parenthood on her own, she would have to secure her life financially. In furthering her own education, she would further her daughter's.

Silversong wanted to stop her. She just wanted to keep her little sister forever, and protect her from life. Motherhood, for a young woman on her own like Pat, could be lonely. Silversong knew the pain inherent in growing up and going out into the world where no one was as nice as Pat; but she also knew she had to honor Pat's dreams, as Pat had always honored Silversong's.

Silversong thought about the world. Pat thought about family. They never explained it to each other; they just knew they would always love one another in spite of everything. Pat would walk twenty miles to vote for something, give blood, or make you a cup of tea. Silversong envied how "centered" Pat was, and felt that it was something she could learn from her.

"Yeah, to hell with it, let's go have a cup of tea!" Patty would say with a big grin on her face.

A good cup of tea could cure any ailment in the family.

It seemed to Silversong that she always had so many choices, and none of them appealed to her. Her sister Pat liked everything, considered only living. She took care of the family's hearts many times, helping them to bypass anger. She was just plain safe. She would laugh and get excited when Silversong would tell her about the things she suspected were possible in life.

"You can do anything," Patty would tell Silversong, and she believed her.

Patty knew that Anne's generation was different than hers and Silversong's, and Anne would get exasperated, saying it wasn't worth trying to figure out why she and Silversong disagreed. It was good advice. Silversong was an independent individual and Pat accepted that, and loved her. Silversong learned a lot from her little sister . . . there are many stories, many memories.

It was a cold February morning when Patty died. She never knew or struggled. The fire inspector told Silversong that the oxygen was used up so slowly, she just went from her sleep, deeper and deeper

. . . until she walked on in the spirit. He said they estimated that she passed away at least a half hour before the flames reached her body. To this day she is deeply missed.

> *My sister, I remember her.*
>
> *Our kind of sistering is a gift, you don't care what other people think. You're loved deeply no matter what and I always seemed to need a lot of that desperately. I learned a lot from my sister . . . there are many stories, many memories. She lives every time a tea bag hits the hot steamy water, each time the cookies come out of the oven, each time someone washes in Dove soap, or packs a picnic lunch for the park.*
>
> *You see, she died. I miss her.*
>
> *But I know none of us are going to get out of this alive. We will surely be there when it happens and we will do it our own way. I learned a lot from my sister and I intend to spend my life doing the things I like to do that encourage me to feel, experience, and to think, while always aware and awake in full consciousness honoring the greatness of life and walking on when it's time. Knowing Pat, she'll have a cup of tea waiting for me.*

The day was February 6, 1972. Silversong, J.J., Loree, and Monica were all at Terry and Anne's house in Kingston. Monica had come down from Canada with Nickel to stay while Ron went to blasting school in Fort McMurray, Alberta.

They sang "Happy Birthday" and Silversong blew out the candles. They were teasing her when they heard footsteps coming up the stairs. There stood two very serious state troopers asking for Terry. Everyone got very quiet when they realized that the police were at the door looking for him.

Terry and Loree were standing in the doorway when Anne ran up and looked at their faces. Before they even spoke, she turned to her bedroom and began her mourning. She knew Patty was dead. She didn't need to hear their words.

They stayed for a long time and called a doctor who came to the house and gave Anne a shot. Then they talked to her and the rest of the family. They tried to answer everyone's questions, but knew few actual details. They gave the family names and numbers of people in Edmonton who might have some of the answers.

Silversong never opened her birthday presents. The cake sat on the counter, uncut. And Loree could not help but think how cruel life could be for her mother to lose her baby sister on her birthday.

The church was packed, standing room only. Her entire nursing class traveled from Edmonton to Edson, where she was buried. She was laid to rest in a beautifully embossed, mauve-colored casket. It was the one time in Anne's life that the three men she had shared her life with came together in love and respect: Terry Lawsen, Dan Walker, and Chaz Belcour. Anne had lost her youngest child, and the men in her life had come to honor her grief.

Jason was working in Paris when Patty died. He was contacted and flew home for the funeral. "Look, it's over ... she's gone. Shit happens ... it's part of life. Everyone dies, Baby, now it's time to get back to work ... cryin' ain't gonna change it."

Jason's words weren't exactly the soothing salve Silversong's soul was searching for. Patty's death was a real inconvenience for him. Jason had a very simple and uncomplicated view of life—if it feels good, do it; if it doesn't, screw it. All the crying and gnashing of teeth got on his nerves.

J.J., Amethest, and Loree were cared for by family friends. The twelve-hundred-mile trip back to Edson in the winter for the funeral would have been too difficult with the children. And the family was too overcome with grief to see any other solution.

Jason booked his flight back to Paris before leaving Edson. He didn't even unpack. There had been a time when he'd picked cotton, but he no longer claimed those memories, he was a man of the world and an international executive. No longer the little boy who lived at the edge of a dirt road leading to nowhere, Jason had arrived, he was somebody. He demanded respect and was willing to intimidate anyone who wouldn't give it to him. Life was ripe for the picking with a few credit cards in his wallet and an unlimited expense account to entertain himself on.

Jason was rarely lonely or alone when away from home. With Silversong busy at home taking care of the children and licking her wounds, Jason was free, white, and well over twenty-one.

Jason's colleague Pete had heard that Silversong's sister died unexpectedly, and assumed Jason would take a liberal leave of absence, but Jason was not one to fret over something as matter-of-fact as death.

Pete had thought of Silversong often, more often than he cared to admit. After knowing and working with Jason, he was simply amazed to see a woman like Silversong with a man like Jason. Pete had always assumed Jason preferred them tall and blonde. At least, that was the type Jason was usually drawn to, and had more than once taken back to his hotel room.

But it wasn't only Silversong's physical description that didn't seem appropriate, it went deeper than that. In the time Pete had spent speaking to Silversong, he sensed a quality Jason was a stranger to: class. Her lovely paintings showed a vulnerability and beauty that extended beyond the canvas and touched a quiet place in him. Finding himself in a daze, Pete would try to erase her from his mind, but she always came back.

Dear Silversong,

With sincere sympathy, I think of you, of your loss and all you have to offer, all you possess—a simple smile and the world becomes a beautiful place.

Your art . . . that beauty captured and placed in a frame . . . You have great spirit, and strength. I know you'll heal.

Love,

Pete

When he finished writing the note, he placed it on his dresser and left to meet Jason for a drink in the hotel lounge. The weight of the note haunted him, and he wondered if he was crazy to think of such things, even more so for having written them down. He felt the need to reach out to her, yet feared doing so, afraid he might somehow damage her further. He feared that if he were to break the silence he'd imposed on his emotions, something would come and take away the beauty. He felt maybe it should stay in silence, in safety. He would simply throw the note away.

Pete entered the hotel lounge and squinted his eyes, beginning to focus on faces in the room. Jason's sandy blonde hair caught his eye. He was sitting in a far corner with one hand resting on a large breast, the other around a drink. Like most of the woman Pete had seen Jason with, she was blonde and seemed to respond eagerly to Jason's generosity as he pulled out his wallet and paid for their drinks with a hundred dollar bill.

Seeing the situation for what it was, Pete wanted to return to his room, but as he turned to leave, Jason yelled out his name.

"Pete! Hey buddy, come on over, drinks are on me tonight."

"Hi, how you doing tonight?" Pete said as he sat down and motioned to the cocktail waitress.

"I'll have a rum and coke."

Quickly putting away the drink he'd ordered, Pete excused himself and stepped back out into the brightly lit lobby. A long sigh escaped from his throat as the sounds of brittle laughter and scratchy juke box music faded comfortably into the background.

He went to his room, picked up the note he had written to Silversong and read it once more, pausing when he finished, to add a couple of lines:

I'll be returning home on the sixth, if you should need anything at all, please call.

Silversong first met Pete at a small party at her house. He was still married to an obnoxious little blonde woman named Karen.

First, there were the wigs she used to wear—platinum blonde, always sitting on her head a little crooked. She spent most of her time rearranging either her hair or the large falsies she wore, and she was none too happy when Loree walked in on her as she was straightening her boobs.

"What are those?" Loree asked.

"None of your business. Didn't your parents teach you to knock before entering a room?" she spat.

"Yes, they did ma'am . . . but this room's mine."

Loree pointed out a few stray strands of hair that had managed to escape at the base of her thick little neck. She was rather red in the face and sweaty all over and Loree was going to suggest that she try a little face powder, but bit her tongue. She figured that might be pushing her luck.

Even though the two families began spending quite a lot of time together, Karen never seemed to like Silversong or Loree that much. But that didn't stop her from using Loree as a baby-sitter when she was desperate.

Loree checked out her underwear drawer when Karen had gone. She had a lot of fun trying on her falsies and thinking she looked pretty good with breasts.

The first time Silversong saw Pete, he was wearing a fur coat. She had never seen anything like him before in her entire life.

He was tall and thin, with long black hair and blue eyes, and sideburns that would make Elvis drool.

But it was his personality and his flair for fashion—long, embroidered, fur-collared coats, bell bottoms, and lots of leather—that made him interesting. Silversong had never seen a man who dressed with so much flair before, and it embarrassed her slightly, but she decided it was kind of . . . cool.

Jason spent more and more time overseas with his work. Often he would fly in and stay for less than a week before Silversong drove him back to Sea-Tac Airport, the car quiet and desperately tense. Silversong would watch him walk across the sky bridge to his plane.

It was hard for the family to hide their lack of disappointment at his departure. Once he was gone, they were safe to resume their more natural behaviors. It was as if the tension in their shoulders lifted as his plane lifted off the runway. They were free again, even if it was only for a few months.

Silversong would flip on the radio and turn it up loud as they drove toward home. There were two worlds: one when Jason was home, and another when he was away. They differed dramatically from one another. In one, they were happy, in the other . . . at least they had each other.

Loree began to notice Pete coming by the house alone more often to visit Silversong. She cried a lot after Patty died and it always seemed to cheer her up when he came by.

Pete was always considerate of Loree's feelings, often taking time to talk to her, asking if she needed anything. He always looked as if he wanted to stay a little longer when it came time for him to leave.

Silversong would play Rod Stewart songs on the stereo over and over after he left. She had been through phases like this before so Loree was used to it, but it still got on her nerves, playing them to death the way her mother did. Loree would wake up in the morning singing "Maggie May," or dreaming that she had learned to play the mandolin, although she didn't even know what a mandolin was. Pete took care of that too, though; he arrived home from a trip to Switzerland with a mandolin for her.

Loree wandered down the stairs at the crack of dawn one morning, just as a flash of red passed through the back gate, heading out. There was no mistaking it; it was Pete's tiny sports car.

Rounding the corner, she walked through the kitchen, startling her mother, who was coming up the stairs from the basement.

She looked extremely guilty, and she stopped humming "Every Picture Tells a Story" when she saw Loree.

Aha! A light bulb went on in Loree's head. She began the interrogation.

Her mother's eyes got real big at the mention of one little red sports car belonging to "you know who," but she feigned innocence. Loree was only ten years old, but she was nobody's fool.

Loree was scared beyond words at the thought of her Great White Father coming home and finding out. She'd always been afraid that Jason might kill her mother at some point. This would make him feel he had good reason.

Several days passed in utter silence as she gave her mother her own version of the silent treatment.

During this time, while going through Silversong's jewelry box looking for a pair of earrings, she came across a marijuana joint. As if she didn't have enough problems . . . Great, now on top of everything else, Loree thought, my mom's a drug addict.

She was really sick about it. She hadn't heard much about drugs, but knew that they did strange things to people. She wasn't sure what to do, but finally decided to put the small velvet jewelry box in her pocket and talk it over with her grandmother. It was Friday, so she didn't have to wait long before seeing her. On Fridays, J.J. and Loree would meet Anne and Amethest at the ferry dock in Edmonds, and head toward Kingston for the weekend. Silversong drove her down to the Edmonds ferry dock at 5:00 P.M. and Grandma Anne was on the Illahee, which docked at 5:15. Greeting Loree with a big smile, she took Loree's hand, and they walked back onto the ferry. They always enjoyed the time they spent suspended on the water, but on this day, Loree didn't feel much like talking.

Anne had come prepared for the trip with a pocket full of quarters.

"Can I get you a hot chocolate, Lor?"

"That would be nice, Grandma. I don't feel very good."

Coming back several minutes later with a cup of watery hot chocolate, Anne handed it to her, and with a concerned look, asked if she was okay.

Loree burst into tears and handed her the small velvet box. Anne opened it carefully, and then slammed it shut.

"What are we gonna do, Gram?"

She was so relieved that it was no longer up to her and her alone.

"We'll walk outside to that railing right there," she said pointing, "and I'll stand right next to you while you throw it into the ocean."

Loree was worried that her mom might get mad when she found out, but she took a deep breath and flung it far out into the waves. If only all their problems were this easily taken care of, Loree thought as they walked down the narrow steel stairway that led to the loading dock, off the ferry, and down the main drag in Kingston.

Loree returned home at the end of that weekend to find her mother happily playing "Mandolin Wind" on the stereo again. Pete was going back to Paris for a few weeks.

Although he seemed to make her mother happy, it scared her. She wondered what would become of all of them. Loree thought perhaps they would forget about each other while Pete was gone.

Loree was not as thrilled as her mother when Pete returned to their front door exactly two weeks later, with a gold-plated key to a castle and a copy of "Every Picture Tells a Story" for Silversong.

She thought, God, not only is he back here to further complicate my life, but there's another Rod Stewart record!

Long before Patty's death, Silversong and Jason's marriage had gone sour; but Patty's death accelerated and intensified the conflicts that had existed for years. The general atmosphere of confusion, hysteria, and grief that Silversong experienced after Patty's death gained momentum.

Families have problems, I told myself, trying to minimize what was going on.

Something clicked inside of me after my sister died. I was no longer able to comply. There was a lot of drinking and little agreement between Jason and me. Many heated arguments escalated in overwhelming violence. It seemed my feelings had become problems.

I felt God was punishing me, that I was guilty of something. I started to cry at night, often. I didn't want to be married any longer, but, economically, Jason held the hammer.

I was continually frightened, I felt as if I were dying and I feared losing my life. Panic attacks began. I couldn't eat. Everything was out of control, yet everything was about control. Power and control. Jason couldn't control me and I wasn't smart enough to act stupid.

I knew Loree was talking to mom a lot, and that made me withdraw from Loree and the rest of the family even further.

Loree knew how Alice must have felt when she fell through the looking glass. It happened to her, she thought, and it was all real. Everything was backward. No one could give her a straight answer. All the mirrors in the house were distorted, and she couldn't see herself anywhere. Her mother's eyes could no longer tell her who she was. They were either blank with resignation and despair, or somewhat frightening, like the Mad Hatter. The only person who could comfort her was her grandmother Anne, which strained her relationship with her mother to the breaking point. It was like they had become the enemy.

Anne made Loree feel better on the weekends. Loree spent all of them in Kingston with Anne and Grandpa Lawsen. They would escape to the beach, and it was beautiful and peaceful there. Often, they would just sit and watch the ferries pull into the dock. They came and went almost silently, along with their thoughts. It was a special place and their special time; no one seemed to bother them there. Loree was able to tell Anne how unhappy she was and they would have long talks about how someday this would be far, far behind them, all a distant memory.

Amethest was four and J.J. was five years old, little free spirits moving in and out of the water, finding treasures and playing games, as Anne and Loree talked.

Many times, Anne also romped in and out of the water with the kids, sand everywhere, a big grin on her face, her warm brown eyes also smiling, and a big bucket of clams in both hands. Anne gave Loree more strength then she could ever know.

"Only eight more years honey, and you'll be all grown up and then you can make your life your own and live it the way you think is right, Lor, you'll see . . . We come from a long line of strong women with a lot of backbone, Loree. You're a Lawsen woman and Lawsen women are strong. We are survivors."

She gave Loree a hug that said what she spoke was the truth.

Often, we stayed at the beach in Kingston until the sun set, trying to hold back the reality that lay beyond our little beach. Afterwards, Grandma and I would walk up the long hill that led to Kingston, a town composed of four bars, a couple of restaurants, a Laundromat, a marina, and the Kingston ferry dock that took people to Edmonds.

When we got back to the house, Grandpa would be at the bar, or worse, he would be at home and pick a fight with Grandma, so he could get out of the house and go down to the bar stool that was beckoning him. Grandpa was a wonderful man but he had a terminal disease—alcoholism.

He had a big heart and I think because he felt so much so deeply, it terrified him at times. If he stayed sober for too long, he might just break into a million pieces. Patty's death had hit him hard; it penetrated through his shield of alcohol. He was confused by my mother's behavior, and he was worried.

I loved Grandma and Grandpa, but he was hard on her. When he passed through the initial "warming-up" period, the first couple drinks, then came the darkness, usually directed at Grandma. She took the abuse so typically dished out by an alcoholic; she became the focus of his anger, disappointment, and fear. The rest of the family was spared his dark side.

Not everyone in the family understood Grandma's pain and resentment. She had lived in the shadow of his alcoholism for thirty years. The rest of us basked in the afterglow of the first couple of drinks. After a couple of drinks he was my Grandpa, he called me "Little Loree" and looked at me in a way only Grandpa could. He held my hand and tried to tell me what I meant to him.

He was in pain. He would try to communicate through the confusion and touch the part of himself that felt, the part he was trying to drown in alcohol. Finally, he would get quiet and just hold my hand with tears in his eyes. I would always know what he was trying to say, and he would try to focus his eyes on my face, trying to see clearly, searching for the contact point.

Like many alcoholics, Grandpa held down a job at the lumber mill for years. It was his lifeline. As long as he had a job, it counteracted the other realities of his life.

"Real alcoholics can't hold down a job, everyone knows that, right?"

So here was another way for the family and Grandpa to deny a problem. Things had to get really bad before any of us were going to admit it. We were tough, strong women, survivors, right?

So it was that Grandpa played the game with Grandma that only an alcoholic can. Of course, Grandma never won because it's a drinker's game and Grandpa could change the rules as his disease dictated.

I could see how tired and worn out Grandma had become since Patty died. I would wake up in the middle of the night sometimes and hear her out on the back balcony in the dark, wrapped in a down jacket, lying in a lawn chair crying to the moon, looking for Patty.

I never heard anyone make sounds like she did, or see pain etched so deeply in someone's face as it was in hers. I stood and watched her through the sliding glass doors. How sad she was. I realized there was nothing I could do to bring her baby back, but it was hard to walk away and leave her alone to cry.

Grandma had told me a story about a Moon Bird. She said

the Moon Bird was like an angel, and that if our intent was pure she would help us, guide us, and comfort us.

"She'll make a brand new day."

Grandma said I am just sad that Patty won't see the sunrise.

She was a Lawsen woman, she was a grandmother who would now become her grandchild's mother as she had in the past. She would pray for strength, guidance, and the courage to raise a child through tragedy.

"Gotta go get a haircut," Grandpa would say after taking his shower and changing into his weekend clothes. This was typically at about noon, when the bars opened.

"Yeah, yeah...dinner's at five," Grandma would say. And Grandpa would practically skip out of the house and down to his extended family at the "Sail In," a little hole-in-the-wall bar that Grandma couldn't stand.

One time after Grandpa left, Grandma could not contain herself.

"As if I believe that little patch of hair on top of his head needs to be trimmed every Saturday for the rest of his life and it takes five hours to do it! I know damn well he's on his merry way to the bar."

"Well, why don't you just say something to him, Gram?"

"Well the truth of the matter is this, if it gets him out of my hair for the afternoon, I am all for it. If he didn't lie, he would be moping around here all afternoon looking for a way to pick a fight with me and go stomping off to the bar anyway," Grandma said.

I could see this made a certain sense and let it be at that.

Once in awhile, Grandma would give in and go down for a few drinks herself. There weren't a lot of places to go in Kingston other than the beach. It was only a matter of choosing which bar— definitely not the ideal town for an alcoholic to live in, especially Grandpa. He didn't drive, but their apartment was nestled between two of the local taverns.

Grandpa made good money but often had trouble paying his

bills, which were relatively few. He rarely paid the phone or electricity until the disconnect notice arrived. If the notice was stashed
away, it would sometimes be too late and the lights and phone
would be cut off. Grandma would get angry but it never made
any difference. He wouldn't hear of Grandma taking over the bill
paying. He would dole her out money as he saw fit, five bucks
here, five bucks there, often just enough to do the laundry at the
Coin Mart.

Sometimes Grandma would do the laundry by hand, like she
did in the old days. It was a lot of work but it allowed her a few
extra bucks to take us out for an ice cream or hot chocolate. It was
frustrating for Grandma. She rarely even got to go to the grocery
store; it was too far to go without a car. She would rely on whatever food Grandpa brought home. There were rarely more than
two grocery bags full at one given time, as that was all he could
manage. But he would walk in proud, his arms seemingly over-
flowing with food, and I couldn't understand why Grandma wasn't
thrilled.

It became clear that something had to change, and it wasn't
going to be Grandpa. Grandma began to realize that the security
Grandpa had to offer wasn't enough. She started building up the
courage to leave. She said she just couldn't stand to see Grandpa
"piss his life away" any longer, and she now had Amethest to
think about. She owed it to Patty. She had nothing, but she would
walk alone if need be, with Amethest's little hand in hers giving
her new purpose.

I don't remember when it was that Amethest stopped calling
her "Grandma" and started calling her "Mommy," but I imagine
that day was filled with both joy and sorrow for her.

Amethest was a mirror image of Patty. She had the same large
brown eyes and a head so full of hair you could lose small objects
in it.

Grandma would spend an hour putting Amethest's hair into
ringlets with soft rags she could sleep on comfortably; and

Amethest would look like a little doll the next day running through the house, her little black ringlets bouncing from room to room.

When Amethest began to cry and pull at her skin, Grandma discovered enormous boils breaking out in several different areas on her body. The doctor was unable to tell what was causing these sores to develop, so together Grandma and the doctors began to search for clues as to what was causing her illness.

"Until we find the cause, that is if we do, you're going to have to live with it the best you can. Dress the wounds, keep them clean so they don't become infected, and use hot rags to bring the boils to the surface to relieve the pressure and pain," the doctor said.

Long, nightmarish nights for Amethest and Grandma followed. They would finally get the boils to heal only to have them mysteriously reappear, and the whole process would begin again. Grandma read everything she could get her hands on, and continued to take Amethest through a round of doctors that offered as little as the first had. Grandma began a process of elimination, thinking perhaps a food or something around the house was causing Amethest to have this violent reaction. Then she found an article in a magazine about people who are hypersensitive to detergents and chemicals and even dyes in clothing. She figured anything was worth a try, and slowly, Amethest began to improve, but Grandma still feared she might need further medical care that they couldn't afford in the United States.

The mounting medical bills weren't the only thing worrying Grandma. Her own health was beginning to suffer. She realized that in order to afford medical care, she and Amethest would have to return to Canada, where medical expenses were funded by the government.

Patty's death had been so sudden, so unexpected, she feared someone would challenge her authority in regard to being Amethest's guardian. She had no legal papers giving her custody. My mother had spoken to Grandma, telling her that she would raise Amethest as her own, with J.J. and me. To Mom it seemed natural, and she would have gladly taken the responsibility, but Grandma already feared for J.J. and me, knowing the instability and uncertainty of our future with Jason.

Grandma explained her fears to Grandpa and he reassured her that he would stand by them and help as much as he possibly could. They began to plan for Grandma to take Amethest to Canada, unannounced to the rest of the family, and hoped like hell it would all work out.

CHAPTER TWENTY~ONE

Chaos

Ron *was five years younger than Silversong. They once took a train* trip with their mother when Ron was just a baby. Anne swept him up in his blanket and into her arms as she began rocking him, hoping to quiet his cries. As his high-pitched shrills grew louder, Anne kept rocking, more and more vigorously.

This went on for some time with no improvement, until Anne opened the flap of Ron's baby blanket and found his feet staring straight up at her. She was holding him upside down.

They had a good laugh over that one.

Generally, Ron was pretty quiet. As a child, he always played as if it were real life, not play. When he drove his toy trucks they became real. When one of them would get stuck, he never cheated and pulled them out like most kids would, he'd go off and find just the right size scrap of wood and jack it under the tires, rocking the truck patiently back and forth until it was free.

Unlike the rest of the Lawsens, he wasn't a problem solver. It was as if he'd been born knowing "things happen." He never seemed to get sucked into heated family debates like the rest of the family.

As the children grew older, Silversong's life was in such confusion that she never really knew what Ron had gone through, but they had many, many long talks over the years, always about the spirit.

Being Indian, they knew and understood on a different level, and lived in a world apart from non-Indians. She knew Ron's spirit and he knew hers.

When Ron had trouble with his relationship with Monica, he came and lived in Seattle with Silversong. Jason was rarely at home. He taught her a lot about roots and herbs and how they worked. He talked about soul travel and getting in touch with other realms that he felt were available to them.

It upset her.

"For God's sake, Ron! I can't deal with the present, let alone any other realm!"

"One of these days Silversong, I'm really gonna blow your mind."

They also spent a lot of time talking about art. Ron knew nothing about painting, but he knew how he felt, what he saw, and what it said to him. Silversong treasured that about Ron. He never hesitated to express himself, especially when he didn't like something.

"You need to show more dimensions in your paintings. Look, you have a background and an object. There is way, way more . . . and when you can paint *that*, you'll have a painting."

Silversong was perfectly happy with her two-dimensional world.

"Three-dimensional art means sculptures," she told him.

"Don't believe everything you read," he said. "Just because they say that's what a painting is, doesn't mean it's so. You're thinking 'mainstream' again. I thought you wanted to paint like an Indian? At least, that's what you told me. Remember, Sis? No art degrees for you—how did you put it? Eurocentric Certification?"

He laughed, long and low.

Regardless of their differing opinions, Ron and Silversong agreed that artists were way ahead of scientists when it came to the needs of the spirit.

Sometimes when Ron talked, Silversong would sense a futility as he'd sit back and look around the room, as if he saw the span of humanity from beginning to end.

"You just don't get it," he said, "but if anyone can, you will."

He always left her feeling that he still had confidence in her, no matter how short-sighted she was.

When Ron lived with Silversong, they covered every newspaper and television report that aired concerning John Trudell, Dennis Banks, Leonard Peltier, Dino Butler, Russell Means; all those who were fighting for freedom, honoring the old ways, and trying to breathe a new spirit back into a tired people.

They honored all the young Indians who, like them, questioned authority. They knew the truth about the genocide and extermination perpetrated against the Tribes. This was one area in which Ron and Silversong agreed. Every skirmish, every confrontation, and every warrior was purposefully and intently held up in prayer and in spirit.

Ron would have gone down and joined the brothers, except for one reason—he was sure Silversong would go too.

"You've got kids to raise, and that's your first and foremost duty."

"But it's the children's world we're fighting for," she would argue.

They went to rallies and were outspoken wherever there was an ear. They supported Nisqually fishing rights, and at Fort Lawton, Washington, the protests often got violent.

Leonard Peltier, then well recognized in the Indian community, was jailed. Jane Fonda and Marlon Brando, along with other celebrities, stood in truth and made an effort to shed some light on the situation for the American public.

Silversong had a lot of hope. She donated paintings to the Indian education center in her community, and saw powwows resurge and take shape once again. She worked with Billy Mills, who was campaigning for gyms to be built on reservations.

Indian people did not have an equivalent of "God," the way the black community did. Martin Luther King had a vehicle; he was a minister and held the key to the Guilt of America. With free access to communicate in scripture, upon scripture, he had a place to stand.

No one understood "Great Spirit." Their ceremonies were demons that made America uneasy. Silversong thought that blacks had it better than Indians because they had been worth something as slaves, they had value, whereas an Indian wasn't "worth a red cent," whatever that's supposed to mean.

One time Ron eyebrowed her real long.

"Alcatraz, that's not too far."

The occupation of Alcatraz was a major move. They seriously considered going, but Ron said it was probably more helpful to stay where they were, as the presence of more people might become a burden.

They decided they would support the effort in spirit. Alcatraz was an important social comment.

"All us Indians on Alcatraz," Ron laughed.

It really seemed like the People were in their truth, and going in the right direction, but then it became terribly *real* again—people were dying.

Neutralize the Indian leaders. You could stand on the sidelines and see it happen one by one, as America locked up their worst fears.

John Trudell's family was murdered in an arson fire. There was no freedom, no justice, no truth. It was also February, the anniversary month of Patty's death.

Between the injustice in the outer world and the chaos in Silversong's inner world—alcohol, physical abuse, a pending divorce, and the fire that had taken her sister—she couldn't go any farther. She couldn't see, feel, or think. She was close to no longer being able to function at all. Everything had become vacant, void, and lifeless. She felt as stripped and colorless as the naked winter trees.

Loree was trying to figure out what was happening to her family. The were all wrapped up in this space and time and they were all a mess, each in his or her own way.

Silversong and Pete were seeing each other regularly. Loree couldn't help but resent both of them, and she was happiest when she was in Kingston.

Anne was trying to figure out what was going on in the family.

She thought Silversong was acting strangely, and she was worried. Anne and Loree talked as usual, and Loree confided in her about Silversong and Pete, and how scared she was about what would happen if Jason came home and found out.

Pete was a regular visitor at the house and wanted Loree to be comfortable. He attempted to be her friend and they even went out for pizza together. It went well, but Loree was having a hard time understanding what was going on.

Something clicked inside of Loree. She knew Pete was trying his best, but she was so unhappy there was no way she was going to let Pete and her mother forget about keeping this information from her.

That particular Friday after dinner, J.J. and Loree met Anne at the ferry, and headed to Kingston for the weekend. Anne wasn't happy about the events taking place, either. Loree thought that she might be afraid of what could happen now that Silversong was seeing Pete.

The following Saturday night, Pete and Silversong took the ferry over to Kingston, unannounced.

Anne and Terry were not happy to see them together at all. Everything was becoming very intense. The tension was building, becoming threatening.

Silversong had so sheltered her mother and stepfather from the realities of her marriage—Jason's infidelities and abuse—that they thought *she* was the bad guy. Worse, they thought she was going crazy.

Silversong was not apologetic, nor would she defend herself or explain her actions. She felt no one ever heard her anyway, so why should she keep trying? Her actions began to appear even more bizarre because of her unwillingness to express her feelings. She was paralyzed and desperate.

Terry came up the stairs and gave Anne the news: Pete and Silversong were down at the tavern together.

"Come on down, we need to talk."

"How dare she flaunt this in town in front of God and everyone? She must be crazy!" Anne said.

Terry was mad too, and he told Anne to hurry up, because Silversong was "acting strange and dressed like some kind of freak." Maybe they could get her to come up to the house and figure out what was going on. They headed down to the bar, where Silversong and Pete were waiting. Loree stayed and baby-sat the kids, J.J. and Amethest, who were already sleeping when they left.

Loree loved her grandpa's apartment. It was like living on top of a cloud. Everything was cream-colored and tan. The apartment was on the second floor above a small store, and to get to his suite, you had to walk up a steep flight of stairs. The stairs were paneled in a dark wood that absorbed the light and it looked more like the entrance to a dungeon. It was always a surprise to open the door and see all the lightness and beauty.

One could see the ferry approach the dock from the living room windows, and also the marina from the balcony out back. It always smelled salty in Kingston, like the sea.

The adults had been gone for about an hour or so when Loree heard her grandma coming up the stairs. When Anne entered the living room where Loree was watching TV, she told her Pete and her mom would be coming up any minute.

Anne was unable to sit still; she walked back and forth, gathering her thoughts. She told Loree she was too upset to sit there at the bar with them any longer and came home without them. Terry, of course, had stayed to have "one more."

Loree felt panic set in. She thought her grandma was trying to prepare her—something was very wrong with her mother. Even the way Silversong dressed was worrying Anne—she wore bell bottoms that hung off her hips and were decorated with a native design. Her was hair long and straight ... she wore *feathers and beads* tonight. This was symbolic, she wore her regalia, her protection.

The phone rang and Loree answered it. Jason was on the other end. It had been a long time since she talked to him. He said her name in that southern drawl of his.

"Hi, Loree baby, where's your mom? What's going on? . . . Something's wrong, isn't it? Tell me, Loree."

She could hear her heart beating in her ears. She was so scared, she couldn't talk. She looked at her grandma.

"Find out where he is; if he's close by, don't tell him anything," Anne whispered to Loree, while she held her hand over the phone.

Jason said he would be flying home from New York and it would take him five or six hours to arrive. He would see them real soon, he said, and then he asked if Silversong and Pete were in Kingston, or at the house in north Seattle.

She told him they were in Kingston. She thought he must have already found out they were seeing each other. Maybe he had already talked about this with her mom? She hung up the phone.

Anne and Loree were grateful that he was still in New York. Now there would be time to talk to Silversong and see what she had planned. They had much to be grateful for. He sounded so calm on the phone, it was reassuring.

About a half hour after she got off the phone with Jason, Silversong, Pete, and Terry came back from the tavern. They sat in the kitchen, Silversong on Pete's lap. Terry made his way down the hall to the bathroom muttering, "Jesus Christ."

The conversation in the kitchen was sarcastic and tense. Silversong and Pete wanted to take J.J. and Loree home. Anne was stalling.

"Let them stay until Sunday, like we planned." Anne knew it was only a matter of hours before Jason arrived home and there was a bad scene.

Loree heard footsteps coming up the stairs, and there was a knock on the door. She ran to answer it, opened the door, and there stood Jason, smiling at her.

"Hi baby, Daddy's home," he said as he bent over and picked her up. Her heart was beating in her ears again. He had told her he was in New York. He had lied. He had actually been at the ferry dock in Edmonds when he called.

As they entered the kitchen, Jason was still smiling. He set her down. Silversong was still seated on Pete's lap. As he approached them, he appeared calm, and again Loree felt reassured. Anne and Terry looked horrified. They weren't expecting Jason either.

At first, Silversong seemed sure of herself, not in the mood to put up with any more than she already had. Deciding to divorce Jason was probably one of the healthiest choices she had made in years, even if no one else seemed to think so.

God only knows what poor Pete thought at that moment. There was only one way out of the apartment.

Jason extended his hand for Pete to shake.

"Hey, buddy! How you doing?" he said, still smiling.

They shook hands, and then Jason grabbed Pete, dragged him through the hall, pausing to punch him a few times, and threw him down the long flight of stairs that led outside. The glass window at the bottom of the stairs shattered as Pete's body hit it with full force, and Jason was at the bottom of the stairs soon enough to smash him into the jagged pieces remaining in the window frame.

Silversong was screaming. She wanted to leave, but Jason wouldn't allow her to take J.J. or Loree.

"Oh, Jesus," Terry said.

Anne was trying to get a handle on the situation, still taken aback by the swiftness of Jason's actions. She tried to calm Silversong down.

"If you would only settle down and try to appease Jason, and cooperate." But Silversong had been doing that for almost thirty years now. She was through cooperating with anyone.

That's when she stepped into another dimension—they were all the enemy, now more then ever.

The police didn't care, the Wheelers didn't care, and her own family didn't care. "Well, fuck them all, if they think I am crazy for not wanting to stay in this marriage then *I want to be crazy!*"

She was not going to stay with Jason. He was not going to let her go.

For the first time, Anne and Terry saw him grab Silversong by her hair and drag her through the house, slapping her. He got a punch in; she fought back like an animal.

"For God's sake, Jason, stop!" Anne and Terry took turns screaming.

Anne threw her body in between them as Jason beat Silversong, demanding him to stop.

Jason threw Anne against a wall and told her that she had better stay out of it, or she would be next. They all knew it was no empty threat; he meant every word he spoke. Silversong screamed at everyone.

"You think *I'm* nuts? Look at him! Look at what he's doing to me!"

She looked at Loree, searching for something. She was bleeding but didn't seem to notice.

"They're right, Loree, because if I'm not crazy it means they are all crazy, and I don't want to be like them. I want to be crazy. I'm insane. They're right, Loree, what they've been telling you. I'm the dangerous one, the one who should be taken away . . . I'm the crazy one . . . Loree?" She spoke in a pleading question.

And Jason began beating her again.

Terry was crying. He could barely speak but he kept trying to stop the violence anyway. Anne tried too, but it was so out of control and ugly. They were playing by Jason's rules again and nobody else was going to win.

It was after one in the morning when Anne took Amethest, J.J., and Loree into the back bedroom. She put all the furniture she could move in front of the door. It was the only thing she could do to protect them. Silversong was on her own tonight, except for Terry's pleading.

"Oh, for God's sake, Jason, please stop. . . ."

Loree didn't want to be in there. She knew what was happening outside that room. She sat and listened to her mother scream. It went on all night long, until sunrise.

It was decided, sometime during the night, that her mom should be institutionalized.

Silversong and Jason left on the first morning ferry.

When Loree walked out of the bedroom in the morning the house was silent. It was like a death had taken place. She watched as Anne picked up the pieces of the broken furniture and glass that encompassed the murder scene. The only thing missing was the body. It was on its way to the University of Washington mental ward.

Loree remembered what Silversong had said to her the night before.

"I wish you were dead like your Aunt Patty. You'd be safe and wouldn't have to deal with all this shit."

Loree was hopeful that wherever Aunt Patty was, it was better than this.

J.J. and Loree spent the week in Kingston with Anne, and then it came time to go back home. It was just J.J., Loree, and Jason now.

CHAPTER TWENTY~TWO

Nervous Breakthrough

I mourned for my mother. I had looked into her eyes the last night I saw her. She wasn't there. I wanted her back. I wanted her to be okay.

I heard the adults all talking, but nobody that I remember at least ever came right out and told me my mom was in the mental ward at the University of Washington.

It was such a difficult time for everyone, I don't think anyone knew how to deal with it. My stepfather, however, seemed quite pleased with himself and the events that had taken place. Mom was in the nut house, and he was in full control.

My mother was gone for three months. I was allowed to see her in the hospital only once. I wondered why she didn't want to see me or J.J. Didn't she miss us? Or were we just two more people she was trying to get away from?

I didn't realize then that my stepfather was the one keeping us away from her. There are a lot of things I didn't learn until many years later.

During this time, my stepfather was trying to have my mother officially declared insane and institutionalized for life, or for as many years as possible. This would guarantee that she would not be granted custody of J.J. or me, and he would never have to give her a penny in support or compensation of any kind—the perfect plan. He would always be in control, always the winner.

No one told me anything directly or prepared me for the visit

273

to see my mother in the hospital. I remember the drive very well. It was already dark out. We got to stay up late on a school night. My stepfather laughed and joked with me. He thought it was funny that I was going to get to see all the weirdoes, and see what the inside of a nut house looked like. He had always said Mom was crazy and belonged in a mental ward. Now that she was there, he couldn't help but enjoy the show, nor could he contain his satisfaction at seeing his prophecy come true.

I walked in the front door excited to see my mother; it had been a long time since that last night we were all together in Kingston. There were times I had wondered if she had died and they didn't want to tell me, or that she was dying more slowly, perhaps from a disease, and that's why I couldn't see her. Nobody would talk to me about her, but I felt it would all be okay somehow, if I could just see her for a little while. Maybe we would take her home?

We stepped off the elevator, and onto the seventh floor. Everyone knew what Seven North was—the mental ward. We walked toward the visiting area, and as I walked I looked for my mother. Funny, I thought as I looked around Seven North, that's the same as our street address . . . Seventh Avenue North, Seattle.

As far as I was concerned, we all lived in a nut house.

I didn't see her anywhere. I scanned the room again, waiting. There were several people, some visiting in small groups, some reading. They didn't look crazy to me, just very sad. And so was I.

Maybe I will end up in the mental ward like my mother someday. I better be good. I better be careful. I better not upset anyone. I better not act sad.

"Here she comes, over there," Jason said.

I turned and saw a woman moving toward us in slow motion. She was very thin and her black hair hung down partially covering her eyes. She lifted her head and looked at us, but her eyes never focused. It was as if she were looking through my body at the painting on the wall behind me, but it was too far away, and she couldn't understand what she was looking at.

Suddenly I became unnerved. I felt afraid of her.

Death had been frightening me since Aunt Patty had walked on in the fire. I had nightmares about it. The family was never allowed to see her body because it was too horrifying.

"Burned beyond recognition," they said—I could only imagine what that meant.

Sometimes I would close my eyes at night in the bed I had shared with Aunt Patty before she died, when Amethest was a baby.

Suddenly I would see a monster coming at me, something so terrifying, I would cry and run down the stairs and turn on the lights in my bedroom.

I had come to hate my upstairs bedroom. It wasn't beautiful or special anymore, it was just another frightening room.

I would pray. I knew Aunt Patty loved me and for a minute I would see her beautiful face telling me not to be scared, and that she was sorry she had left me alone, but it only lasted a minute, and I would begin to imagine something coming toward me again.

I looked into my mother's eyes, and saw the living dead.

"Oh God, please let me wake up. Please let my mother see me standing here."

Silversong shifted her gaze upward and looked at Jason.

"I hate you."

That's all she said, nothing else.

We walked her back to her bed because it was time for more Thorazine. The nurse brought it in, and Mom took the pills and laid down on the bed, her hands crossed on her chest, eyes staring at the stars through the ceiling of her room.

We left and drove home. It was a long drive and I knew it was going to be a long time before my mom would come back home, if she ever did.

It was the ending of the *old*, painfully accentuated by the blows Jason had inflicted upon Silversong's body. And the pain inflicted upon her mind when Patty died. The *new* would come slowly and would not be without birthing pains. A real person was about to be born, no longer trapped by her own mental reservations. It would be a long labor.

Silversong started asking what the pills were and she heard names like Cogentin and Thorazine. She was living in a world of shadows, recognizing only that from time to time, there was movement around her, and that there were light and dark times also. She didn't know who she was, only who she thought she might be.

As she struggled to think it through, she came to the conclusion that she was a woman, possibly a spirit, and maybe even a ghost or someone's dream. All she knew was that something terrible had happened, that she had experienced some kind of trauma, and that she was now in the hospital.

She tried to figure out why she was there. Was it because she didn't know who she was? Some type of amnesia that had left her feeling so mixed up? She thought her name was Silversong, but she wasn't sure. All she knew was that she had experienced something awful, something she didn't have words for. She knew she had experienced an indescribable trauma and was now being punished for it.

The hospital worker who helped her dress had called her "Barbara." When she got out of bed alone for the first time and felt her way to the bathroom, she noticed upon returning that the name posted on the foot of the bed was Barbara Burnie.

Oh, that's who I am, she thought, and fell promptly asleep mouthing "Burnie . . . Burnie . . . ." The word transformed as she slept, "Burnie . . . burn . . . fire . . . " and she woke up screaming.

They forced more pills into her mouth and put her in a padded room that was soundproof. The room was all one color; there was no reference point, nothing even remotely familiar to comfort her.

The following morning, she was returned to her original room. She told them her name was not Barbara Burnie and they apologized and changed the name on the bed.

"My sister burned to death in a fire, you know...it is true, isn't it?"

Silversong wasn't sure of anything. Maybe she had just gone crazy and *thought* Patty died. That was a reassuring thought. It felt good, and she hung onto it until she noticed Patty's housecoat lying on the bed near the window. She was sure it was the one she bought her the previous Christmas. Silversong put on the housecoat and reached her hands deep into the soft pockets. She felt something and pulled it out. It was a tea bag and it made her laugh. "Of course, Patty always carried tea bags in her pockets. She's probably here right now, come to help me get well," Silversong mused.

Suddenly, another patient entered the room and started screaming at her.

"How dare you?! Give me that housecoat!"

She began clawing at Silversong and a nurse rushed to her aid.

"You mustn't take other people's things, Silversong. We wouldn't want to go back to the holding room, would we?"

"No, we wouldn't," she said.

Loree felt sick.

She thought that she might throw up, so she went downstairs and slept with J.J. She woke up again feeling even worse. The sun was just beginning to rise. She walked to her parents' bedroom door and opened it.

"Dad, I feel sick."

She was holding her stomach, sweating and shivering at the same time, as another wave of nausea swept over her.

"Come lay down here, and try to get to sleep," Jason said, still half asleep himself.

"If you need anything wake me up."

She felt safe. If I get sicker, he'll take care of me, she thought. There was no one else to turn to.

Then the nightmare returned.

The monster looks like my father. His face is red, he sounds strange ... he's talking ... he's breathing funny ... now he can't talk.

What is he doing?! Oh God, what am I going to do?! I am scared again, no one is home, and I want him to stop this. This is wrong! How can he be doing this to me? He's my father.

No, Loree, he's your stepfather.

But he raised me since I was three years old. He's the only father I've ever known....

I've never seen a penis before. I am frozen. He's hurting me, and I've got to do something.

If I do something, he might hurt me more. What if he gets mad at me, remember what he did to Mom? I'm leaving now. I'm going away somewhere and there's nobody else there ... not even me. Just a grey sky outside the window over the bed. There is nothing but tiny birds flying away from their regular nests built in the rafters above the house. My spirit went with them.

I awoke from my nightmare and immediately began forgetting the details, shaking them from my consciousness. I saw the sky out the bedroom window, it was still grey. The neighborhood was still asleep.

I quietly got up and went into J.J.'s room and laid back down, J.J.'s little body in front of me, protecting me. I had to go to the bathroom, but I laid there for a long time, not wanting to move ... something else might happen. I felt safe with J.J.

I walked to the bathroom slowly, so as not to make the wood floor creak, trying to remember where all the loose boards were. I looked to my right; his bedroom door was still closed. I turned the doorknob to the bathroom quietly while I looked at the impression my mother's teeth left in the door when Jason slammed her face into it a few months before.

I opened the door, closed it again quietly, and locked it. Everything is fine. I'm okay. But then I saw my face in the bathroom mirror. I stared at myself for a long time, holding my face and

*crying. I realized it wasn't a nightmare; it was real, and I prom-
ised myself I would remember forever.*

*How could he do this to me? He was the only father I ever
knew.*

I hated him. I really hated him.

*Okay, get a grip, I told myself. There's a little blood and I'm
swollen but I'll live. I haven't had a period yet and you can only
get pregnant if you've had your period . . . yeah, that's right, okay,
fine. I'm not pregnant. Yes, that's better. Just keep telling yourself
you're okay and you're alive. Act like everything's okay and it'll
go away. . . .*

*If I sleep with J.J., he won't bother me, he wouldn't come in
here with J.J. and all, right? He'll forget too. Only a few more
days and I'll get to go to Kingston. If I can just see my grandma,
I know it'll be all right. If I can just see Grandma. . . .*

*Maybe I'll go live with Grandma. Grandma said we were
strong, and survivors, we Lawsen women. I have a strong backbone. Yes Grandma, I'm a Lawsen woman. I'll live. We forget all
the other bad times don't we? We always forget, we'll forget this
too. Jason always makes it easy to forget.*

My Great White Father. . . .

*Jason had always been a master manipulator. He knew all
my mother's weaknesses. She was a squaw, a woman, and totally
worthless. His mission was to convince her of this, and show her
that he would always win. He had begun to develop the control he
held over my mother years before this. We all watched as it escalated beyond the brink of insanity.*

Jason grew frustrated. His attempts to persuade the doctors in
charge of Silversong's care to administer shock treatments failed.
Nevertheless, he proceeded as planned with the commitment procedure. It all looked fairly uncomplicated, and if Silversong's record
counted for anything, Jason was confident that she would be found
incapable of caring for herself or her children.

He chuckled thinking about the day he had Silversong admitted to the psychiatric ward. The ride over to the hospital had been hell. Silversong had actually jumped out of the car while it was moving. The vehicle wasn't traveling very fast at the time, but she still got pretty scraped up. It took a police officer thirty minutes to persuade Silversong to come out from the middle of the highway. Aurora Avenue was busy that afternoon, but it didn't seem to faze Silversong. She walked alone in her mind down the middle of the thin yellow strips that divided the highway.

At the hospital, when they undressed Silversong, they found to their amazement that she had completely wrapped herself, from armpits to thighs, in thick Silversong duct tape.

Jason was brutal . . . no one knew what I'd been through . . . it may have seemed stupid or in fact downright crazy to the people who saw how I taped myself up. No one understood I was protecting myself, and I guess I decided it wasn't worth explaining . . . or telling perfect strangers how he used to hurt me. When they asked me what was wrong with me, I told them I was injured . . . that was all I was able to say . . . because all I did was cry. When your injuries are all on the inside they call it a nervous breakdown.

"Did you know about this?" one of the interns asked Jason.

"No, but it doesn't surprise me. I told you she was nuts," Jason said, his lips curled in amusement.

Silversong sat silently and stared at the blank wall in front of her.

Loree didn't remember much over the next few months. Bits and pieces floated around in her memory.

"No one will believe you. They'll say you're crazy like your mother. You'll never go to Kingston again. Be a good girl. You're just sick, honey. I'll take J.J. away and you'll never see him again, and it'll be all your fault." Jason recited these words over and over until Loree truly believed them.

To Loree, it seemed an eternity before she was allowed to return to Kingston. By then, she was so scared that she didn't know what to do or say, but broached the subject with her grandma as best she could.

"I'm unhappy, Grandma, I'm scared . . . I want to come live with you. But I don't want Jason to know, and I want J.J. to come with us."

She waited for Anne's reply.

Gently, Anne rocked her as they sat with the salty wind blowing in their faces, watching Amethest play in the sand. Jason had kept J.J. at home with him, and Loree knew what that meant: "If you ever want to see your brother again, you'd better not tell."

"Oh, honey, how I wish Grandma could make your life all better. I know how hard this must be on you. But we'll get through it, Lor, we'll make it." Grandma said, looking her straight in the eye, as if to answer the question she had not yet asked . . . "Will we, Grandma, will we really?"

That afternoon, Anne told Loree that she and Amethest were going to be leaving where they were living in Kingston and returning to Canada soon. There was no other choice. She said Loree could go with them, but they both knew Jason would never allow J.J. to go.

She never told her grandmother what had happened.

She never told anyone.

Silversong was beginning to feel much better. In her private therapy sessions she told her doctor that she was ready to face the world again. She had found a new lawyer to handle the divorce, and her doctor was confident that with time she would be perfectly fine, so she was totally unprepared for what she heard the following day.

Her therapist entered her room, sweating with outrage. Holding her arms, eyes moist, he told her that they had a problem.

"Your husband wants you committed to a state mental institution. There will be a sanity hearing. He even had the nerve to suggest shock treatments and possibly a lobotomy. Your husband talked as if he were taming a wild horse.

"I'm so sorry, Silversong, but there's not a damn thing I can do about this. I can't spare you the process. You'll be taken to Harborview for twenty-four hours before the hearing. It's standard process—no drugs. I don't know how you're expected to appear normal after pulling you off medication suddenly but, there's no option."

Great. They're sentencing me to death. Jason is laying out all his cards and he won't stop at anything. How the hell am I going to pull this off?

Twenty-four hours before her sanity hearing, Silversong was taken from her hospital room and held in the county jail. As required by law, all medications were abruptly withdrawn. After two months of a diet consisting of little more than Thorazine, Lithium, and Valium, Silversong was going cold turkey. She knew at that moment that she was fighting for her life, her future, and what was left of her dreams.

The large steel cage slammed shut and her world came crashing down around her. She was told nothing about the hearing, and as her body began withdrawing from the drugs she'd been given, a frightening reality was awakened.

As the drugs left her body, the first memory that came was that of Pat. "My little sister's dead."

Then she doubted herself . . . she couldn't really be sure. Maybe she had made it all up? Maybe she had just gone crazy and dreamed that Patty died?

"No . . . no . . . no," Silversong cried. But it was all too true.

And Jason wouldn't stop until he'd taken everything from her, even her mind.

Realizing that she only had twenty-four hours before the hearing, she struggled to pull herself together. Surrounded by others waiting for their hearings, she listened to the woman in the cell next to her describe how she was going to murder Silversong while she slept.

Oh my God, Silversong thought, these people are really crazy.

The thought of being institutionalized became frighteningly real to her. She knew that she would surely lose her mind if she was sent to live among people whom she feared.

Closing her eyes, Silversong tried to sleep but the sounds, the awful sounds coming from the other cells, were too disturbing. Seeing the sky slowly fade to a light shade of blue at the horizon, she stared out the barred window of her cell.

My cell was small, and only thin steel bars separated me from a raving woman in the cell next to me. Her wrists were bandaged, stained red with her blood. She was a heroine addict who had attempted suicide. She said if she killed us both it would be better for us, and I knew she meant it and it was terrifying. All night long she ranted and raged on insanely through the night.

There was a full moon that night, it was the only light in the cell. It shone so brilliantly, casting lines, shadows from the bars, slicing across her face. I had my reference point . . . all night long the moon was there shining down in my darkest night. I had to stay awake, I was scared to sleep, scared of this woman next to me and the strange sounds coming from the other cells . . . and the strange sound of steel doors echoing through the dark hallways. I'll be okay . . . I've got to be okay . . . please let me be okay . . . I chanted my prayer until sunrise.

It was ten o'clock in the morning when Silversong was led from her cell through a maze of bright fluorescent lights to the dark wooden door that opened to the large hearing room. It was packed to capacity—Jason had given his permission for a group of twenty students to observe the commitment procedure.

As Silversong entered the room, the crowd grew silent as she was escorted before a panel of five psychiatrists and five psychologists for her sanity hearing. No one spoke, but one doctor kept tapping his pencil on the desk in front of him as she approached.

The constant tapping echoed through the room and increased the tension that filled the air. Scanning the room lined with strangers, it took a moment for Silversong to locate Jason, who was seated and poised for the show to begin.

Finally, the man with the pencil spoke.

"Do you hear voices, Mrs. Lowe?"

"Yes, I hear voices, don't you?" she replied.

"Do you know where you were born?" he inquired.

The room quietly awaited her reply. Silversong flipped her long black hair from her eyes and looked directly at the panel, making eye contact with each one as she spoke.

"You're damn right I do. My name is Silversong, I was born in the Indian community of Marlboro, Alberta, in 1944. I was in a flood two years ago, trapped on the roof with my two children, and we almost lost our lives. My baby sister Pat burned to death on my birthday, and that son-of-a-bitch right there—" Silversong pointed at Jason, "has been beating the shit out of me since the day we were married."

The crowd stirred and stared momentarily at Jason, who shifted uncomfortably in his seat. He was no longer wearing the bemused and arrogant grin on his freshly shaven face. It was apparent that the proceedings so far were failing to meet his expectations.

When Silversong finished speaking, the doctors spoke in hushed tones among themselves.

"Mrs. Lowe, I would first like to apologize to you for having to go through these procedures this morning. It is obvious to both my colleagues and myself that you are of sound mind and body. The fact that you have withstood such tragedy and misfortune in the last several years is to your credit. You are obviously coping to the best of your ability, considering the amount of stress you've been subjected to. It is our belief that what you've experienced was an acute attack of anxiety, and a well-deserved one at that. All you need, young lady, is a good rest."

And with that, he handed Silversong a document confirming her sanity.

Silversong rose to her feet, unsteadily at first, and felt her backbone turn to steel. She walked directly to where Jason sat in shock. Shaking the paper she'd been given in his face, Silversong looked down at him.

"I have a piece of paper proving my sanity...now it's your turn."

CHAPTER TWENTY~THREE
I'm Alive

*S*omething inside of me had finally clicked back into place. I don't know where or how it happens, but you're all you've really got. And whatever anyone else says is theirs, is not yours. From this moment on, I became very quiet and intent. When I was given pills, I didn't fuss. I just pretended to take them and then spit them out. Within one week, the cold hard reality of my life had returned. I was no longer drugged, but I did continue to take the sleeping pills they brought me at night.

I suffered shaking, nausea, weakness, dizziness, shortness of breath, and panic attacks, along with all kinds of sensations. But I decided it was not good to sedate my feelings any longer, and if I ever wanted to find out what was really wrong with me I knew I had to be free from the mind-altering, chemically induced haze I'd walked through. I never realized that I was kicking drugs, I thought it was me, just all me, and I would be omitting the truth if I said I didn't think of suicide.

I took the elevator up to the top floor of the building. I wasn't locked up anymore and so I had been free to roam. I went and stood at an open window. When a janitor appeared and said "What are you doing here?" I just looked at him. "I got lost," I said, and then looked back out the window for a long moment before going back to my room.

I knew I needed to function ... I knew I was in trouble,

waiting to shake some sense into myself. I thought back at the ridiculous manner I had chosen to protect myself and communicate. No, I said to myself, now I must get out of this marriage and find my own way, my own life. I wanted my children to have a life built on real love and caring ... whatever that was supposed to mean. I tried to figure it out.

One of the nurses said I was well enough to take one of the classes they were having. We were supposed to write our life history as we knew it and then share it with the group. Man, did I get excited, finally something that might shed some light on the patterns and implications of my life. I wrote and wrote and wrote, with the belief that perhaps the psychologist would be able to find my fatal flaw and I'd have someplace to start.

Baring my soul like never before, I handed in my life story to the doctor and began looking forward to the day we would begin. I waited patiently while the doctor discussed one life history after the other until finally the last one was read. I was choked. "What about mine?" I asked. "Oh, yeah, it got lost," he replied, rather annoyed. "My office got cleaned. It must have been thrown in the trash. Besides, this class hasn't shown any real potential ... it's not really that important."

Once again I had put so much into "it," painfully exorcising every demon I possessed, hoping for insight ... only to have my life thrown in the trash. Perhaps the Great Spirit is with me and has intervened? Perhaps I would have been spending so much time considering every word, and what was, that I wouldn't have been able to respond to the moment. And then I laughed. It was all in the garbage anyway, and now it's all behind me. I decided to concentrate on the future and what could be.

When Loree first overheard talk about her mother coming home, she was frightened—it was too good to be true. She tried not to get too happy about it, just in case it didn't happen. Jason was obviously unhappy and angry about it.

"She should be in a state institution. She's crazy and they're letting her out!"

Jason was accustomed to winning. Now, Silversong was finally mastering the game.

There were long talks: "You're mother's fragile. She's coming home but we have to be careful. No matter what, we mustn't upset her."

The threat hung heavy in the air. If Silversong gets upset, she'll go away again, and next time she may not come back.

The first day that Silversong was home from the hospital, Loree walked in from school and found her sleeping in her bedroom. At first, her mother barely spoke and was very tired. Loree wondered if they were still giving her a lot of medication. Yet even with the uncertain quality of her homecoming, she welcomed her presence, but she worried. What if she couldn't handle being back home?

A week passed and Jason was busy being Mr. Nice Guy again, but this time was different.

He had won many battles and Silversong bore the scars of defeat, yet the war she had fought within herself had ended in her favor. No one could take this victory from her. She had spent the past three months building a brick wall around herself. Although she appeared fragile, something had been transformed. She'd had a nervous *breakthrough*, and she told Jason to leave.

He said no, but she wasn't budging. A month went by, and Jason couldn't understand. He'd been so nice for weeks. For what? She's not acting normal, not responding. She's still crazy, that's it. Yeah, she's still a nut. She's always been into that strange Indian shit, he thought. He was confused. Silversong wasn't playing by his rules. They had a new game. For the first time in her life, Silversong knew the rules and they were hers.

When Jason protested, she stood firm and smiled at him, a smile for herself.

"Remember, Jason, I'm crazy."

This was actually the greatest thing that had ever happened to her. People don't tend to bother with a crazy person much. There's a certain odd respect that results. She had paid her dues; ten years married to Jason Lowe, and three months in the University of Washington psychiatric ward. Finally she could see the light at the end of a very long, dark tunnel. The light was emanating from within her spirit. And when Jason could no longer stand her light, he left.

Suddenly, Silversong was allowed to do all of the things that in the past had resulted in confrontations, arguments, disapproval, or unwanted advice.

"If I leave this house, she'll be sorry," Jason had said.

"But Dad, she *wants* you to leave, doesn't that mean anything?"

"I'm leaving when I'm ready to leave, when I decide it's time to leave! She never has, and never will, be able to make me do anything. No one can make me do anything."

He squinted his eyes and his lips curled around the words as he spoke.

"But Dad, what about child support? The judge said he can make you pay it," Loree said, proud that she had found something he would have to do.

"Baby, no one can make me pay it. I won't do it."

"Then they'll put you in jail."

Jason laughed.

"Then they put me in jail. I'll go to jail but I still won't pay. They still can't make me."

It was simple in Jason's mind. He would always win. It seemed as if that was the only thing he believed in. True to his word, he never gave her a cent.

All the years that Silversong had spent investing in the family's future meant nothing. Jason had been the one going to school, upgrading his education and getting his commercial pilot license. Silversong was only qualified to waitress.

Whenever Jason would call the house, Loree was very polite and reassuring.

"Oh yeah, Dad, I miss you, too. Can't wait to see you."

He was soon living with another woman and her five children.

He would make arrangements over the phone to meet Loree on Friday after school, and then to go on to his house to spend the weekend. When Friday rolled around, Loree was nowhere to be found. And Silversong would catch hell from Jason.

"Well, where is she? What have you told her? What have you done?"

Loree would wander in some time after six o'clock in the evening, confident that by that time Jason had left without her. She knew they all thought it was strange that she would do something like that, but she couldn't explain it to anyone. She didn't really understand it herself. Had she acted as if there were a problem when she spoke to him on the phone, she knew she would have had to face it, and she simply couldn't do that—not yet.

Finally, Jason got so mad that he and Silversong tricked Loree. They decided not to tell her he was coming to take J.J. and her for the weekend. Loree unsuspectingly walked directly in the front door to find him standing there. Her mother didn't understand. Silversong had always thought that the problems the family had were only between the *two* of them, and Loree never said any different. She was mad, but smiled; she was angry, but complied.

It was the last time she would smile or comply for a long, long time. Her mother could handle it; she was strong. Now it was her turn to rebel—it was *her* turn to be crazy.

Loree was twelve years old and she felt as if her parents had died. Their marriage had been dissolved. The people she had known no longer seemed to exist. It wasn't actually a bad thing, considering how much pain and violence surrounded the family when they were "alive." They still lived and breathed in the outside world, but the two people she knew as parents became null and void for her.

She was so relieved that Jason was actually gone that it became easy for her to pretend he had never existed.

Her mother was kind of empty-looking by the time it was all over. Loree didn't realize what strength it had taken for her to get through the dark descent. With Jason gone, it was as if they were all born again. In most ways, life was much better, but financially, it was a disaster. They were struggling, not only to heal, but to pay the bills.

No one was being beaten. No one was bloody.

They had become the walking wounded. Each one wore their unique battle scars; some were more evident than others.

J.J. was almost six years old, and he still had problems speaking clearly. It had been that way ever since he watched Jason slam Silversong's face into the bathroom door.

Silversong worked two jobs, went to school full-time, and tried to keep going. She established a steady routine, which seemed to help the family survive. Perhaps because she needed to escape in some way, Loree made the conscious decision to check out for awhile. The first time she did drugs she was thirteen years old.

It was a real discovery for her—a way to turn off the world and turn up the stereo that Ron had given to her. She found a way to kill the pain.

After Loree figured out that her mother was strong enough to handle Loree's anger, Loree unknowingly, or at least unconsciously, participated in a little payback. Have a nervous breakdown? I'll run away. Leave me alone with Jason? I'll do drugs. Play the victim? I'll run away again.

From the time she was twelve until she was fourteen years old, Loree put her mother through hell. She hurt her, screamed at her, and disobeyed her in every way possible. Finally, though, Loree realized that she could trust her again. No matter what Loree did, no matter how hard she pushed, Silversong pushed back, and showed Loree that she was strong enough for her to lean on. The two of them managed to salvage some good memories; however, one argument stood out in Loree's mind.

Loree had just returned home from being tricked into spending the weekend at Jason's. His girlfriend's sister was pregnant. It gave her an idea. Returning home, she confronted Silversong.

"Mother, I think I'd like to get pregnant."

She was leaning against the wall on the front porch, decked out in her army-issue green combat jacket with the words "Life Sucks" elaborately emblazoned on the back, and bell bottoms that hung three inches past her platform shoes.

Silversong played it very cool.

"Oh really? Well, that's news to me."

She raised her eyebrows and scanned her daughter's abdomen. Evidently, Loree's statement did not carry the shock value that she was looking for. So Loree decided to ask her a question that had genuinely been on her mind. The timing seemed right.

"Well, Mother, how would you feel if I started dating a black man?"

Silversong smiled instantly.

"Loree honey, all I want is for you to be happy. As far as I'm concerned, you can marry Smokey the Bear, as long as you're happy and he takes good care of you and your little cubs."

Loree was furious; she quickly responded.

"Oh, I didn't say I wanted to get married. I just want to get pregnant."

Loree felt a little satisfaction when Silversong was momentarily unable to respond. She saw her mother's eyes darting about in the air looking for answers.

"Well Lor, you know if you have a baby you probably won't be able to wear a bikini again, you know, stretch marks and all—"

Aha! Finally, she has hit on something Loree can get really pissed about.

"So that's it! That's why you hate me, I gave you stretch marks!"

She stomped toward her room.

Being a mother is sometimes a rotten job. It's kind of like being an artist's kid: No one really appreciates what you've been through. You always hear about those poor "starving artists" and what they go through in pursuit of their "art." I was a starving artist's kid, and that meant that even when things got ugly, I was surrounded by my mother's beautiful paintings, and was forced to participate in life in unusual ways.

A year after my parents divorced, I received my spirit name from a hereditary Cheyenne chief called Chief Antelope. I was thirteen years old.

We left early in the morning to travel to a powwow; the sun had not even begun to rise. I was tired as we traveled, yet excited because my mother had told me that today I would receive my Indian name.

I wore the shell earrings that Chief Antelope's wife, Princess White Lily, had given to me. I felt very special because Chief Antelope and White Lily had chosen to take me, alone, with them this day.

I sat quietly in the back seat listening to the chief's stories, which were always entertaining and full of wisdom. Chief Antelope was quick to smile and extend his hand in friendship, yet he always looked a little sad in some way, even as he smiled. He carried much in his heart; I was lucky to learn a little of it.

We arrived at the powwow—at last I would learn the name he had chosen for me. He thoroughly enjoyed my lack of patience as we walked toward the gathering. I tried to reason with the chief as only a pre-teen can.

"At the end of today's ceremonies I'll tell you, little grasshopper. I'm not ready yet." He smiled broadly, and chuckled.

"But Chief Antelope, who will I tell them I am when they ask me today?"

I wrapped my shawl around my shoulders. The sun had just begun to rise and it was still chilly in the dim morning light. The chief stopped, looked down at me, and smiled again.

"Yes, that would be a problem for you today. Let me look at you now."

He looked at me closely, said a prayer, then lifted his face from mine to the Great Spirit in the sky with his arms outstretched. There was still a star shining brightly as the sun was rising.

"You are Starlight," he said, looking down on me again. "In the old way your name is 'Light from the Morning Star.' I will call you Starlight."

And so it has been that my medicine has always had a strong spirit connection to light, and throughout my life that would be affirmed again and again.

I remember the story of Chief Antelope to this day.

Chief Antelope was the great grandson of the Cheyenne chief White Antelope. In 1864, the Reverend J. M. Chivington, colonel of the Colorado volunteers, reported to state headquarters that the Cheyenne had stolen government cattle. Every time cattle were missing it was said to be the work of Indians, whether there was sufficient proof or not. This was the unwritten law of the land. So as before, this was an accusation, not a fact.

The colonel proceeded to attack the unsuspecting Cheyenne, and the Cheyenne retaliated in the spirit in which they were attacked. Another war had begun.

It was autumn. Leaves were turning colors and falling to the ground. A chill already present in the wind, the People knew they would be at war with the white man through the winter season.

The governor of Colorado was persuasive when it came time for peace talks. He assured the peace party headed by Chief White Antelope and Black Kettle that it was imperative to attend.

The Cheyenne peace party set up their camp thirty miles from Fort Lyon, at a place known as Sand Creek. Then approximately eight hundred troops moved in, unannounced, and began murdering. Their orders were to "kill big and little—nits make lice." They did their job well.

In a desperate attempt to stop the killing, Black Kettle ran up not only the white flag, but also the American flag. But the troops continued on until the only Indians in sight were dead ones. They then began to mutilate the bodies, taking trophies of the "glorious battle."

Chief White Antelope stood in front of his tipi and sang his death song.

"Nothing lives long, except the earth and mountains," he sang, defiantly and honorably.

And then he was shot to death.

He was over seventy years old when he died at Sand Creek, looking for peace and instead, embracing his death.

Over two hundred women and children were massacred without mercy at Sand Creek that day.

Back in Denver, severed arms, legs, and scalps were exhibited in a theater by the proud troops to whom thirteen Congressional Medals of Honor were awarded. Sand Creek would be the greatest victory recorded in terms of Indian deaths during the Indian wars of the plains. And so it was . . . another proud moment in American history.

After Jason left, Silversong took down all the family portraits that made Sears famous and the six-by-two-foot painting of the Vikings coming to conquer the new world.

She laid down a heavy coat of moss green paint on the deck. For hours, she gathered pieces of plants and flowers from the yard and decoupaged them onto her "canvas," before bringing J.J. and Loree on to the back deck for the finishing touches. There, with bare feet, they each chose a color and as Silversong held their hands, they stepped into the paint, wiggled their toes, and walked across the length of "their" painting.

It went well until J.J. lost his footing and skidded off the end of the painting. As it turned out, it became one of those happy little accidents, and made the painting much more charming.

Loree felt very lucky to have as many caring people around her as she did during that time. She got strong again. Once she began to heal somewhat, her need to alter her reality with drugs disappeared. Her feelings were no longer something that frightened her so badly that she had to hide them from herself with drugs.

Silversong, like many women in her position, had gone, as a last resort, to a state agency in hopes of getting some kind of aid until she could get fully on her feet again.

"I need help, I need training so I can support my children," Silversong said.

"Do you have a drug or alcohol problem?" the woman behind the desk inquired.

"No."

"Well, have you ever been in trouble with the law, perhaps arrested?"

Silversong shook her head no, and the welfare worker shifted her weight in the chair.

"We can't help you then, except for food stamps and information about child support enforcement."

Silversong left the building wondering how many women were in her position: "Sorry, you're not screwed-up enough yet."

Money was sparse, but the house had become a warm place again, even if there wasn't any oil to heat it. They all waddled around the house, wrapped up like human sleeping bags, only their noses peeking out. They made it through some long winter nights that way, making the best of it. Luckily, Anne had a way of popping in unexpectedly and offering them money from the Lawsen Emergency Fund for fuel. They would celebrate then, as they gladly shed their second skins on the floor, and felt the warm air fill all the cold little corners of the house.

Friends stopped by, and that helped a lot in the encouragement department. They knew many people from different backgrounds and ethnic groups. The house was a place where people would converge. It was interesting to see how everyone related to each other being different in age, race, and lifestyle.

The conversations that took place at that time were insightful and full of energy. Often, Loree would recognize the intense look in her mother's eyes as she shared bits and pieces of her past. Even as she smiled, one could see that life had been hard on her, and Loree would watch as she'd slip into that dark place where Loree couldn't go. No one else seemed to notice, but Loree always knew.

"It's not that the world doesn't care, Mom, it's just that people don't know," Loree would say to her when she was feeling blue. Loree always felt that it was a matter of education versus ignorance.

"There are a lot of good people out there and I have faith in them. If they knew the truth of what has and is happening to our people, I think they'd be with us, Mom. They just don't know any better."

Judging by the look on her mother's face, Loree was sure that she sounded very much like the naive, cocky kid that she was.

"Well Lor, I'm happy *somebody* has some faith left."

Somehow, Silversong kept hanging in there financially by selling paintings for a fraction of what she should have charged, and cleaning houses and offices on the weekends.

Ron was the one who would gently say, "You're *not* insane, Silversong, *that's* your problem."

After her divorce, Ron and Silversong hung out together. When they saw something terrible, stupid, or insane, they would just laugh. Survival humor had kicked in.

"Yeah ... right ... uh huh ... " they'd say, mocking the stupidity and ignorance that surrounded them. They liked pretending to agree with absurdities, and "talking backward"—saying the opposite of what you really mean—gave them a lot of personal satisfaction.

Ron helped her to heal and deal with the world. It wasn't as hard as she thought it would be at times, because she felt that she had an ally in her brother. They were both black sheep, but it was okay because each walked in the other's spirit. When Ron felt confident that Silversong was once again on her feet, and he returned to Canada.

Ron was right there by Silversong's side when the moment came that she realized she had transcended; the sun had not come up, but her world had turned around.

I knew I would miss him, but I was never more happy to hear that he and Monica were going to try to save their marriage. I knew how much he loved her and their beautiful daughter Noel. Ron had been hired to drive a truck up in the interior of British Columbia in a small town called Ashcroft. He'd only been gone four months when he called to tell me that he and Monica were going to be parents for the second time. "Boy, that's one lucky kid," I remember telling him, meaning every word I spoke.

CHAPTER TWENTY~FOUR
The Midnight Wind

Ashford, British Columbia, 1975

With Amethest, a few small suitcases, and her bus fare, Anne finally left the United States and returned to Canada to the small mining town of Ashcroft, British Columbia, where Ron, Monica, and Little Nickel were living.

Except for the absence of a salty sea breeze and the sound of a distant ferry ready to dock, Ashcroft was similar to Kingston. It had a downtown consisting of several bars and the basics. The town's economic mainstay was the mine, whereas Kingston's had been the lumber mill.

Feeling the dry heat catch in her throat as she stepped off the bus, Anne squinted into the bright sun and through the haze of dry dust kicked up by vehicles as they passed. The journey had been a long one, but little Amethest was a real trooper, and Anne was proud of the way she had behaved herself on the long bus ride.

Sensing something familiar out of the corner of her eye, Anne turned to see a lean figure dressed in jeans with a leather vest and black hat, complete with eagle feather. Like the warriors in South Dakota, Ron had on his regalia.

"It's good to see you, Ron," Anne said. She reached her arms up high to hug him and, holding on for a long moment, she tried in vain to be strong and stop the tears that rushed to the surface.

"You did the right thing. Welcome home, Mom."

Ron looked past his mother's shoulders and down to where Amethest sat waiting patiently on top of her suitcase.

"So how about coming over here and giving your uncle a hug, kid?"

And with that Amethest ran to him, and he picked her up in loving arms, and gently placed her on his shoulders as she giggled.

Ron and Monica's apartment was in town so it didn't take long before they arrived home. Monica had the apartment spotless and a meal prepared and waiting for them when they walked in. Anne thanked her for welcoming Amethest and her into their home, and laughed as she tried desperately to wrap her arms around Monica's once-tiny waist that had grown beyond belief.

"How are you feeling, dear?"

Anne knew very well what the last weeks of pregnancy were like.

"About like you'd suspect: bitchy, hot, and exhausted," Monica replied.

She rose from her chair awkwardly at the sound of Little Nickel's voice coming from the bedroom where she'd been napping.

"I'm happy you're here, Mom, we could sure use some help," said Ron. "It's been hard these last few months. I've been no help, working long hours and all. I worry about her."

The concern on Ron's face showed the weight of his responsibilities.

"We'll make it, Ron, it'll be okay."

Anne soon realized that the long days Ron spent at work were indeed brutal and taking a considerable toll not only on her son, but on his marriage. Driving trucks through the dangerous and dusty backroads took skill, but like his older brother Lance, it seemed as if it were in Ron's blood. He drove his big eighteen-wheel iron pony at full speed down winding roads that barely hugged the mountainsides with which he'd grown familiar. No longer did he allow himself to peer off the narrow ledge. It took all his concentration to hug the side of the tiny road and look out for incoming loads. He always sighed with silent thanks every time he felt the bite of the large truck's brakes cutting into the gravel beneath the wheels. There were no guardrails, not that they would have provided any real protection should he lose his brakes and have to ride her in, out of control.

The runaway truck lanes were in place, spaced out and constructed in the areas that had been deemed the most dangerous. But all the men knew that if the time ever came when they needed such a set up, they would first have to make it there; and the reality was, few did.

Like any occupation that involves risk, there were many tales shared among the proud tribe of truck drivers who worked the land. Day and night, night and day, they traveled through the hairpin curves, through canyons such as the Frazer, and down steep mountainsides. Like old warriors recounting feats of bravery, they would tell their tales.

As far back as Loree could remember, she sat and listened to the men share their stories. Strong and stoic, their eyes would betray their feelings as they slugged back their black coffee and smoked their cigarettes. She would listen as one of her uncles or their friends recounted the moments leading up to one of many tragedies or triumphs that they had witnessed firsthand.

They were often first on the scene of an accident, usually long before the mounties or ambulances arrived. They were truck drivers, but they were often called upon to be paramedics, priests, or heroes. Loree was always very proud because she knew that her uncles were all of these things.

Ron always said the first time is always the hardest. Loree knew this to be true from the stories Lance would tell her. She recalls the time he would suddenly be brought fast-forward into reality when triggered by a recent incident. Sometimes when the pressure got to be too much, he'd take a night off and come and find her at Anne's house. Sipping tea, he'd tell Loree stories.

"What's wrong, Lance?"

Loree could see something was heavy on his heart. Word had come that a dear friend he'd known for many years had died in a trucking accident. He told her about the first time he'd come upon the unexpected.

It was late, he was driving down the highway, and he saw something glowing off to his right. He slowed down and saw that it was a car, or what was left of a car, crumpled off the side of the road, upside down at the bottom of an embankment. Lance was only twenty.

He slid down the embankment. It was pretty dark except for his headlights, which he had tried to use to guide his way, but they weren't much help to him. As he neared the wreck, Lance heard the voice.

"I think I'm going to die," it said.

Lance tried to locate the young man.

"Are you in pain?"

"No, it doesn't hurt, but you know, my dad's gonna be real mad at me. I really wrecked his car up bad and this is the first time he lent it to me. I graduated tonight, that's why I'm all dressed up. I was on my way home from the dance."

Following the sound of his voice, Lance felt his way through the crumpled metal that surrounded the soft-spoken voice.

"I don't think your dad's gonna be upset about that, son. You'll see, we'll get you out of here and it'll be all right. You trust me, eh?"

Lance whispered softly as he felt his way though the dark. He could feel that the young man's legs were crushed.

"I'm going to have to leave for a minute and go radio for some help here. We're gonna get you out."

Lance was scared. When he reached in to feel around the young man's body, his arms became damp with warm blood and he knew that the young man didn't have long to live.

"I'll be right back," Lance said calmly. The climb back up the embankment was difficult; he had to claw into the ground as he made his way up to the road.

"This is the Midnight Wind calling," Lance said, as he quickly put out the distress call over his C.B. radio. After the call, he slid back down the embankment to be by the young man's side.

"They'll be here soon. I'll just hang out here with you until they get here."

He worked his way back to where he'd felt the warmth draining and tried to hold back the blood, grateful that the young man was not feeling much pain, but sad at the thought that he would most likely be paralyzed.

"Thank you," the young man said. His voice was getting weaker. "I'm getting cold . . . I don't want to die alone."

"Oh, come on now there, buddy, you're not gonna die, you hang in there, they're on their way and I'm right here."

Twenty years had passed since the night Lance rocked a dying man in his arms, yet my uncle talked about it as if it were yesterday; to him I'm sure it will always be that way—a few hours spent on the side of a dark road, holding a stranger in his arms while he died.

"You okay, Lance?"

"Oh yeah, honey. I just needed to talk tonight."

Later that night I wrote Lance this poem:

Looking into your hazel eyes, I see your history. Like tiny road maps winding around, the folds of skin near your kind eyes. Always so strong, and somebody's dad, when do you ever have time to be sad?

The Midnight Wind calls your name, echoing through the steep canyons, wheels turning in the night, seeing dawn break . . . it's a beautiful sight. Living is love and loving the light, one more shift, I made it through the night. Morning's finally come at last, and all those memories fade into the past, like a Peterbilt—made to last, special places in the past.

Record keeping on radio waves, voices invisible float through

*a maze, hitting a smooth patch of highway I fly, like an eagle
through a brilliant blue sky.*

*Rolling down the window, the breeze captures me, a special
place to live, behind a wheel, a large truck made of steel—a modern day warrior . . . who's real.*

The months that Anne spent in Ashcroft were difficult. Like
her, Ron and Monica were struggling financially; they were also
trying to stabilize the power struggle in their marriage. The birth of
their second daughter came, and although it was not something
Ron discussed, he asked that she be named Patricia. Unlike Patty,
she would be called Trisha.

It was only a week after the baby's birth that Monica's mother
arrived, along with several other family members, to see the new
baby. The apartment was small, and it took only a few days for Anne
to realize that things were going to come to a head. It didn't look
pretty. The fact that Ron was native had not set well with Monica's
mother. Ron knew . . . he would never be good enough for her.

Anne was fed up. Monica's mother, a strict Jehovah's Witness,
treated Ron like he was some pagan savage. She was a retired army
sergeant, and had carried that "take charge" persona into her civilian life.

Already raw from months of uncertainty, Anne was impatient
with her. The family always fought the only way people who really
love each other can fight, and it got pretty vicious at times. They
were a dysfunctional family and didn't know it. No one had coined
the phrase yet. They *cared*, they were going to keep *trying* . . . and if
necessary, they would *will* things better . . . because *they were Lawsens, damn it.* . . . Most of the time this approach didn't work, but it
was all they knew.

After the scene was played out and the dust temporarily settled,
Anne decided it would be best to leave, hoping that Ron and Monica
would stand a better chance of working through their problems on
their own.

Terry Lawsen sent whatever money he could to help Anne while she was in Canada. It was an unconventional relationship, with Anne living in Canada and Terry in the United States. But it worked, and that was all that mattered. The money was never the same amount, but it was all she had, and she was grateful to Terry, who had basically taken on the role of Amethest's dad.

Catching a ride into the city of Kamloops with Ron, Anne began to look for a new home. As fate would have it, she answered an ad to rent a room and was shocked to see Ron's old friend, Sandy, answer the door.

"Well, I'll be damned," Ron said, as they shook hands and Sandy led them into the house.

"It's been a long time, eh? I heard about Patty, I'm sorry. I tried to get in touch, but nobody seemed to know where you'd all gone off to."

Anne smiled and reached out to squeeze Sandy's arm, remembering how much he had thought of Patty. He had always wanted to marry her.

"And then here you are one day on my front doorstep. I'll be damned."

He too considered himself a Lawsen, another foster kid. He'd been one of the young guys who hung out long enough to feel adopted. Like Teddy, he'd basically been alone in the world; his family had abandoned him while dealing with their own problems. Whenever anyone would ask about his family, he would look at them proudly and tell them that he had been adopted by a Cree Indian family named Lawsen.

Sandy's girlfriend, Robin, was a nurse at Inland Royal Hospital and she told Anne that she could use her as a job reference. There was an opening on the hospital's housekeeping staff and Anne wanted the job badly. Not only would the pay and benefits be good, but she and Amethest would be secure.

Receiving the good news that she'd been hired, Anne squealed like a young girl and ran to share the news with Sandy and Robin.

The walk up the hill to the hospital was steep, and the work inside demanding, so it seemed natural that Anne would be sore while her body grew accustomed to her new schedule, but soon her gratitude turned to fear.

Waking one morning a week later, Anne found that she was unable to move. Her body ached deep inside. It took all her strength to force her body onto its side, and holding her breath to stop herself from crying out and waking Amethest, she coaxed her stiff joints from the bed.

"No . . . no . . . no, this can't happen, not now, not ever," Anne said out loud. She wondered what was happening to her, and feared for Amethest's future. It was true she was the child's grandmother, but no paperwork had been put through, so the question of legal guardianship was still not determined. Anne feared that if she was found to be sick, her chances of raising her granddaughter would be slim.

Unable to work and without medical coverage, Anne was desperate, and with Robin's help, she made an appointment with Human Resources—Canada's equivalent to the U.S. Department of Welfare.

Although she was treated kindly, Anne refused to tell the authorities that she was raising Amethest, and in return they had no idea that Anne would be attempting to raise a small child on the one hundred and fifty dollars a month they allotted to her while her medical condition was under evaluation.

It wasn't much, but Terry Lawsen was still doing his best to send what money he could. Rent was cheap in Kamloops in the early seventies, and Anne felt lucky to find a larger place to rent that she was able to afford. It was a big old house in downtown Kamloops, located on St. Paul Street within easy walking distance of anything she or Amethest needed, which was important because they didn't own a car.

Her landlady was a nice woman, happy to find someone older and responsible enough to oversee things for her. There was a large suite downstairs and another separate apartment above that was smaller. The house wasn't in the best of condition, but because Anne agreed to oversee the place and collect rent, as well as restore the yard, her landlady reduced her rent dramatically.

While Anne was working at the hospital, she met Nell, who quickly became her good friend and visited her often. When Anne walked stiffly to her door, Nell came to help her with her coat.

"You'd better run, Anne, or you'll be late for your doctor's appointment," Nell said, and Anne shot her a look.

"Pretty sick joke, Nell."

"Now you don't worry about a thing. I'll take good care of Amethest," she said, and placed a ten-dollar bill in Anne's hand.

"I know it's not far, but you're taking a cab, and I don't want any back talk."

Anne didn't want to hurt Nell's feelings, but she decided to walk anyway, even if it hurt. Anne could think of much better ways to spend ten dollars than on cab rides.

When she arrived at the clinic, Anne was ushered by a nurse into a room where she waited for over an hour before a young man dressed in a white coat entered. Without even so much as an introduction, he flipped through Anne's chart and began his examination. Hesitant to tell him how severe her symptoms were, Anne grimaced as his hands touched her in a careless way. Abruptly, he told her that the only thing she needed was two aspirins and a job.

Anne recognized the look immediately—"Welcome back to Canada, you lazy Indian"—and feeling ashamed and embarrassed, she dressed herself as best she could and made her way home.

"Well, what did he say?" Nell asked as Anne entered.

"You don't want to know, and I don't want to talk about it."

"You get some rest, Anne. I'll be back in the morning and we can talk about it then if you like."

Waking in the night, Anne decided in tears to move the furniture around to block off the living room from the rest of the house. Her body hurt worse than it ever had, and she knew that unless she partitioned off the living room, she'd have no way of keeping up with Amethest when she woke up in the morning.

Amethest looked so little, camped out on the living room floor, and Anne felt very alone as she stared at her baby's little girl. Lying down on the couch, she prayed that when the time came, she'd be able to get back up. Early in the morning, the door bell rang, and it was Nell. Anne was unable to get up.

"Push hard, Nell, I've blocked the door," Anne yelled.

Opening the door, Nell gasped.

"Anne, oh, Anne, what is it?"

"It hurts all over, Nell," Anne was crying, and couldn't stop. "They'll take her away from me, I just know they will."

"Take her away, where? What do you mean, Anne?"

"Well, just look at me, just look! I didn't tell the resource people about Amethest. I couldn't . . . I mean how could I? Just look what I've had to do just to make sure she's safe."

Nell saw how Anne had partitioned off the living room.

"Anne, you've got to listen to me. Nobody is going to take your granddaughter away from you. You have to believe me; they want to keep children with their flesh and blood, but you've got to tell them, so they can help you. But first we've got to get you to a doctor."

"It won't do any good, Nell. He said there's nothing wrong with me."

"Well, I'm telling you, he was wrong. For heaven's sake, Anne. Doctors aren't God! I'm calling up my doctor right now and making you an appointment."

"Can I do that?" Anne asked in surprise.

"You're damn right you can."

Nell slammed her fist down hard on the table, making her point.

"Dr. Knox has been good to me and my family. I've known her for years and you'll see, it will work out."

Relieved, Anne began preparing herself as Nell secured an immediate appointment. Several hours later when Anne met with Dr. Knox, she was still in quite a lot of pain, partially immobilized.

Dr. Knox was a sweet, round woman with soft edges and short grey hair. She looked at Anne from over her wire-rimmed glasses. She smiled as she introduced herself and led Anne into an examination room.

Her manner was gentle as she examined Anne and questioned her about the treatment she'd been receiving.

"Aspirin and job hunting? You've got to be kidding!"

"I wish I was. All I want is to feel better. I've tried but it's just getting worse."

"Well, by the looks of it, Anne, you have rheumatoid arthritis. I'm sorry you've had to suffer like this, but we're going to begin some treatments today to help you get through it. It's sometimes linked to a major infection or illness."

Anne thought back to her days in Edmonton, and the cobalt treatments she received when it was discovered that she had advanced cervical cancer. Perhaps the two were connected. She was grateful to be alive after the cancer treatment; this pain was something she could learn to live with.

Anne learned that in its severest form, the arthritis could deform her joints and that it was not unusual for some people to eventually become wheelchair-bound. She vowed that this would not be the case with her.

They began the treatments that day, but it took time for the medication to take effect. Dr. Knox explained to Anne that once they got this bout under control, it would be easier to stave off future episodes with preventative medication.

As soon as she was able, Anne called the Human Resource office, explaining her predicament, and a social worker was sent over. It was frightening, but Anne had no choice but to tell them about Amethest and her daughter's death. She had prepared herself for the worst.

Seating the social worker down for tea, Anne recounted the time her daughter died. She became emotional.

Maria, the social worker who sat across from Anne, listened

respectfully, and reassured Anne that Amethest would not be taken from her. She commended Anne for the commitment she'd made to raise Patty's daughter, and further assured Anne that she would no longer be expected to raise Amethest on one hundred and fifty dollars a month. It was an incredible relief when the threat of losing Amethest no longer hung over her.

Her body, unfortunately, held a new threat. Refusing to surrender and become a victim of the disease that had her in its grip, Anne kept moving, refusing to be idle. She fought back hard, sometimes crying while she tried to comb her hair or dress. The people at the Human Resources office sent an aid to help through Anne's toughest time, but she chose to do most things herself. She was afraid of what would happen to her if she ever slowed down, so she pushed herself, never allowing this new threat to take root, and never admitting to herself how badly it hurt at times.

Months passed before she was back on her feet, physically and financially. The extra income had gone far; Anne was a master at managing money. Saving her pennies, she purchased a used freezer and filled it with staples, and stocked her pantry with canned goods. Knowing there was plenty for all, Anne called Silversong long distance and urged her to bring the children to Kamloops and spend the summer. Silversong packed up her car, loaded the children, and headed up I-5 north to the border.

Kamloops, British Columbia

It was summertime, school had just ended, and the yard was full of flowers. It was a hopeful time. Silversong was home to stay, and Loree no longer lived with the fear that Silversong would leave the family.

Anne and Amethest had been in Canada for over a year. Like Silversong, J.J., and Loree, they were beginning their lives again, rebuilding and replanting whatever could be salvaged from the previous years.

They pulled up in front of a great, huge house. It needed a paint job something awful, but it was charming, and Anne had made her presence known. The yard was well kept, spotted with pansies and wildflowers everywhere. In the backyard, she had planted a large garden. It was beautiful, but it did look odd, considering she lived right downtown and her backyard was unfenced and surrounded by a parking lot.

They hadn't even stepped out of the car door when Amethest and Anne came running out to greet them. Loree felt good again, seeing big smiles on everyone's faces as they hugged and laughed their way into the house, where they spent most of the time just sitting and staring at one another. Anne had decorated the house for their arrival with large welcome signs and special treats for everyone.

That year, Loree learned there's no place like Kamloops in the summertime. Like her grandmother, the weather, lakes, and the people were welcoming. Warm nights and hot days down at Riverside Park felt great . . . they were a family again.

Still, there were a few missing pieces.

It had been well over a year since Ron had disappeared. Monica had left him, taken their daughters, and supposedly moved to Edmonton, though no one knew for sure.

It was hard on Ron, not knowing where his girls were. He didn't know himself anymore—he had had a major crisis, and just seemed to cut out of the human race for awhile. Anne told Silversong that he had gone to live with some elders somewhere up north, but she never got the whole story. All she knew for sure was that he spent his time trying to recapture his perspective and reconnect with his spirit, so he'd have the strength to return home.

He arrived unexpectedly at Anne's door, looking leaner than Silversong had ever seen him, and darkly tanned. Loree thought he looked really handsome, even if he did need a haircut and a clean change of clothes. He only had one little bag with him; since the kids were gone, he was traveling light.

He never spoke much about where he'd been for the last year or why he had left; he simply said it was something he had to do. The rest was off limits and no one pushed him. They were just happy that he was home and safe.

Ron had a new calmness about him when he came home. He'd always been quiet, but this was different, and they all knew there was a lot going on beneath those still waters. Ron's presence always demanded respect, and unlike others who sometimes demand respect and don't deserve it, Ron did.

The family loved having him home. They spent days up at Paul Lake, taking out a small boat that Sandy had. They'd play all day, it was good medicine for them all, being together and smiling and enjoying the warm summer days.

Ron and Sandy were wild men when they got together. They once took the top off a picnic table and used it to water ski. It was pure comic relief, as Anne would say. Loree always listened to Ron, he was her elder, yet treated her as an equal and never talked down to her, unless he was pulling her leg. He liked to laugh a lot, and luckily the family was blessed with a great sense of humor. The only bad part about Ron was that sometimes he drank too much.

Ron hadn't been home too long when he and Sandy were in the backyard starting up the barbecue and, out of the blue, Ron came bolting into the house, slamming the door so hard that the glass shattered across the floor. Loree recognized that sound and it frightened her. She ran into the hallway to see what had happened. Her uncle looked shaken, like he'd seen a ghost. Anne ran to see what had happened.

"What is it, Ron, what the hell is going on?"

"Mom, I just saw Monica and Noel," Ron said.

He looked lost and began to cry as he paced the living room. Loree was frightened to see him so distraught.

"Are you sure it was them?"

Anne had missed the girls, and it seemed odd that they would suddenly be driving through her alleyway.

"Yes, damn it. Yes, I know what my own kid looks like. I have to find them, Mom, I have to find them and know if they're okay. I'm their father."

No one was able to stop him. They watched as Ron grabbed his coat and ran out the door. Through the whole scene, Sandy stood quietly in the background, as he often did.

"Is it true, Sandy? Or has he gone crazy? Was it really them, did you see them?" Anne asked.

She missed her grandchildren, and the prospect of never seeing them again had haunted her for a year.

"He's not crazy, I saw them too, and I'm sure it was Monica and Little Nickel."

Strong emotions swept through the household quickly and without warning. Ron's intensity was frightening when he came home. He began to calm down as he talked about it.

"When I saw them, I couldn't believe it. She drove by slowly, but as I approached the car she took off."

Pausing, his head hung low.

"You know, I just realized—it wasn't Noel I saw, it was Trisha. It's been so long."

The family stood in silence. It was an odd situation and no one knew exactly what to do. Monica had her reasons for leaving, some that the family weren't even aware of, and although they missed the girls, they always knew that Monica would see to it that they were safe and well cared for.

Loree woke up later that night when she heard Ron come into the house again. She laid in bed, and listened to him as he cried. He couldn't stand not knowing where his children were, not being able to see them. And he wanted to talk to Monica. Ron loved her, but he just couldn't get it right.

As the pain became deeper, Ron turned to what he knew, what he had learned many years before: When you're in pain, when you don't know what to do, when you don't like yourself anymore, drink some more . . . pretty soon it'll be tomorrow.

In spite of their concern for Ron, the family had a great visit in Canada. They all needed the rest, especially now that Silversong was on her own. The kids and Silversong were on welfare and food stamps, and she was supposed to return to accounting school. They were demanding times, but she was determined. After touching such deep despair, Silversong knew there was only one way left to go, and that was up. Things were getting better every day, and she became stronger. For the first time in her life she felt like a sovereign being. And she liked it.

When they returned from Canada, Silversong opened the door to discover that the house had been vandalized. Someone had taken an ax and destroyed everything, even the cuckoo clock Jason had brought back from Germany for J.J.

In shock, she tried to comfort the kids. They made do as best they could for the night, and the next morning she called the insurance company.

"Oh, Mrs. Lowe," the insurance representative said, "Mr. Lowe took care of everything. He just picked up a check for eight thousand dollars."

It hurt Silversong that Jason had no consideration for the children's welfare, but she decided then and there that it was worth it, if it meant that the family was, finally, free of him. It really didn't matter to her anymore. Silversong had everything she wanted. She was alive.

BOOK THREE

Loree

Would there be . . .

Light without darkness? Truth without lie?

Sound without silence? A tear without a sigh?

Would there be . . .

Joy without sorrow? Today without tomorrow?

Life without pain, or sunshine without rain?

Would there be . . .

Man without woman? Song without poem?

Life without death? Dreams without desires?

Land without ocean? Air without breath? Art without emptiness?

Would there be . . .

Music without tune? Sun without moon?

Good without bad? Happy without sad?

Or would there be me without you?

CHAPTER TWENTY-FIVE
In Loree's Words

When I needed my grandma, I would go to Canada.

It wasn't unusual to find me living with her on and off over the years. I spent the early years with her while my mother was in the United States, and I also lived with her while I was a teenager and attended Kamloops Senior Secondary, a Canadian high school.

It never seemed to matter where Gram was, I always had a home and a room wherever she lived. On St. Paul Street, my room was called "the buttercup cubby hole," because it was so small and cozy. Grandma worked for days fixing it up for me, covering the walls with yellow roses and making matching curtains. She didn't have much money, but she always made ends meet. There never failed to be a little something left over.

1975

Amethest Lee Ann was five years old the year I came to live with Gram and go to ninth grade in Canada. It was amazing to see how well Grandma had managed to carve out a life for Amethest and herself after Patty's death. Grandma believes in miracles, and they don't have to be big ones. There were always a lot of little miracles around the "homestead" (as Grandma referred to the house on St. Paul Street). Sometimes it was a miracle to have the money to pay the electrical bill. It was a miracle that bought me a winter coat. The family used to joke about how Grandma had money growing in her walls. It never seemed to fail; no matter how broke she was, if someone had a financial crisis, Grandma could be relied upon to pull money out from behind some knick-knack hanging on the wall. We would crack up as we watched Gram hunt it down.

"Where has she hidden the Lawsen Emergency Fund this time?"

My Grandma made me believe in miracles. It was nothing short of a true miracle, the way she managed to forever pull things off.

Back home in North Seattle I spent most of my free time with my friend Lynn. She lived half way up Motorcycle Hill, a steep hill dotted with trees, flowering bushes, and houses of every shape and color peeking out from odd angles. From a distance, it resembled a patchwork quilt: colorful little rectangles and squares surrounded by an evergreen border.

When we'd get brave and drive the car straight up Motorcycle Hill, it always made the hair on the back of my neck stand on end. No matter how many times we had done it, there was always a little fear about what we might find once we reached the top ... would the land really level out again? Or would we perhaps drop off the edge of our world? Or better yet, continue straight up into the hazy blue sky and into the spirit world?

Since I was several months shy of receiving my driver's license, I had to walk up the hill and I hated it. My thighs were burning by the time I reached the top to begin the descent into the little lights of North City, which was what the area north of Seattle was called.

Lynn and I had a pretty good system worked out. Usually she'd call from her place and we'd meet halfway between our houses. Lynn was getting the good part of that deal, considering it was all downhill from her place, but Lynn had a way of sweet-talking that made you feel like it was all fair and square. I suppose it was; she had to walk back up the damn hill to get home.

Sometimes, when we didn't have anything going on, we'd sit across the street from the 7-11, under an archway to a real estate building that had closed hours before. We'd watch our friends and neighbors come and go with all the little necessities they had to have before Safeway reopened in the morning.

Lynn's mom worked at Safeway. She was a pretty lady with short, dark hair, in sharp contrast to her daughter's blondness. Other than hair color, they had a strong resemblance.

Like me, Lynn had a stepfather; but unlike me, hers still lived with them. They had inherited the problems most "second" families face. Lynn resented him, but what teenager doesn't resent the authority figures in her life?

I do pity them for having to put up with Lynn and me. Often when I was up at Lynn's, I would catch a glimpse of her little brother Don as he dashed in or out of his room with one of his buddies, usually with a skateboard under his arm. He was a sweet kid and reminded me of my brother, but older. Again, like mine, Lynn's little brother meant the world to her.

It's difficult to describe Lynn. She was blonde with big brown eyes and a huge, wonderful smile that was charged with energy, but she was more than that—she was bigger than her smile, she seemed bigger than life, although she stood only four-foot-eight.

Her height was a bone of contention, with "platform" everything in fashion. We used to tease her about trying to sneak a couple of inches onto her height. "We" being Sue, Rick, Jim, Russ, Steve, Kerry, Dawn, Terry, Blaine, Tyrone, and Gina—our gang.

Anyone of the gang would say Lynn had a special energy about her that you couldn't help but feel. It was electric, infectious—she could recharge you in a matter of seconds . . . or verbally scalp you, depending on the situation.

That quality may have been what caused my mother to appreciate her so. In a world full of imitations, Lynn was the real thing, not afraid to laugh, cry, or cut out of a situation if it wasn't happening for her. She was a very brave teenager, never afraid of living her life to the fullest.

Lynn and I were frustrated. All dressed up and no place to go.

We were fifteen and sixteen. In our moments of dark, dank teenage despair, we felt trapped and misunderstood by the world.

Lynn would say, "Lor, if we're together, no one can stop us. We have twice the power, twice the determination, and we can do anything we want. We just can't ever give up is all . . . ."

Looking at Lynn, seeing her confidence in herself, and in me as her friend, I believed her.

Our social life took up much of our time and energy, and we'd spend our "free" time trying to figure out the world and where we fit into the big picture.

Our friends were in similar situations as far as jobs, college and career plans went, but Lynn and I wanted to know why we were here, on earth. I guess Lynn was my first "metaphysical" friend; she understood the spirit and thought about concepts that no one else felt compelled to discuss at length.

We once got lost in downtown Seattle for five hours while a local radio station had an all-night Led Zeppelin marathon. Another time, we took off in Rick's old beater and drove eight hundred miles to Idaho to see our buddy Kerry, so he'd know we hadn't forgotten about him.

I remember lying in the back of Rick's station wagon—Lynn, Rick, and I—watching the stars. Lynn and I were convinced that some of the lights in the celestial light show were UFOs. As usual, Rick thought we were both crazy. I think that's what he liked about us.

Lynn's favorite color was blue, and her favorite wine was Jaquray, "White Rose." It came in a frosty white bottle (with a real cork and everything), and it was only slightly more potent than soda pop.

Many times, Rick and another close friend, Jim Clark, saved us from boredom or worse. Day or night, they were there, good buddies. Jim would die before admitting it, but he could be very sweet and thoughtful, but he was hung up on being a bad guy; he took a perverse pleasure in it.

"Jim, you're being an asshole," Lynn would say.

Jim's expression of unreasonable, bull-headed stubbornness would instantly melt, and an ear-to-ear grin would cover his face.

"Yeah, I know I am; ain't it great?!"

Luckily for him, Lynn and I didn't scare off easily.

"Yeah, we know you're an asshole, Jim, but we love you."

I think Jim really needed to hear that, and I know he loved us too, in addition to loving to terrorize us.

Jim could make you crazy, and so could Lynn. How I got flung in the middle of those two, I'll never know, but I can tell you, it was not always a comfortable position. Jim drove a 280z, no back seat, and as one can imagine, it got pretty cozy.

My mom liked my friends a lot. She knew that as long as we were together, all was well.

Some nights, Lynn and I would just walk alone in the dark for hours and talk. It didn't matter if the restaurant we picked that evening was five miles away, we always felt the walks were time well spent. We talked about sad and silly stuff, and about life and death.

"Get over here!" Lynn said. "You know I always walk on the side closest to the street."

Dutifully obeying her request, I wanted to argue the point.

"Lynn, that's silly. Why should you always walk on that side?"

"Because I'm older."

"Older? Lynn, you're only a year older than me!"

"It doesn't matter, Loree. If a car suddenly goes out of control, swerves and broadsides us, it's only right that I should go first because I'm older."

Life never frightened Lynn; she knew that no matter what happened, it was "meant to be." She seemed to know instinctively that the only thing we could do was to live as fully in the moment as possible, and go after what we wanted.

Uncle Ron was similar in that way. Like my grandmother, he

was gifted and had a way of making memories, not the fleeting kind, but the type that last a lifetime. He could put on a production that would make Bill Graham proud, and the party he threw for my seventeenth birthday was no exception. No holds barred, this one was going to be for the memory book.

For three days straight, Ron worked day and night, stringing up colored lights that would illuminate the large pine trees in our backyard, converting the tennis court into a dance floor, and stringing speakers in strange places while routinely running into the kitchen to oversee the hors d'oeuvres he had hand-picked for the menu.

"Damn, Ron, how many people are you expecting at this party anyway?" I asked, amazed at the effort he was putting forth.

"Well, Lor, let me put it this way—the next-door neighbors are not going to be the least bit happy with us, however . . . I guarantee that you won't forget the day you turned seventeen," he said, grinning, as he raised his hand over his mouth and began to chuckle.

"You see, Lor, this is just between you and me now kid, but the way I see it, there are two really cool people in this family, and it just so happens I'm throwing a party for the other one. Besides—"

"Oh I know, I know," I interrupted, "it's a rotten job but somebody's got to do it."

Ron joined me in this old Indian saying that he had become famous for.

Ron's planning and preparation was worth the effort. The party was a smashing success, and just as Ron had predicted, the neighbors were none too happy.

June brought not only my birthday, but a time for Lynn and me to go our separate ways.

While I headed north for Canada, Lynn rode the ferry to Alaska with Sue's older sister, Dawn. It was a strange feeling, knowing Lynn would not be there, but that energy field of hers was real, she had a strong spirit, and I felt it often when we were apart.

"You can do it, Lor, you can do anything. I believe in you."

I received a card in the mail from her when she reached Alaska. It was a bright orange sunset and the poem on the cover quickly etched itself indelibly into my memory.

I haven't seen you in awhile, yet I often
*   imagine all of your expressions.*
I haven't spoken to you recently, but many
*   times I hear your thoughts.*
Good friends must not always be together, it's
*   the feeling of oneness when distant, that proves a*
lasting friendship.

Lynn had written these words inside the card:

I thought this card was a lot like us.
I'm going through a lot of changes, I'm sure
*   you are too, but I feel really good about it.*
Well Lor, enjoy your trip and I'll see you
*   when you get back.*
When the sun sets, I'll be there. Think of me,
*   and know that in that moment I'll be thinking of*
*   you, no matter where we are.*

That summer, I learned that "inseparable" is a state of mind.

The month I spent in Canada was good for my spirit. The warm winds caressed me as I watched the beautiful sky fade into darkness, made bright by a million stars.

Kamloops, British Columbia, is known as Canada's own version of California. Many evenings, my friends and I would walk through the warm nights, down along the Thompson River that ran through the city, stopping to admire the meteor showers that were occurring. The news said that there were over a hundred "shooting stars" per hour, raining down from the sky in sheets during this phenomenon. It was an amazing sight. Apparently, Kamloops was situated in the ideal location to view the meteors as they burned through the sky before fading into the night. It was a magical time.

Grandma had done a good job in coming to Kamloops to build a new life for her and Amethest. I was proud of how much she had accomplished over the six years since she'd traveled alone with Amethest and a few suitcases across the border, out into a new and uncertain future.

It always amazed me how someone who had known so little security in her own life could be such a stronghold for an entire family. Grandma had learned a lot of lessons over the years, not to mention a few good Indian tricks. Talk about stretching dollars— my grandmother could make them into rubber bands.

Never losing sight of her goal, Grandma moved with Amethest, out of their "old homestead" on St. Paul Street, into their very own condominium in North Kamloops. To Grandma, the home she bought represented much more than a mere roof over their heads, it meant a safe place, a place where the entire family could go. No matter what we were struggling with, or going through, Gram's door was wide open, full of hope, encouragement . . . and an occasional, well-deserved kick-in-the-ass.

I came home from Canada a month later, just in time for Kingston's big annual Fourth of July celebration. I was well rested, deeply tanned, and didn't have a worry in the world. Lynn had a new boyfriend, someone she had been crazy about for a long time, and I had also met someone.

The next thing I knew, Lynn's boyfriend Dave was killed in an automobile accident.

Lynn was distraught and grieving. I didn't know how to help her—all she wanted was Dave, and Dave was dead and I couldn't bring him back.

"We were going to be together forever, Loree," she said, looking at me like a child who had been told a lie.

I worked in a little coffee shop that summer. One day, when summer was almost over, Rick walked in.

"Hey! Can I get you a cup of coffee?"

I was happy to see his familiar face.

"We need to talk," he said. The expression on his face frightened me.

"Let's go in the back," I said, and motioned my boss to take over.

After closing the door I turned to look at Rick, afraid of what he was going to say. Hugging me, he began to cry.

"There's been an accident . . . it's Lynn . . . we have to go right now."

"But she's alive . . . she's alive, isn't she, Rick?"

I didn't want to move until I heard him say yes.

"Yes, but we have to go now."

Lynn had fallen, hurting her back. During surgery to repair the damage, she had experienced complications with the anesthesia. By the time we arrived at the hospital, she was gone; her brain had died. Although her body was being forced to breathe by a cold machine, her energy had walked on.

Two days after her eighteenth birthday, the machines that had kept her body alive against its will were turned off. Letting her go was the greatest gesture of love her parents could make.

Saying good-bye is hard. Maybe that's why there is no word in the Lakota language for good-bye. The Lakota were smart people—never creating a word that is so easy to say and so hard to accept.

Pain and sorrow are sometimes paths we must walk alone in order to find our way. Lynn and I had spent a lot of time together, searching for the questions and the answers. Now I spend more time looking for those in some far-off place, just beyond where the sun sets. I know I have to believe that her death was meant to be.

Maybe it was the Indian in me that spoke to my spirit and told me such lessons of understanding from the natural world. Like a gift from my grandmother and my mother, I was born with perceptive instincts.

Loree was my angel with large, warm brown eyes and copper-colored curls framing her face. Even when she was little, I knew she had what the old people called a "grandmother spirit."

I remember one warm summer night when the family sat out on the old wooden porch. The moon was full and hung low, just barely above the black shadow of the trees. Mom had country music on the radio in the kitchen as she washed the dinner dishes, and she paused occasionally to yell at Ron and Patty, who were still full of mischief.

Surprisingly, Loree, who was not yet five years old, sat quietly on Dad's lap. (Even though Dad was Loree's grandfather, she called him "Dad" just like the rest of us.) Her brown eyes grew wide with wonderment as she intently stared at the moon, so full and bright that it gave her skin a bright baby blue complexion. She was clearly mesmerized by the moon, and I, by the expression on my child's face.

This time of silence came to an abrupt end when Ron and Patty came trotting out the door and Ron leapt off the porch, his sister in hot pursuit. Loree pointed her chubby little finger into the sky.

"See that up there? What is it?"

"That's the moon, Loree," Dad said.

"Well, I want it. Can you get it for me, Dad?"

"But Loree, it's up there too high for me to reach."

Loree put her small hands on her hips and shook her head back and forth slowly.

"Get a ladder, Dad, just get a ladder."

CHAPTER TWENTY~SIX
Buried Treasures, Unbroken Bonds

*W*hen Loree first met her future husband, she was a thirteen-year-old seventh-grader attending Kellogg Junior High School. He was the cute new guy with huge hazel eyes and jet black hair.

She found out that his name was Marshall, and that he was one year older than her. Loree was depressed because she knew that they wouldn't have any classes together. They were introduced by a mutual friend named Billy, who brought Marshall to her front door on Halloween night.

It wasn't long before they were going steady. Loree soon learned that Marshall's immediate family was experiencing a major shakeup, and it had been decided that it would be best if he lived with his Aunt Christy and Uncle Dan until things settled down. They had moved to the area with their three children, his cousins, of whom Marshall was very fond.

Loree was walking slowly near their house when a tall, skinny kid with white blonde hair popped up next to her. It was Marshall's little brother, Mike.

"I know what your name is, it's Loree, and you're in love with Marshall aren't you?" he said.

"And who are you?".

"I'm Marshall's brother."

Then he ran off.

Loree and Marshall never really talked about personal problems then—they were thirteen and fourteen years old, and too embarrassed to admit they had any. But one thing they both knew was that "happily ever after" was a fairy tale. Somehow, the fact that they both came from troubled families seemed to be partly why they were drawn to each other.

Just before Marshall's aunt moved, they saw each other on Christmas Eve. He had stopped by the house earlier and asked if he could leave a bike he'd bought as a gift for his brother Mike beside the house until he could pick it up. That night about midnight, Loree heard a tap on the glass and there was Marshall with his dad, whom she had never met. They packed Mike's bicycle into the car, and it touched Loree that it was so important to Marshall that his brother have a good Christmas because his parents had just divorced, and Mike was the youngest. She could see that Marshall wanted to make things right for him.

She lay there after they left, trying to fall asleep. She imagined the smile on Mike's face in the morning when he woke up to find his bike.

Through friends at school, Loree heard that Marshall had moved back in with his mother, who lived in Edmonds. From that point on, they had a knack for running into each other once a year or so.

It was four years later, at a large street fair in Seattle, in the midst of a crowd of thousands, that Loree walked directly into Marshall.

He was with one of his friends and Loree was with her girlfriend, Sue. Marshall and Loree were eye-locked, but Sue finally managed to pull her away. It wasn't long before he asked for her phone number. They were now seventeen and eighteen years old, no longer mere children. Dating had taken on a whole new meaning.

Following proper protocol, Marshall waited an entire twenty-four hours before phoning her, and when he did, she could hear his older brother, Mitch, playing guitar in the background.

He came to the door with a bouquet of fresh wildflowers, and they went to a Grateful Dead concert. There, Loree met his older brother, Mitch, the family musician and tie-dyed T-shirt expert. And shortly after that, she was introduced to his mother, Lana, and her boyfriend, Matt.

Being typical teenagers, Marshall and Loree seemed to break up every other week for about a year. She usually felt justified, having discovered Marshall had a rotten temper. Loree instinctively knew which buttons *not* to push with Marshall, but she went ahead and pushed them anyway.

"It was a 'wicious circle'. . . ." her Grandpa Lawsen would say, his Scandinavian accent making it impossible to pronounce the letter *v*.

Typically, Marshall would go roaring off on his motorcycle, and Loree would pack her bags and head to Canada for a couple of weeks, both thinking they would "show" each other. Before long, they would each come home, take one look at each other, and do it all over again.

After one such breakup, Loree was shocked when she came home from Canada and heard that while she was gone, Marshall had joined the navy.

Brokenhearted, Loree cried for three days, after which time she wrote him a letter, called Mike for his address in boot camp, licked the stamp, placed it on the envelope, and then promptly ripped the letter in half and threw it in the garbage.

Loree was very angry when, two weeks later, she learned that Marshall had only joined the reserves and would be home in time for Thanksgiving. All those days that she had cried because she was never going to see him again, and he would be home in two weeks!

"Ha! Who needs it?"

Again, they took one look at each other when he got home, and started dating the next day. It was all so agonizing, she knew it had to be the real thing.

Although Loree was always curious about life in general, high school could not keep her attention. She opted for an alternative education program, with the hopes that she could define her own education. The free time she had afforded her the opportunity to begin to explore who she was creatively. She began modeling, although she was in the petite category. For a time it was a good experience, satisfying her teenage narcissism. But something was missing. She wanted to be challenged, she wanted to be in charge of her own creative process.

Still the sole provider for the household, Silversong graduated from accounting school and got a job working for a CPA. She still painted, but it was hard enough being an artist, let alone a starving artist with kids. Raising a teenager getting ready to leave the nest is never easy, and Loree was ready to fly solo. Silversong did her best to encourage and guide Loree, all the while knowing that Loree would most likely do the opposite of what she suggested.

Besides money, the only thing separating the family was the U.S./Canadian border. They all became intimately familiar with every little twist, turn, and bump in the road between Seattle and Kamloops. Although everyone was working hard and raising families, there was rarely a holiday or birthday that went by without some sort of family celebration.

1980

When she was eighteen, Loree began working for a modeling agency as the assistant director, coordinating fashion shows. When the director decided to move on, Loree lacked the basic business skills to take over the business. Going to business college seemed a good bet.

On a business school field trip to a large medical insurance company, Loree "accidentally" got a job offer. As part of the field trip, the students had to fill out employment applications. They didn't know the applications were going to be evaluated by the company, and Loree was quite surprised when the personnel manager called her later with a job offer.

The job paid little and she still had three months to go in school, so Loree declined. But the manager liked the fact that Loree had been honest about her situation, and called back with another offer, this time a good position with considerably higher pay. Although Loree didn't want to take it, everyone, including her college job counselor, said they'd kill her if she didn't, so she did. She should have followed her own instincts, though, because it definitely wasn't her cup of tea. She stuck with it for about a year, and then she quit, frustrated by the bureaucracy and lack of human contact.

Unfortunately, she had no car and no money. She was definitely lacking in direction and financially destitute.

Meanwhile, Silversong was still struggling financially and Marshall knew that soon he would have to make some decisions concerning his future. Ever since he was a little boy, he had wanted to be a deep sea diver. After looking into different grants and loans (only to be denied because his parents made too much money, when in fact they were simply getting by), he made the decision to join the navy full-time so he could get the training he sought.

Loree was nineteen when she became pregnant. She found out just one month before Marshall shipped out for a six-month West Pacific tour.

The first person she told about the pregnancy was her uncle Ron. She was scared. He knew something was up when Loree asked if they could go somewhere else, somewhere out of the house, and talk privately.

As they sat directly across from one another, Ron waited patiently for her to spit it out, which she finally managed to do, nervously. To Loree's delight, Ron smiled.

Without even blinking, he said, "Lor, this is the best thing that's happened to this family since the invention of popcorn. A child is exactly what this family needs."

Loree would not forget his loving acceptance of her and her unborn child.

"It's going to be okay, Lor. You just take good care of yourself and that baby. We'll work it out together."

Always so strong, Ron never once showed any fear or reservations about the future. Loree and Ron had always been close in age and understanding. There just never seemed to be a generation gap.

She had told someone in the family, and had survived.

Loree was anxious about telling Silversong and totally unprepared for what Ron did when they got back to the house. Striding through the front door, he tilted his chin up and smiled at Silversong.

"Hey, Silversong, you're going to be a grandma!"

Silversong leaned sideways, then became stiff. Ron simply stood there, looking at her. He raised his eyebrows and spoke in a very low voice.

"Listen, Grandma, knock it off. This is the best thing that's happened to this family in a long, long time. Deal with it."

Loree was very uncomfortable, but she had to smile at Ron. He was so cool.

Ron and Loree spent the next couple of days talking about what she should do, and decided that it would be best for her to have "Mikey" in Canada. At the time, there was a popular television commercial based on a finicky eater named Mikey. Ron liked to call the baby "Mikey."

"Whatever you do, Lor, as long as Mikey likes it," was the refrain.

Two weeks after she told Ron the news they went to Kamloops. As Ron and Loree were heading north, Marshall was heading south on his motorcycle to San Diego, where he would be stationed before shipping out.

Loree knew that it was just one of those times when she had to be strong, and to believe that everything would ultimately work out as it was meant to be. Although she and Marshall loved each other, and had talked about marriage before she became pregnant, she simply could see no point in getting married at that time in their lives. Her pride entered into it too; she had seen and heard it too many times: "He was forced into marriage" or "They only got married because she was pregnant."

Worst of all, she worried that someday Marshall would feel trapped, and she couldn't have lived with that.

After a long day's drive across the U.S./Canadian border and up through Frazer Canyon in British Columbia, they arrived at Anne's house in Kamloops. Loree didn't know it, but Ron had already broken the news to her. Anne later told Loree that Ron was pretty shaken up about it, but he never let Loree know. Together, he and Anne remained silent, while Loree gathered her courage to tell her grandmother the news herself.

Hugging Loree tightly as they cried, Anne told her that every child is a miracle, a gift from God, and something to celebrate.

The family always referred to Anne's place in Kamloops as Camp David. They had special names for every place that she had lived. In a moment of crisis, Anne was gifted. She always said that the words came from God, and wouldn't take personal credit for them. She couldn't explain why people of all ages and races were, at different times, inexplicably drawn to her, but those that know her, know that she is special.

Amethest was almost thirteen when Loree came to live with them. Ten years had already passed since Patty had walked on in the fire. Amethest was the spitting image of her mother. Somewhere out there, Patty must be very proud.

Loree arrived in May, turned twenty years old on June 2, and Ron threw her another great birthday party. This time, it was a barbecue in Anne's backyard. As a gift, she received the most adorable playpen—white with pink, blue, and yellow designs, and little portholes. Someday she would see her baby's face peeking out from these; she was thrilled.

A magical thing happened that day. Just as the hamburgers were getting done on the grill, the wind swept into the backyard, sending thousands of tiny white flowers from the tree branches circling around them, like snow dancing in the warm June air. They all ran into the house, laughing, and began picking miniature white petals off the hamburgers and out of their hair.

But the light note on which summer began subtly changed. Ron and Monica split up again. It wasn't seen as Monica's fault, or Ron's. They were just two people trying to have a life, preferably together, and they were running into problems.

Now it was Loree, Ron, Anne, and Amethest living at Camp David, trying to come up with a new game plan.

In addition to the separation, Ron was laid off from his job and he became depressed and confused. It seemed he had come to a crossroads in his life; the family sensed it just from being near him.

The self-inflicted solitude Ron sometimes endured was never evident in the presence of his daughters. Nothing could dampen the glow of love that was present when he hugged his children. He wouldn't just take them to the park; he'd drive them to a field full of wildflowers.

Those were the good times, the good days. Then nightfall would come, and with it, the weight of the world, as all of Ron's worries would become too real.

He was drinking too much, and probably always had. The family worried about him, yet felt helpless. Sometimes all you can give is love, and sometimes it doesn't seem to be enough.

Off he'd roar on his motorcycle, saying "fuck them all," and he'd have a few beers, escaping for a day.

For the most part, his mood was heavy throughout the summer, until he drove a friend to Edmonton. He was gone for a week, then walked in the front door one evening to find Anne and Loree sitting quietly, enjoying the soft country music on the radio while Anne sewed and Loree read a magazine. When Loree looked up, she saw an expression on Ron's face that was a mixture of excitement and deep peace. She had never seen that look before.

"I stopped in Edson on the way back," Ron said.

"Oh, I see, "said Anne. "Did you see Patty?"

"Yes, Mom, I did."

Anne began to shake softly.

"And how is she?"

"She's good, Mom. She's fine."

This was the first time either Anne or Loree had heard Ron talk about his sister, and they both knew it was the first time since the funeral that he'd been able to go to her grave.

"It was the most incredible thing, Lor. I figured I'd park the car and see if I could just look around and find her. I'd just about given up, and then, you'll never believe it, as I was walking back to the car, I looked down and saw that I had parked right next to Pat's grave."

Never once did his mood waver. He was at peace, and spoke of Patty in an easy way.

Several nights later, Loree stood in her dark room, eight months pregnant, staring out the window. The wind was warm as she stood looking at a full moon, hung high.

She saw Ron start up his motorcycle and ride it slowly up the street and around the corner heading toward Westsyde. She stood there for a long time, first watching, and then only listening, until the sound of his motorcycle disappeared.

After midnight, Loree awoke from a restless sleep and heard the sound of sirens heading toward Westsyde. Westsyde Road had a bad reputation when it came to accidents. When they occurred, they were usually fatal, and it always made her uneasy when she saw the twirling red lights of an ambulance speeding to someone's aid.

Unable to fall back asleep, she lay in bed until one-thirty in the morning, then the phone rang and startled her. Anne hadn't been able to sleep either, and when Loree answered the phone, she quickly realized that Anne had already picked it up and was talking to one of Ron's friends named Sonny.

"Mom . . . Mom, this is Sonny." Like so many others, he called Anne "Mom" too. "Sorry to call so late but I was wondering if Ron was home?"

Interrupting their conversation, Loree spoke up.

"Gram, I've got the extension upstairs. Is everything okay?"

I could hear her take a deep breath, and then, in a small voice, she spoke.

"What's going on, Sonny? Has something happened to Ron?"

"Mom, please don't get upset . . . it may be nothing, but I need to know . . . was Ron riding his motorcycle tonight?".

Anne's voice sounded strained as she replied, like a little girl pleading.

"Yes, Sonny—oh God, Sonny, it's a blue and black bike. Is he hurt? Is it bad?"

"Slow down, Mom. Now look, it may be nothing, nothing at all. My girlfriend was driving home from work on Westsyde Road and she saw an accident and thought she might have seen Ron's bike. Look, I'm going down to check it out. As soon as I know what's going on, I'll call you."

"Okay, Sonny, call me right away."

Loree met Anne at the base of the stairs. Walking into the dimly lit kitchen, they hesitantly made eye contact.

"Oh, Loree, I heard an ambulance going out to Westsyde Road about an hour ago."

She grimaced as Loree told her that she had heard it, too.

"Did you hear it come back Loree? Were there any sirens?"

"No Grandma, I didn't, but if it wasn't serious, they wouldn't have needed sirens on the way back, right?"

They stood in the kitchen, waiting for a word, and wondering if perhaps he was already gone.

The phone didn't ring again. Anne's house was at the end of a very long street, and they saw three police cars with their lights flashing. As if in slow motion, they watched as the cars moved up the street. Anne and Loree prayed that they would pass by their house; but to their horror, the cars turned into their driveway. They saw Lyle, Ron's best friend, in the lead car. They needed no words to tell them that Ron was dead.

Walking out onto the driveway, Loree wrapped a robe around her big belly and watched as Anne stood, waiting.

"Lyle, how bad is it?" Anne asked, as he stepped out of the squad car.

Unable to speak, Lyle's knees began to give way as he moved toward them.

"He's dead, isn't he, Lyle? Please tell me what's happened to Ron."

"Lyle, is it true?" Loree asked.

Sill unable to speak, he nodded yes.

Ron was giving an old friend a ride home. They lost their balance, ran up onto a curb, and into a light pole. His friend sustained minor injuries; Ron had died instantly.

Lyle had seen it all. He had been driving behind them when they crashed. In shock after witnessing the death of his best friend, Lyle was led into the house.

Loree watched Anne pick up a pack of matches from the table. The matches were from the local gas company. Ron had left them on the table before he left that night. Squeezing them tightly in her hand, she shook her head, as a long moaning "no" escaped from her lips. Turning toward Loree, she opened up her tightly clenched fist, and showed Loree where Ron had circled the words, "A Light in the Night."

Amethest woke up. More tears. Everyone was in shock. The baby began to roll in Loree's belly and her stomach hurt. Someone had to call Lance, someone had to call Monica, someone had to tell the girls that their daddy was dead. And Silversong was so close to Ron. Would she simply fall apart when she heard the news?

Dialing all the numbers that were necessary to call long distance, Loree listened to the phone ring once, then handed it to Anne. Silversong answered in a groggy voice, but it would be okay. Soon, Silversong would be with them.

I had a quiet evening at home and went to bed early knowing I had a busy morning to look forward to. As I lay down in bed, I had a feeling of being in a state of crystal-clear consciousness. There was a clarity like never before. I could hear the frogs trying to harmonize; every car that passed by seemed to grow louder.

I've always fallen asleep easily. I had no major problems at the time; my life was going smoothly for a change. Life had been unfolding gently and there was no stressful situation trying to steal my thoughts.

I'll just close my eyes, I said to myself.

The moment my eyes closed, I saw Ron. His face was right there in front of me, as if I were looking through a glass, one that was slightly tinted, like a veil.

He had no ears, no hair, just his facial features, and he had that determined expression on his face, like the time he drove through a washout in the Frazer Canyon against all advice. "No sweat, I can make it through."

I thought about that impassable road where he bypassed the barricades and broke through; it revealed Ron's true essence.

In front of Ron's face, on my side of the glass, was a pure white feather and two abstract images that hovered in space. They were colored, fire red and water blue, like soul blossoms. They resembled roses. There was a symbology present that I couldn't decipher.

I felt a real excitement—wow, wow, wow! Nothing like this had ever happened to me before, something powerful is happening and it's for Ron, I thought.

He was right when he said, "Someday I'm really going to blow your mind, Silversong."

He got it right, he really did it, I kept thinking as my heart leapt with excitement. I wanted to phone him right then and there. I was sure this meant he was going to get the job he wanted. I felt this was a turning point for Ron; everything was going to be okay now.

Crawling out of bed, I made my way to the kitchen. 1:15 A.M., too late to call. I would have to do it in the morning.

I turned on the television, but left the volume off. The house was silent. I read the newspaper. My mind was still so clear and alert. I decided to warm some milk in an attempt to make myself sleepy. After drinking it, I went and lay back down in my bed.

"I'll just close my eyes again," I repeated out loud, exactly as before, and Ron was right there. It was the same imagery. I was in another dimension—no time, no space, no judgments, no considerations.

For the first time in my life, I knew how much I didn't know. That's when the phone rang.

"Ron's gone. He died about an hour ago."

The pain rolled over me in violent waves.

It wasn't until I laid down my white eagle feather on his chest that I fully realized I was seeing the exact same vision for the third time.

I was holding my feather for strength, and I spontaneously laid it on his chest. I kissed him, with deeply, deeply felt loss, moved down to his feet and rubbed them as I looked up at him. The vision held. Because of his injuries, his face was wrapped so I couldn't see his ears or hair, only his face, and one white feather.

That night, the radio played until sunrise. Amethest and Loree stood together, staring out the window, waiting for the rest of the family to arrive. Dolly Parton sang, "I will always love you."

"It's true, isn't it, Lor—we'll always love Ron, won't we?"

"Always, honey, that's one thing that never dies."

It was a long, long night. Anne, Lance, and Monica were especially bereaved. They drove up to the hospital emergency room, and Loree got out of the car and explained to the doctor that the family had just experienced a death and needed tranquilizers. Handing her a small brown envelope, he offered his sympathy.

"Were you the doctor who saw Ron when he was brought in? Did he suffer? Is he still here?" she asked, unable to censor her thoughts.

"He died instantly. He never knew."

"I would like his jacket . . . black leather?"

"I'm sorry. They wanted to get to him quickly. The paramedics had to cut it off."

He shifted uncomfortably and gazed off toward an empty hallway.

Handing over the little brown envelope, Loree had brought Anne and Monica something that would help them make it through the night. She wished that she could take one, but that was not an option, she still had to have "Mikey." Ron had died, but the world did not stand still. Loree couldn't understand it; everything had changed, yet the sun still rose anyway.

I thought about the next time I would be returning to this hospital; it would be to have my baby. It was all so bittersweet, death and birth, one dies and another is born. It was hard to feel so full of life and know that Ron was gone. The baby moved. I wanted Ron to see "Little Mikey's" face so badly. If only . . . one more month. That's all I had left Ron, goddamnit, just one lousy fucking month.

Taking a deep breath, Loree tried to calm herself down. The last thing Ron did before he left that day was fix the baby's cradle board. As he walked out the door, she had run to thank him, but he was already on his bike so she just stood there and stared out the window at him, thinking it could wait. She would thank him when he got home.

He never came home. In pain Loree began to panic. Think about good things, remember good things, hold onto the light—were the only thoughts her mind could hold. Reciting a silent prayer, she began to chant as she searched her mind for memories . . . memories that would keep Ron forever alive in her heart. Memories that would eliminate the shock.

I remember Ron in the bathtub race on the Fourth of July in Kingston, a yellow slip-n-slide, long talks, and my seventeenth birthday; but most of all, I remember how he told me how special my coming child would be to our family. He was always so sure of that. Maybe God began whispering in Ron's ear over those last few months, getting him ready for the trip Home. It's almost as if Ron knew our family needed this baby because nothing except this new little life could have made my family smile.

Oh, God, or Jesus, or whoever you are, I know you couldn't be that cruel. You'll let Ron peek down from heaven and see my baby's face, won't you?

And when the girls graduate . . . and get married . . . and Christmas—Ron liked Christmas, all the pretty lights and the way the snow fell silently and how the moon made the snow glow blue at night. . . .

If you'll do that, God, maybe someday I'll be able to forgive you.

As the family walked into McCloud's Funeral Home several days later, Silversong paused in awe. There were thousands of small, white feathers dropping out of the sky. They lined the streets and rode the gentle wind that minded the day. Many of the mourners who gathered in the pews had picked up and held onto the feathers while they said good-bye to Ron. The feathers mysteriously dropped from the sky all day long.

Silversong had a large picture of Ron that she had taken only a month before his death when he'd ridden his bike down to Seattle. He and his pony, his black leather jacket and that look that said so much.

That evening on the news, the anchors discussed why feathers had suddenly fallen all over the city. The weather forecaster explained that certain birds had inadvertently deviated from their usual migratory pattern and were molting over the city of Kamloops, releasing any extra weight for their long journey.

As her final gesture of love and respect, Silversong wrote Ron's eulogy:

Ron knew what love was. His relationships were one-to-one, from heart to heart, another kind of language, a language of love.

Wildflower bouquets were his favorite. A hero's medal was nothing to him compared to an eagle's feather. He didn't think much about the things he'd done, but of all the things he planned to do, his hopes and dreams.

When he arranged something, nothing was overlooked. It had to be perfect, very special.

He liked pictures because they held on to moments to be enjoyed again and again.

He liked to look long and hard at the horizon, and go to the very top of the hill to see as much as he could see.

His time was short, but he taught the people near him love. Nothing earthly tied him down. His path was unfamiliar to us, but he had the courage to seek it, the honesty to be humble, and sincerity was his guide.

Ron passed through our lives like the wind on the grass. You couldn't help but be touched, however little you knew him. The sky and mountains were the roof and pillars of his temple. His children and his family were in every beat of his heart.

Ron wanted to be remembered as though he'd left something in life, not taken something from it. Life could only be meaningful to him in terms of the love and laughter that he could leave in the hearts of other people.

He wanted life to be simple, uncluttered. He knew Jesus was the Great Spirit. He never disregarded his heritage. He enjoyed music, paintings, and an old Indian trick now and then.

Ron lived every day to the fullest.

We can be thankful he passed our way. He spoke little, but a few well-chosen words would always stay with you. Ron had perfect timing. This was his favorite poem:

Friends give flowers
To mark the hours
Each changing season
As they roll . . .
Thoughts we give
By them we live,
As thoughts are
Blossoms of the soul,
Count your garden
By its flowers,
So count your days
By golden hours.
Count your nights
By stars not tears.
And count your life
By friends, not years.

One month after Ron died, Loree went into labor. *Well, Ron, I always told you Mikey might be a girl.*

It was a long labor, starting at midnight and continuing on until the following afternoon. Anne never left Loree's side. She wore the surgical greens the doctor had given her, holding Loree's hand and wiping the perspiration from her face. Loree entered a "twilight" state and felt Ron's presence, urging her on, telling her to be strong, and comforting her. He told her he was very proud, that things would be okay, and that it was all right for her to be happy.

At 1:20 on a beautiful fall afternoon, October 13, 1982, while the sky was a bright shade of blue and the trees were turning colors, her daughter, Danaelle, was born. Looking out the window, Loree thought about how strange time was; one minute it could speed by in an indiscernible flash, and the next, it could tick by in slow motion, where long, quiet days seemed to last forever.

Anne walked out of the delivery room. She saw a group of young student nurses who were touring the facility. Pulling off the green cap that covered her head, she shook out her deep black hair, and smiled broadly.

"Girls, I just became a great-grandmother!"

Anne had made history that day at Royal Inland Hospital. She was the first to assist in the birth of her own great-grandchild.

Loree spent a week in the hospital before returning home. Silversong made the trip up the Frazer Canyon in record time, after borrowing a Cadillac. She wanted her grandbaby to have a smooth ride home, which really cracked Loree up. "Nothing but the best for that baby girl!" she grinned, as she climbed into the driver's seat, looking very much like a little girl herself, as she propped herself up on a pillow so she could see over the large front end of the car.

She had arrived at Loree's hospital bedside with her characteristic flair, sporting a bright purple satin jacket and jeans. She had teased her hair to an unnatural height before spraying it with purple glitter, and as a finishing touch she donned a pair of clown-sized purple sunglasses and clutched a beautifully woven baby basket. Never one to make a spectacle of herself, she made her way inconspicuously down the quiet hospital corridors to Loree's room.

"I may be a grandma now, but I'm not going down easy!" She giggled as she spun around on her heels, giving Loree a good view of her new look, which she'd aptly named "Punk Grandma."

It was good to see everyone smiling; Amethest and Anne had also come with Silversong to bring Loree home. Looking very grown up, perhaps because of all the sorrow she'd been surrounded by the last month, Amethest looked into Danaelle's little face, "I'm your Auntie Amethest. . . ." Squeezing her arm gently, Loree whispered to her, "I couldn't have done it without you and Grandma."

"Oh yeah, Lor . . . what's Marshall gonna say about that?!" Amethest shot back with a grin. Cracking up, Loree had to admit she had a point. "You know, Amethest . . . your mom was really special to me. And I have a feeling you're going to be very special to Danaelle . . . you already are to me."

"It's not easy, is it, Lor?"

She was only thirteen years old, and had already lost her mother and an uncle who had helped raise her; no phony smile or wishy-washy words were going to fool this kid. "No, Amethest, it isn't easy, but we're family and we'll always have each other . . . we'll always have our memories and sometimes you just have to be very brave."

Smiling, Loree nodded her head . . . although she hadn't said it, Loree knew that, like her, Amethest was thinking how much more real everything had seemed since Ron died.

We had to move on . . . we had to keep living.

Two weeks after the baby was born, Loree returned with Silver-song to Seattle. She felt a lot of guilt leaving Anne and Amethest at home, they'd stuck with her through thick and thin. And she couldn't help but feel somehow like she was abandoning them, al-though they all knew that wasn't the case. She just needed to get away. There was so much pain that she thought at times she might go crazy herself. It was all she could do, with what little strength she had left, to watch Anne wash, iron, and mend Ron's clothes before giving them away.

The drive to Seattle felt good, as they cruised through the Frazer Canyon in Silversong's borrowed Cadillac. The leather seats seemed to comfort Loree's body; she was still sore and tied in knots by stored tension and raging hormones.

Looking out at all the beauty that surrounded her, Loree knew that there was a Great Spirit, and she thought back over the last few weeks before Ron died and the conversations they'd had. Recaptur-ing those moments frozen in time, she found some peace at last that she could hold onto while the world whizzed by.

I thought about the night he told us about going to see Patty, and

it comforted me. I also remembered talking to him the day before
he died. We were standing in the kitchen washing dishes and talk-
ing about his future plans. "I'm going on a trip soon, Lor," he
said. That was sure news to me, and I looked up at him and raised
my eyebrows. "Oh yeah, Ron, where to? You heading back North
again to work in Yellow Knife?"

He looked at me in a rather amused way that he often had and
he said, "No, Lor, I've been North and I've been South . . . this
time I'm heading East."

"What's in the East?" I asked, genuinely puzzled by his
reply.

"I honestly don't know, Lor, that's why I'm goin'. . . . I've never
been there before."

It seemed like a strange conversation at the time . . . but now I
think maybe heaven is somewhere in the East.

Back in Seattle, Silversong and Loree entered Silversong's new
apartment. It was really attractive, done in shades of cream, and
with a nice view overlooking the grocery store and the Handy Dandy
Tavern. It reminded Loree of Terry Lawsen's old place.

Like the rest of the family, Terry took Ron's death hard. He
didn't live in Kingston anymore; since Anne and Amethest were in
Canada it made little sense to keep the big apartment so he moved
into a little one-room place. So many things had been changing so
fast. Laying on Silversong's couch that night, Loree felt overpow-
ered by the world.

"I just don't feel like I'm here anymore, Mom, it's like nothing's
here anymore . . . and I'm scared." Holding Loree close, Silversong
told her that she was going to be okay and that no matter what
crazy feelings were coursing through her body it was normal.

"You know, Lor, if someone, anyone, had told me after the flood,
Pat's death, and my problems with Jason that the feelings I was
experiencing were normal, considering the amount of stress I was
under, I would have been okay. But because I didn't have anyone to

tell me these things, I thought I was crazy . . . and I wasn't. I was a healthy person, reacting normally to overwhelming circumstances. The way you feel is normal, Lor, for what you've been through," she said as she stroked Loree's hair.

Loree spent a month in Seattle before heading back to Kamloops. Her cousin Sierra met her at the border and they took turns holding the baby as they chatted with a young guy on the bus as they went through the canyon. "Holy Christ!" she said, "If that damn bus driver doesn't watch it we just might make the 11 o'clock news yet." He was right. It was a wild ride through the canyon that night.

Amethest met Loree at the door of Anne's house with her usual bear hug, which always felt great. Anne smiled, genuinely happy to have Loree and the baby home, but Loree could see at the same time she was subdued. It was Christmastime and Anne had knocked herself out decorating and stringing lights and hanging mistletoe. Loree knew Anne was brave, there was no doubt about it. . . . "Well, girls, I've got to go be Grandma Claus," she said as she winked at Loree, and then Loree saw her eyes give way to a far-off look as she gathered up the grandkids' parcels, straightened up her shoulders, and headed out the door to visit her other grandchildren.

CHAPTER TWENTY~SEVEN
A New Generation

It was almost spring when Loree found a little apartment that seemed perfect for her and Danaelle. The interior was painted in a pale shade of blue, the floors were covered with thick royal blue carpeting, and there was a fireplace which Loree thought was wonderful. Although Amethest, Anne, and Loree were sad to be parting, they all knew she was only a mile away and it was time for Loree to be on her own. Yet the comfort of knowing her family was near gave Loree a lot of security.

Even though it was just Loree and Danaelle, they seldom got lonely. It seemed someone was always popping over to see them, be it Amethest, who used to routinely make her pit stop on her way home from school, or one of Loree's cousins, aunts, or her Uncle Lance, who always seemed to bring with him something that would make her life easier.

Marshall had received word of Danaelle's birth while overseas, and his letters and parcels full of exotic gifts continued to arrive for months, along with an occasional telephone call from his foreign destination. It was summertime when he arrived back in Pearl Harbor and he and Loree were able to speak to each other more often. He sounded good, and Loree missed him terribly. When Marshall asked Loree to marry him, she said yes.

Because he had so little time in the military, they had to arrange to meet in Seattle and be married on short notice whenever

Marshall's leave orders came in. Both their parents were supportive, and all it took on their part was a few telephone calls and their
parents saw to it that all of the arrangements were taken care of.
Loree arrived in Seattle three days before Marshall flew in from
Hawaii. His mother, Lana, and her now-husband, Matt, drove
Danaelle and Loree to the airport to meet Marshall. Walking up to
the gate where he'd be arriving, Marshall's father, Michael, and Aunt
Violet came to join them.... Loree imagined the look on Marshall's
face when he first would meet his daughter.

*I had sent many pictures ... but I'm sure none of them could take
the place of having and holding the real thing. Stepping off the
airplane, he didn't look at anyone else but me ... as he walked toward me and then placed a beautiful lei around my neck, kissed
me and then took Danaelle out of my arms as if it was the most
natural thing in the world. It had been a long haul leading up
to this day, Danaelle was ten months old ... and I was only two
months pregnant when he left. Not even knowing if we were ever
to be ... we'd let time figure that one out, and now here we were
after not even seeing each other in eighteen months ... getting
married in a week.*

*Grandma and Amethest bought my wedding dress for me ...
and as it turned out, we were married one year and one day after
Ron walked on. Everyone in the family made it down from Canada
for my wedding, and it really meant a lot to me that they were
there for me. My best friend, Sue, sold her car so she could fly
down and surprise me ... we'd always said we'd be there for each
other as maids of honor when we got married ... but I sure never
expected her to do something like that, just for me. We partied
until sunrise with all our friends and family and then made it to
the pier just in time to catch the Queen Victoria, and we sailed to
Vancouver Island for our honeymoon.*

Two weeks after they were married, Marshall drove Danaelle

and Loree back to Kamloops and left for Hawaii, where he would be going through diving school, which was three and a half months long. It wouldn't be that bad, Loree thought.... What's three months? ...then of course they'd be stationed somewhere and sure, he'd have to go out to sea, but they'd have a home and family.

After Marshall graduated from diving school, he and Loree and Marshall's little brother, Mike, drove up to Kamloops. They drove up the canyon together to bring Loree's belongings back to the States. Loree felt a lot of excitement about moving back to the States, but it seemed as if she had a lot of memories still tugging on her heartstrings as she left. The year and a half she'd spent in Canada had been special. The miracle of her baby's birth and watching her grow, surrounded by the love of family and friends, had made some precious memories. The joy, tinged with sadness after Ron's death, gave a new and larger meaning to life. Loree imagined that those petty little things that drive people crazy must seem pretty minuscule once you've walked on.

The first two years Loree and Marshall were married, Marshall was stationed at Bangor Submarine Base in Washington State. It was only twenty miles from Terry Lawsen's old place in Kingston. Many times they'd drive past his old apartment and it never failed to bring back many memories for Loree. Terry died of cancer six months after Loree got married. He walked on while she was somewhere between Seattle and Kamloops, only hours before she made it home to see him. She walked in the front door, and they looked at her...too late. She knew her grandpa would understand...she was empty, something just clicked off. She couldn't mourn for him like she had for Ron...it wasn't that she didn't love him, or loved him less...it was just that it would have killed her to go to that place inside herself once again so soon after barely being able to escape last time.

He always called her Little Loree and she always knew he loved her, as she loved him, deeply. She walked into the front door of the David Thompson Lounge, and sat down at the bar. "Make it a Blue," she told the cocktail waitress. As she stared at all the empty beer glasses sitting on the bar she thought of the tough little Swede with steel blue eyes, a missing middle finger, and the fact that he never did learn how to pronounce his *v*'s properly.

The waiting list for base housing at Bangor was eight months long, so Loree and Marshall decided to rent a cabin on the Puget Sound. It was beautiful, with both an ocean and mountain view, a tiny fireplace, and a large field full of wildflowers. . . . They'd found their first home. Located only eight miles from Kingston, it seemed like a good place to be, but it was lonely. At the end of their stay at the beach house they moved onto the base.

I guess you could say I'd begun my assimilation into the military lifestyle. I had begun to comprehend my situation.

My girlfriend, Sue, came to visit me from Alaska.

"How can you stand it? Just look around you, Loree. There's not one single thing in sight that doesn't 'fit in.' It's like a maze . . . a cage."

The truth in Sue's words cut deep.

"We're all different, Sue; it's not that bad."

"Well, I couldn't stand it. I don't see how you can. Just look around you. God, Loree, I'm sorry but I have to get out of here."

And before I knew it, Sue was bolting out the door, her bags in hand, heading for the hills. Her words lingered in the empty rooms of my house for a long time. How could she say such things?

Deep inside, I knew that I was asking myself the same questions Sue was asking. There was a sense of isolation creeping into my consciousness. I felt as if I was expected to somehow conform, but conform to whom? Conform to what? I was surrounded by sterile walls and strict military codes that were foreign to me.

I was now required to travel with a "military dependent card" which I had to show in order to drive through the base gate (where I lived), go grocery shopping in the commissary, see a movie, work out at the gym, or visit the doctor.

Writing checks became an ordeal, requiring not only my "card," but my husband's social security number, his rank, rate, and location of his command. Try as I did to take it all in stride, it began to get to me. The navy owned my husband, and in turn owned me. I was now officially termed "dependent," which in itself rubbed me the wrong way. Every time someone referred to me as the dependent, my self-esteem took another subtle blow. It wasn't Marshall's fault, it was just part of the program.

With time, Loree became an efficient military wife, comfortable with the routine, even though it irked her. Her family was the number one priority, and when Marshall and Loree discovered Loree was pregnant again, they were overjoyed with excitement and expectation.

Loree's second daughter was born on August 13, 1985. She had jet black hair and a spirited disposition right from the start. They named her Layla, after Marshall's great-grandmother, and because they both loved the Eric Clapton song of the same name. Loree passed the first three months after her birth in a zombie-like state, adjusting to the caretaking of two small children.

Five months after little Layla was born, with infant in one arm and a three-year-old in the other, Loree watched as the movers packed their lives in plain brown boxes—Marshall was being reassigned.

First, he would go through the navy's second-class diving school in Panama City, Florida, and once that was completed, he would learn where they would be moving next. The household would be put into storage for four months while Marshall was in training. Loree and the girls would spend this time in Canada with Anne and Amethest.

Four months turned into five, then word came that Marshall would be stationed in Panama City for another four months before beginning a special services training school in San Diego.

Loree was getting tired, up all night with the baby and chasing a three-year-old around much of the time. She did what she could to alleviate the guilt that Marshall expressed about not being with the family, but it was a lot easier to be cheerful and positive on the phone to Marshall than it was after she hung up.

Once again, Anne and Amethest were supportive to Loree through the tough times, giving her encouragement and praise, and always offering her a place to live and a shoulder to cry on. She was learning the hardest lesson about being a good military dependent: Be strong and don't complain. Don't ever, ever be sad. But nobody ever pinned a medal on *her* chest.

The children and Loree lived like gypsies, roaming from Anne's place in Kamloops to her mother-in-law's place in Seattle. Like Anne, Marshall's mother was there for her in whatever way she could be, even taking time off work to fly to Kamloops in a little twin-engine airplane, so that Loree wouldn't have to drive to Seattle alone with the children.

After spending several months in Seattle, the girls and Loree flew down to Panama City and rented a furnished condominium for three months. It was like a long, strange vacation. The weather was hot and humid, but the area was beautiful. Loree hadn't realized that while she was up in Canada, freezing, her husband's training facility happened to be located in a lovely resort area. The sandy beach was pure white, the sparkling water was turquoise blue, and the people, mainly tourists, flocked to the seashore and to the hotels and beach bars that made up the majority of what is known as Panama City Beach.

When it came time to leave, they packed up the little truck Marshall had originally driven to Florida and headed for the West Coast. Silversong and J.J. were living in a little town on the Oregon coast called Bandon and she figured it would be a good place to spend Christmas.

Marshall had a month off before going into training. They planned to rent a house in San Diego, so they wouldn't have to be separated any longer than they had been already.

The day before they left Florida, a doctor who had performed a physical on Marshall called with bad news. There was an abnormality on one of his x-rays and they weren't sure what it was or if it would disqualify him from the training program he was getting ready to begin.

In a panic, Marshall picked up the x-rays and drove to Pensicola, Florida, to have a specialist make a diagnosis.

Later that afternoon, Marshall called Loree.

"It's going to be fine. The doctor said it was a developmental abnormality, and isn't anything to worry about. We can still leave in the morning."

Feeling like they had been granted a new lease on life, they stopped at the bank before heading out of town and quickly withdrew the four thousand dollars that would see them through Christmas and provide the down payment for a home in San Diego.

They stopped in New Orleans for the night, wandering around the cobblestone streets while the rain poured down, then continued on their way. By the time they made it to Texas, they were all exhausted, and downright sick of traveling. The kids were cranky, and so were Loree and Marshall. Loree promised herself that once they made it to Silversong's house, the kid's talking toy, Teddy Ruxpin, would never be heard again. Several thousand miles of listening to Teddy Ruxpin spin his tales was more than any parent should be subjected to, but unfortunately, it was the only thing that would appease little Layla.

Wearily, they pulled over for a pit stop at a restaurant called the Black Kettle. After enjoying a few minutes of peace and quiet while the kids feasted on french fries, they hit the road again. They had been flying down the freeway for about half an hour before realizing Marshall's coat was missing. Looking distraught, he said that he had placed the money they had inside his jacket.

Racing back to the restaurant, they were disappointed to find that both the waitress who had served them and her supervisor had gone home sick. How convenient, Loree thought; they'll split the money. Not bad for an afternoon's work.

Feeling sick, they called the police, who merely confirmed their fears. There wasn't a damn thing they could do about it. Looking at Marshall's face, Loree shook her head in disbelief.

"It's only money. It can be replaced," she said.

They spent a quiet, painful night in a hotel, hoping that a miracle would happen. It was almost Christmas; Loree kept hoping maybe that would make a difference. She called her mother and said they were on their way. Silversong was solid as a rock.

"Don't worry about a thing. We'll work it all out when you get here. Tell Marshall not to worry."

The rest of the drive was intense, as their future flashed before their eyes and they wondered what was going to happen now that they had no money.

When they finally arrived in Bandon the whole family pitched in, doing their best to cheer them up. Anne called and sent a note with a check tucked inside of it. Loree couldn't help but chuckle; the good ole' Lawsen Emergency Fund kicked in once again.

Sitting alone one night after the children were tucked into bed and Silversong and J.J. had gone out for the evening, Marshall and Loree flipped on the TV. Merle Haggard was singing, "If we can make it through December, it's going to be all right. I know, it's the coldest time of winter . . ." and on he sang, the sad December story about his love for his two little girls.

When it was over, Marshall and Loree looked at each other.

"Boy, ain't that the truth," she said.

They both cracked up—how poignant that song had suddenly become. This was a good sign; they hadn't lost their sense of humor.

When the realization came that she would once again be left alone with the girls while Marshall went through training, however, Loree was not laughing. Scraping together what money they could, it became evident that Christmas would be skinny this year, and there was no way they would be able to afford a home in San Diego.

They came to the conclusion that Loree would stay in Bandon with the girls. Rent in the little town was cheap, and they found a nice, three-bedroom place they could afford and furnished it temporarily with lawn furniture, a picnic table, folding chairs, and an air mattress. The baby would sleep in the playpen, and they borrowed a mattress from Silversong for Danaelle.

Loree found it difficult saying good-bye to Marshall again. She felt as if the past year had lasted a very long time, but again, she was lucky to have family nearby for support. Loree tried hard to dwell on the positive. Bandon, Oregon, was a charming oceanfront town. Both Loree and the girls enjoyed walks along the beach, beautiful sunsets, and the time they spent with Silversong and J.J.

J.J. was in his senior year in high school, and Loree knew that this would be an opportunity for the two of them to spend time together alone as brother and big sister.

J.J. was anxious to get on with his life, and it was hard for him to hang in there those last few months before graduating. He was a man now, and he was ready to move on and see all those things that a young man dreams about.

It was a turning point in Silversong's life also; her last child was ready to leave home. It was as if her nest had a flashing vacancy sign posted. Reacting like any normal parent, she was torn. Letting someone you love go is a hard job.

Having his sister around helped J.J. get through a rough spot. Many nights he'd come and camp out with Loree on the carpet, watching rented movies as they talked casually about life in a meaningful way.

It didn't take Loree long to see that the Great Spirit had given her a wonderful gift, and that she had been blessed the day they lost the money. Coming to that realization made the time she spent separated from her husband easier to bear. Everyone makes trade-offs in life, and she felt it was no accident that she had the opportunity to share with her brother and mother on a daily basis once again. It had been years since they had been together in this way.

The entire family had a sense of gratitude for the way things had come to be.

One late afternoon, J.J. swept into Loree's house, his face lit up brightly. She knew when she looked into his eyes that he had something to tell her.

"Sis, Dad just called me," he said.

He stared at her, expectantly.

"Dad? . . . You mean, Jason Lowe? Are you sure, J.J.?"

"I always knew it, Lor. I knew when I turned eighteen, he'd find me."

J.J.'s lip shook as brushed a happy tear off his cheek.

"I thought he was dead, Loree."

Loree wrapped her arms around her brother and whispered in his ear.

"So did I, J.J., so did I."

J.J. had always believed that one day his father would find him. It hurt Loree to see how much he believed, and to know how much he didn't know about his father; but in this moment, she was happy for him. He had kept the faith.

"How long has it been, J.J.?"

"Thirteen years, Sis. He's calling back at eight o'clock and he said he wants to talk to you. I told him you'd be there."

Holding J.J. close to her, Loree looked into his warm, brown eyes. They were still large and luminescent, just like when he was little.

"Love you, J.J."

"Love you, too, Sis."

Loree walked to Silversong's house that evening, and waited for the phone call. Silversong and Loree knew that no matter what had happened in the past, it was J.J. that mattered now. He was only five years old when Jason left, leaving nothing behind except an old work boot that his only son slept with for months. Finally, it too disappeared.

It wasn't easy, but they knew that if there was a chance that J.J. might be able to fulfill the fantasies he had of having a father, they wouldn't stand in his way.

This choice wasn't made strictly out of kindness; somewhere inside, they both knew that if they were to stand in J.J.'s way, he would hate them for it.

The telephone rang and tension filled the room. J.J. handed Loree the phone, and for a moment, she was a little girl again, and Jason was her dad. She found it hard to speak.

"Loree baby, I've missed you so much. There's so much I need to say, so much I want to say . . . I love you and I'm sorry. All I want to do is be a grandpa, if you'll let me."

She watched as her brother hung up the phone. He looked so happy.

"Got to go to town! Love you, Mom. Love ya, Sis. See you later," J.J. yelled as he headed out the door.

Loree glanced at her mother, who looked bewildered.

"It's scary isn't it, Mom?"

"Yes it is, Loree. All I can say is he's got one chance. He'd better not blow it."

Looking long and hard into her mother's eyes, Loree spoke.

"I swear to God, I'll kill him if he hurts J.J."

"I'll help you. . . ."

Silversong went into the kitchen to take the teapot off the stove. It was making a shrill sound, like an alarm clock going off at midnight.

Two weeks before J.J. graduated from high school, Marshall received his orders, and Loree and the girls moved to San Francisco. After eighteen months of uncertainty, they had finally found a home, and retrieved their belongings from storage.

Loree was sad to have missed J.J.'s graduation, but the time they had spent together had meant a great deal to her. She was pleased to postpone coming face-to-face with her stepfather once again.

Marshall knew about Silversong and Jason's marriage, but Loree had never gone into great depth or detail about what those days were like. It was in their new home in San Francisco that Jason's telephone calls began. He would call once a month or so from Alaska.

At first, it was a minor inconvenience. When he called, Loree *performed*; she was artificially polite. But as time went on and he kept calling, her resolve slowly began to crumble. So deeply rooted was her denial of the past, that she finally agreed to allow him to come to San Francisco and spend two days with the family. She wanted to get it over with so it would go away. She was a bit curious, too.

It was awkward and frightening for Loree, but Marshall was there and she knew that she and Jason wouldn't be left alone together.

They picked him up at the airport. He was, of course, much older, and appeared smaller than Loree had remembered him. It was hard to believe that this was the man who had made her life so miserable and had filled her childhood with unexpressed fears. She thought of those things only on the most superficial level now. She couldn't allow herself to go any deeper; it would have made it too real, and she was still not able to face the truth of her past with Jason.

It didn't take long for Jason to become relaxed, once he realized that Loree was not a threat to him. For a moment, he let down his guard, and she recognized his true colors. All of a sudden, this stranger became familiar as he began bragging about the women he had taken to bed while still married to Silversong; they were women Loree had known, women she'd loved.

Still, neither Jason nor Loree sensed the level of pain his words were inflicting. He continued on, telling her that his body may have aged, "but all the important parts were still functioning at peak level."

She lay in her bed, frightened that first night, but not under-standing (or wanting to know) why.

They all had breakfast at Denny's, and as they sipped coffee, Loree smiled politely. Then she drove him to the airport and said good-bye.

As the months went by, J.J. and Loree rarely talked about Jason, but when they did, she could sense the disappointment and bitter-ness that evolved as he got to know his father. Like her, J.J. found it easy to be polite on the phone, and then forget about it. But for her, forgetting was becoming much harder. One day, when she couldn't stand it any longer, she made an appointment with a counselor.

JANUARY 8, 1990

I WOKE UP TODAY IN A PANIC. I GOT THE CHILDREN OFF TO SCHOOL, AND TRIED TO GET A GRIP ON MYSELF AND CALM DOWN. IT'S SO GRAY, I JUST WISH IT WOULD RAIN OR DO SOMETHING. THE AIR IS SO HEAVY.

AT LEAST I FOUND STEPHEN, AND I FEEL REALLY COMFORTABLE WITH HIM. A LOT OF HIS CLIENTS HAVE EXPERIENCED THINGS THAT I'M EXPERIENCING; BUT EVEN THOUGH I HAVE A COUNSELOR TO HELP ME SORT THIS OUT, I STILL HATE THE FEELINGS—MY PALMS SWEATING, FEELING SO TIRED AND ESTRANGED FROM MYSELF.

FOR WHAT APPEARS TO BE NO REASON AT ALL, I GET THIS UNCON-TROLLABLE FEELING OF FEAR THAT SOMETHING SCARY IS HAPPENING. I'M AFRAID I'M GOING TO GET IN TROUBLE FOR TALKING ABOUT THIS.

I KNOW THERE ARE REASONS THAT I FEEL THIS WAY, AND STEPHEN SAYS IT'LL TAKE TIME.

Loree had been seeing Stephen steadily now, and she had never phoned him before. But this day was different. She wondered why. She had to really push herself to get into the shower and get going. She was actually feeling ill. She forced herself to exercise a little; it always seemed to help.

She had been reading survivors' stories in the book, *The Courage to Heal,* which Stephen had recommended. Silversong bought it for her. It was very painful for Silversong to find out after all these years what had happened to Loree when her mother was away. Loree didn't want her to feel badly; they had all done the best they could to survive.

FEBRUARY 5, 1990

I ALWAYS THOUGHT I HAD PUT THE PAST BEHIND ME A LONG TIME AGO. I WISH I WAS ANGRY, EVEN FURIOUS WITH MY DAD. I'M CALLING HIM "DAD" NOW BECAUSE THAT'S WHAT HE WAS, THE ONLY ONE I EVER KNEW, ANYWAY. MAYBE I'LL FINALLY GET MAD.

I'M WONDERING IF I THINK SO LITTLE OF MYSELF THAT I CAN'T JUSTIFY GETTING ANGRY IN MY OWN DEFENSE. I THINK ABOUT HIS PAIN. I MAKE EXCUSES FOR HIM.

HE BEAT MY MOTHER, HE SLAMMED HER FACE INTO DOORS, HE DANGLED MY LITTLE BROTHER ABOVE A FLIGHT OF STAIRS, HOLDING HIM WITH ONE HAND AND A SHOTGUN IN THE OTHER. THE YEAR THOSE THINGS HAPPENED, I FOUND OUT JASON WASN'T REALLY MY FATHER. THE WORD "STEPFATHER" MEANT SO MUCH; HE WASN'T MY FATHER, HE WASN'T A PART OF ME. BUT SOMEHOW, THAT "AW-FULNESS" IS A PART OF ME. I WANT TO FORGET IT ALL, BUT SOME-THING INSIDE WON'T LET ME DO THAT ANY LONGER. I'VE BEEN TOLD ONCE YOU START THE PROCESS OF HEALING AND BEGIN REMEMBER-ING, IT TAKES ON A LIFE OF ITS OWN; THERE'S NO STOPPING IT. THERE REALLY IS NO CHOICE. THE ONLY WAY OUT IS THE WAY THROUGH.

HOW MUCH DO YOU HAVE TO REHASH OLD PAINFUL MEMORIES? UNTIL YOU DON'T CRY OVER THEM ANYMORE? THE PAIN RUNS SO DEEP THAT I'M SCARED THERE WILL BE NOTHING LEFT IF IT GOES AWAY. MAYBE THAT'S WHY I'M HOLDING ONTO IT.

MARCH 10, 1990

I FEEL PANICKY, AND SAY TO MYSELF, OKAY, OKAY, I GIVE UP . . . HE RAPED ME, HE RAPED ME, HE RAPED ME. ALL RIGHT, I ACCEPT THAT. NOW MAKE IT GO AWAY.

I ALMOST FEEL LIKE I'M GOING TO BE FORCED TO REMEMBER MORE, IT FEELS LIKE IT'S BUILDING UP AND IF I LET IT GO, IT'LL ALL BLOW APART. I WANT TO PROTECT MYSELF FROM PAIN.

I DON'T ADJUST WELL ANY MORE. EVERY POTENTIAL CHANGE THREATENS ME. I'M AFRAID I WILL LOSE MY GRIP AND IT'LL ALL COME TUMBLING DOWN. I WONDER IF I'M USING EVERY OUNCE OF ENERGY NOW, TO NOT REMEMBER ANYTHING ELSE.

I'M TRYING, AND I WANT TO BE HEALTHY.

Everyday life went on. Loree took care of her responsibilities and the superficial issues of her normal routine. But once a week she would talk to Stephen about incidents that had laid unspoken for years. Those days were hard work. Although not physically demanding, the emotional aerobics required an entirely new level of exertion.

The effects from the time Loree spent with Stephen were not limited to the one hour they spoke in his office every week. Often these meetings would trigger a kaleidoscope of emotions. Tucking the children in bed, Loree would turn her bedroom radio on and pick up her pen and paper. As the music drifted in the background, she began to empty her mind.

MARCH 18, 1990

SCHOOL IS VERY DEMANDING. I FEEL LIKE I'M JUGGLING SO MUCH, I DON'T KNOW WHAT'S NEXT, WHERE TO START OR STOP, BOTH PHYSICALLY AND FINANCIALLY. I HOPE I'M GIVING MY GIRLS ENOUGH OF ME, MY TIME IS THE MOST VALUABLE THING I HAVE TO OFFER THEM. I MUST NOT FORGET THAT.

APRIL 8, 1990

THE LAST FEW WEEKS HAVE BEEN MUCH BETTER. I'M STILL READING *THE COURAGE TO HEAL*, AND THINKING A LOT. IT SEEMS THIS ISN'T ALWAYS THE BEST TIME OF YEAR FOR ME. IT MUST HAVE BEEN ABOUT THIS SAME TIME OF YEAR WHEN MY STEPDAD ABUSED ME. AUNT

PATTY DIED IN FEBRUARY, AND MOM WAS HOSPITALIZED ABOUT TWO MONTHS AFTER THAT, SOMEWHERE AROUND THERE ANYWAY.

I'M TRYING TO FIGURE OUT WHY I'M HAVING SUCH A HARD TIME SORTING OUT MY FEELINGS ABOUT JASON LOWE. SOMEHOW, I STILL FEEL LIKE I OWE HIM SOMETHING AND THAT HE WAS GOOD TO ME ONCE UPON A TIME, BUT I DON'T REMEMBER HIM EVER REALLY HELPING ME OUT, OR EVEN REALLY SPENDING ANY TIME WITH ME. I DON'T HAVE ONE SINGLE MEMORY OF ANYTHING SPECIAL, OR SPECIAL TIMES. I GUESS WHAT I REMEMBER AS "GOOD" WAS A FEW KIND WORDS ONCE IN AWHILE.

THE OTHER THINGS I REMEMBER ARE NOT NICE OR KIND, AND I HAVE MANY OF THOSE. I REMEMBER WHEN HE SPLIT MY MOM'S HEAD OPEN IN CUCAMUNGA. SO DOES SHE, SHE STILL HAS THE SCAR. I REMEMBER HIM POUNDING ON MY MOM, DRAGGING HER THROUGH THE HOUSE. I REMEMBER HIM BEING DRUNK. . . .

I REMEMBER HOW *YOUR* VOICE SOUNDED WHEN YOU SAID, "LOREE." I REMEMBER THE NIGHTS I THOUGHT YOU WOULD KILL US, MOM AND ME THAT IS. AND MAYBE JUST DROP J.J. ON HIS HEAD DOWN A FLIGHT OF STAIRS, EH?

I REMEMBER THE TEETH PRINTS THAT WERE IN THE BATHROOM DOOR UNTIL THE DAY WE MOVED OUT OF SEVENTH AVENUE NORTH. I REMEMBER YOU CHASING ME AND GRABBING MY ANKLE WHILE I RAN FOR HELP. YOU GRABBED MY ANKLE WHEN YOU SLIPPED IN BLOOD. MOM BEGGED YOU NOT TO HURT ME. I GOT OUT OF THE HOUSE WHILE YOU WERE BEATING HER AGAINST ANOTHER DOOR. I REMEMBER YOUR BLOODY FISTS HITTING HER STOMACH, ONE AFTER THE OTHER, UNTIL BLOOD SMUDGES OUTLINED HER WAIST. I REMEMBER, DAD.

I REMEMBER BEING TERRIFIED, THEN EVERYTHING WOULD BE GOOD FOR ABOUT A WEEK, REMEMBER?

I REMEMBER WAKING UP AND HEARING GLASS BREAKING. I REMEMBER HOW MOM'S FACE LOOKED IN THE MORNING . . . AND NOW I REMEMBER HOW MUCH I HATE YOU.

THE ONLY THING ABOUT YOU I LOVE IS J.J. HE'S THE ONLY GOOD THING I CAN REMEMBER YOU BEING RESPONSIBLE FOR. SOMETIMES IT

AMAZES ME THAT HE'S YOURS, BUT YOU CAN'T REALLY TAKE MUCH CREDIT FOR THAT CAN YOU, DAD? WHAT YOU CAN TAKE CREDIT FOR IS THE FACT I'M IN THERAPY AND BEGINNING TO REMEMBER YOU. YOU'RE STARTING TO BE REAL AGAIN. I MADE YOU DISAPPEAR FOR WHAT WAS IT, TWELVE OR THIRTEEN YEARS?

YOU CAN TAKE CREDIT FOR THAT ONE TOO, AND CREDIT FOR NOT KILLING MY MOTHER OR ME. MAYBE YOU KILLED HER SPIRIT FOR AWHILE, AND DEFINITELY MY CHILDHOOD, AND ANY FANTASIES I EVER HAD ABOUT HAVING A FATHER.

YOU WERE MY *STEP*FATHER, AND I CHERISHED THAT WORD. IT LET ME BELIEVE THAT MY REAL FATHER WOULD NEVER HAVE DONE TO ME, TO US, WHAT YOU DID.

THANK YOU FOR BUYING J.J. A CAR. HE CAN ACTUALLY SAY HIS FATHER DID SOMETHING FOR HIM, AT LEAST ONCE. I THINK YOU PROBABLY REALIZED IT WAS YOUR LAST CHANCE TO EVER REALLY BE ABLE TO HELP HIM OUT. YOU LOST PLENTY; YOUR ONLY SON AND A LITTLE GIRL WHO USED TO LOVE YOU VERY MUCH, IN SPITE OF YOURSELF.

I CAN'T BELIEVE AFTER ALL THIS TIME, THIRTEEN YEARS, YOU'D CALL ONE DAY AND SHOW UP IN OUR LIVES.

YOU SCARE ME STILL. WHAT WAS THAT YOU SAID WHEN I TALKED TO YOU? YOUR BODY'S GOING OUT ON YOU, BUT AGE HASN'T AFFECTED ANY OF THE IMPORTANT PARTS YET?

IT'S TERRIFIC THAT YOU'RE SO HAPPY NOW. REMARRIED, EH? I'M HAPPY SHE HAS A LITTLE BOY AND NOT A LITTLE GIRL.

YOU SAY NOW ALL YOU WANT IS TO BE A GRANDFATHER TO MY TWO DAUGHTERS. THAT'S THE ONE THAT DID IT, DAD. THAT'S THE ONE STATEMENT THAT MADE ME REMEMBER.

ALL YOU WANT AFTER ALL THESE YEARS IS THE TWO MOST PRECIOUS THINGS IN MY LIFE. THIS TIME, DAD, YOU LOSE. WHAT SCARES ME NOW IS ALL THE THINGS I DON'T REMEMBER, BUT I BET YOU DO. . . .

Loree had found her anger after all.

Reading her journal entries, she realized that she was still connected to Jason through hate. It's strange how both love and hate can bind people to one another. She had to let this last tie go, to release it. She decided to burn some sage and say a special prayer. *The Creator knows what's in my heart, and I know now that I don't need hate to survive. I'm just a little sad, that's all.*

APRIL 11, 1990

TODAY HAS BEEN A GOOD DAY. I WENT AND WORKED OUT AT THE GYM, AND PAID FOR MY AIRLINE TICKET TO MOM'S ART SHOW IN PORTLAND. I ALSO HAD QUITE A SESSION WITH STEPHEN. I THINK I'VE GOTTEN A LOT OF THIS OUT OF MY SYSTEM. I FEEL LIKE I'M STARTING TO OPEN UP, AND BECAUSE OF THAT, ALSO LETTING GO. I GUESS WHEN YOU BURY THINGS SO DEEPLY INSIDE, YOU CAN'T LET GO WITHOUT FIRST REMEMBERING. IT JUST DOESN'T GO AWAY. I ALREADY TRIED THAT.

UNFORTUNATELY, WHEN I WAS GROWING UP MY MOM WAS HAVING A HARD TIME OF IT. IT AMAZES ME SHE'S COME THROUGH IT ALL AS INTACT AS SHE HAS; IT'S TO HER CREDIT. MOM WAS NEVER AN ORDINARY MOTHER, SHE NEVER BAKED COOKIES OR WAS VERY DOMESTIC. SHE PAINTED MASTERPIECES INSTEAD.

WHEN I WAS YOUNGER, I USED TO WISH FOR "ORDINARY" A LOT. I USED TO THINK THAT BEING REAL ORDINARY WAS WHERE IT WAS AT.

MOM CARRIED A LOT OF PAIN AND SHAME. SHE ALWAYS HAD SO MUCH TO PROVE TO HERSELF AND THE WORLD—THAT SHE WAS VALUABLE, NOT JUST A SQUAW.

THE PART THAT REALLY MAKES ME SAD IS SHE CAN'T JUST BE AN OKAY ARTIST, SHE HAS TO BE AWESOME. AND SHE IS, BUT DOESN'T REALIZE IT. SHE STILL NEEDS TO HEAR IT FROM SOMEONE WHO SHE FEELS HAS ACCOMPLISHED SOMETHING JUST OUT OF HER REACH, WHETHER IT BE A FAMOUS PHOTOGRAPHER OR A WORLD-RENOWNED ARTIST SHE ADMIRES. SHE'S GETTING BETTER, BUT I STILL LOOK FORWARD TO THE DAY SHE CAN VALIDATE HER OWN EXISTENCE BY BEING, NOT JUST BY DOING.

I WISH HER SUCCESS WERE AN ENHANCEMENT OF HER LIFE, NOT SOMETHING HER HAPPINESS DEPENDED UPON.

Maybe the Creator invented tortured souls for that very reason, to be driven to be more than human, to achieve more than was ever expected of them. I hope I can get beyond that feeling and be happy being myself, just as I am. Let everything else just be "extras."

Something more than human—a native girl from Marlboro, sold by her father over a barroom table, with a family who could never figure her out, a mother who tried to force her to accept the realities of life, when the only thing keeping her alive was her dream—becoming a world-class artist.

I'm afraid we would not be where we are today in the world if it were not for these driven people. When I say, "where we are today," I'm referring to the progress we've made.

When I think of my mother and grandmother, and my own experiences of trying to let it all go, it seems like an awful lot to ask. Life's been so hard. It's too easy to stop struggling, give it up, and let it go.

They must be right—the struggle to survive is in our DNA. Here we are, trying to balance the scales of justice, the Bad versus Good scenario, and the bad has been so bad that the good is never good enough. I hope that isn't true.

I wish I were a black and white TV. I wish I were ignorant and didn't care. I wish I could see myself content to be pregnant, with a large package of M&M's and a Big Gulp from 7-11. I wish I wasn't so hard on myself.

Sometimes I can't believe I'm studying dentistry, to become what they call an RDA. It's what I like to call my "security job." If all else fails, I'll be an RDA and make fifteen dollars per hour.

I always hated dentists and the dental environment, so structured and antiseptic, not many human elements.

Don't get me wrong. RDA's are great, fantastic.

What can I say? My mother cursed me—I'm a big-screen color TV.

UNCLE RON ALWAYS SAID IT'S A ROTTEN JOB, BUT SOMEONE'S GOT TO DO IT. THANKS A LOT, RON.

Around the time that Loree's writing began to have meaning and she found solace and healing in the writing process, Silversong began to focus intently on her art once again. She was showing her work more and more, first locally around Seattle, and then in major metropolitan cities like Dallas, Los Angeles, and San Francisco. Her work was becoming known amongst dealers and select collectors, and the turning-out crowd was always an odd mixture of art connoisseurs, local followers, and business personalities. One such gala event in Portland turned out to be more than just an art showing. It was a true reflection of Silversong's family and how spirit moves.

The art show ebbed and flowed with many different stars. Silversong looked fantastic—she was definitely in her element. Loree thought about how cute she looked, only four-feet-nine inches tall, standing next to a huge limousine that the art gallery sent for her.

Sue even flew in from Alaska. She and Loree had been friends since the fifth grade. Loree thought about how good it was to have someone familiar there—a little unconditional love and acceptance sure does go a long way.

Loree walked into the gallery; it was her mother's first show in Portland and Loree's first impression of the gallery itself exceeded any preconceived notions she had. The marble floors, spiral staircases, and incredible sculptures fed her senses as she walked to where Silversong stood. She was discussing her paintings with a group of people. As Loree neared, that group dispersed and another took its place.

Loree looked around, and there, before her eyes, was her own family. They were all there in spirit, manifested through the paintings that had captured their essence. She wasn't expecting to have such a strong emotional reaction. She touched her mother's arm. Silversong knew Loree's thoughts immediately, and smiled.

"We're all there, Mom."

She realized that for her mother, life and art *were* one; there is no separation.

The powerful emotions captured in vibrant colors demanded a response. As Loree looked at "Spirit of the Salmon Women," she knew this was her grandmother, Anne, struggling instinctively upstream in a turbulent sea of emotions, looking for her rightful place.

Then there was Loree herself, in "Holding Up the Sky," doing what she's done all her life, trying to bridge her mother's and grandmother's worlds, holding them together.

"Thanks, Mom; but don't you think my arms are getting tired?"

Loree was only partially joking when she said this, and Silversong knew it.

"I knew you could handle it. See how her head is in the sky yet her feet are firmly set upon the earth as the ocean creates her dress designed with the waves crashing and continual cyclical movement of nature?"

Loree admitted she had a point, although it still angered her that she had to hold up the sky for everyone else; especially when she looked over to see Silversong's self-portrait, appropriately titled, "So Be It," otherwise translated as "Deal with It."

Her eyes were closed, head tilted toward the sky, and a single, perfect purple tear dropped from her eye.

J.J. was represented by the eagle in "The Many Flights of Freedom." There he was, just flying through the sky, as if saying, "Hey man, I'm up here having a great time and I really love ya Lor, Mom, and Grandma; but I think you women are all nuts."

J.J. always had his own sense of humor and his unique view of the world. Loree once asked him to describe his childhood to her. He replied that he was orphaned at age five and adopted by a family of clams that lived on Kingston Beach.

Loree felt that people are mysteries to one another, but that if love is present, this is never a problem. Loree worried about the things she had not told J.J. that had divided the family, yet feared he wouldn't understand if she did tell him. While she didn't want to hurt him, she felt by keeping this part of herself secret from him she was taking away an opportunity for the two of them to *really* know each other. She didn't want J.J. to be just another acquaintance. She wanted to know him.

J.J. was such a nice guy, hardly a ripple, protecting the family from his feelings, or protecting himself. Loree imagined that it was not very easy growing up surrounded by women; she saw peacefulness in the eagle's flight, and a solitude that she hoped was not from loneliness.

Just remember J.J., while on your flight of freedom, I'll be holding up the sky for you and my arms shall never become tired until you reach your destination, or my feet no longer rest upon the solid earth, until my body joins my mind and I become the sun that sets in the East, where the spirits live.

Silversong was speaking to her friend, Steve. He was a renowned photographer whose work had been praised by many. He was also the only one at the art show who was not wearing a tuxedo, which spoke volumes to Loree, and she was impressed. He wore his good Levi 501's and a new T-shirt. For Loree, the most entertaining aspect of the show was watching the line of tuxedoed men, waiting for introductions. Steve doesn't watch the news, he makes it; yet he had never lost his humanity or sense of humor.

While watching them engaged in a form of mental intercourse, Loree and Sue felt like voyeurs. It wasn't that their conversation was sexual in content, but it was obvious that these two intense minds were so passionately in need of communication with each other.

Sue and Loree kept glancing at each other, each one hoping the other would be able to translate what was taking place in the conversation. Their eyebrows raised in unison—their own, unique form of communication, perfected over the years since they had met in fifth grade—when they realized that everything they had ever heard about artists and other creative types must be true.

"Let's get out of here for a little while," Loree whispered to Sue. Sue looked relieved.

On their way out the door, they stopped long enough to grab Steve. They wandered down the street and stopped in a restaurant. He thought it was particularly funny when Sue told him at the restaurant that she had forgotten the five-thousand-dollar camera she had been holding for him. She had handed it to Loree under the table, and Loree played along. Steve didn't get picked on very much and he seemed to enjoy the joke, realizing they only picked on people they really liked.

They returned to the gallery an hour later, ready for round two. Silversong was swaying a little and her eyes were starting to get a glazed look, which told Loree it was only a matter of minutes before she would be stiff from exhaustion. It had been a long, demanding day for her, yet a good one, and Loree and Sue tried to get her to say her good-byes. But she didn't want to leave without seeing Marty Bluewater, a friend who had traveled from Seattle with his girlfriend for the show. She had spoken to him earlier and knew he had arrived in town, so she asked Sue and Loree to keep an eye out for him.

"He's just a real little guy," she said, "and that's why I'm afraid I might just miss him here with all these people around."

She continued to describe him: shoulder-length dark hair, brown eyes, native.

"He's just a little fella; you'll know him when you see him," she assured her daughter.

Five minutes later, as Sue and Loree were caught up in conversation, the room suddenly became dark, as if the sun had been blotted from the sky. Loree turned toward the shadow that had fallen across the room and saw a giant warrior.

"Loree, I'd like you to meet Marty Bluewater," her mother said. "Didn't I tell you he's just a little guy?"

Loree was stunned. That's an old Indian trick, talking "backward" like that, and Loree swore she could hear Ron laughing down at her. She missed him. She missed getting picked on by him as much as she missed having him to pick on.

All the intellectual chatter was definitely taking its toll on Loree. She suggested they all go order a pizza or something. Didn't these people realize that it's inhumane to make someone who is unaccustomed to their ways think so hard? Didn't they realize that she's the mother of two young children who has to return home and communicate on something other than a subatomic particle level? And cruelest of all, how have they, with all their knowledge, forgotten that her husband is out to sea and she will be unable to communicate with another grown-up on subjects other than Tupperware!

She convinced Steve and Silversong to leave the "higher plane of awareness," but before the waitress at the pizza place made it to their table, they were at it again.

Silversong is very spiritually oriented, whereas Steve is a child of science. Silversong began calling him "Top Soil," finally words Sue and Loree thought they could understand, although they weren't quite sure what she meant by it. They looked at Silversong, and raised their eyebrows in unison.

"Well, girls, it's obvious; I'm going to the happy hunting ground, and Steve here is going to be Top Soil."

We were roaring with laughter at this point, exhausted by the mental aerobics of the evening.

At four in the morning, they called it a night.

Hamilton Air Force Base, exit one mile. Loree saw the main gate, pulled into the driveway and parked the car. As she got out of the car, the children came running up.

"Mommy, you look different!" they both said.

"Yes, little darlings, it's been three whole days."

Later, she unpacked, tucked the children into their beds, and turned on the tube to watch a movie, *The Stepford Wives*. Loree decided this is cosmic humor; the Great Spirit's way of telling her to hit the sack.

She was disappointed in the morning when she realized that there wouldn't be a limousine to drive her to school, but she managed to get there regardless. She could never fit that limo in one of those little parking spaces anyway.

A rainbow followed her to school. It made her feel a little better; the kids had been paying her back for being gone over the weekend. They screamed and fought. She just didn't know what they wanted sometimes. She couldn't give them their dad. She tried so hard, but there was so much to do and too little time. She felt like she was being punished.

Loree had only two more months left of school. She hoped she would make it.

MAY 12, 1990

I'M KIND OF DEPRESSED. I THINK NEXT TIME ONE OF THE FAMILY CALLS I'LL TELL THEM THE TRUTH: EVERYTHING IS NOT FINE.

I SPEND SO MUCH TIME ALONE. I'M TAKING EIGHTEEN CREDITS THIS SEMESTER, AND TRYING TO RAISE TWO CHILDREN IN MY SPARE TIME. I ALSO FEEL BAD FOR COMPLAINING ABOUT IT. I GAVE INFORMED CONSENT WHEN I MARRIED MARSHALL. I KNEW HE WAS IN THE NAVY AND I HAD AN IDEA OF WHAT WAS IN STORE. IDEAS AND REALITY, HOWEVER, ARE NOT THE SAME THING.

BE A GOOD LITTLE GIRL. BE A GOOD NAVY WIFE. DON'T BE SAD.

I HATE THIS FEELING. I FEEL AS IF IT WOULD OVERWHELM ME IF I GAVE INTO IT. I'M JUGGLING SO MUCH, I DON'T KNOW WHAT'S NEXT OR WHERE TO START OR STOP, BOTH PHYSICALLY AND FINANCIALLY. I WISH THE GIRLS WOULD MELLOW OUT A LITTLE.

BE GOOD LITTLE GIRLS. BE GOOD LITTLE MILITARY DEPENDENTS. DON'T BE SAD.

I KNOW ITS HARD ON MARSHALL, TOO. HE MADE A BRAVE CHOICE BY GOING AWAY AND JOINING THE NAVY; HE COULD HAVE JUST STAYED HOME AND GOTTEN HIGH.

THE NAVY DIDN'T ISSUE YOU A WIFE AND KIDS IN A SEA BAG. YOU'RE THE PROPERTY OF THE U.S. NAVY NOW.

DON'T BE SAD; IN FACT, WE'D PREFER IT IF YOU DIDN'T FEEL ANYTHING AT ALL.

CHAPTER TWENTY~EIGHT

Chasing Monsters

August 26, 1990

It was official: Loree was finally an RDA. She thanked God it was over.

Silversong called to tell her that the gallery was hosting an art show in Los Angeles at one of the major movie studios.

"Loree, you know I've never been the type of mother who made you feel like you had to do something just for me, or tried to pull rank on you, but you're going. You will be there, because this is your mother and, for once, I'm going to make you feel guilty and responsible for my happiness, kid. I need you there.... Well?"

She finally stopped talking and took a breath.

"Gee, Mom, thanks for never being that kind of mother."

"I'll be the good-looking one with the sunglasses on, sitting in the airport lounge."

About half an hour after Loree's plane had landed, Silversong came floating into the lounge. She looked great as usual, once again in her element.

They stepped outside after getting her bags, and were trying to decide whether they should wait for the gallery limousine to pick them up in an hour when it became available, or catch one of the shuttles that ran every fifteen minutes. Then a very polite man came over and asked where they were headed. He seemed so pleasant that they decided to take advantage of his offer.

Never had they seen anyone undergo such a dramatic personality change before their eyes. In a matter of moments, this sweet driver had become some kind of maniac, screeching in and out of traffic, profanity streaming from his lips, and hands gesturing old Indian sign language that Loree recognized instantly.

As Silversong and Loree clung to the walls of the van, he hit various curbs and large bumps, and Loree could see a pained expression on her mother's face becoming ever more acute by the second.

Finally, as they took another corner on two wheels, and their bodies pressed against each other, experiencing a closeness they'd never known before, Silversong whispered that she had to pee.

Loree had to laugh at the irony of the situation: They flew hundreds of miles to arrive in L.A., only to be killed when Silversong asks the Ayatollah if he wouldn't mind stopping for a minute so she could powder her nose!

Silversong could stand it no longer. It didn't matter that the driver was now incensed because he'd gotten lost; she used the sweetest tone of voice Loree had ever heard her use, and politely requested that he stop and let her use the facilities.

A minute later, they pulled to an abrupt stop in front of a hospital emergency room entrance.

"Just in through those two doors, and hang a right," the driver said.

He stepped out from behind the wheel and instantaneously became the sweet guy who had gotten them into all this in the first place! He graciously extended his hand to help Silversong step down out of the van.

She returned, sat back down, and off they went again, screeching back out into traffic. He was a regular Dr. Jekyl/Mr. Hyde.

"Where the hell is that hotel?"

Silversong was getting stiff; she did that sometimes when she was nervous. Loree knew that if this was any indication, it was going to be a long, strange trip.

Next time, they definitely would wait for the limo.

The hotel that the gallery had put them up in was great. They were on the seventeenth floor with a view of Hollywood at their feet. There was a wall bar, and even a gold phone in the bathroom, which really amused both of them.

They began to get ready for the art show, and catch up on the latest news since they had last seen each other.

They arrived late, but they didn't care; they were having entirely too much fun, that's all there was to it. These art shows have their appeal, but one can only handle mingling and acting the intellectual for so long; then it's time to cut out and be cheap and superficial for awhile.

Giani, a good friend of Silversong's, was waiting for them with his girlfriend, Tanya, when they arrived. Loree had met Giani at another art show, and she liked him immediately. He was very sweet and sincere. She had never met his girlfriend, however, and noticed that she had an unidentifiable accent. Clearly, she had lived somewhere else before settling in Los Angeles.

Giani had recently lost a family member, and apparently Tanya had been there and helped him find some direction and security in his life again.

Loree noticed the power Tanya seemed to have over Giani; it didn't seem healthy to her.

When they showed up late, and the movie stars who were supposed to be in attendance didn't arrive, Tanya reminded Giani of her prediction.

"Mercury's in retrograde. Nothing you plan is going to work out as expected."

Tanya billed herself as a spiritual counselor. She had her talk down pat, and it was obvious she had some college psychology classes under her belt. Loree decided, for Giani's sake, that she would try her best to keep her opinions to herself. It became evident early on that Tanya was not accustomed to anyone questioning her more than superficially about her prophecies. She was plugged directly into the universe. Who where they to question her celestial authority? After all, she had *big* medicine.

Loree thought it was more like bad medicine.

Silversong's agent, of course, was also in attendance. He was a cross between Rhett Butler and Rambo, in a tux.

Later in the evening, Silversong and Loree took off and ran around the city with "Rhett" and his girlfriend, who was also his personal assistant. They went back to their hotel and discussed Silversong's art career over drinks in the lounge.

"You've got to produce, Silversong. You know, this Indian thing's only going to last so long. You've got to grab it while you can before it's passé."

He was so sure of himself; he reeked of authority.

Silversong desperately tried to explain to this man what her art meant to her, that the Creator had given her this gift as a child, that it was worth more than money, it was her medicine; it was not a fad.

"I envision you in buckskin and beads," Rhett responded.

What a jerk, Loree thought. Next, he'll have her painting little pastel pots. She couldn't stand it any longer and pulled her mother aside.

"Listen, Mom, you've got to stop giving it away. These people don't understand and they don't care. Save it for the ones who do."

She hated seeing Silversong give so much of herself away to people who saw art as a commodity, rather than an act of beauty that pleased the Creator.

As if being born Indian were some kind of fad.

"Gee, you're white, how cool. You know, you should really capitalize on that this year; pale faces are really in fashion!"

That evening when they returned to their room, Silversong's eyes grew wide as she watched Loree dial Rhett's number on the gold bathroom phone. She waited for him to pick it up, then she held the receiver over the toilet and flushed. It was a nice bit of symbolism. They were both suddenly caught up in hysterical laughter.

It didn't take long to figure out that this place, or at least these people, could eat you up and spit you out, real fast.

Loree thought it would be nice to get away for awhile; Giani had invited them to spend the day together and she thought it would be nice, even if she did get the feeling Tanya wished she would go back to San Francisco and vanish.

Giani looked distraught when they picked him up. They collected Tanya and were on their way. Giani and Tanya had a business meeting with a group of people who were putting together a big project. They were building a resort town; they described it as a "Disneyland with a soul."

As they neared their destination, Giani kept telling them about Gabrielle, the lady they would be meeting, and how important it was that they be totally honest and sincere with her. Apparently, Gabrielle could see the sincerity of one's soul and there were no second chances. Screw up once and that's it; you're off her "preferred persons" list.

The conversation was getting kind of weird for Loree. Who the hell was this lady anyway? She could tell Silversong was thinking the same thing. If these people were so "in truth," as Giani and Tanya professed to be, why were they so anxious, and why were they telling them all this? Silversong and Loree were presumably just along for the ride.

This was a business meeting, so Giani decided to introduce them and then drop them off at a nearby restaurant on the beach, where they could relax while the others took care of business.

Well, when Tanya heard Giani's plan, her voice became high and shrill.

"No, no, no, Giani, this is business. We'll drop them off first, and pick them up after the meeting."

Her tone was unusually insistent. Silversong and Loree looked at each other again. Weirder by the moment, for sure.

Giani insisted.

"No, we'll take them in, introduce them, and then I'll drop them off."

Tanya seemed to stiffen, but Giani had his way.

The group walked up to the front door and a beautiful lady came to greet them. She looked familiar to Loree. She had seen her before in a magazine. So this was Gabrielle. Any apprehension she had felt earlier quickly dissipated and their hostess not only made them feel comfortable, but very welcome. There were quite a few people gathered at the house when they arrived, and everyone was caught up in conversation.

The afternoon went by quickly and Gabrielle insisted they stay for dinner after the meeting. Silversong had been in the living room, showing her artwork to one of Gabrielle's other guests. They were still deep in conversation when they came onto the porch, where many of the guests had begun to congregate.

"This is absolutely an incredible story; this is a mini-series. Producers chase all over the country looking for stories that aren't half as good as this," he said.

It wasn't until later that Loree discovered that the man who had been talking to the others about her mother happened to be a well-known composer who had recently won his second Oscar.

They had been discussing Silversong's art and what it was like for her growing up in Canada.

For a moment, Silversong looked at her daughter in a way only Loree would understand.

"He's right, Loree, it is a goddamn mini-series, only thing is, we really lived it," she said.

"I know, Mom."

They both laughed and resumed socializing, but something had happened. For a moment, they fully remembered their painful past; for them, the lightheartedness of the evening wouldn't be recaptured.

Gabrielle had also experienced some of the harsh realities life has to offer. She'd lost a child and had known hard financial times, among other things.

She had the need to bond with Loree that night, and she wrapped her arms around her and said, "You're very special, Loree. I feel like you're a little sister to me."

Loree had always wanted to have a big sister.

She smiled and twirled her around, "Isn't she just beautiful?" she said to Tanya.

"Oh, yes. Loree's very special," Tanya replied.

It amazed Loree how Tanya had warmed up to her in the presence of Gabrielle. Loree didn't care. She had made a friend that night, and that's all that mattered.

Gabrielle insisted that Silversong and Loree should be involved in her resort idea. She asked if they would be willing to relocate.

"We'll have to think long and hard on that one."

She had it all figured out in a matter of minutes—their lives, that is.

First, Silversong would be commissioned to paint a large mural in the main entrance, and Gabrielle would carry Loree's line of contemporary and traditional Native American jewelry and accessories.

It was all very nice, but they weren't going to bet the house on it.

When they arrived back at the hotel that night, they talked about what had happened, and cried. Somehow the idea of their lives being seen as some kind of soap opera, or mini-series, was less than appealing when they considered the reality of it, and they realized that not everyone's reality had been the same as their own. They had taken it in stride, and now it had caught up with them.

The taxi driver who took them to the airport was quite a conversationalist. He pointed out several locations of recent drive-by shootings and a few other points of interest.

Silversong and Loree parted at the airport where they had met three days earlier, and boarded their individual planes, both feeling like they had been run over by a large truck. Loree figured they should consider themselves lucky to be alive.

Back home, Loree's heart was a little heavy; she was acutely aware of the scars her family still bore after all these years.

She thought back over the conversations, the stories they had shared, the stories they hadn't shared. And she thought about how close the family was, how much each one cared for the others. They didn't always agree, but they loved each other even when they didn't.

She thought about what had taken place when they were in L.A., and how devastating it was for her mother and her to realize that yes, that really *was* their past. They had all been there, represented in her art.

For many years, they had enabled one another to pretend that somehow that was not really *them*, that somehow it was someone else's life, and so they lived two lives really, and neither one fully.

Monsters are always the most threatening in the dark.

SEPTEMBER 1990

THESE WRITINGS HAVE BEEN PRESSED SO STRONGLY UPON MY HEART, THAT AT THIS POINT I CANNOT IMAGINE NOT WRITING IT ALL OUT AND SEEING IT THROUGH. I THINK THE ELDERS WOULD UNDERSTAND THE NEED FOR RECORDING OUR LIVES IN WORDS, IN THIS DAY AND AGE. THE TIMES HAVE PASSED WHERE OUR HISTORY WAS KEPT ONLY IN OUR HEARTS, AND SHARED ONLY IN THE FORM OF ORAL STORYTELLING. NOW, IT'S ON FLOPPY DISK.

THANKFULLY, THE STORYTELLING IS KEPT ALIVE ONE WAY OR ANOTHER, AND WE ARE RICHER FOR THE INSIGHTS AND PERCEPTIONS THAT ARE OFFERED TO US IN THIS WAY.

MANY OF THE ELDERS ARE ONLY NOW BEGINNING TO TELL THEIR STORIES AGAIN, AND MANY HAVE WALKED ON WITHOUT RELATING THEIR STORIES TO ANYONE WILLING TO CARRY THEM TO FUTURE GENERATIONS.

MUCH IS LOST THROUGH ASSIMILATION; WHO DOES IT BENEFIT IF WE BECOME INVISIBLE?

I UNDERSTAND THE FEAR, THEY WERE TRYING TO PROTECT WHAT THEY HAD LEFT, WHAT WAS SACRED, WHAT WAS IN THEIR HEARTS. THEY FEARED IF THESE THINGS WERE KNOWN, THEY MIGHT BE TAKEN FROM THEM.

IT IS TIME TO PUT AWAY YOUR FEAR. THIS PART OF YOU CAN
NEVER BE DESTROYED. IT COMES FROM A MISTRUST OF WHITE WORDS,
YET WORDS ARE ONLY TOOLS. WHAT IS CREATED DEPENDS UPON THE
VISION OF THE BUILDER; AND WHAT IS IN THE BUILDER'S HEART IS
WHAT WILL DETERMINE THE OUTCOME OF HER EFFORTS.

I LOVE MY FAMILY. I WANT TO BUILD THEM A PLACE WHERE THEY'LL
BE SAFE, WHERE THEIR PAIN WON'T BE FORGOTTEN, WHERE IT CAN
LIVE INSIDE OF A BOOK, AND SEEING IT THERE, THEY WILL KNOW IT
WASN'T ALL IN VAIN, THAT IT MEANT SOMETHING.

PERHAPS, IF IT'S INSIDE OF A BOOK, WE CAN SET IT GENTLY UPON
A SHELF, AND FINALLY LET IT REST.

It was a quiet morning. Loree's girls were at school, the sun was
shining, and Loree had the radio turned up real loud as she straightened up the house. She heard the odd, out-of-tune ring of the phone
make its way over the music. It was Silversong.

"Loree, are you okay?"

Her voice was full of concern.

"Yeah, Mom, I'm doing great. Did you get any of the writings
I've sent you yet?"

"Yes, honey, I did and I'm worried about you. I never should
have encouraged you to do this. I'm worried it's going to be too hard
on you. I feel like it's just too much, and I can't imagine how you're
feeling down there, reliving the past as you write, and trying to deal
with all of it."

Loree could hardly believe what she was hearing.

"Mom, really, I'm dealing with it fine. Sure, I get sad at times,
but when it starts getting heavy, I put it away and go play for awhile,
come back, and give 'er some more. Honestly, it's okay, Mom."

"Well, it's just that I think maybe this isn't a good idea. I'm
scared and I'm sorry I encouraged you to go through all this shit. I
don't want you to be doing this just for me."

Loree was getting angry.

"Mom, I'm telling you, if you wanted to worry about me, you

should have done it two years ago when I first started dealing with these things, head-on. I've been working my ass off for two years now to be healthy. For two years I've seen a therapist, read books, and cried. I'm healthy now. If you want to worry about someone, make an appointment with a counselor for yourself, damn it.

"I'll understand if you find that you can't deal with it, but at this point, I'm not stopping. I've been in training my entire life to write this book; now I'm ready to graduate. It's all new for you, though, and I understand. I didn't want to remember at first, either."

Loree felt bad realizing that she was the one putting her mother through things that she wasn't as prepared for as Loree was.

"I love you, Mom," she said.

"I just needed to know you're okay and this is something you really want. Love you, Lor. I'll talk to you soon."

Loree hung up the phone and stared at the wall for awhile. "It's more than *want* to; it's *need* to," she said aloud to herself.

It had been two weeks since Loree last spoke to Silversong. Loree was beginning to get the feeling that Silversong was avoiding her, and she wasn't sure why.

OCTOBER 26, 1990

THE PHONE RANG AND I WENT TO ANSWER IT.

"LOREE, IT'S MOM," SHE SAYS QUIETLY.

I CAN TELL SHE'S BEEN CRYING.

"HI, MOM. WHAT'S WRONG?"

NO REPLY.

"MOM, TELL ME. WHAT IS IT?"

I CAN BARELY HEAR HER, BUT I KNOW SHE'S CRYING. FINALLY, SHE BEGINS TO TALK.

"LOR, THERE ARE THINGS YOU DON'T KNOW, THINGS NOBODY KNOWS. I NEVER WANTED ANYONE TO KNOW. I WAS TOO ASHAMED AND I DIDN'T WANT TO CAUSE ANY PAIN."

"MOM, I HOPE YOU WEREN'T UPSET BY ANYTHING I WROTE."

"IT WASN'T ANYTHING YOU DID. I JUST STARTED TO REMEM-
BER. . . ."

AFTER REASSURING HER THAT I COULD HANDLE ANYTHING SHE
WANTED TO TELL ME, SHE FELT SAFE ENOUGH TO TELL ME THAT WHEN
SHE WAS SIXTEEN YEARS OLD, SHE HAD BEEN RAPED BY A GROUP OF
BOYS WITH WHOM SHE WENT TO HIGH SCHOOL.

SHE HAD NEVER TOLD ANYONE EXCEPT FOR TEDDY, AND THE
SECRET DIED WITH HIM; SHE ALONE HAD CARRIED THE SHAME FOR
THIRTY YEARS.

ONCE AGAIN, WE CRIED TOGETHER, AND REALIZED WE UNDER-
STOOD EACH OTHER ALL TOO WELL.

SHE READ ME WHAT SHE HAD WRITTEN THAT DAY:

*IT'S IN THE DARKNESS OUR GREATEST FEARS BECOME STRONG. IN
THE LIGHT, AND THROUGH SHARING, WE SEE THEM, SOMETIMES AFTER
MANY YEARS . . . BECOME POWERLESS BEFORE OUR VERY EYES.*

I TOLD HER HOW MUCH I LOVED HER AND HOW PROUD I WAS
OF HER. SHE HAD NOTHING TO FEAR ANYMORE; THE TRUTH WOULD
MAKE HER STRONG.

I COULD TELL SHE WAS BEGINNING TO FEEL BETTER. EVEN HER
TEARS WERE HELPING TO LIFT THE LAST OF A BURDEN SHE'D CARRIED
FAR TOO LONG.

I WAS MORE PROUD OF HER THAN EVER BEFORE. I REALIZED SHE
HAD THE COURAGE TO HEAL.

WE BEGAN TO SEE, MORE AND MORE, HOW MUCH WE HAD IN
COMMON, AND OUR UNDERSTANDING OF EACH OTHER HAS CONTIN-
UED TO GROW—UNDERSTANDING EACH OTHER'S SHAME, EACH SET-
TING THE OTHER FREE.

CHAPTER TWENTY~NINE
Healing

After almost two years of counseling, Loree finally found the words and the courage to come home one afternoon and call up her brother.

But first, she phoned her mother.

"It can't wait any longer, Mom. I feel this wall between J.J. and me, and I know it's not going to go away until I tell him. Besides, he's getting married soon, someday he'll have children—"

"It scares me, Loree, but I know you've got to do what you think is right."

"I want to know him, Mom. He means too much to me to become some kind of acquaintance. He can't really know me if I keep hiding this from him. Until I tell him the truth, we're living a lie.

"It's my biggest fear, Mom, I've been having a hard time with this one—scared, wondering what would happen if J.J. ever found out.

"I think I need to tell him myself, my way. I just wanted you to give him a call when I'm done. He'll need you."

"I will, honey. Your brother...he's all grown up now, you know."

"Yeah, I know, Mom. I really like the way he turned out."

Loree hung up the phone, and heard the quiet day scream, as she picked up the receiver again, and dialed her brother's number.

"J.J., it's Loree...how you doing? Caught you at home from work, eh? Still on the night shift?"

She tried her best to sound casual.

"Lor, what's up? Is something wrong, Sis?"

"I need to talk to you, J.J. It's about something serious."

"Am I in trouble?"

"No, you're not in trouble, geez."

"Whew! Had me scared there for a moment, Sis. Thought I did something wrong."

"Why? What have you been doing lately?"

"Nothing! That's why I was worried. Couldn't figure out why I'd be getting in trouble."

He relaxed once they got that one out of the way.

"So what is it, Lor?"

Oh ... they were getting serious again, and the phone suddenly became hard for Loree to hold onto. She considered changing her mind, but then it was as if the energy began to move, and she just kind of let it go.

At first, she just sat there crying. She was sure she scared the hell out of J.J., but he was very loving.

"Whatever it is, Lor ... I love you and it'll be okay. I'm not a kid anymore, Sis, and I'm here for you."

She then told him what Jason had done to her when she was a child. She explained to him why she needed to tell him, that it was something that has been extremely hard on her, and that telling him was her biggest fear, because Jason had told her many times, in many ways, that if she told anyone, he would take J.J. away and she would never see him again.

Somewhere along the line, the idea of telling the truth became tied into losing her brother.

They talked for a long time, and before hanging up the phone, he said, "I love you, Lor ... and you know what I wish? I wish I could be there to give you a hug. I'm really sorry you had to go through all that. I don't remember the stuff that you remember."

She knew that J.J. meant what he said, and she felt that hug as it traveled in a second, through a thousand miles of wire, and wrapped itself around her.

"You've done a lot for me just listening, J.J. Even when you were a little boy, I always felt safe with you. I'm happy you don't remember, but you were there, J.J. You were there."

There was a moment before they hung up where J.J. told her he was worried about something. His voice was very soft. He asked her if she thought this sort of thing was hereditary.

Beyond the simple question he was asking, Loree heard the real one, the scary one, the one question he needed answered.

"Am I okay? Am I worthy? . . . Am I still good, even if my father wasn't?"

It really hurt Loree to know her brother would ever have reason to question himself.

"Anyone can have a child, J.J.—Jason fathered you, but he didn't form you. You're a good person and that's never going to change, because, honey, God took only the best from both of our parents and made you."

"I hope you're right, Sis."

"If there's ever been one thing in my life I've been right about, this is it. There's good in everyone, J.J., including Jason. A lot of bad things happened to him, some we'll probably never know about, but there's no reason for you to question yourself. Please promise me that you won't, because I mean it, J.J., you've got nothing but good in you."

Her voice was strong, it didn't waver and it was easy to say, because she knew the things she told her brother were true.

"Besides, J.J., don't you think it's kind of odd that both of us look like Mom?"

"Them there's some strong genes, eh, Lor?"

"Well, you know, Mom. She's always been a powerful, dominating little enigma!"

They both launched into an imaginary scenario involving a showdown between Silversong's and Jason's genes.

"Yeah, I can see it now," J.J. said. "Mom's genes walk up to center court, they're toe-to-toe with Jason's."

"And Mom's gene says, 'Listen sucker, I said brown hair and brown eyes. You got that? Otherwise, I'm out of here!'"

Good medicine.

"We've got a lot of good people in our family, J.J. People who love us."

"I'm really proud of you, Lor. You're the best sister I've ever had."

"I'm the only sister you've ever had, J.J."

"Well, it's a good thing that God got it right."

"I love you, J.J."

It was a long time before Loree was able to answer the phone and politely tell Jason that she didn't want to speak to him.

"I'm beginning to remember a lot of things. The . . . and . . . I'm not ready to talk to you about them yet. I'll call you when I am."

It wasn't ugly or earth-shaking. It was just the way it was, and for once it seemed as if Jason heard what she said. He never called back after that, and for that she was grateful. But before that last telephone call ended, Jason told Loree how bizarre his last two weeks had been.

"You know . . . I've really been sick. I just about died."

"Oh really . . . Dad . . . wow . . . how unfortunate. What happened?"

"Well, it's been just the strangest thing," he said.

Loree had never heard such genuine concern in his voice before. She was curious.

"The doctors couldn't figure it out. They pretty well told me there was nothing more they could do for me. I was scared.

"You see, I was working outside, the sky had been overcast . . . anyway I was only outside for two hours when I came in the house and began breaking out in large, weeping boils on my arms and face, anywhere my skin had been exposed to sunlight. Plus, it was like I'd been burned, my skin felt like it was on fire, and then the swelling started."

"So what was it?" she asked.

"They didn't know ... no one could figure it out. I was dying and they had pretty much given up on me. The only thing I could think of that I'd done differently was that I had begun taking a new medicine. But when I asked my doctor if that could be the cause, he said that there was nothing to correlate that particular drug and the reaction I was having. I was desperate."

Numbly, and very slowly, Loree responded.

"How absolutely terrifying. You must have been really frightened, Dad. No one to help you, no one to make it all better, all alone and helpless. It must have been really frightening for you."

She spoke slowly, deliberately, and honestly—not being mean, but wanting him to fully experience the feelings that were so foreign to him, and so familiar to her. Feelings he had so callously inflicted upon her for years.

"Well, I thought perhaps if I called the pharmaceutical company that manufactured the medication directly, they might know something my doctor didn't.

"It worked. The guy I spoke to on the phone couldn't believe it, and neither could I, but he told me that I was having a one-in-a-million reaction to the medication I had taken and that it was so rare, it wasn't even printed on the insert enclosed with the pills.

"It's been over two weeks now and I still can't go outside. We had to cover up all the windows, and when I go into town to see the doctor, I have to cover every inch of my body. It's a photo-sensitive reaction, or allergy, to light. I even have to wear gloves on my hands."

"What about your face?"

"Well, I have to wear a hat, of course, and they gave me special makeup. I have to paint any exposed areas of my face black and wear sunglasses," Jason said.

"Black face paint, eh?"

Loree could hardly believe what she was hearing, and could only imagine what this hard lesson was like for him: a Southern man, proud, arrogant, and prejudiced, now forced to paint his face black and live in the dark like a monster.

And to know, after all these years, what it's like to feel scared.

"You know what the worst part is, Lor?"

"What, Dad?"

"It's sunny here, twenty-four hours a day."

"That's right Dad, you're living in Alaska. Well, just think, eventually it'll be replaced by an endless night."

She shook her head as she hung up the phone.

Light has always been her medicine; monsters are only scary in the dark.

There have been several well-meaning people over the years who suggested that she confront Jason. They figured it would do her good to scream and yell at him. But to Loree, it seemed so futile. Nothing can change the past, and it was just too damn easy for people to say they're sorry all the time.

She always believed that someday Jason would receive the retribution he deserved. Call it karma, or fate; the Universe saw to it that justice was done. It wasn't up to her alone.

"Wherever you are out there, Dad, I forgive you. I don't need to hate, but I can never again forget."

Still, it was easier for Loree to face the world than it was to face Jason, and look him in the eye. With him, she would always feel like a ten-year-old girl. That's why she chose not to see him.

She, herself, had a ten-year-old daughter. How can two ten-year-olds protect themselves? Protecting her daughters was more important than protecting the past.

JANUARY 1992

I GOT HOME FROM WORK TONIGHT AROUND SIX. IT HAD BEEN A LONG DAY AND IT WAS GOOD TO SEE MY CHILDREN'S SMILING FACES AND FEEL THEIR LITTLE ARMS WRAPPED AROUND ME.

"I LOVE YOU, MOMMY!" DANAELLE SAID, AS SHE SWUNG HER COPPER-COLORED HAIR OVER ONE EYE AND SMILED.

"I LOVE YOU TOO, MOMMY, AND I EVEN MISSED YOU!" LAYLA, MY YOUNGEST, SAID, AS SHE SPRANG UP TO GIVE ME A LITTLE BEAR HUG.

I GOT MYSELF SOMETHING WARM TO DRINK AND SAT DOWN.

I FELT GOOD ABOUT THE JOB I'D RECENTLY TAKEN. YES, IT WAS A DIFFERENT WORLD IN THE CLINIC, SO SCIENTIFIC AND ANTISEPTIC; BUT I'D BEEN WRONG ABOUT A LACK OF HUMANITY IN THE FIELD. I GUESS ANYWHERE THAT HAS PEOPLE CAN'T HELP BUT BE GENUINE IN SOME RESPECT. THE PEOPLE WITH WHOM I WORK, AND THE PATIENTS, GIVE MY JOB A BALANCE I FIND COMFORTABLE.

THE CLINIC IS FUNDED BY THE COUNTY WHERE I LIVE, AND SERVES THOSE WHO ARE EMOTIONALLY, PHYSICALLY, OR FINANCIALLY CHALLENGED. THEY RECEIVE CARE AT A DISCOUNT RATE AND PAY IN CASH.

THEIR STORIES I MAY NEVER KNOW, BUT THEIR FACES TELL ME MUCH. MANY HAVE STRUGGLED WITH ADDICTIONS AND OTHER UNTOLD STORIES, I'M SURE.

MANY ARE HOMELESS, OR IMMIGRANTS, HAPPY TO HAVE NOTHING MORE THAN A PLACE TO CALL HOME. SOME DO NOT SPEAK ENGLISH, BUT WE COMMUNICATE REGARDLESS OF THE BARRIERS BETWEEN US.

SOMETIMES I SEE NOTHING BUT HATE AND ANGER WAITING FOR AN OPPORTUNITY TO HURT, TO LASH OUT. I WONDER IF MY OWN ANGER HAS BURNT ITSELF OUT; I WONDER IF HURT AND ANGER ARE ALL THEY ARE CAPABLE OF FEELING. WITH PAIN COMES THE ATTEMPT TO RELEASE IT: LASHING OUT, HATING, HURTING THEMSELVES AND, OFTEN, HURTING OTHERS. ARE THEY TRYING, SOMEHOW, TO HEAL THEMSELVES? CAN YOU HATE AND HURT AT THE SAME TIME?

IT'S SAD TO SEE SOMEONE WHO HAS SO ABANDONED THE SELF AND THE BODY, BUT IT HAPPENS. I'VE SEEN IT TOO MANY TIMES.

OTHERS AT THE CLINIC HAVE BEEN IN CAR ACCIDENTS OR HAVE BEEN STRICKEN BY A SERIOUS ILLNESS OF MIND OR BODY, SOMETIMES BOTH, AND THERE ARE CHILDREN WHO HAVE NO STORIES YET, AND

ARE STILL BOUND TO THEIR PARENTS' PATH, WHICH WAS LAID OUT BEFORE THEM, EVEN BEFORE THEIR BIRTHS.

NOW, I KNOW AIDS IS REAL. I'VE SEEN ITS REALITIES, AND I'VE SEEN HOPE AND FAITH IN ITS VICTIMS' FACES, AND I'VE DECIDED THAT IF THEY CAN BELIEVE IN HAPPY ENDINGS, SO CAN I.

TODAY, WE EXAMINED A LITTLE VIETNAMESE LADY. IT HURT ME TO SEE WHAT SHE HAD ENDURED, THE SCARS HER BODY BORE, HER SMILE SHOWING ONLY THE JAGGED, EXPOSED ROOT TIPS WHERE TEETH ONCE WERE.

HER SMILE WAS SO GRATEFUL AND GENUINE. SHE SPOKE LITTLE ENGLISH, BUT WHEN WE WERE ALONE, SHE LOOKED UP AT ME AND SAID, "YOU ARE SO BEAUTIFUL."

I THOUGHT TO MYSELF HOW BEAUTIFUL SHE WAS, AND SHE DIDN'T EVEN REALIZE IT.

THESE GIFTS DON'T COME WRAPPED IN PRETTY LITTLE PACKAGES, BUT I DON'T CARE.

I TOOK THIS JOB TO EARN ENOUGH MONEY TO BUY A COMPUTER TO HELP ME FINISH MY BOOK, BUT I SUSPECT THERE'S MORE TO IT THAN THAT. I'VE LEARNED A LOT, AND REMEMBERED A LOT. I REMEMBERED WHAT IT FELT LIKE TO BE YOUNG, ABUSED, AND POOR AFTER MY MOTHER'S DIVORCE, WHEN WE WERE TRYING TO REBUILD OUR LIVES. I REMEMBER WHAT IT FELT LIKE TO HAVE A SECRET, UNTOLD STORY.

I COULD SENSE, EVEN AS A CHILD, THAT MY PEOPLE WERE CONSIDERED SOMEHOW SUBHUMAN, OF LESS VALUE THAN OTHERS. IT SEEMS TO BE A SIN IN THIS COUNTRY TO BE POOR, UNHEALTHY, OR UNEDUCATED.

"THERE, BUT FOR THE GRACE OF GOD, GO I."

I CHOOSE TO RESPECT THESE PATIENTS, MANY WHO WORK MUCH HARDER THAN I, JUST TO SURVIVE. I CHOOSE TO HONOR THEIR UNTOLD STORIES.

Loree sipped on the last of her tea and felt it warm her. She felt very lucky to have a home, her children, her health and sanity, and an opportunity to tell her family's story.

Loree had a hard time putting her finger on it, but she sensed that something was moving, something that was bigger than her. Some intangible force began to move her spirit, guiding her action, and clearing the path that lay before her. Although much of what she was experiencing was a mystery, she had a strange sense of peace. She knew that her decision to tell her family's story was inspired by love, pure and simple. And maybe the belief that this book will also help another person heal played a bigger part in Loree's thought processes than she fully realized.

I picked up the newspaper at my feet, and read that Alex Haley, the author of Roots, *had died in Seattle.*

I felt an impact that was hard to describe, and again felt deep gratitude and respect. I felt a loss for a man I had never even met, yet knew so well in my heart.

I thought of the peace he must have had. His life had made a difference, changed the world; he lived to see his family honored and a national holiday proclaimed for Dr. Martin Luther King, Jr.

I thought about my mother, and our own elusive "roots," becoming known now, after many years in anonymity.

My mother always had a great respect for Mr. Haley's work, and for Black culture and history, in general.

I'll never forget when my daughter Danaelle was born and Mom held her up to the sky, asking for special blessings to be bestowed upon her grandchild.

She always told me it was right to honor and respect what was good in the world. Tribal people have many similarities in their beliefs and ceremonies, even though sometimes they are oceans apart. We all live on the same sacred circle.

Unfortunately, some people choose to be comfortably blind, rather than face truths that don't come easy.

Several months after Alex Haley died, I picked up the Sunday paper and came across an article in the newspaper's weekly magazine.

It was called something like, "Writer with a Hundred Faces."

As I sat studying the cover photo, I wondered what I might find that had been written about this man. I could see from the photo that he was from an indigenous family, and I assumed he would have an identity as well formed as his striking features.

I recognized him as either Indian or Mexican, which I feel are one and the same in many ways. I believe all indigenous inhabitants of this continent share the same history when it comes to the genocide perpetrated against us. Although we are not uniform, we are all rich . . . in our own customs, beliefs, and languages.

I believe we are, and were, all in this together, and that we've all experienced in one way or another, directly or indirectly, what it's like to deal with issues that have nothing to do with who we are as individuals.

At the same time, I realize that we are not yet assimilated into world culture enough to be viewed as a non-minority.

We do not all have ivory skin, light brown hair, and clear blue eyes. And if, by chance, we do, our parents may not; in this case, you may now find yourself suspect for being of "mixed" blood. It's another "vicious circle." When will it end? I suppose when we all have the same definition of a human being, but it's not quite that easy . . . is it?

What happened to my grandmother and my mother affects me, hurts me, as a human being. There's an idea that has come to the forefront lately, of an Earth Tribe, that all of us are part of one big tribe. I would like to see that become a reality.

We share some basic common truths. Mortality makes us all equal, but as in any large group of people, or small, such as a family unit, it is our diversity that makes us rich. We are all unique individuals, yet on some level, we are the same. We are an amalgam of good and bad, we are humans and sometimes we are afraid to face the truths, especially about ourselves.

Being Native Americans, or coming from indigenous families, forces us to search beyond the shallow, generalized consensus of who we are, in an attempt to define ourselves.

It is not easy for a native, or any minority person, to find the inherent goodness we are all granted at birth, yet it's easy to find the bad. This is, in part, due to the fact that we did not write the history books, and those who did often didn't paint an accurate picture, and sometimes no picture at all.

Not much has changed when it comes to minority issues receiving accurate news coverage. "No news coverage" would be more accurate.

Every day, most of us read newspapers or turn on the news, only to learn about the atrocities that are taking place around the world, but rarely is the camera turned to focus on what is happening in our own homeland.

Hunger-strikers in Ireland enter their seventeenth day, but what about Eddy Hatcher? He's from home, he's Indian, and he's considered to be an American Prisoner of War. Apparently, no one wants to know about him.

Then, there's Norma Jean Croy. She was convicted of being an accessory to murder. The supposed murderer was released when they found he had acted in self-defense. That was seventeen years ago, and Norma Jean is still in jail serving time. Norma Jean is an Indian, and a gay one at that.

Justice for some, but not for all . . . just ask Leonard Peltier . . . if you've heard of him. He's another well-kept secret, another political prisoner, praying for a miracle. Few people are aware of the fact that this prisoner who is held in Levenworth Penitentiary has been nominated for a Nobel Peace Prize for the work and understanding he has shared with the world from his prison cell. Robert Redford knows. In fact, he produced a documentary about Leonard, entitled Incident at Ogala. To the best of my knowledge, this documentary has never been aired nationally. Like Marlon Brando, Mr. Redford has been brave enough to use his celebrity status to give a voice to indigenous people. In doing so, he has lessened the pain of such inhumanities.

Minority people have been manipulated into believing they are of less value, that they must prove themselves, not only to the world, but, more importantly, to themselves, so that they can raise healthy children that have inherited a damaged world and a divided tribe.

As we become healthier as a People, we are able to take our rightful place, out of the shadows of shame and prejudice, and into the light.

We're angry, we're hurt, for all of us who share a common story. We can't help it. It happened to our grandmothers, our mothers and brothers . . . it's happening to our children now.

Our anger is in vain unless it is acknowledged. Until it has been acknowledged, we cannot heal.

When we heal, we can once again feel the bonds we share by virtue of our birth on planet earth.

In order for this to take place, something extraordinary needs to happen, something that is very rare: people must listen. People must care, not only about what has happened historically, but about what is still happening today.

People must care enough to be uncomfortable, enough to face the truths we all know so intimately. People must be brave enough to put the real stories on the six o'clock news. People need to be brave enough to watch it.

We are individuals born with an inherent struggle to make the world a better place for our children. We know that they will face the mirror one day, and ask if they are worthy of a place in the tribe.

Our number-one priority must be our concern and action to restore our Mother Earth; this world is what we bequeath to our children. It's time to stop talking about it and take action.

If you believe the government will take care of these things, ask any native person you know, and he'll tell you that you're playing Russian roulette with your grandchildren's world.

Naiveté and Ignorance are no longer the acceptable excuses they once were. There is only Apathy or Action left to choose from.

I have used the word "Indian" to describe the native people who inhabit this land, but only because it is identifiable.

One night after a benefit concert for political prisoners-of-war sponsored by the American Indian Movement, I spoke privately with John Trudell.

"We were never Indians, man; they made up 'Indians.' We're Lakota, Cree, Blackfoot, the People, the Tribes. Indians were invented by them. 'Indians' are losers, drunks; who the hell wants to be an Indian, man?

"We know who we are . . . and we are not Indians."

Grandma and Lance had been right all along. I thought how sad it was, all those years that had passed that they were never able to be proud of being Indian.

Suddenly, I saw what they had been trying to explain all along.

The "Indian" that society had created was a mean, savage, hedonistic, subhuman creature who has no real value. Grandma and Lance always knew that they were more than that. In that moment, I found a new and deep respect for my uncle and grandmother. They never surrendered; they never, ever retreated; and they never bought into the party line. They knew who they were, are, and always have been: Blackfoot, Cree, the People, the Tribes.

CHAPTER THIRTY

Cat's Eye

Never underestimate an animal.

If there is anything about the Tribes that the general population is aware of, it would probably be the way they honor Great Spirit through nature and animals.

Honoring the spirit's daily gifts to them, whether it be the air they breathe, the clothes they wear, or the food that nourishes their bodies and minds, they know that all originate from the earth.

They give thanks to the spirit of the animal they have killed to show their respect, and to acknowledge the animal's sacrifice. In turn, they know that they complete another sacred circle in life. If they honor this animal's gift, their own spirit is also nurtured, along with their body. Like children and the elders, animals are powerful teachers.

March 1992

Once again, Marshall had left with the navy. Loree knew he would be back soon, and that there would be many future separations of greater length. Things had not gone very well between them, but it was as if they had hung a sign on the front door of the house the day they were married that said, "If it makes you uncomfortable, don't talk about it."

It was two and a half years before, on a visit to Silversong's house in Bandon, that they adopted a cat. His name was Smokey;

he was light gray, with long hair and bright green eyes. Layla and Danaelle fell in love instantly and renamed him "Purdy," because he was so "purdy."

Silversong had been taking care of Smokey for a dear friend, Mary, a person with a beautiful heart. Smokey had been her grandmother's cat before her grandmother walked on. Unable to care for Smokey, Mary asked Silversong to find him a new home. The grandmother had spent many hours holding Smokey, rocking him in the night, through the long days of her illness, giving and receiving love with no strings attached.

Marshall was not particularly happy about having a cat, but he could see it wouldn't be an inconvenience to him. The cat was clean and trained. He was leaving with the navy again soon, anyway.

They had been married for almost eight years, so Loree knew how it worked. She always thought it would get easier, that they would all get used to the separations with time, but she was wrong.

No, it had not been easy, yet she was unable to express her unhappiness. It was that damn sign on the front door again.

Purdy gave that special kind of love to Loree and her children that only an animal can give.

One day, while Loree was visiting her friend Eva, her daughter Danaelle came running into the house and collapsed on the rug crying. She could barely speak.

"Purdy's dead! I know he's dead, Mommy. I couldn't get it off! There's something around his neck! Hurry, Mom!"

Danaelle curled her little body up into a ball.

As she ran home, Loree's heart was pounding hard in her chest. She swung the front door open hard, and began searching for Purdy. She found him tangled in a cord, choking.

It was hard; her mind and hands were not cooperating with each other, but she managed to free him. Too scared to come home, Danaelle waited at Eva's for Loree to return.

"He's dead. I know he's dead. I tried, Mommy," Danaelle began to cry as she saw her come in the door.

"No, Danaelle, Purdy's going to be fine—scared, but fine. You must have loosened the cord enough, honey, so that he was still able to breathe."

Danaelle began to cry with relief. Loree realized what it must have been like for her. She'd never experienced death or even fear in her world.

It was a happy ending . . . Purdy was alive.

Danaelle and Purdy would always share those intense moments when Danaelle alone fought for Purdy's life. Purdy loved her for that. They had bonded on a new, deeper level that day.

Over the next two years, Purdy's personality became imprinted upon the family. He fit the family and they fit him.

Loree believed that everyone is made up of a special energy, life force, or spirit. It's the spark that makes something alive; animals, too, have their own special energy.

Purdy knew how to get his needs met. If he was hungry and the family was insensitive to the fact, he would first rub up against Loree's ankle. If she was busy and didn't respond, he would become more agitated and whack her leg. And if she was still too preoccupied with what she was doing, he would bite her, and then run like hell. He never broke the skin or left a mark, but she got the message.

Sometimes, if he was impatient with Loree, they would get into a fight, and she would send him downstairs and close the door until he behaved. Usually, he'd apologize by timidly coming upstairs and rubbing her ankles softly.

Purdy never left the yard. He was loyal to the family, and more than that, he'd earned his place in the family. He protected them from stray animals that threatened to invade the home. He chased away a lot of skunks. Purdy stood his ground fearlessly. This was his home and he would protect them all.

Loree began working part-time at the county clinic in December. It didn't take long before it developed into a full-time job. It had been a long time since she had worked outside the home, and worked so many hours. The patient load at the clinic was incredible. Five doctors worked in rotation and two RDA's assisted. She was lucky number two.

Although Loree didn't want to keep working full-time—and she was exhausted by the end of the day—the time flew by in that clinic. At least she felt as if they had helped some people. Plus, the clinic promised to hire someone else so Loree could reduce her hours.

Carmen, the lead RDA, was a hard worker, like Loree. They made a good team, and managed to laugh a lot despite the stress they were under.

No one in the family was accustomed to her being gone so much. They were all running on empty. Her job was demanding, and on top of that, her relationship with Marshall was slowly draining her, too.

Everyone in the family except Loree seemed to take; no one was giving, at least not emotionally. Loree was starving to death spiritually, but was too weak and scared to face the truths in her life, to face her own feelings.

Purdy began to have "accidents." He would urinate on a blanket or clothing that had been left on the floor. It was upsetting and unpleasant, and it had never happened before.

One night, Loree came home from work very, very tired, all used up. Marshall was mad.

He began complaining about Purdy. Loree, being the smartass that she can sometimes be, said, "Fine, Marshall. What do you want me to do about it? Take him to the humane society, and have him put to sleep?"

Sometimes people say things they don't mean, assuming the other person knows they don't mean it. It wasn't the right thing to say, but she was too tired to argue the point. It seemed like the quickest way to stop the conversation.

"No, Loree, I could never do something like that."

She believed him, and the conversation came to an end. That week, Marshall left for San Diego on a week-long business trip.

A month later, he shipped out with the navy once again, this time on a two-week assignment. When he was on assignment, he was gone; there was no communication. (Not that there was much communication between them when he was home.) The family was not allowed to call or write letters.

Be alone. Cope. Cope. Cope, and deal with it some more, Loree.

It was March: "Beware the ides of March." Her life was hell once again.

They couldn't find a replacement to hire at work, so Loree continued to work a full-time schedule. The last week had pushed the family too far. The children missed her, and she felt guilty for being gone.

At the same time, she felt a responsibility to her employer to stay until they found a replacement. It became obvious that the children needed her more, and it was then that she realized that all the time she had been working, her children had saved up their problems, worries, concerns, fears, and anger for her. Slowly, it all began to pour out.

They were on a roller-coaster ride, she was their safety net, and she was alone.

Danaelle would have fits of crying and be overwhelmed with emotion until she would scream, "I hate you, I hate you!"

She would cry as Loree held her and told her that she didn't have to be tough all the time; she had a mother to stick up for her, to yell at, and sometimes, to say things she didn't mean.

Loree wanted her to trust the fact that she had a mother who could handle it; and Danaelle could be a little girl.

There was a boy at school who sat next to her. He was terrorizing her. Loree spoke to the teacher and had Danaelle moved. Everything was fine for about two hours, and then another crying jag would start—this time, her best friend hated her. They would work through that one, and everything would be fine again for another two hours. Then Danaelle and her sister would start fighting. More yelling, more anger.

"It's all your fault, Mom. You just go to work when you want, go to bed when you want, do anything you want to!"

They were mad at their mother for not being there; they were mad because their dad was gone, but they never said so. Loree thought they could read that sign on the front door.

During Marshall's ten-day period at sea, they realized Purdy was missing. Once they solved one problem, another seemed to crop up.

Purdy never left the yard. Loree feared that one of the children might find him somewhere, hit by a car or hurt by an animal. It was impossible to know what had happened, so until she knew, she filled up his cat bowl and hoped he'd come home.

Before Loree could gather her thoughts on how to handle the missing cat, another tension-bearing situation would arise. Danaelle was ten and about to become a young lady. Loree and her daughter had spoken about adolescence and Danaelle's body changing, but children don't always appreciate the games their bodies play when they begin to grow up. Danaelle couldn't trust her own body, it was changing; her emotions were strong. She trusted that her mother could handle it, and Loree did the best she could. Every morning after dealing with the latest crisis, she went to work, drove home, and dealt with yet another crisis, as well as the shared grief over their missing cat.

Loree was always left alone to deal with the family's emotional crises. The day before Marshall left, he was feeling guilty about not being around for the girls, so in typical Boyd fashion, he gave the girls the day off from school and took them to the mall. Danaelle got her ears pierced, they picked out toys, had a Happy Meal at McDonalds, and at the end of the day he brought them home. He left the next day. He assuaged his feelings of guilt with toys for the children, and left Loree behind to deal with all of their emotions. Time to call Silversong: SOS, emotional support needed, ASAP!

Silversong talked her through it; Loree would survive this, it would be okay. Silversong also spoke to Danaelle and told her she was like a beautiful flower, blossoming. Danaelle liked that a lot. She explained to the children that instead of feeling bad about Purdy, they could "bless" him; and she was considerate enough to ask both girls if there was anything around the house that they could do to help their mother out.

Finally, Loree and the children felt some relief. Even the simple act of "blessing" the cat when they thought about him made them feel less like helpless victims, more capable of dealing with their lives.

Later, Silversong called back to see how things were going. She said she was drumming and praying for Loree. She explained a lot of things, and comforted Loree through her crisis. She let Loree cry. She let her know she could handle it, and another sacred circle was complete. Daughter, mother, mother, daughter; Great Spirit super-gluing them all together.

Loree took two days off work, one for the children and one for herself. She felt bad about not being at work those days. She had given them an opportunity to find a replacement for months, but instead of honoring the agreement that she would only work three days a week, they had taken advantage of her sense of responsibility. She was angry when she realized they had not so much as put an ad in the paper. Loree was prepared to quit, even though she liked the job. She realized it was using her energy up, and her children were more important than work.

When Loree called, the office manager was very sincere and understanding. She said, "Loree, we can't ask much more of you than we already have."

She was right. Loree didn't have any more to give. She felt better, knowing she had done the right thing and felt some long, overdue peace.

One day after the girls got home from school, Loree took Layla and her friend Joey to the Humane Society to look for Purdy. As they walked slowly down the cool corridors anxiously looking into cage after cage, Loree told the attendant how Purdy had come into their lives three years before, and that her husband was in the navy and out to sea.

"He's such a good cat. We love him. We're worried about him," Loree told her. They would have to check the list of dead animals that had been brought to the shelter. It was an unpleasant thought.

"There's one more place we can check," the attendant said, "it's a long shot, but we have a few animals in our isolation room, where we keep animals that have symptoms of illness."

As they walked into the warm little room, Layla let out a scream of delight. Purdy was curled up in a floor-level cage. He was quiet and still when he heard Loree's voice, as if he had just awakened from a long, long nap.

"That's my cat, that's him," Loree said, as Layla and Joey began to jump up and down. Layla wanted to take him home immediately, and so did Loree, thinking of the look on Danaelle's face when she told her the news. It was hard to concentrate on what the attendant was saying to her.

"We'll need to go up front and check the paperwork, and see if he was picked up in your neighborhood.

"You're very lucky, you know. He's been here past the limit and was scheduled to be put to sleep, but someone fell in love with him and fought for him, so they brought him here to recover from an upper respiratory infection," she said.

"We've had Purdy for three years. He's a part of our family. I'm so grateful that he's still alive and someone saw to it that he was spared."

Relief flooded Layla's little face. Even little Joey was beaming, a large ear-to-ear grin.

They were standing in the main front office when the attendant brought out Purdy's paperwork. Looking puzzled, she asked Loree again where she lived.

"250 San Jose Drive."

"Well, it says here that Purdy was picked up at 250 San Jose Drive."

"Oh, there must have been a mistake, perhaps a stray in the neighborhood was mistaken for our cat," she said, uninterested in the details.

Holding up a yellow slip of paper, the attendant began to read, "It says here that he was turned in as a stray, Friday, March 13th, by a Marshall Boyd."

Marshall Boyd . . . Marshall Boyd . . . at first, Loree couldn't speak. Her eyes were wet.

"We have a problem," she said.

"Well, it says right here, that he was dropped off by a Marshall Boyd who said the cat was a stray who had been hanging around the house for about a month."

Oh, please, stop saying his name, Loree thought, not wanting Layla to understand what she now knew.

Loree held her hand to her mouth, and began to cry.

"You don't understand, we have a really big problem here. Please, stop saying his name; that's my husband."

By this time, she couldn't stop crying.

Communication, trust, responsibility . . . how could he leave them there to lick their wounds? Leave the children with the wife, who will make it all better by the time he gets home.

"I could never do anything like that," she recalled him saying. And she had believed him.

Loree could read the attendant's thoughts: Your husband did this?

Layla was crying because she wanted to bring Purdy home. Loree calmed her as she cried herself, for different reasons. Perhaps they wouldn't return him to the family.

"I have to figure this out. Please promise me that no matter what happens, you won't let them put him to sleep. He's a good cat, and even if you won't give him back to us, I'll find him a home."

Loree walked out the door with tears still streaming down her face, and a roomful of bewildered people behind her.

"What's wrong, Mommy?" Layla asked.

"People cry sometimes when they're happy. I'm just really happy we found Purdy, Layla. I'm just really happy he's alive," she said as they walked to the car.

Joey put his arm around Layla, and gave her a hug.

"Yeah Layla, your mom sure is happy."

Loree had finally found the courage, through the Purdy ordeal, to face her own denial. She went home and called Silversong again. Another crisis, an "emotional breakthrough," as her mother would call it.

She asked Loree how she really felt about what had happened, so she sat down and wrote this letter:

Marshall,

The truth is, over a month ago, I told you to take Purdy to the Humane Society if you couldn't put up with him.

The truth is, I didn't mean it.

The truth is, you know I didn't mean it.

The truth is, I feel betrayed, hurt, dumped on, mistrustful, shocked, scared, humiliated.

The truth is, you've done this to me before, in other ways. You mess with my mind.

The truth is, you control me and treat me like a child.

The truth is, you keep secrets.

The truth is, we don't communicate.

The truth is, I think you're an emotional coward. You never even discussed this with me. You dropped Purdy off and left. You left me once again to pick up the pieces, and try to grow healthy children. You left so that once again, you could be spared any display of unpleasant emotion.

The truth is, there isn't enough left in this relationship to keep me going.

The truth is, I don't know if I want to stay married.

The truth is, I want to make my own decisions, based on my own convictions.

I want you to tell the truth.

The truth is, I've spent the last ten days comforting crying kids, being yelled at, and generally abused. Everything is my fault.

The truth is, you're not here and I'm all alone.

The truth is, when you're home, I'm still alone.

The truth is, the children are scared of you, your yelling and spanking, your moods.

The truth is, they love you.

The truth is, I'm very unhappy and I don't know what to do. I want the chance to decide. I want to separate for awhile and see if we can learn to communicate and be happy. I need more.

The truth is, this is very scary for me. I am also an emotional coward in many ways.

Loree

She sent the letter.

Loree took the children and went to her friend Eva's house. She was scared, but the action she took was empowering—the truth often is.

It was a powerful lesson her Purdy taught her. He almost lost his life, showing her things she didn't want to see. Strange lessons that a cat can teach.

It was comical, too. She had one friend who, upon hearing what had happened, arrived at her child's daycare center, decked out in cat regalia from head to toe. There was a gray cat motif on her T-shirt, a cat on her wrist band, a lapel pin, and even cats dangling from her earlobes. Was she trying to cheer her up? Make her smile? Perhaps, and perhaps she also didn't realize how sad Loree was or how much it had hurt her.

Loree laughed. For awhile, she wasn't sure what to do, laugh or cry, so somehow she managed to do both.

Humor, the Sacred Clown, the Coyote. There's a reason for all this, she told herself, as she tried to disengage from her darker emotions.

Upon receiving her letter, Marshall called to suggest they get together to talk. He had taken what she had said seriously, and for that, she was grateful.

It was sometime during this conversation that he mentioned having a problem with peer pressure.

Weird, she thought momentarily, what would peer pressure have to do with anything? But she didn't really think much about it until later that day.

They were standing in their bedroom when Marshall looked at her, as if she knew something, as if she had a secret. With a strange expression on his face, he began looking through her jewelry.

"You haven't seen my wedding ring, have you, Loree?"

Surprised by such a question, she turned toward him and shook her head no.

"Well, if you found it, you'd give it to me wouldn't you, Loree?"

This was getting really strange. She looked down at his hand and realized that his ring was indeed missing.

"Of course I would, Marshall."

Still looking weird, he walked into the bathroom to shave. Loree sat on the bed, beginning to realize what this was really all about. She remained calm.

"So, when did you lose your wedding ring?"

Marshall stared at her for a long moment, as if deciding whether or not to tell the truth.

"The last time I had it was when I was in San Diego . . . I know it doesn't sound very good."

"You're damn right it doesn't sound very good."

He had probably thought she had known all along that his ring was missing. She highly doubted that the cat had anything to do with the real issue they were dealing with here.

With a nervous smile on his face, he stared at her, waiting. For what, she didn't know.

"That was two months ago. Anything else you forgot to tell me about? Children that I don't know about, perhaps?"

She turned to walk out the front door.

"You mean you never noticed it was gone?" he asked. Looking directly at him, she shook her head.

"No, Marshall, I never noticed, I don't look for things like that. When the time comes that I have to look for things like that, it won't be the kind of relationship I want anymore."

There were many more words exchanged.

The morning he had taken Purdy, a violent storm had erupted. Big, black clouds gathered, and the wind had slapped him in the face hard when he walked out the door of the shelter. He told her, "I know that damn cat's going to get me. . . ."

He had actually told her that she was a terrible person for suspecting him of infidelity. After all, he was down there with how many other happily married men?

Loree knew for a fact that his roommate was feeling pretty neglected. Poor guy. His wife was not only working full-time, but trying to get her law degree. She missed one of his basketball games or something, and he was hurt.

"Yeah, Marshall, well, all those men at Tail Hook were happily married too, weren't they?

"I've been to places where I couldn't trust my own feelings, where I didn't even know what my own feelings were, and I will never, never allow anyone to put me there again. Right now, I know how I feel; and I do not feel good about this."

Loree began to experience intense F.E.A.R.—False Evidence Appearing Real, otherwise known as Fuck Everything And Run.

Which was it going to be? There were too many things that didn't ring true. He hadn't mentioned the missing ring for two months—if its loss had been an accident, she could have spent that time searching as she cleaned, and perhaps found it under a rug somewhere. And although he'd never admit it, he knew it wasn't where he pretended to look for it.

Too bad he couldn't tell the truth. Had he actually told her the truth, they may have had a new place to start, a solid foundation, a place where trust grows.

But Loree already knew that he could lie well. She thought of how nonchalant he had been the weekend before he left. It would have been easier to think that he had taken Purdy and gone straight out to sea. But he hadn't. He took Purdy Friday morning, then returned home and spent the weekend with the family, as if nothing were wrong.

Several months later, Marshall's ring was found. The discovery did not answer the questions that had been raised, nor did it restore the trust that had been violated.

Bitter love
Casting shadows, falling from your lies
Where does love go when it dies?
Is it a fire within that just burns out so slowly that the light becomes dim? Is it as the Moon Bird, with wings to fly away? Or with soft, sweet understanding, will it stay another day?
Is every feather of its wing hate and hurt and pain? Slowly, day by day, the wings are feathered in the rain?
When the final feather is put in the right place, love saves itself.
Love takes to flight.
Love leads me to the light.

CHAPTER THIRTY~ONE
Light in the Night

The woman Loree sat next to at the pool on the naval base one day was the perfect definition of *wasi'chu*—someone with no thought of others, or of the consequences of their actions. Later, she realized that Silversong had been right; she should have been more careful.

The encounter started out innocently enough.

"How are you today?" Loree asked.

The woman nodded her head while wrapping her lips tightly around her cigarette and taking a long drag. She had five children, her husband was out to sea, and she quickly let Loree know that his rank was Lieutenant Commander.

She had done a lot of traveling, seen the world, and she liked it that way—to keep moving.

She said that she liked Marin County—where the base was located—because it was "clean, no visible trash." It was modern, unlike the farm in Montana where her husband wanted to move. It was important to her to raise her children in a "pretty" place, where she could shield them from the "ugliness" out there.

Loree told her about the beaded jewelry she made, and that she was writing a book. She asked what the book was about.

"Six generations of native women in my family, my mother's side."

"So, what would that make you, then?"

"Blackfoot/Cree. I was born in Canada."

"What's it like up in Canada for you people?"

"Well, they seem to be picking on East Indians now, so the natives are consequently getting a little more slack. It's unfortunate though; wherever you go, the 'majority minority' are the ones who get the most flack."

This ruffled her feathers. She vigorously stamped out her cigarette and looked directly at Loree in a challenging way.

"You know, there are reasons for that."

Yeah, Loree thought, they were raised by prejudiced parents. No value for human life. No humanity.

"As a writer, I know there are many reasons people feel the way they do. I've been forced to step back and observe. I see that most issues are more complex than we would like them to be."

She lit up another cigarette, and challenged her with that expression again.

"You know, I just don't understand these Indians. It's so pitiful. I mean, why on earth would they want to live on some desolate little reservation, in the middle of nowhere, barren and filthy? The problem is, they just refuse to change. They are stubborn people. As if their primitive technology is better than what *we* have. It's just so ... sad ... sitting on their little rocks, clutching their beads."

Loree thought of John Trudell, who said, "It's a war that nobody wins," a wasted effort to even "attempt" to converse on the subject.

Loree talked it over with herself. She figured the likelihood of this woman understanding her or her people was probably nil. In spite of this, however, her mouth suddenly flew open. Some things just have to be said.

"You really don't get it, do you? I mean, you just don't have a clue, do you?"

The woman was too shocked to answer.

"First off, it has absolutely nothing to do with technology, it's about spirituality."

"Well, what about those little cliques or clans, whatever they call those groups they gather in?"

"Well how about this," Loree leaned in closely, peering at the woman over her sunglasses. "You want to hear something really sad? How about those Catholics sitting on their hard little benches, clutching their rosary beads, praying their little butts off while staring at graven images steeped in religious symbolism?

"And as far as little cliques or clans go, well, I hate to shock you, but we're surrounded by those right here on base. Let's see, we have the Enlisted Men's Club, the Officers' Club, and, of course, the Wives' Club."

"Uh . . . well . . . what are you saying? Are you trying to tell me there are little groups of militant dependents living on base?"

"That's right lady. I'm a Militant Dependent."

"Well, it's like I said, they refuse to do anything for themselves besides clutching their little beads, as if that's going to save them."

"You know, it didn't start out that way—sitting on a piece of crap land clutching their 'little beads.' There were treaties. In fact, they're kept in the same room as the United States Constitution. You know, the Constitution that our husbands are risking their lives to protect, so that we can have freedom of religion? Freedom of speech?

"Well, unlike the Constitution, the other legal documents and treaties that belong to my people are continually discounted, overlooked, and ignored, but no one wants to hear about it. Instead, people flip on the news and point their fingers at the world.

"Indians didn't start out living on a little piece of crap land, but that's what they ended up with, which was fine with our government until it was discovered that the crap land held valuable minerals and other resources, so they took the crap land, too, and left the Indians a rock and some little beads.

"You're damn right it gets 'ugly' out there. That's why a lot of native people don't make it. They commit suicide or drink themselves to death, not that there's a real difference between the two. They end up falling off the rock, either way.

"I'll tell you what America needs. America needs a twelve-step program. America needs to make amends. America needs a soul. So you tell me, what's so bad about beads, or any religious freedom, if it helps someone want to wake up in the morning? If it fills them with strength and makes them happy to be alive? Why does that upset you? Indians have a *right* to see God through their own eyes.

"Did you ever notice that the Statue of Liberty has her back turned on America? The Indian people live in her shadow, while she welcomes the hungry, the poor, and the oppressed."

Loree was still angry when she returned home, but it was good to be there in her own basement, surrounded by the thick walls that formed her Thunder Bird egg that protected her heart.

She felt safe there. Safe enough to sometimes believe she *was* safe.

That day, her Thunder Bird egg split open, and instead of a brave warrior there to protect her, she found a *wasi'chu* sitting next to her, and she wanted to throw all Loree's beautiful beads away.

Our family existed somehow within a state of extreme denial. It's only at this point in my life that I can see the blame is not upon any one person's shoulders. Denial is generational and takes many forms. I have been denied because I was a child, a girl, a woman, and an Indian. I could make this list a lot longer, but I choose not to; I'm sure you get the point. Often we are denied for simply being the way we are, a mass of questions yet to be asked and answers yet to be given. I've even been denied for being positive, powerful, pretty, and having a clue as to what the hell I want out of life.

Yes, even good things can scare people; they're so frightened by every little ripple in their fish bowl. It makes the big fish uncomfortable when their little schools get out of line. Some have very pretty worlds, supported by the sense of their own aliveness. For them, there is a continual flow of fresh water—their fish bowl's connected to something much bigger, and they sense the ocean's continual movement and flow and are at ease. Whereas some fish bowls have become so stagnant, the water so still, that a heavy cloudiness has covered them, as they are supported by no cause other than themselves . . . they have no vision. Having lost their perspective, their fish bowl becomes a scary little place. Don't make waves, they think, because you never know when you're going to piss that "big fish" off, by reminding him that he is not alone in this fish bowl. If we allow our fears to rule us, we become terrified, fearing the big fish will make the quiet water move, and your bowl may tip and shatter as you die, flopping on the floor.

Teddy would have been an "Angel Fish."

Jason would have been a "Man-of-War."

Grandma would have been a "Salmon."

Purdy would have been a "Catfish."

Up near Kelowna, British Columbia, there is the most beautiful lake I have ever seen. It is called Okanagan, which in native language means "the lake of a million colors." And there is a legend of a mysterious creature who inhabits the rainbow waters, and it is called the "Ogo-pogo."

Mom would have been the "Ogo-pogo."

And me, well right now I feel like a cross between a sting-ray and a jellyfish . . . looking for a new fish bowl.

My mother and grandmother have also experienced denial for their very "being." This is one family tradition I do not want my daughters to carry on—being victims. I will empower them by mirroring back to them their undeniable right to "be." I'll teach them the only power any other person has over us is that which we have given that person by choice—consciously or unconsciously. I want to be fully conscious . . . sounds funny, doesn't it? But you would be surprised how many people I know who are walking around comatose.

I'll try to teach them to value themselves so the choices they face in life will not be ones that deplete their power base. Then, as they grow up I'll try to let them go and make mistakes. Mistakes are positive, they mean you're trying. But of course I still am and always will be a mother, and in "being" so will not be able to repress the urge to let them know it isn't necessary to struggle—learn the hard way—unless we choose that as the way we need to learn personally. Which, it seems, many of us have chosen to do in the past. I know this, that one day when my daughters are grown and I look upon their faces and see my little babies that are now women, I will be happy knowing that they have been raised with the knowledge that they are not anybody's victim.

Denial—keeps alive that which we are too afraid of and ashamed of to face.

Guilt—is not a part of love—it is not loving. It motivates us to deny.

Shame—does not accept human qualities—it seeks judgment—against ourselves.

I think if this shame is present and not able to be internalized sufficiently—a dysfunctional state in which we victimize ourselves—it seeks a release and a victim which it can be transferred upon.

Love—denies nothing if it is unconditional—love accepts reality—it is a positive motivator—love empowers us and enables us to empower one another . . . love is not color blind—it sees in Technicolor the brilliance and beauty of our "being."

I feel sorry for those who see in only pale shades of gray.

I guess that is what life is about for me . . . to learn how to utilize the full spectrum; who needs a frame if you've got the whole picture anyway?

I want to teach myself and my children to play by our own rules. And I hope that if they are raised with acceptance, they will make rules that are not judgments about other people, or in any way diminish another in order to make themselves feel good.

I realize now that my family and People have lived with the effects of "Trans-generational, Post-Traumatic Stress Disorder." Like Vietnam veterans, we have been shell-shocked and have experienced atrocities that wounded our spirit. Only our jungle was not in Vietnam; our jungle was the North American continent.

I am thirty years old and I just reread what I had last written and again I have my own personal realization of "spirit moving" and helping me through life. It never occurred to me that someday I would need so badly to find strength in my own words. All the answers are there . . . but it still hurts.

I have never realized such a level of pain and love in my life.

My fish bowl tipped over, and I'm flopping big time, and it's frightening.

You see, I started writing a book—only this book has taken on a life of its own and now it has even changed the ending. I knew from the beginning this book was about denial. Yet I didn't have a clue about how much information I had been denied, at least none that was recognizable until now. Many hours I have spent here with my thoughts and my family, until finally I came face-to-face with the monster who chased me throughout my life.

Ever since I began my sessions with Stephen, we knew there was always something more, something that frightened me, something so horrible I could never possibly survive it. An awful fear would sometimes reach out and touch me for a moment . . . and threaten my very existence.

When Stephen and I would begin to talk about Jason, it began to get better. I thought finally . . . I'll be free, finally the past will no longer threaten me. Yet still I had fear.

It was so deep that somehow it lived inside of me without a name, without a face.

"There's something going on here," Stephen would say. . . . "Yeah, I know," I would say. "What is it? What do you feel?" Stephen says as I attempt to answer his questions. "Fear," I reply. He's pushing me and won't stop, and now he says I need to "go into it." He urges, looking for answers, and for a minute, I attempt to do as he asks.

"Now, what do you feel?"

"Absolutely nothing."

It worked.

EPILOGUE

Loree's Spirit Moves

It was August 8, 1992, when Grandma flew down from Canada to help me with this book. For three weeks before she arrived, the streetlights that line the road in front of my home never went out. They shone twenty-four hours a day—it made me glad—I felt my spirit connection, and I knew I was where I should be—happy good medicine, I knew this time would be remembered. It was a very special time for us . . . a time to laugh and a time to cry . . . a healing time.

We talked for hours, for days, and taped all of our conversations so they could be put into words that would later build the lives and stories represented in this book. After a particularly great day, we gently went into the evening sitting on my front porch, sipping coffee and laughing as the stars began peeking out of the light blue sky until ever so slowly, it became night. And there in the darkness we discovered the beauty of the night as the stars stood silent, hung in perfect order from the sky while the warm wind gently caressed the large oak trees, illuminated by the warm peach glow of the street lights. I so fully felt my own presence and that of my grandmother's that I believe I reached yet another level of aliveness and feeling of really being whole. I was reminded of something my mother had said:

Moments frozen in time, memories that hang in the gallery of your heart. . . .

And this portrait I hold in my mind of that night is truly a masterpiece in the gallery of my life. It was almost eleven o'clock by the time we reluctantly bid the day farewell and left the porch and returned inside. I felt a still peacefulness within me and I slept.

As we continued to piece together the puzzle of our lives, I tried as I had for the last year to make it all fit together somehow—until the pieces created not only something we recognized, but something of the beauty that carried my family through some pretty ugly times.

Many, many times I have added and subtracted from these pages. I have spent hours contemplating the words upon the screen in front of me—and the feelings they evoked. And a new question began being asked in my mind . . . but I still did not hear it. Instead, I felt only its uneasy presence pressing on my heart. This is the scariest monster of all . . . and I saved it for last.

We began talking about when Mom was raped and I mentioned Edson; Grandma became visibly shaken at the mention of this little town, and spoke oddly of the town, as if it were a person. Grandma told me that I must have been mistaken because Edson never would have hurt my mother—Edson was the little town everyone loved. Everyone except my mother. I was confused, the rape had taken place in Cashe Creek, B.C., when Mom ran away from home. Oh . . . and for a moment, I faced my worst fear and I heard for the first time clearly the question that had finally found a voice to be spoken.

I was working on a picture I was drawing as we talked. As I listened, I picked up pencil after pencil until finally it seemed that with every pencil I grasped came a new question until finally I realized this "puzzle" was gaping with missing pieces.

The picture I am drawing is the face of a girl, her eyes are wide open . . . seeing clearly . . . seeing all. Yet her hands are spread out over her ears so she can't hear—yet somehow I know this does not matter because I know the question is not being asked outside of herself; it comes from within.

Voids—dark places I hide from myself—today is a strong day, today I discovered my question and gave it a voice.

Could I have possibly been conceived through a brutal, violent sexual attack . . . that night in Edson thirty years ago?

The dates, the places—it's not right, something is very wrong. I feel it. I look at my grandma and we touch—"Grandma, was Teddy really my father?" She stood silent. I search for an answer and once again I speak.

"What really happened? Please tell me, Grandma." At first she's quiet, but I see her body gently begin to shake and I know in my heart. I stop and feel the intensity . . . before she even answers. "Loree, I honestly don't know." Everything's in motion now, moving, breathing, thinking, not thinking, hurting, needing. Needing to know the truth, needing to talk to my mother. . . .

I felt sadness for my grandma as I set my pencils down and began to walk up the stairs. "You're a grown woman now, Lor, and you have a right to know, I understand." I could see how hard this was by the look on her face as she tried to give me something, only there was really nothing she could do but be there, and I really appreciated that. I couldn't help but think that if this could somehow be true, and if Grandma never really knew any details, would this all somehow even affect the relationship we have had? I couldn't help but feel somehow I was to blame, I existed.

"I've got to talk to my mother," I told Grandma, hoping she understood it somehow could not wait one second longer. Grandma looked at me and quietly said, "Now, Loree, right now?" I could tell she wanted me to wait awhile and think things through more before talking to my mother, but I just could not wait one more minute. I know she realized that it had to be now. She stepped aside and let me go. As I walked into my bedroom and shut the door, all the electricity and lights in the house went out. I felt both the weight of my own fear and also that of my grandmother's as I walked toward the phone. A million thoughts plagued me, but only one stood still. . . .

Am I the family secret?

I thought of how I cried when I wrote the section of my book—this book—detailing how my mother had been violated—desecrated—and humiliated that night in Edson, when she'd been gang raped. I thought of how many times I read it, it always made me cry, but then it was for a different reason. I can see she tried to tell me the truth—she wanted me to understand, and I think now I finally do. She just never quite got that far. I remember the first time I heard the details and how she cried and told me there were things she could tell me that I just could never believe, things she never wanted anyone to know, and that she just never, never wanted to hurt anyone. At the time, I thought I understood; I can see now I didn't have a clue. My body literally ached with compassion and pain for my mother, for my family, for myself.

I never really realized how much you loved me, Mom. I dialed the phone.

How there were so many thoughts and feelings in what only amounted to minutes, I'm not sure, all I know is that they were all there.

Some moments are frozen in time—arms stretched out like Jesus . . . I wonder if they'll kill her . . . I'll never be sixteen years old again . . . I'll never be innocent . . . Is it a game? a sporting event? a competition? . . . and so I made my vow of silence to the Creator . . . and asked why was I born. . . .

I was really going into it—God, where's Stephen when I need him? Nobody's gonna hold your hand through this one, Loree. Once again, the script began to read itself out loud inside my head.

Silversong hovers above . . . speaking softly, yet not speaking to anyone at all . . . how could God be a part of this. . . . I really wanted to leave, please . . . go numb or maybe even stiff, but this time it didn't work. Something inside of me made the decision to stay, to stay and see denial die.

The phone's ringing now.

She answers it. "Mom, it's Loree, we need to talk about something . . . and it's really serious," I said. There was a pause and then she told me that a customer had just walked in and she would call me right back. She asked me what it was about and I told her it had to do with the book. "Oh, okay, umm, I'll talk to you in a minute," she said as we hung up the phone. The neighborhood was silent; you could hear the trees outside, no televisions or radios blaring out due to the power outage, and for the first time in five weeks even the streetlights were dead. A few more minutes passed that seemed like an eternity before the phone rang again. I could hear Grandma moving nervously around the quiet house and I noticed that today my mother's voice is different; she wants to know what it is, but she can't speak it, she already knows and so do I.

I try to begin, I know she's scared so I assure her that I can handle it, we can handle it. I tell her I think maybe there is something she has not *told me about my father.... "What do you mean?" she asks. "I mean maybe it really didn't happen that way, Mom. Maybe Teddy really isn't my father ... I really need to know the truth, Mom, please, I know this must be very painful for you, but you don't have to be alone, you don't have to keep secrets anymore."*

A long silence ... a pause, accentuating a vow of silence that lasted for thirty years.

"Mom ... Mom, please, it's gonna be okay—we'll face it together," I said, hoping somehow to reach out to her and make it somehow a little better. It was never going to be easy, we both knew that. "Life's so hard, I never wanted you to have to deal with this ... it just never seemed fair, you were just an innocent, beautiful little baby. You didn't deserve any of this...." She is crying now and I am silent. It's true, it's true, oh my God, it's really true. Everything hurts. "It must have been really hard on you, Mom—I could understand any emotion you may have experienced, how easy it would have been for you to give me up. I wouldn't have blamed you, no one would have," I said. "No, Loree, it wasn't that easy for me, you were a living being, you never asked for any of this and it was never, never your fault." She must have guessed how I would feel; she was answering questions that I couldn't ask yet.

"When you were first born, I was really scared, really freaked out, but then I began to heal and I fell absolutely in love with you, Loree, you were so cute, so sweet, just an innocent little doll, honey, and I decided that regardless of what they had done to me, I was going to have something from it, something that was all mine, and that was you.

"I thank God for you every day, honey."

God, Mom, I love you, too ... but how could you love me? I thought to myself, knowing that things sure could have been a lot different. And the funny part of it is I realized how lucky I was. I hung up the phone as the lights came back on and the radio began to play, but for the length of our talk it had just been the two of us. You know, I realize some people might think it's kind of weird but I don't care; without spirit connections you're an empty well. It was very powerfully affirming to me, that because of my spirit connection to light ... that while my fish bowl stood still, for a few minutes the ocean did, too. You know? Like that feeling someone's watching over you and really cares a lot? I sure hope you do.

I guess I wasn't kidding when I said I'd been in training to write this book—I'd never known the need to know myself more desperately than I did now. As the pendulum swung out far and frighteningly, I stood silently until it returned to center. Somebody knocked down all her sand castles and she doesn't know why, and she doesn't know why, John Trudell sang in the background, and I thought, boy, ain't that the truth.

Sometimes the changes we face force us, we have to make a decision that involves no one other than ourselves. I had to make one of those decisions, I chose to love myself. It helped a lot knowing that my mother had made the same decision, many years ago.

The next three days were hard, hard to function, hard to face the world, hard to face myself. But you know it had to be, it was meant to be. I found out that my grandmother had known all along that I was conceived violently, she just hadn't known the details. She thought it had happened when Mom ran away from home and traveled to Cashe Creek. Whenever she would try to speak to my mother about the circumstances of my conception, my mother would become so distraught, it became no longer important.

But Grandma faced her own pain in finding out after all these years that it had happened in Edson, and for reasons my mother felt were important to only her and me, she chose never to tell anyone exactly what had happened that night, except for me. She said it was important to her that if it was to be that someday I should know that she could tell me; I was the first person who ever really knew what had actually happened. At the same time, no one ever knew enough to allow it to become distorted in any way or hurt me unintentionally.

Grandma, not knowing the full story, but knowing that Silversong had become pregnant after being raped, swore that she would never tell. Until the day she died, she would protect me. It was a very sad time for her, so many years, so many secrets, so many times I'd ask her to tell me about Teddy. Knowing she knew, and our relationship was based on truth— even if I wasn't let in on it—comforted me. My grandmother's affections *were genuine and wouldn't change. She loves me, no one can ever take that away. And once again, it helped rescue me when the pendulum would swing out violently, seeming to turn itself threateningly toward me. Grandma is an honest person, and we never kept any secrets, except for this one. I was glad she too no longer had this burden to carry alone, none of us were alone anymore, now we could start helping each other. I really needed a lot of help. I felt so bad for them, but I just wanted so badly to be maybe in one of their positions rather than the one I found myself in. I had no other choice except simply to accept it and keep living.*

I thought about all the painful questions people think about when they don't have a father present, and how in a funny way those painful questions are comforting.... Would he have really loved me? Things would have been different, he never would have done something like that to me. I couldn't ask myself those questions anymore. I knew my father never loved me. I grieved for Teddy, I never knew much about him, only a few stories and one picture ... it's a side view. He's sitting on the couch at the old S&N with my mom, Uncle Lance, and Aunt Karen. They all look so happy. You know, it's surprising how tightly you hold onto these things through your life when you have so little to define yourself growing up.

I realize that Teddy was never my father—but I still know in my heart that he helped protect me all my life, until finally I was strong enough to look inside of myself and seek the monster I had always feared and never been able to face. Now I see it wasn't even my monster.

Teddy will always be special to me, just like he was special to my family before he died. I don't think he'd mind, and what Mom said was true, "A single act of kindness will forever immortalize the giver." I guess kindness and love are what spirit moving is all about, it sure isn't done with this era's cool ... indifference.

He was my Guardian Angel ... and one of my protectors.

For thirty years he was my father, now he's my friend.

Bittersweet feelings ... once again.

I know I had and have many people who loved and protected me so I could grow up and have a chance to get to know who Loree was. They say things happen in life to teach us lessons—if that is true, I can tell you this, that this family has loved me so well . . . I fully realize what hearts are for. . . .

My family did the right thing; they did the only thing possible. And I love them more today than I can possibly express. But it still sure must have been hard. . . . I'm just thankful that you all chose love as the highest emotion, and so have I.

Still, the shock rolls over me in waves. I have all the answers, but there are so many questions that won't be ignored now. That someone could have done this to my family, we were all victims of one night over thirty years ago in a little town called Edson, a little town . . . so loved by my family—cherished for the special memories of growing up. The place we buried Ron and Patty. How could you have done this to my family? You'll never know how lucky I was to be born a Lawsen.

I know their names. Someday, I may knock on your door and ask which one of you thinks you're my father.

The truth is, we all have to live with it.

There's a certain kind of feeling sneaking up on me, but this time I know it's no monster. It's a feeling of peace and of putting things in the past. I'm no longer holding up the sky—and now I know I never really did, my family just let me think I was so I would feel my own strength, when actually they were the ones holding up the sky for me all along.

My brother called today. . . . "Lor, we may not be able to be proud of our fathers, but we can be proud of ourselves," he said. And I know that it's true. In some of my hardest times, I drew close to my family and they never let me down. I'm lucky, I know what I believe. I know that my brother is special and kind; I know he's a good man with a big heart. I know I love him. And because I know these things so well, and that they are true about my brother regardless of who fathered him—I know I can believe the same about myself.

Jesus said . . . "Your sins are as scarlet . . . I will make them white as snow. . . ."

And so I remember good things . . . playing superball with Aunt Patty. Uncle Ron buying me a yellow slip-n-slide with his first paycheck.

Spending days at the beach in Kingston and digging for clams with Grandma. Building bonfires, and gluing eyes that wiggled onto rocks and shells. My mother's smile, my little brother, and Teddy, my little angel.

Facing your past can be brutal. It took a long time and many baby steps before I came to where I am today.

I recently read a book entitled Women Who Run with the Wolves. Here is one section of many that had special meaning for me:

If you have a deep scar, that is a door. If you have an old, old story, that is a door. If you love the sky and the water so much that you almost cannot bear it, that is a door. If you yearn for a deeper life, a full life, a sane life, that is a door.

I believe that only by opening these doors will we ever truly know who we are. It's only now, in my thirtieth year, that I've begun to do that.

Like my Grandma Lawsen, I, too, am one of the lucky ones. I made it. I've given birth, I've helped bury the dead, and have seen life spring forth triumphantly within my body once again. No matter what today may hold, there will always be a tomorrow.

I choose to release the past, and I release the future as well. I choose not to live in tomorrow, but am comforted knowing it is there.

Living only in this moment, I often see the face of tomorrow in my daughters' eyes, and the future is filled with hope.

Because of my grandmother, my mother, and myself, my daughters may not be merely "survivors," but will thrive. If it is possible, the buck will stop here. Generations of abuse, and what has often been a painful family legacy, will fade out of existence.

To my daughters, Danaelle and Layla—
Take the good things of your past. Even through ugly times, there was beauty.

Gather up the pretty little packages, the precious gifts that are sometimes wrapped in plain brown paper. Take them to *tomorrow. You are the hope for the future, a new day and a new way.*

My Little Moon Bird, with your birth you illuminated a path into my past and that of your grandmothers. A messenger flying between heaven and earth, you helped me unravel a part of my Great Mystery.

Little Brown Bear, you've given me balance when I've been lost in the solitude of my spirit life. You've brought me "home" with a little bear hug. You are strong and very brave.

It is said that a curse lasts three generations but a blessing lasts forever.

I've been twice blessed.

New World library is dedicated to
publishing books and audio cassettes
that improve the quality of our lives. Our books
and tapes are available in bookstores everywhere.
For a catalog of our complete library
of fine books and cassettes, contact:

New World Library
14 Pamaron Way
Novato, CA 94949

Phone: 415 • 884-2100
Fax: 415 • 884-2199

Or call toll-free: 800 • 227-3900